The Linux Internet Server

Kevin Reichard

Series Editors: Patrick Volkerding & Kevin Reichard

The
Linux Internet
Server

Kevin Reichard

Series Editors: Patrick Volkerding & Kevin Reichard

A Subsidiary of
Henry Holt and Co., Inc.

MIS:Press
A Subsidiary of Henry Holt and Company, Inc.
115 West 18th Street
New York, New York 10011
http://www.mispress.com

First Edition—1997

ISBN: 1-55828-545-8

MIS:Press and M&T Books are available at special discounts for bulk purchases for sales promotions, premiums, and fundraising. Special editions or book excerpts can also be created to specification.

For details contact: Special Sales Director
                         MIS:Press and M&T Books
                         Subsidiaries of Henry Holt and Company, Inc.
                         115 West 18th Street
                         New York, New York 10011

10 9 8 7 6 5 4 3 2 1

Associate Publisher: *Paul Farrell*

Managing Editor: *Shari Chappell*   **Editor:** *Laura Lewin*

Copy Edit Manager: *Karen Tongish*   **Copy Editor:** *Sara Black*

Production Editor: *Maya Riddick*

The MIS:Press *Slackware* series:

LINUX: Configuration and Installation, 2/e
1-55828-492-3   Available now

LINUX Programming
1-55828-507-5   Available now

The LINUX Database
1-55828-491-5   Available now

LINUX in Plain English
1-55828-542-3   April 1997

Dedication

To Sean

CONTENTS-IN-BRIEF

CONTENTS

Section I: Welcome to the Internet

Section II: Setting Up Internet Services

Section III: Creating Content

Section IV: Security

INTRODUCTION

Linux and Your Internet Server

Welcome to the worlds of the Slackware Linux operating system and the Internet! This book covers using Slackware Linux as an Internet server, beginning with the installation of Slackware Linux and its configuration as a network server, following through with the configuration of several powerful Internet servers, including an emphasis on the most popular Web server on the Internet, the Apache Web server.

Why Linux? The primarily goal of any Internet server is reliability, pure and simple. You don't want to have an Internet server that can be overwhelmed by a high number of users, each asking for a slew of data. You'll want an Internet server that's pretty much bullet-proof, and that's where Linux comes in. Developed by people around the world, Linux has evolved into this ultrareliable UNIX workalike that provides high performance with an amazingly low failure rate. Slackware Linux is like the proverbial Energizer bunny—it keeps going and going and going.

Add to that the relatively affordability of Slackware Linux. By purchasing this book, you've already purchased *the entire operating system*. No reason to pony up hundreds or thousands of more dollars from the likes of Microsoft or SCO. Plus, Slackware Linux can be run on most PC configurations. Small firms may find that a relatively inexpensive Pentium or even an older 486 can handle their Internet server needs, while medium-sized company can invest in one of the new multiple-Pentium servers hitting the market.

This book specifically covers using Slackware Linux as an Internet server, not just a Web server. The Internet is made up of many services, and the World Wide Web is only one of the many services. There's more to the Internet than the Web, as there are World Wide Web, Gopher, mail, news, and FTP servers included with Slackware Linux.

Who Should Read This Book?

This book isn't a hardcore look at networking with Slackware Linux, but there's enough information here to get your system up and running. However, advanced network design is a subject better left to the network engineers and really hardcore system administrators, so if you're looking for an in-depth guide to Slackware Linux networking, you won't find it here.

Luckily, most of us don't need to know about hardcore system administration and network engineering, and this book is for us. You'll find this book useful if:

- You are a Webmaster who is evaluating Internet publishing platforms.
- You are a UNIX system administrator who is looking to build or extend an Slackware Linux network onto the Internet.
- You are evaluating Slackware Linux as an Internet publishing platform.
- You are evaluating Slackware Linux as an intranet publishing platform.

The Accompanying CD-ROM

The accompanying CD-ROM contains all the software you'll need to get a Linux Internet server up and running, including:

- A full version of Slackware Linux.
- The Apache Web server—the most popular Web server on the Internet—as well as other Web servers.
- The WU-FTP server.
- Programming tools like Perl, Java, and Tcl.
- Other server tools detailed throughout the course of this book.

Chapter 3 covers the installation of Slackware Linux and its configuration for usage on the Internet, while Chapter 4 covers the Apache Web server in some detail. Though this book covers Slackware Linux in some depth, it can also be applied to other Linux distributions to some extent; for instance, the Red Hat distribution of Linux also features the Apache Web server, and so Chapter 4 can be applied to Red Hat Linux as well as Slackware Linux.

Feedback

You're welcome to drop me a line at *reichard@mr.net*, and you're invited to visit my Web site at *http://www.kreichard.com* for more information. However, because of the volume of electronic mail I receive, you might not receive an answer promptly.

SECTION I

Welcome to the Internet

Before you can actually begin offering your services via a Linux Internet server, you'll need to determine your connection method to the Internet, as well as install Slackware Linux. This entire process, which is more involved than you might think, is covered in this section.

Chapter 1 provides a basic overview of the Internet, intranets, and the Slackware Linux operating system. The information here is rather rudimentary; we start with the very basics and move to more advanced topics.

Chapter 2 covers how you can connect your Linux Internet server to the Internet. These methods would include dialup connections, ISDN, frame-relay connections, and T1 and T3 lines. Along the same lines, you'll learn about the bureaucracy involved in obtaining a domain name and InterNIC policies on domain names. In addition, you'll learn about Internet service providers (ISPs) and why they'll be important to your Internet experience.

Chapter 3 covers the installation of Slackware Linux for use as an Internet server, including network configuration and some basic X Window configuration.

THE INTERNET, INTRANETS AND SLACKWARE LINUX

This chapter covers:

- The Internet
- The World Wide Web
- Web servers
- Electronic-mail serves
- Gopher servers
- FTP servers
- Chat/discussion servers
- A short history of the Internet
- Hardware issues
- Setting up an intranet

One Big, Happy Network

If you bought this book, you've probably already either used the Internet to some extent or worked with Linux on a networking level. You'll be able to put this experience to good use as you chart your way onto the Internet or a corporate intranet using Linux as your server—or, rather, using Linux to run your *servers*. (Put simply, there is one box and many servers.) This viewpoint requires some new orientation on your part. When you map out your Internet server in your mind, you're probably using a single box to denote your Internet server. However, in reality, there are many different servers that comprise Internet connectivity, even though they may reside on the same Linux box.

Here's a quick philosophy lesson. Conceptually, Linux shares a lot with UNIX, as you might expect. Put simply, UNIX is basically a series of smaller tools that are combined to provide power to users. As such, Linux/UNIX is designed to break larger tasks into smaller tasks, each of which can be individually manipulated.

Coincidentally, the Internet shares the same philosophy with UNIX and Linux. (There's no surprise here—in its early days, the Internet was essentially run on a largish UNIX network.) What comprises the Internet—electronic mail, the World Wide Web, Usenet newsgroups, Gopher, FTP—can actually be broken down quite easily into smaller services, which have their own servers.

Therefore, when you're planning your Internet connectivity, you'll need to decide which servers you want to run. There are World Wide Web (HTTP) servers, Gopher servers, mail servers, and electronic-mail servers. As Webmaster, you'll not be administering a single Internet tool, but rather (potentially) a whole set of services. Each server handles some aspect of the Internet. A Web server serves Web pages to Web browsers. A Gopher server serves Gopher menus and data files to Web browsers and Gopher clients. An electronic-mail server serves electronic mail to e-mail clients and Web browsers that can handle mail (such as Netscape Navigator). An FTP server serves files via the File Transfer Protocol (FTP). A chat server allows multiple users to chat via IRC clients. A news server sends Usenet news postings to news clients and Web browsers that can handle the news (like Netscape Navigator).

Sound daunting? It should. On one level, setting up these services can be a pain—less so if you are not necessarily responsible for content (like coding your own Web pages)—but still a good amount of work, especially when you don't know anything about the service and don't know what's available for Linux. And, depending on your needs, you may find that your users are best served by mixing and matching individual services, using a Web server to route requests to a Gopher server that's better equipped to handle large databases.

The good news here is that these individual services are actually pretty simple in and of themselves. They're not going to overwhelm you with their complexity. And getting a basic Internet system with a Linux server up and running can be a quick process.

Detail Work

If you bought this book expecting to open your own Internet site for business immediately after skimming through this text, you'll be disappointed. Like any largish computing task, using Linux for an Internet server requires some basic planning. In this case, a review of what actually comprises the Internet is in order.

You might be able to get your arms around the immensity of the Internet by breaking it down to its basic components: clients and servers. *Clients,* which include Web browsers like Netscape Navigator, ask for data from servers. This data is (usually) rendered on the client's local computer; when a Web page is sent to Netscape Navigator, Netscape Navigator takes that page and applies local fonts and colors to the page. *Servers* are responsible for sending the data to the clients, basically sitting there and waiting for a request to come its way. A server is also responsible for making sure that the request is valid; if a secure document is requested, then the server must make sure that the originator of the request has the correct authorization to receive the document. Similarly, the server must protect sensitive areas of the server (such as program files and protected data files) from users who may want to access these area for nefarious purposes.

If you come from the world of big iron, the notion of client/server should be familiar to you. If you've spent any time at all working with a

Linux network, you're familiar with the notion of client/server. And if you've administered databases using SQL Server, you already are familiar with the notion of client/server.

These transactions all occur under the context of TCP/IP (Transmission Control Protocol/Internet Protocol). TCP/IP is the unifying network standard that unites the Internet as well as the protocol upon which Linux is based. If you have a Linux box already connected to the Internet, you have a large part of the puzzle already in place.

Past that, however, there are protocols specific to different services. The HyperText Transfer Protocol (HTTP) governs the transfer of Web pages to Web browsers. The File Transfer Protocol (FTP) governs file transfers between FTP servers and FTP clients. The most popular service on the Internet in terms of traffic is HTTP (electronic mail actually has more users, but it generates less traffic and less overhead than a Web server), which is why a closer look is warranted.

An HTTP Overview

Much has been made about the fact that the World Wide Web is a *hypertext* medium, where documents are linked, and that to move to a new document, you just need to click on a link. The theorists argue that this represents an end to Western-style linear thinking, that this represents an entirely new way of organizing information. Other theorists who decry the Web argue that it's the electronic equivalent of Short Attention Span Theater, an activity perfectly suited to the MTV Generation, who merely substitute their remote controls for a mouse.

Whatever.

You're going to discover that your documents are going to be amazingly linear when viewed under the cold light of the Web server. Indeed, if there weren't some logic to their organization, there would be no way that you could keep track of them. The user may be able to hop from document to document and to various points within documents, but it's up to you and your organizational methods to make sure that hopping is an option.

Still, it's amazing that the World Wide Web has stayed basically true to its roots, as first outlined by Tim Berners-Lee in March 1989 when he was at the European Particle Physics Laboratory, or CERN. Berners-

Lee's original plans were much more modest in scope, involving an academic system where researchers could easily browse through the words of other academic researchers around the world.

Berners-Lee outlined his plans in a paper, where he acknowledged the pioneering ideas of Ted Nelson, who first visualized a hypertext system way back in 1967, which he dubbed Xanadu. (Xanadu, amazingly enough, is still under development; you can check out the details at *http://xanadu.net/the.project*.) Nelson's theories are rather grandiose, involving both hypertext transactions and ways to protect copyrights in hypertext transactions (it's amazing how well Nelson anticipated the problems posed by hypertext in the real world, however), and it's to Berners-Lee's credit that he cut through all the conceptual baggage to come up with what was basically the world's first workable hypertext system.

By October 1990, CERN had embarked on the creation of such a system, and in December 1990 the first Web browsers were available. By that time, Berners-Lee had fleshed out his hypertext medium with some basic building blocks. The Web documents were to be formatted in the HyperText Markup Language (HTML), which is basically a subset of the larger Standard Generalized Markup Language (SGML), which had already been developed by the U.S. government as a way to standardize documentation. HTML is basically a text medium, where portions of the documents are defined by tags. These tags are then interpreted by the Web browser, which then applies local resources to the document. Instead of providing a specific typeface for text, an HTML page merely provides a text tag, and the browser then uses a locally specified text tag to render the page.

 You'll learn more about HTML in Chapter 11.

NOTE

The other important block provided by Berners-Lee is the HTTP, which governs how servers send documents to browsers. Basically, a Web browser sends information to the server, including a Uniform Resource Locator (URL). If you've spent any time around the Internet, you know the basic makeup of a URL:

http://www.kreichard.com

refers to a Web server run by yours truly, whereas

ftp://ftp.sun.com

refers to an FTP server at Sun Microsystems. Contrary to public belief, a Web browser isn't limited to connecting to Web servers—it can also be used to connect to almost any other Internet service (except for the retrieval of mail, although Netscape Communicator and Microsoft Internet Explorer do include mail modules).

Basically, the URL specifies how a document should be transferred, as well as the location of the document itself. Let's break down the following URL:

http://www.kreichard.com/linux/linux.html

This is a real Internet address. Go ahead and try it if you're connected to the Internet.

N O T E

The parts break down as follows:

- *http://* refers to the protocol used to transmit the document. In this case, the browser asks that the document be sent using HTTP, and the connection is being made to an HTTP server (also known as a Web server).

- *www.kreichard.com* refers to the machine storing the document. In addition, some addresses contain a colon and numeral at the end (such as *:80*), which refers to a specific port used to transmit the information.

- *ature* is the path to the document. On a Web server, documents are stored in an hierarchical format just like your local computer.

- *linux.html* is the document.

These transactions are *stateless*, since the Web server sends off the document and then ends the transaction. This is actually a reflection of the Web's roots in UNIX, where the UNIX operating system is built to spin off processes upon processes as a natural course of events. In terms of overhead, each HTTP request is actually pretty light in computational resources—there's not a whole lot needed to ship a file and (perhaps) other associated graphics files to a remote client. The transaction is logged, and that's about it.

NOTE The move in the World Wide Web is toward persistent connections between a browser and a server. However, this technology hasn't yet reached the Linux world.

That's the theory, and it worked fine in the early days of the World Wide Web. Today, a lot more is expected from these transactions. CGI scripts and programs may tailor output to the input provided by a client, and even though these scripts may be fairly lightweight (Perl and Tcl are not exceptionally demanding scripting languages), it still adds up when multiplied by a thousand or ten thousand. With the advent of advertising, users need to be tracked. To do so, they may be asked to register and then supply a password and username upon subsequent visits, which adds a whole new level of authentication overhead. Similarly, many Web sites are toying with the idea of charging for access; although there's a lot of doubt within the Internet community whether these plans will fly, there's no doubt that enhancing revenue streams will be an important issue in the future of the Internet.

NOTE Will you be expected to implement some sort of payment scheme on your Internet site? Probably not, unless you're running a very large site. The Internet will inevitably be transformed into some revenue-producing system—there's no way that companies like The *New York Times* and the *Washington Post* will continue to be free of charge in the future. At the time this book was written, there were several plans in the works from third parties, which would handle billing duties for other Web sites. CompuServe, the large online service, was working on such a site where CompuServe subscribers would have full access to large for-profit Web sites; access wouldn't need to be done through the CompuServe service, but billing would be done through CompuServe. If these plans become popular—and in terms of economics, they make the most sense—then the future Internet would most resemble cable television, where users pay per month for access to a wide variety of channels (or, in this case, Web sites). Users wouldn't need to worry about watching the clock as they hop from site to site, and billing wouldn't need to done on a complicated transaction basis.

The explosion of the Web is rather breath-taking. Back in January 1993, there were only 50 World Wide Web servers online (although, admittedly, there were a great many mail, news, and FTP servers available). What fueled the Internet explosion wasn't necessarily the development of Web servers—indeed, a basic Web server doesn't represent a stupendous programming task—but the development of Web browsers. February 1993 saw the release of NCSA Mosaic for X Window from the National Center for Supercomputing Applications (NCSA) at the University of Illinois at Urbana-Champaign. Macintosh and Windows versions soon ensued. The software development team at NCSA did a lot to shape how we view the Web today, with its support of multimedia additions to Web documents (through the MIME protocol), the incorporation of graphics into documents, and the addition of protocols like mail and news. In the early days, the Internet was a UNIX beast.

The Internet exploded in popularity thanks to NCSA Mosaic. Of course, NCSA Mosaic didn't remain the only Web browser in town for long, as other Windows Web browsers like Cello soon claimed their fair share of users. Today, NCSA Mosaic is still available via the Internet, but commercial versions of Mosaic are overseen by Spyglass. (Microsoft Internet Explorer is actually based on the venerable Mosaic, although Microsoft has made enough enhancements to the browser to allow it to be considered a new and separate product.)

In March 1994, several people who worked on the development of NCSA Mosaic left the Midwest for the sunnier climes of California to work at a small startup called Mosaic Communications. (The name was changed to Netscape Communications after a few phone calls from University of Illinois lawyers.) Their first product, Netscape Navigator, set the tone for the next generation of Web browsers—fast, slick, and colorful. Depending on who you ask, Netscape Navigator accounts for between 50 and 80 percent of all Web usage—which is why you'll need to consider at some point whether to tailor your site for Netscape Navigator or to remain neutral in the browser wars.

HTTP is still a technology in development. One new development currently in limited use is Secure HTTP (S-HTTP). It uses public-key technology from RSA Data Security in order to facilitate secure Internet transactions.

The big brains guiding Internet development are working on HTTP-NG, which is short for Next Generation. (Apparently there are too many Trekkies out there.) If you want the specifics, you can check out the World Wide Web Consortium (W3C) at MIT, where Berners-Lee currently holds court. The Web address is

http://www.w3c.com

Enough history of HTTP, HTML, and the like—while there are other fascinating tales of how the Net developed, they're not terribly relevant to your administration of a Linux Internet server.

Your Server and the Internet

Where will your Linux Internet server fit in the larger scheme of things? It will fit like any other server on any other network. Basically, the Internet is the world's largest network, all connected with TCP/IP. There's a main backbone, administered by MCI, Sprint, Ameritech, and other firms. Basically, this is an MCI network made up of high-speed switches and fiber-optic cabling. There's really not a part of this backbone that's specifically designated as "Internet-only"; this backbone is also used for voice and video transmissions.

The things to note about this backbone are its speed (600 million bits per second, or Mbps, or more than 20,000 times faster than the average 28.8-Kbps modem) and its capacity, or bandwidth. The backbone represents the largest capacity of the Internet at any point; as the Internet gets closer to your particular server, the bandwidth winnows as more users clamor for access. Your Internet connection will probably be through a local Internet service provider (ISP) or telecommunications firm.

NOTE   You'll learn about these connections in Chapter 2.

Internet transmissions are meant to be broken up and sent as part of other sets of transmissions. This is opposed to the typical telephone call, which commandeers control of an entire circuit for the entire call, meaning that others cannot use the circuit for other purposes. Internet communications are divided into *packets*—smaller chunks of data with a source address and a destination address—and then sent from router to router before they end up at a final destination. When a Web browser sends a request to a server, that request is sent from router to router until it arrives at the server. That's one transaction. Your server responds to the request with a new transaction. There's no open connection between the server and the browser.

The complexity of this model can't be overstated. There are millions of bits flying from here to there on the Internet, and the fact that most transactions are completed satisfactorily says something about the reliability of the Internet. There's actually data redundancy built into these transactions: When a packet is dropped from a transmission, the recipient of the transmission will ask for a retransmission.

N O T E Currently there's a huge debate among Internet journalists as to how reliable the Internet really is. Bob Metcalfe of *InfoWorld Magazine* is a naysayer, a prophet whose voice in the wilderness argues that the Internet collapse is nigh and that Internet reliability is decreasing based on some server measurements of dropped packets. On the other hand, many Internet journalists argue that the Internet is growing just fine (albeit with some growing pains), and all it takes is some fine-tuning to ameliorate these growing pains.

The protocol governing these transmissions is TCP/IP. When you break it down, TCP/IP oversees the following:

- The address of the packet.
- The data size of the packet.
- Error-detection information.
- Routing information.

As a networking protocol, TCP/IP isn't regarded as robust or as complex as other networking protocols, like those used in Novell NetWare networks. However, for the purposes of the Internet, TCP/IP is the perfect solution, for the following reasons:

- **No one owns it.** TCP/IP was developed by the U.S. government, as part of the Defense Advanced Research Projects Agency (DARPA), to be used on the DARPAnet (the predecessor to the Internet). There's no royalty structure to deal with, which allows the computer world to avoid nasty fights over dueling proprietary networking protocols.

- **Routing information is built into a packet.** DARPA was built to have data redundancy; if one military site needed to connect to another in times of war, TCP/IP packets had the option of being transmitted via several different routes. In other words, there would be no singular data center during times of war; if Washington, D.C., were to be wiped out, a transmission between Atlanta and Boston would not rely on Washington as a conduit to the transmission. Today, there are some alternative routine schemes on the Internet that are used. However, the routing options available to DARPAnet aren't available to the Internet world at large, and you shouldn't assume that massive rerouting capabilities are available. (Indeed, one of the side effects of the commercialization of the Internet has been to cut down on these routing options for economic reasons.)

- **TCP/IP is available on all operating systems.** TCP/IP was not designed for any particular operating system. It was first implemented heavily on UNIX-based computers, with the result that TCP/IP became the networking protocol of choice in UNIXdom. The Internet evolved in the academic world, where UNIX computers dominate. As the Internet grew, schemes that turn personal computers into Internet-ready systems sprang up (like Trumpet Winsock, which allows connections to the Internet without the overhead of TCP/IP), making the Internet accessible to virtually any computer user with a connection and a modem. And, of course, Linux is built around TCP/IP, which makes it the perfect choice to use as an Internet server.

These same factors can also be applied to internal computer networks that won't interact with the rest of the world. These networks can be found in the corporate world, and they go by the name of intranets. You'll learn about intranets later in this chapter.

N O T E

Hardware Tips

Linux purists love to brag about how little hardware power is needed to adequately run Linux. However, evaluating hardware needs for a Linux Internet server requires a little different orientation than the average Linux installation.

This is true for two reasons: the nature of an Internet server and using Linux purely as an Internet server.

Unless you're using a lot of fancy programs based on CGI, your Linux box won't spend a lot of time responding to individual Internet requests. Basically, an Internet request comes to your Linux box, which then begins a new process to deal with the request. After the request, the transaction is completed (for the most part). For instance, a Web browser may ask your Web server for a Web page. After the Web page is sent to the browser, the transaction is complete. The Web browser may place information on this Web page and send it back to the server, but this is considered another separate transaction, with its own process.

These multiple processes don't really eat up a ton of CPU power, unless you have some pretty involved CGI scripts running. And in and of themselves, they don't eat up a lot of RAM, either. However, a good Web server—like the Apache Web Server—will cache frequently requested Web pages so that they can be sent directly from RAM instead of from hard disk. This speeds up the transaction time—RAM is always faster than hard disk—and decreases the wear and tear on your hard drive. Still, you'll find that a Web server that's used even moderately will require a goodly amount of time going to hard disk.

However, if you're running a Linux Web server, one factor will actually decrease the amount of RAM and firepower you'll need: there will be no purpose to running the X Window System. Let's face it— XFree86 is a memory hog. While some tools will require X (like tkHTML for creating Web pages), there's actually no need to be running the X Window System on your server. Since X on its own requires at least 4 Megabytes of RAM (and up to 8MB if you're running multiple tasks), you can subtract this amount from your Web server.

With all these factors in mind, here are some hardware tips if you're buying a new Linux box or adapting an older PC for Linux:

- **Buy enough RAM.** You'll want to cache as much information as you can in RAM. Since the price of RAM is so low these days, you'll want to consider having at least 16MB of RAM, and perhaps even 32MB. Since you're not running X (at least not running it consistently), you'll have a lot of RAM freed up both for Linux and Internet requests.

- **Go for the fastest hard drive you can.** Since there's an inevitable amount of churn to your hard drive, you'll want to make sure it's as fast as possible. Like RAM prices, hard-drive prices have been decreasing lately. In the PC world, the fastest hard drives are SCSI hard drives, which are a tad more expensive than standard IDE drives. However, the extra expense will be worth it.

- **Don't sweat out the processor speed.** Most Internet transactions are remarkably simple and don't require a ton of processing power. If you've got an older 90-MHz Pentium that you want to adapt for your Internet server, go ahead. Your users won't notice the difference between a 90-MHz Pentium box and a Pentium Pro box.

- **Don't invest in an expensive graphics card.** Most of the time you won't be using the Linux Internet box for your daily computing chores. Why invest in a Matrox Millennium graphics card on a box where the monitor will be turned off most of the time?

Linux on the Network

When you're running a Linux box purely as a network server, you probably aren't going to be using it much as a terminal. If this is the case, you don't need to factor in the X Window System (in the form of XFree86) as a factor when evaluating your hardware needs.

As a matter of fact, you can get by with old 486 boxes if you're planning on multiple boxes running multiple servers. If you are planning on using Linux on the enterprise, you'll want to divide the computing tasks among several PCs. Managing a news feed, for instance, requires a lot of computing resources, both in RAM and in hard-disk space.

If you're providing a full news feed, electronic mail, and World Wide Web access on your server, you'll probably want to look at two and maybe three PCs for all the traffic. The news should probably reside on its own machine if you're providing a full feed, and you should place the other services (mail, Web daemon) on another. In this case, you'll definitely want to go with a router and a direct network feed. (These are things you'll cover in Chapter 2.)

Some Constants

In other respects, however, there are some universal rules when you look at a hardware installation.

When it comes to increasing the performance of your Linux Internet server, two things directly aid performance: RAM and speedy hard-disk space. Web servers love to cache frequently accessed pages, and the more RAM available, the more caching can occur. Even though Internet servers and content don't actually eat up that much hard-disk space, there's a lot of churning to hard drive as Web documents are summoned for sending down the network. In these cases, the fastest access to the hard disk is the best, and you can get the best performance from high-performance (read: expensive) SCSI boards and hard drives. Throw a high-performance PCI bus into the mix, and you've got the makings of a really fast server.

This book doesn't pretend to be a hardware guide to servers. Basically, buy as much computer as you can get away with. If you're been given a rather liberal budget because the marketing weasels in your firm have deemed it absolutely necessary to get a fast presence on the Internet, go ahead and spring for that dual-Pentium Pro system with 32 megs of EDO RAM, a PCI bus, and a 2 gig SCSI disk. If your resources are more modest, consider overhauling an older Pentium PC with a PCI bus and expanding its RAM and hard-disk space to as much as you can afford.

Some Planning Criteria

You shouldn't assume that you can just throw a server on the Internet and achieve instant success. Indeed, you'll need to make some important decisions as you plan your Internet server. Many of these criteria will be explained more fully throughout this book. As you begin your Internet server journey, however, keep in mind the following questions:

- **What services should I offer?** A Web server is mandatory, since most Internet Web usage is now funneled through a Web browser. In addition, electronic mail is also mandatory, since electronic mail represents an easy way for your users to communicate with each other and your customers. Past that, you'll need to make some important decisions. Do your data needs call for a Gopher server, which can be handy for larger text documents? Should you incorporate a search engine for indexing the contents of your Web site? Should you have a Usenet feed, and what newsgroups should that feed incorporate?

- **Do I need to be connected to the Internet at all?** Internet technology can be used to create in-house intranets, which are used to connect users within your corporation. However, there's no connection to the outside world, or perhaps a partial connection (such as electronic mail). The advantage is that your workers won't be wasting their time perusing the Playboy, Penthouse, and Screw Web sites. The disadvantage is that the vast resources of the Internet won't be available to your workers.

- **What development tools should I look at?** So far, Web development tools have relied on scripting languages like Perl and Tcl, which you'll learn about in Chapter 12. For many simple tasks, like the gathering of user information and simple forms, these two scripting languages are more than adequate, and they both ship as part of Slackware Linux. When it comes to more complicated tasks such as multimedia and more elaborate data-acquisition needs, you may want to consider next-generation tools like Java (as promoted by Sun Microsystems and Netscape Communications). The Java Developers' Kit is included on the accompanying CD-ROM, and it too will be covered in Chapter 12.

- **Am I aware of all the legal issues involved?** The Internet poses a stiff challenge to many of the premises of legal theory developed in the United States. Some of the challenges have been successfully decided (for instance, the courts have generally agreed that trademark law can be applied to the Internet), while others are still in a state of evolution, such as obscenity. So, the best advice is to protect yourself and your company. Put a disclaimer on every page open for outside comment, telling Internet surfers that the views there are not necessarily those of the company running the site. Tell your users to respect the Internet as a business tool—inappropriate use of the Internet is considered grounds for dismissal in many companies, and you should decide if this is a policy you want to adopt.

An Overview of Services

In this book, we'll discuss almost all the possible services in their own chapters. Here, we'll introduce each. In each of these cases, both clients and servers and included on the accompanying CD-ROM.

The Web

So far this book, as well as the rest of the world, has focused on the World Wide Web as the engine fueling the growth of the Internet. And indeed, the Web is one of the most exciting developments in recent years, and potentially a harbinger of tomorrow's media.

As you already know from the beginning of this chapter, the Word Wide Web is nothing more than a series of file transfers between a Web server and a Web browser. To implement the World Wide Web on your site, you must be running a Web server. One such Web server, the Apache Web Server, is included as part of Slackware Linux. In Chapter 4, the majority of the discussion will focus on the Apache Web Server, which is the most popular Web server on the Internet (according to the research site of ServerWatch, run by CMP). However, alternatives to the Apache Web Server are discussed in Chapter 4, both commercial and noncommercial.

In addition, there are noncommercial Web browsers included on the accompanying CD-ROM, which you can distribute to your Linux users. The Arena Web browser is shown on Figure 1.1.

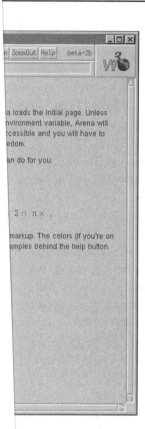

...rser.

Electronic Ma...

The true engine b... c mail, which is close to universal among l... allows a user to send a text message to a... is done by combining a username with the... e. A user named *reichard* at *mr.net* would ha...

reichard@mr.n...

Electronic mail is simple: You set up a mail server on your machine. This machine receives mail from your service provider. Your users connect to the mail server, which then sends their mail messages (if any) to them. In turn, their outgoing messages are also sent to the mail server, which then routes them to your service provider.

However, electronic mail can be a little trickier than this. Slackware Linux includes a slew of electronic-mail options, ranging from the venerable **sendmail** to newer alternatives designed for the greater Internet world. Chapter 8 covers your options.

Gopher

In many ways, Gopher can be seen as a rough predecessor to the World Wide Web as it attempts to supply user-friendly tools to Internet users. Basically, Gopher allows users to connect to a Gopher server, which then sends them a menu of possible choices. These choices can be other Gopher menus or documents stored on the local Gopher server, or documents stored on a remote Gopher server. When the user selects a menu item, a new request is sent to the Gopher server, and the process continues until the user receives enough data.

However, in many other ways Gopher is turning into a legacy system, as indexing tools like Glimpse combined with the flexibility of the World Wide Web are making it irrelevant. If you're starting to design data structures from scratch, you're probably not going to want to go with Gopher. However, if you already have a lot of data already organized using Gopher, you'll want to maintain that format.

There are no native Gopher servers for Linux. However, it's possible to take the original source code from the University of Minnesota (where Gopher was originally developed) and compile it for usage on Linux. In addition, the accompanying CD-ROM contains an excellent Gopher Server, GN. Chapter 5 covers Gopher.

The Usenet

The Usenet is a collection of discussion groups, organized around various topics, such as programming, folk dancing, or politics. Some of the topics can be mainstream (such as *rec.folkdancing*) or they can be dreadfully obscure (such as *alt.barney.dinosaur.die.die.die*). Anyone with access to the Usenet can post to a newsgroup and join in the discussion (unless the group is moderated, a situation you'll learn about in Chapter 9).

Your connection to the Usenet would come if you set up a NNTP server, which handles a feed from another Usenet news server, continuously updating the postings. You can choose to handle only a limited number of newsgroups, or else you can provide a total feed.

Be careful, though, as the Usenet can be a voracious pit when it comes to computing resources. A *full* Usenet feed is about 400MB *per day*, which can tie up a lot of your bandwidth even when using a 56K frame relay, never mind a dialup connection or ISDN. You're best off limiting your Usenet feed to purely essential groups (such as *alt.os.linux.slackware*), instead of providing every newsgroup under the sun (which includes many that provide nothing but pornography, useless information, and racist rants and raves).

There are a slew of Usenet tools that ship with Slackware Linux, and they are covered in Chapter 9.

Indexing Tools

If your Web site has a lot of information, you may want to install software that indexes the contents of your Web site. You would then set up a Web page where users submit a search term to the indexing software. The indexing software then takes the result of your request and sends it along to a client, either in the form of a Gopher page or an HTML page. They are covered in Chapter 6.

FTP

FTP stands for File Transfer Protocol, and it's the mechanism for sending files back and forth from your Internet site to an Internet user. This user doesn't need to be running a Web browser—they could be running an FTP client.

An FTP server is built into the Slackware Linux operating system, which means that there's relatively little for you to do in terms of configuration. (In fact, the directory */home/ftp/pub* is designed for FTP access.) You'll learn more about FTP in Chapter 7.

Internet vs. Intranet

So far in this chapter we've discussed the Internet, assuming that you'll want to connect your Linux network to the rest of the world.

It's not mandatory that you connect your network to the rest of the world in order to use Internet technology. One of the hotter trends in the computer world, as a matter of fact, is using Internet technology on internal networks, the result being an *intranet*.

If you've used Linux for any amount of time, you've been using an intranet for a while *and didn't even know it*. An intranet is basically using network-based tools like electronic mail, remote logins, and TCP/IP to interconnect computers. This sounds just like the typical Linux network!

So, dear Linux reader, your evaluation process of intranet is a lot less complicated than for Windows geeks debating whether or not to connect to the Internet. As they sit and twiddle their thumbs about implementing intranet technology (contemplating using TCP/IP instead of Novell— what a concept!), you've already made the decision in favor of the intranet if you've already settled on Linux. Your only decision is whether or not to connect to the wider Internet and in what format.

This probably isn't a difficult decision. Let's face it—if your company works in a sensitive area, chances are good that you really don't want the outside world to be poking around your Linux Web site. If your company is in a nonglamorous manufacturing field with a defined audience, you may decide that the cost of connecting to the Internet just isn't worth the cost of said connection, since the number of potential customers stumbling across your site will be rather small. Or you could partially connect to the Internet, perhaps only with electronic mail.

What kind of information can be published on your intranet?

- Personal Web pages, so that workers can learn a little about other company workers through self-published pages.
- Group schedules. A new breed of group-scheduling programs uses the Internet to coordinate schedules among workgroups.
- Clear delineation of company policies. Instead of printing corporate policy handbooks, the information can be posted on an intranet.
- Electronic mail, both for internal employees and for the benefit of the world at large.

- Forms used for routine matters, such as payment and vacation requests.

- Access to company documentation. If your company creates widgets for the nursing market, the documentation can be placed online and updated as needed. Instead of creating a limited set of printed manuals, each user can have access to the documentation online.

- Threaded discussions of company developments.

- Corporate phone information.

Creating documents for an intranet isn't that complex; to be honest, a document prepared for dissemination within a company doesn't need to be as elaborate or as showy as Web documents prepared for the world at large. In these cases, using a text editor like emacs or an HTML editor like tkHTML is perfectly adequately.

The Intranet Layout

An intranet will look like any company network when mapped out. Your clients will use TCP/IP to connect to the Linux server. There's one big decision you'll need to make: whether or not to maintain a live connection to the Internet. You could easily implement Internet technology within your corporation without ever connecting to the Internet—after all, an intranet is nothing more than client/server computing using Internet technology.

On the flip side, a connection to the Internet can be a valuable thing, as your users can undoubtedly find useful information on the Net. In addition, you can maintain partial links, such as maintaining electronic mail with the Internet without providing Web usage. These situations require you to make some access decisions, but these decisions are not technological issues; rather, they are policy issues that require you to take into account intangibles. As far as technology goes, it's easy to set up a firewall that allows only outgoing data requests from your users while preventing outside requests to your Web server. It's also easy to set up a mail server to process incoming and outgoing mail without including Web access. Again, these are policy decisions.

Intranets and Security

You should have some knowledge of one of the prime considerations of anyone considering an intranet: security.

Chapter 13 will contain more information about security and firewalls.

N O T E

A recent development in the Internet world is the *virtual private network* (VPN). In a VPN, you would set up an Internet connection and use the Internet as your corporate network. In this situation, you wouldn't use private leased lines to connect your corporate sites; you would use the Internet, instead. You would need to establish usernames and passwords for anyone requiring access to your VPN, in much the same way that you would with a regular network. This basically turns the Internet into your own Wide Area Network (WAN), cutting down on your network costs (you don't need those expensive leased lines, except for the ones between your servers and your ISP). The advantages are that Internet technology is open and ubiquitous, and anyone connected anywhere in the world could log in to your VPN. In addition, you could adopt TCP/IP as your networking protocol of choice. Your users could use any operating system that supports TCP/IP—including Windows, Windows 95, UNIX, Linux, and Macintosh.

In this situation, however, privacy must be the first consideration, and you may find that the risk involved isn't worth the money savings. You'll need to adopt some stringent encryption policies, and you'll need to make sure that your browser and your server are well-integrated when it comes to security (in other words, using Microsoft products together or using Netscape products together).

There's also the moral issue of using the Internet as your own network and essentially asking other Internet users to (basically) subsidize your network. I once tangled with a computer consultant on a radio interview over the issue of Internet telephone software, which allows users to avoid paying long-distance telephone bills by using Internet connections. The trouble with arrangements like this is that telephone software packages are bandwidth hogs, and it's profoundly unfair for users to have to wait longer for their Web documents just so that two factory workers can have an Internet telephone connection open 10 hours a day.

N O T E

The Case for Web Browsers

When you decide to go with an intranet, you're really deciding to make a Web browser a prime part of your company information infrastructure. This decision shouldn't be made lightly. There are other corporate computing tools that are better integrated with the everyday tools—like word processors, spreadsheets, database managers, and customized applications—that your users are likely to use.

Still, there are some rather compelling reasons to go with Web browsers in your company. To wit:

- **Browsers are platform-independent.** Both Microsoft and Netscape Communications offer Windows 95/NT, Windows 3.1, and Macintosh versions of their browsers. In addition, Netscape offers UNIX and Linux versions of its browser. You can support a mixed environment of users with few problems—a Linux Web server can serve a mixed environment of PCs, Macintoshes, and UNIX workstations.

- **Browsers are free.** Arena, which ships on the accompanying CD-ROM, is free. Netscape Communications does require payment from corporations who use Navigator.

- **Browsers do not drag on system resources.** You won't need to upgrade hardware just because a browser is running all the time.

- **Browsers are easy to use.** Let's face it, there's not a lot of computing complexity associated with a browser for users. You basically enter a URL and away you go. With the rise of the Internet among home users, you're also assured that a good chunk of your workforce will be somewhat familiar with browser technology. This should cut down on training times and costs.

- **Browsers can help cut down on development costs.** When you develop an application, you usually must develop it for a specific operating system. Sure, we know that cross-platform development occurs, but we also know what a pain it is. This is avoided when you use Web browsers to funnel this technology to users: A Java applet will run the same on any browser supporting Java, no matter if the browsers run on Linux, Windows 95, Windows 3.1, or Macintosh.

Your specific situation will dictate whether or not to go with an intranet.

Administrative Issues

Many of the most important issues you'll face in setting up an intranet will have little to do with technology and more with turf issues. Everyone will want to have a say in how the intranet is run and administered. Let's face it, experience with Internet and intranet technology is a good thing for anyone to have on their resume at this time, so don't be surprised if there are some sharp elbows coming your way as you plan the network.

Still, you'll need to work out logistical issues of all sorts. Who should decide permissions for various domains? Who should be performing the grunt work of the network, doing such things as system backups? How much power should be divided among domains? Once it's set up, Linux is rather easy to maintain—basically, it runs itself—but someone will have to be charge of the network when it comes to the grunge work.

This book isn't going to spend a lot of time on setting up a TCP/IP network. This is an involved topic that's already been the topic of other texts (which you'll learn about in Appendix A). Here, we'll assume that such a network has been set up.

Summary

This chapter introduced the Internet and intranet as they apply to the Slackware Linux operating system. The tools for placing your own server on the Internet are part of Slackware Linux. This chapter detailed the various servers that comprise the Internet: Web servers, electronic-mail servers, Gopher servers, FTP servers, search engines, chat/discussion servers, and more. All these tools are either part of Slackware Linux or contained on the accompanying CD-ROM, so it's possible for you to place a well-rounded site on the Web without having to go out and buy a lot of additional commercial software. Just add your own content, and you're set.

Additional time was spent discussing what sort of hardware configuration you'll need on your Linux box. It's not a complicated process to decide on such a configuration, but spending a little money in the right places will increase performance.

If you've been using Linux on a network, you're already familiar with intranet technology—after all, Linux is built upon the same TCP/IP that fuels the Internet. Your task as a system administrator or Webmaster will be to decide if limiting yourself to intranet technology is important and to what extent you want to connect to the Internet.

Linux Internet Connection Methods

This chapter covers:

- Connecting to the Internet
- Dialup connections
- ISDN
- Frame-relay connections
- T1 lines
- T3 lines
- Working with an ISP
- Addressing issues
- Obtaining a domain name
- InterNIC policies on domain names

Connection Methods

Connecting to the Internet isn't an exceptionally difficult process. There are basically three methods:

- Dialup connection
- Hosting by Internet service provider
- Direct high-speed connection

You can't accomplish any of these connections on your own. You'll need to work with a firm that specializes in Internet connectivity, an *Internet service provider* (ISP). The company will walk you through the process of setting up an Internet connection. Even though all ISPs offer the same thing—Internet connectivity—they differ on their processes and methods. Put another way: There's no one way to connect to the Internet, and each ISP differs, so your exact plan for Internet connectivity will depend to a very large extent on your ISP. Hence, this chapter deals with generalities of connecting to the Internet, rather than specifics (buy a router from Corporation A, configure it in this manner, and so on).

So, your first step in Internet connectivity is to find an ISP. The ISP will be the outfit that provides the direct connection to the Internet, with a domain name and IP addresses.

The advice in this chapter is really meant for smaller to midsized companies and organizations. Larger outfits probably already have a presence on the Internet in some way, and enterprise connectivity to the Internet is beyond the scope of this book.

NOTE

You'll want to get information from a wide range of ISPs. There are several nationwide lists of local ISPs that you can check. The best are

- *http://thelist.com*
- *http://www.primus.com/providers*
- *http://www.stars.com/Vlib/Misc/Providers.html*
- *http://union.ncsa.uiuc.edu/HyperNews/get/www/leasing.html*

- *http://budgetweb.com/budgetweb/*
- *http://budgetweb.com/hndocs/list.shtml*
- *http://www.yahoo.com/Business_and_Economy/Companies/ Internet_Services/Web_Presence_Providers/*

You may also want to check with national Internet service providers, especially if you're located in a large urban area. Some of the leaders include:

- BBN Planet (*http://www.bbnplanet.com*)
- Netcom (*http://www.netcom.com*)
- PSINet (*http://www.psi.com*)

When discussing your situation with an ISP, you should have some idea of how many users your Linux Internet server will support and what services you want to offer. In Chapter 1, you learned about the services; in this chapter, you'll learn about connection methods.

Table 2.1 lists the major connection methods and their optimal speeds.

Table 2.1 Major Connection Methods to the Internet

Connection	Maximum bits per second (bps)	Users Supported
Dialup modem	28,800	3–4
Frame relay	56,000	10–20
ISDN	128,000	10–50
T1	1,500,000	100–500
Fractional T1	Varies as needed	Varies as needed
T3	45,000,000	5000+

Dialup Connections

If you don't expect a lot of traffic on your Linux Web server, you can limp along by connecting to an ISP via modem (with a top speed of 28.8Kbps) or ISDN modem (with an average speed of 128Kbps).

Basically, you dial into an ISP's computer and then leave the connection open 24 hours a day. A dialup connection costs little to set up (basically, all you need is a $120 modem), but you'll need a special arrangement with an ISP that gives you a fixed IP address (as opposed to the dynamically allocated addresses that most Internet dialup users have), probably a leased line (you could try to use a standard line, but reliability becomes an issue), and you'll need to pay for the privilege of such a 24-hour connection (in other words, don't expect to pay $19.95 a month for such an arrangement; expect to pay between $100 and $300 per month).

A connection like this can be expected to support three to four users simultaneously in most situations. For a small Linux network that doesn't need major Usenet access and isn't spending a lot of time transferring large files to and from Internet sites, this connection method is pretty acceptable.

 As this book was written, the telephone industry was on the verge of introducing a new networking technology, ADL, which allows higher-speed dialup connections to the Internet. Because the technology and services are still very new, they are not covered here.

N O T E

ISDN

The Integrated Services Digital Network (ISDN) technology was supposed to be the next great thing when it came to supplying digital information from computer to computer.

Unfortunately, ISDN never took off on a large scale; by the time the telecommunications giants stopped fighting about ISDN standards, newer and more affordable technologies had made ISDN obsolete on a large corporate scale.

Standards die hard in the computer world, however, and with the rise of the Internet ISDN was dusted off and repositioned as a higher-speed digital access tool. It's really a transitional technology—as our telephone and cable systems move toward a merger of sorts, ISDN technology will be obsolete when we all have high-speed access in our homes.

Basically, ISDN works like a regular analog modem. You connect an ISDN modem or an ISDN router to your phone line, which transmits digital signals. It's actually the equivalent of two telephone lines: there are two 64Kbps B channels that can be combined to provide 128Kbps. Or these channels can be maintained separately—one for data and one for voice. (If you're a telephone geek and wonder how this can happen, it's because there's a separate D channel used for signaling. Then again, if you're a telephone geek, you probably know more about this than you can get from a book.)

ISDN offers a higher connection speed but costs even more than a standard dialup connection. ISDN modems are more expensive and, to be honest, most ISPs don't yet support ISDN. In addition, you'll need to contract with your local telephone company for an ISDN line (with setup costs between $50 and $100, depending on your area). Almost every telephone company also charges by the minute for ISDN access, so you're looking at some pretty outrageous bills—probably at least $500 per month. The telephone industry has been slow to see ISDN as a viable business tool, and marketing and availability are spotty.

Because ISDN offers better throughput, you can expect to support up to 40 or 50 users simultaneously. Given the larger number of users you can service, this may be a more attractive alternative. However, both ISDN and dialup analog lines suffer from the same problem: reliability. Connections are frequently dropped, and the current phone system wasn't built to support 24-hour analog connections.

In the next six months, many of you can expect to see cable modems be a factor in these decisions. Basically, a cable modem uses the same wiring used in cable television to connect to the Internet. In these cases, your cable company is your ISP, which should scare the living daylights out of you.

There are different hardware requirements for ISDN. You'll need a network terminator (which costs between $100 and $300) and a router, or you'll need an ISDN modem.

You may need to know about specific configuration options for using an ISDN modem under Linux. More information can be found at *http://www.ix.de/ix/linux/linux-isdn.html*.

Financially, ISDN tariffs range all over the map. Some states have a low monthly charge, with a per-minute charge past a small period. Other states have a higher monthly charge, with more free hours thrown in. The frustrating thing here is that there's no shopping for ISDN service; it's under the auspices of the local telephone company, so they can pretty much set whatever rates they want. If you want a full-time connection to the Internet, you'll need to maintain a 24-hour connection, which can run into serious money.

N O T E There's a constant in the computer world: The user base lurches in one direction, and the computer industry frantically rushes to catch up. Such is the case with ISDN, which uses 1980s technology to provide digital telephone lines. This means that there are many new offerings from vendors hitting the market. In addition, many telephone companies are reevaluating their ISDN tariffs. The prices listed in this section may not be valid by the time you read this book, so you'll want to do some shopping before you either decide on or reject ISDN.

Hosting by an ISP

Many ISPs essentially "rent" space on their server, with rates depending on the amount of hard-disk space you use. The appeal here is that there's no system administration involved; all you need to do is upload HTML and program files via FTP. Of course, there's a corresponding lack of control here—if your ISP goes down, access to your information will also go down. Similarly, you can't fine-tune performance at all.

An alternative that's gained some popularity recently is for you to actually set up your own physical Web server at an ISP. Your server would be directly connected via network to the ISP's system (typically, an ISP will have more than one system involved for Internet access). You don't sacrifice anything in performance (in other words, a connection to your server wouldn't be slowed down like a connection via modem is), and you can administer your site from anywhere—all you need to do is connect to your server via the Internet and log in as an administrator.

Direct High-Speed Connections

You could go digital and get your own high-speed connection to the Internet in the form of a 56K frame relay or T1 line; these connections cost as much as $1,000 per month or so (depending on your location and your local telephone company). If you're working in a smaller community that lacks an assortment of ISPs, you could actually turn around and host Web pages from others on your system.

What can you expect to pay for a direct connection? That depends on your location, to an extent. If you're serious about Internet access, you'll want to look at a leased line between your server and the ISP. (Procuring this line is usually a service offered by the ISP.) This alone may run you about $1,000 a month, depending on the distance between you and the ISP.

In addition, you can expect to pay a setup fee to your ISP, which will cover its costs in allocating IP addresses and bandwidth. You can also expect a monthly fee from your ISP above and beyond the costs of the leased line. You'll also receive separate bills from your telephone company: one bill for setting up the leased line and monthly bills for the leased line itself.

Some ISPs may handle all billings for leased lines. This probably isn't a big deal for most companies.

NOTE

There may be other expenses involved, particularly if you're not in an urban area or if for some reason you decide to go with an ISP outside your local calling area. This tends to be rather complicated, involving leased lines going to other LATAs (Local Access and Transport Areas). Basically, it's rather evil. If you can avoid this, do so. If there's no other alternative to dealing with an ISP outside your local area, you'll want to consider physically placing your own server at the distant ISP or merely leasing space on the ISP's server. (You can run a Linux box in the first instance, but the second instance leaves you at the mercy of your ISP when it comes to an operating system and development tools.)

If you're expecting a middling amount of traffic on your Web site and are also looking to have your own users connect to the outer Internet, you're looking at a leased line, either a 56K frame-relay line or a T1 line. The advantage to 56K in this situation is that it's much cheaper than a T1 line (a 56K line runs $100 to $200 a month, while a T1 line can run $2,000 to $6,000 a month) and more reliable than an analog line used for 28.8 or ISDN connections. Unless you're expecting a high-traffic site, a 56K frame relay should suffice. You will need additional hardware to use a 56K frame-relay line, including a CSU/DSU (Channel Service Unit/Data Service Unit), which handles the interface between your system and the line. Most ISPs will sell you this equipment.

More on T1 Lines

Some of you will find that a T1 line is a necessity—especially if you're setting up a situation where many of your users will also be connecting to the Internet via your network. These leased lines are sold by local telephone companies, and they're charged on the basis of distance from the switching service. Your bandwidth with a T1 line is 1.544 megabits per second.

Physically, the T1 line connects to a router at your office. An Ethernet connection is used between your server and the router. The router allows you to connect other Web servers to the T1 line, as well as any other specialized servers you might have (for example, you may want to install a separate mail server if you experience high electronic-mail traffic). Most ISPs will sell you a router and a CSU/DSU, as well as any other cabling and equipment you may need.

Currently, the manufacturer of most Internet routers is Cisco Systems (*http://www.cisco.com*). However, for one reason or another, Livingston (*http://www.livingston.com*) routers are popular among Linux networking folks (if information in the newsgroups and HOW-TOs is correct).

There are also *fractional T1 lines*, where you don't have full access to an entire T1 line—instead, you have access to 24 channels of 64Kbps. A fractional line represents a good cost savings from a T1 line (although it must be pointed out that the costs of setting up a T1 and a fractional T1 line are the same) and provides your company with a lot of flexibility.

N O T E Networking hardware tends to be a world unto itself, and this book isn't written for the network engineer whose heart pumps a little faster when hardware is discussed. If you're into hardware, you'll want to check out a hardware-oriented networking book (some are listed in Appendix A).

Addressing Important Issues

After you've settled on an ISP and a connection scheme, the next step is obtain a domain name and IP addresses. Every computer on the Internet needs an IP address, including both servers and clients, such as your users who are out surfing the Net.

IP addresses are allocated in two different ways: permanently and dynamically. A permanently assigned IP address is exactly what it sounds like. Your server will need a permanently assigned IP address.

On the flip side, your users can share a range of IP addresses. These can be allocated to them on an as-needed basis; that's why they are *dynamic*.

When you sign up with an ISP, you'll be assigned an IP address for your server. This single address can be tied directly to your server, or it can be tied to a router connected to the server.

NOTE The mysteries of networks and subnetworks are beyond the scope of this book. See Appendix A for a list of additional resources.

Obtaining a Domain Name

Your ISP can arrange for your domain name, or you can apply directly to InterNIC. (Before you do this, you'll need to have an arrangement with an ISP, as you need to tell InterNIC your IP addresses.) You can do this directly from the Internet by connecting to the following address:

http://www.rs.internic.net

This brings up an information screen. Follow the instructions, and you'll get your own domain name. You'll need to provide the following information:

- The name and address of your company or organization.
- Your electronic-mail address.
- Contacts within your company or organization.
- Billing information. (The initial registration cost is $100, which covers the first two years, and $50 per year after that.)
- Server name and IP addresses.
- A short description of your site.

InterNIC is actually an umbrella organization; the actual registration is handled by Network Solutions, Inc. This firm administers domain names in the *com, org, gov, edu,* and *net* domains.

Once your domain name is approved—if there's no conflict with previously registered names—you'll be notified via e-mail in a few days. (If you want to see whether a domain name is taken, point your Web browser to *http://www.rs.internic.net/cgi-bin/whois*.) The domain name is then part of the InterNIC database, which is the official repository of domain names.

NOTE What do you do if your preferred domain name is already taken? It depends. In the early days of the Internet, there was a mad rush to claim common company names for domain names. Back then, you didn't need to provide a link between your domain name and what you wanted to do, so many entrepreneurs registered common names and then held them ransom.

As the Internet grew, it became apparent that this system wouldn't work, as it basically denied the existence of trademark law—why should the Internet be immune to trademark protections? The current InterNIC policy is to award the domain name but to reserve the right to withdraw that permission if the valid holder of a trademark name comes forward with proof of the trademark. If you registered the domain name of *burgerking.com* and the real Burger King corporation came along to register the same domain name, you'd be asked to give it up. As the InterNIC registration page says:

NSI has neither the resources nor the legal obligation to screen requested domain names to determine whether the use of a domain anima by an applicant may infringe upon the right(s) of a third party. As a result, the InterNIC requires that as part of the application process, the applicant must represent and warrant several conditions related to the name.

These conditions include acknowledgment of trademark validity.

The InterNIC has tightened its registration procedures, adding encryption to make the procedure secure with the Guardian service. In addition, the InterNIC has expanded its registration procedure to make sure that contact information is correct. (A full explanation can be found at *ftp://rs.internic.net/templates/contact-templates.txt*.)

How Domain Names Are Organized

We've been tossing around the term *domain* throughout this book without explaining it.

Basically, a *domain name* is a substitute for an IP address. Domain names don't actually exist for technical reasons—they exist because some smart people realized that most people would remember *www.suck.com* rather than its numerical IP address. A Domain Name Server, or DNS, handles these translations. When a user enters **www.suck.com** in Netscape Navigator, a DNS is contacted, and that DNS translates *www.suck.com* to its IP address, facilitating the proper destination for the request.

Basically, these domains are organized in a hierarchical fashion. At the top of the pyramid is the international backbone of the Internet, followed by a national backbone, regional backbones, local routers, and machines where the Internet basically ends (which is where your server will exist).

A domain also refers to a type of a server. Commercial domains end with *com*; network providers, ISPs, and Internet-related domains end with *net*; educational domains end with *edu*; government domains end with *gov*; organizations (nonprofits and noncommercial entities) end with *org*; and military domains end with *mil*. In addition, domains from outside the United States usually end with a country domain—domains in Canada, for example, end with *ca*, while domains in the United Kingdom end with *uk*.

There are DNS servers scattered all around the Internet. If you do go with a service provider, you'll probably go through your ISP's DNS. If you decide to install a DNS at your site, you'll need to make sure that you set up a mirror of another DNS on the Internet, preferably one that is physically near you.

Summary

This chapter summarized the methods of connecting your Internet server to the greater Internet. These connections can be slow and cheap (as in 28.8Kbps dialup connections), fast and expensive (as in the case of T1 and T3 lines), or somewhere in between (as is the case with frame-relay connections and ISDN).

Your specific connection structure will depend largely on your ISP, from whom you buy your own Internet connection.

After you settle on an ISP and your connection method, you'll need to acquire a domain name. You can work with your ISP to purchase a domain name, or you can directly contact InterNIC to claim one. There's no advantage to one or the other, but most ISPs have mechanisms in place to acquire domain names from InterNIC.

In the next chapter, you'll learn about installing Linux and Internet components.

INSTALLING LINUX AND INTERNET COMPONENTS

This chapter covers:

- Linux installation
- Preparing your system
- Installing from CD-ROM after making a bookdisk
- Running the **setup** script
- Running the **netconfig** script
- Configuring X Window
- Using the **xf86config** script
- Checking X Window settings
- Important networking files
- Checking your network connection

Installing Linux

After you finish your planning, it's time to install Linux for use on the Internet. For the most part, installing Slackware Linux from the accompanying CD-ROM is the same as a general-purpose Linux installation. The concern here is that you install the networking components during the main Linux installation. In this chapter, you'll be guided through installation.

Basically, installing Slackware Linux is a multipart process. First, you must prepare the PC for installation (which means wiping out the remnants of previous operating systems and starting from scratch), boot a scaled-down version of Linux, and then proceed with the full installation. After this, you must configure your Linux system in several different ways. The actual installation process is as follows:

- Create your boot and root floppies from the accompanying CD-ROM
- Prepare your hard drive for installation with PC DOS–based tools
- Boot a small implementation of Linux from boot and root floppies
- Install the full version of Linux from the CD-ROM

Starting with a Clean System

It's best if you install Slackware Linux from a clean PC; that is, nothing on the hard drive save the MS-DOS operating system. You can install and use Slackware Linux on a PC that already has another operating system installed (such as Windows 95), and many personal users do opt for this configuration.

However, there's very little reason to have more than one operating system on a Linux box used as an Internet server. You can't use more than one operating system at a time, and if you plan on having a full-time Internet site, you certainly won't be booting up Windows 95 too often. Therefore, for the purposes of an Internet server, you'll want to have a clean PC with only MS-DOS (or PC–DOS; it really doesn't matter) installed.

You'll also want to make sure that the networking hardware is installed and working on your Linux box. When Linux boots for the first time, it senses the hardware in the system (or, more accurately, looks for hardware in the usual spots) and adjusts accordingly.

Preparing Your Hard Drive for Linux

Preparing your hard disk for Linux isn't difficult—you merely wipe out what's there and reinstall DOS. It's best if you actually have two or more partitions on your PC: a small partition for DOS and at least one partition for Linux. (You may want to have two partitions for Linux: one for the operating system and one for swap space. We'll cover each later.)

If you're from the UNIX world, the notion of a partition may seem a little odd. Intel-based PCs can have multiple *partitions* on a hard drive. If you've worked with PCs, you know that you can have several drive letters (such as **C:**, **D:**, and **E:**), even though the PC has only one physical hard drive. This capability exists because early versions of MS-DOS could not recognize hard disks with more than 33MB in a contiguous area, and when 40MB hard drives appeared, Microsoft pulled a quick trick in order to be able to use the entire hard disk. (MS-DOS 4.0 was the first version to do away with this restriction.)

However, you must use DOS tools to create your partitions. You could use OS/2, but there's no reason to go out and buy OS/2 just for creating partitions. When you use these DOS tools, you tell the PC what operating system exists on a given partition.

In our best-case scenario (in a perfect world, of course), you install Linux on a brand-new system, and there's little of importance currently installed on your hard disk. This is the route we try to follow, since there's little chance that you'll damage anything important.

However, if you've been using your PC for a while, you've probably accumulated software, data files, and configurations that you're loathe to give up. In this case, you'll want to retain as much of the DOS configuration as possible, while making room for Linux. You can take two routes:

- Use the **FIPS** utility to partition the hard drive without (theoretically) destroying the existing data.

- Back up the DOS data, creating the new Linux and DOS partitions, and then reinstall the backup. (This is our preferred method.) You'll need to make sure that the new partition is large enough to contain all the data from the old DOS partition, of course.

In either case, you should first make a backup of your hard disk, either on floppy disks or some tape-based medium (Bernoulli drive, SyQuest tape, DAT tape). Depending on your system configuration, you'll want to either back up everything or back up those directories that can't easily be reinstalled from floppy or CD-ROM. (We find that a good system cleansing is desirable once in a while, so we tend to back up data and irreplaceable configuration files, while reinstalling applications from scratch.) Yes, we know that backing up your hard drive is a pain (and we probably don't do it as often as we should), but you should make a backup every time you do something to your hard drive that has the potential to destroy data.

Using FIPS to Divide Your Hard Drive

After you make your backup, you'll need to decide which route to take. The **FIPS** utility described previously is stored in the root directory of the accompanying CD-ROM as **FIPS.EXE**; the guide to using **FIPS** is stored in the same location as **FIPS.DOC**. (If you plan to use the **FIPS** utility, we *strongly* advise that you read through this file several times, as it contains far more information and detail than here.)

Basically, **FIPS** creates a new partition on the physical end of the hard drive. Before the **FIPS** utility does so, you must first *defragment* your hard drive. When a PC writes to a hard disk, it writes to clusters on disk. Generally speaking, this writing is done sequentially; the first clusters appear at the physical beginning of the disk. As you use the system, you inevitably write more and more to the hard drive, and you probably delete a good amount of data. As you delete the data, the clusters they occupied are freed; at the same time, new data are written to the end of the disk. Any hard disk that's been in use for a while will have data scattered throughout the physical drive. (This is why hard drives slow down when they fill with data; the drive head must physically hop around the drive to retrieve scattered data.)

When you defragment your hard drive, you're replacing the freed clusters at the beginning of the drive with data from the end of the drive. While not purely sequential, your data are all crammed at the beginning of the hard drive. This improves disk performance—since your data are physically closer together, the drive head spends less time retrieving data that were scattered in the past.

 Newer versions of MS-DOS and PC DOS (that is, versions 6.0 and better) contain a defragmenting utility. (Check your operating-system documentation for specifics, as the utilities differ.)

N O T E

The **FIPS** utility takes advantage of the fact that the data are crammed at the beginning of the hard drive. It allows you to create a point past the end of DOS data to begin the new Linux partition (if you use this method, remember to leave room for more data in the DOS partition!).

FIPS is more suited for those who are adding Linux to an existing configuration. Generally speaking, this won't be the case with most readers of this book—quite honestly, there's not a lot of use to having multiple operating system on a Linux Internet server, where the vast majority of the time will be spent connected to the Internet as a server, not as a terminal. If you really want to preserve your existing operating system, check out the documentation for **FIPS** on the accompanying CD-ROM.

Using DOS Utilities to Divide Your Hard Drive

The second—and preferable—method to prepare your hard drive for Linux involves various DOS utilities, which you'll use to create new partitions and configure a floppy diskette that you can use to boot your PC with DOS.

The first steps involves creating a DOS boot diskette. This is a rather simple procedure, involving the following command line:

```
C:> format /s A:
```

where **A:** is your boot drive and **C:** is your hard disk containing your operating system. This command formats a floppy disk and adds the system files (**COMMAND.COM**, as well as hidden files **IO.SYS** and **MSDOS.SYS**) needed to boot DOS from the floppy diskette. If you install a DOS partition, booting from this diskette will give you access to that partition (which will appear as drive **C:**). It will *not*, however, give you access to the CD-ROM until you install the CD-ROM drivers on the DOS boot diskette.

After doing this, you'll need to copy some additional utilities to the floppy. You'll need to be fairly selective about what files you copy to the floppy diskette, since the sum of all DOS .**EXE** and .**COM** files (essentially, the utility files) in a typical DOS installation won't fit on a floppy diskette. You'll need to copy the **FDISK.EXE** and **FORMAT.COM** files to the floppy diskette drive with the following command lines:

```
C:> copy \DOS\FDISK.EXE A:
     1 file(s) copied

C:> copy \DOS\FORMAT.COM A:
     1 file(s) copied
```

You may also want to copy onto floppy diskettes the files that restore your system backup, if you used operating-system utilities to create the backup. Check your documentation for the specific files, since they differ among operating systems.

N O T E

What Are FDISK and FORMAT?

FDISK.EXE is the program that creates MS-DOS partitions. Every operating system has a program that does something similarly (you'll use the Linux **fdisk** command later in this process). You'll need to use the partitioning software specific to the operating system—for example, you can't use **FDISK** to create Linux or OS/2 partitions. **FDISK.EXE** works very simply: You delete an existing partition or partitions and create new partitions in their place.

Creating a partition merely leaves a portion of your hard disk devoted to the particular operating system. After you've used **FDISK.EXE** to create a new DOS partition, you'll use the **FORMAT.COM** program to format that partition for use under MS-DOS. If you don't format the MS-DOS partition, the operating system won't be able to recognize it.

Using the DOS FDISK Utility

Now that you've created the system backup and a boot diskette, it's time to destroy the data on your hard drive with the **FDISK** utility. The act of creating new partitions is by definition a destructive act. You must destroy the existing partitions and the records of the data contained therein in order to create the new partitions.

 You can use **FDISK** if your system has more than one hard drive. In this case, you'll want to make sure that you're working on the correct hard drive. **FDISK** does not use the normal DOS drive representations (**C:**, **D:**, **E:**, etc.); rather, **FDISK** uses numerals, such as *1* or *2*.

Begin by booting your PC from the floppy diskette drive you created in the previous section. This vanilla boot will ask you for today's date and time (ignore both; they don't matter) and then give you the following command line:

```
A>
```

You're now ready to run the DOS **FDISK** utility:

```
A> fdisk
```

There are no command-line parameters to **FDISK**.

The program loads and displays something like the screen shown in Figure 3.1.

```
                    MS-DOS Version 5.00
                  Fixed Disk Setup Program
            (C) Copyright Microsoft 1983 - 1991


                      FDISK OPTIONS


Current fixed disk drive: 1

Choose one of the following:

1. Create DOS partition or Logical DOS Drive
2. Set active partition
3. Delete partition or Logical DOS Drive
4. Display partition information


Enter choice: [1]


Press Esc to exit FDISK
```

Figure 3.1 The opening screen to the FDISK utility.

NOTE The figures is this section are for a specific version of MS-DOS. However, most versions of MS-DOS follow the conventions shown and explained here. If the choices on your system aren't exactly like the choices here, read through them carefully and use the similar choice. Remember that you are essentially deleting a partition and creating a new one in this procedure.

At this point you'll need to delete the existing partition, so you'll choose **3**. (If you're not sure about the existing partitions on your disk, or if you're even working on the correct disk should you have more than one, select **4**.)

NOTE

When using the **FDISK** utility, you'll see references to primary and extended partitions, as well as to logical drives. Here's an explanation:

- The **primary** partition is the partition containing the files (**IO.SYS, MSDOS.SYS**, and **COMMAND.COM**) needed to boot MS-DOS. In essence, this is your **C:** drive. The partition cannot be divided into other logical drives.

- The **extended** partition or partitions do not contain these boot files. An extended partition can exist as its own logical drive (such as **D:** or **E:**) or be divided into additional logical drives.

- The **logical drive** is the portion of a partition assigned a drive letter. For instance, an extended partition can be divided up into up to 23 logical drives (**A:** and **B:** are reserved for floppy diskette drives, and **C:** is reserved for the primary partition, leaving 23 letters).

Additionally, the **non-DOS** partition is for another operating system, such as Linux. Chances are that you won't need to deal with more than a primary drive or an extended drive.

After selecting **3**, you'll see the screen shown in Figure 3.2.

```
            Delete DOS Partition or Logical DOS Drive

Current fixed disk drive: 1

Choose one of the following:

1. Delete Primary DOS Partition
2. Delete Extended DOS Partition
3. Delete Logical DOS Drive(s) in the Extended DOS Partition
4. Delete Non-DOS Partition

Enter choice: [ ]


Press Esc to return to FDISK Options
```

Figure 3.2 The delete screen for FDISK.

What you do at this point depends on how your hard drive has been configured. If you have primary and extended partitions, delete them. If you have only a primary drive, delete it. **FDISK** will confirm that you do indeed want to delete a partition. This is your last chance to chicken out and check the DOS partition one more time before actually wiping it out.

After deleting a partition, you'll need to create a new DOS partition— a choice that's listed in Figure 3.1 as option **1**. After choosing **1**, you'll be shown a screen like that in Figure 3.3.

```
            Create DOS Partition or Logical DOS Drive

Current fixed disk drive: 1

Choose one of the following:

1. Create Primary DOS Partition
2. Create Extended DOS Partition
3. Create Logical DOS Drive(s) in the Extended DOS Partition

Enter choice: [1]

Press Esc to return to FDISK Options
```

Figure 3.3 Creating a new partition with FDISK.

Of course, you'll want to create a new primary partition; this is the partition that will be used for DOS.

The next thing you'll need to decide is how much of the hard drive to devote to DOS. There are no hard-and-fast rules concerning partition sizes. In this situation, you'll need to decide if you want to have DOS available. (You probably will, since it comes in handy at times to boot DOS for diagnostic purposes.) Web servers tend to suck up a lot of disk space, especially if you're accessing the Usenet on some level. It won't do your Web server a lot of good to have a DOS partition sitting there with a lot of usable space. Leaving as little as 5MB for DOS is prudent.

Don't bother with any other partitions—at least none for Linux usage. You won't want to create a logical DOS drive, more than likely; if you do, you can't use it for a Linux installation, as all Linux partitions must be created through Linux later in the installation process.

After deciding how much hard-disk space to give to DOS, you'll want to exit **FDISK**. Go ahead and make the DOS partition active (this means that you can boot from it later, which you'll want to do; you can have multiple partitions ready to boot).

After quitting **FDISK**, reboot the system, leaving the DOS diskette in drive **A:**. You'll now want to format drive **C:**—or at least the DOS portion of it—with the DOS **FORMAT** command:

```
A> FORMAT /S C:
```

This command formats the DOS partition with the core of the operating system (the **COMMAND.COM, IO.SYS**, and **MSDOS.SYS** files). The **FORMAT** command makes sure that you want to go ahead with the format (this is to make sure that DOS neophytes don't accidentally format a partition containing valuable information); you'll answer in the affirmative when asked whether you want to proceed with the format.

NOTE
You can use any version of DOS for these steps, as long as it's DOS 4.0 or better. DOS doesn't care if you format the hard drive with one version of DOS and install another versions later.

Now that you've prepared the DOS side of your hard disk (and after looking back, realizing that it's a lot easier than the extended verbiage in the previous sections would make it seem), it's time to actually ainstall Linux.

Creating Boot and Root Floppy Disks

Your first steps will be to create two floppy disks used to boot Linux: the *boot* and *root* diskettes. The boot diskette is the diskette used (as the name implies) to boot the PC, while the root diskette contains a set of Linux commands (actually, a complete mini-Linux system). Creating these disks is probably the best way to install Linux, although it is possible to install Linux without using any floppy disks using **LOADLIN.EXE**, a DOS program that loads Linux from an MS-DOS prompt. We'll cover this option a little later on, but unless your floppy disk doesn't work under Linux, it is recommended to install using a bootdisk and a rootdisk.

Your next step is to determine which bootdisk and rootdisk images you'll be using and to write the images onto formatted floppy disks. Because selecting the disk images to use (especially the bootdisk) can be a relatively large selection, it warrants its own section.

Choosing Bootdisk and Rootdisk Images

Linux needs to know a lot about your PC's hardware, and that knowledge begins the second you boot the system. That's why you need to put some thought into selecting your bootdisk and rootdisk images.

Before we go any further, you need to understand what *bootdisk* and *rootdisk images* are. Linux needs to boot from floppy diskettes initially and needs to know what sort of hardware it's working with. When you boot Linux for the first time, the information is contained on the bootdisk and the rootdisk. To create a bootdisk and a rootdisk, you must select the proper image. Then you'll use the **RAWRITE.EXE** utility to copy the image byte-for-byte to the diskette.

How do you select the proper image? The first step is to determine the disk size of your drive **A:**, which is the drive from which you boot the system. If you're using a 3.5-inch disk drive as **A:**, you'll need to grab an image from the **bootdsks.144** directory. (This is so labeled because the capacity of a 3.5-inch high-density floppy diskette is 1.44MB.) If you're using a 5.25-inch disk drive to boot from, you'll need to grab an image from the **bootdsks.12** directory. (This is so labeled because the capacity of a 5.25-inch high-density floppy is 1.2MB.)

If you look inside either directory, you'll a list of filenames ending in **.I** (for *IDE*) or **.S** (for *SCSI*). (The filenames are the same in both directories; at this point it doesn't matter from which directory you grab the image.) Each image supports a different set of hardware; a listing of the files and the supported hardware appears in Tables 3.1 (for IDE bootdisks) and 3.2 (for SCSI bootdisks).

Table 3.1 Linux IDE Bootdisks and Supported Hardware; All IDE bootdisks support IDE hard drives and CD-ROM drives, plus additional hardware.

Filename	Supported Hardware
aztech.i	CD-ROM drives: Aztech CDA268-01A, Orchid CD-3110, Okano/Wearnes CDD110, Conrad TXC, CyCDROM CR520, CR540
bare.i	IDE hard-drive only
cdu31a.i	Sony CDU31/33a CD-ROM
cdu535.i	Sony CDU531/535 CD-ROM
cm206.i	Philips/LMS cm206 CD-ROM with cm260 adapter card
goldstar.i	Goldstar R420 CD-ROM (sometimes sold in a Reveal Multimedia Kit)
mcd.i	Non-IDE Mitsumi CD-ROM
mcdx.i	Improved non-IDE Mitsumi CD-ROM support
net.i	Ethernet support
optics.i	Optics Storage 8000 AT CD-ROM (know as the "Dolphin" drive)
sanyo.i	Sanyo CDR-H94A CD-ROM
sbpcd.i	Matsushita, Kotobuki, Panasonic, Creative Labs (SoundBlaster), Longshine, and TEAC non-IDE CD-ROM
xt.i	MFM hard drive

Table 3.2 Linux SCSI Bootdisks and Hardware Support; All SCSI bootdisks feature full IDE hard-drive and CD-ROM support, plus additional drivers.

Filename	Supported Hardware
7000fast.s	Western Digital 7000FASST SCSI
advansys.s	AdvanSys SCSI support
aha152x.s	Adaptec 152x SCSI
aha1542.s	Adaptec 1542 SCSI
aha1740.s	Adaptec 1740 SCSI
aha2x4x.s	Adaptec AIC7xxx SCSI (including AHA-274x, AHA-2842, AHA-2940, AHA-2940W, AHA-2940U, AHA-2940UW, AHA-2944D, AHA-2944WD, AHA-3940, AHA-3940W, AHA-3985, AHA-3985W)
am53c974.s	AMD AM53/79C974 SCSI

Table 3.2 Linux SCSI Bootdisks and Hardware Support; All SCSI bootdisks feature full IDE hard-drive and CD-ROM support, plus additional drivers. (continued)

Filename	Supported Hardware
aztech.s	All supported SCSI controllers, plus CD-ROM support for Aztech CDA268-01A, Orchid CD-3110, Okano/Wearnes CDD110, Conrad TXC, CyCDROM CR520, CR540
buslogic.s	Buslogic MultiMaster SCSI
cdu31a.s	All supported SCSI controllers, plus CD-ROM support for Sony CDU31/33a
cdu535.s	All supported SCSI controllers, plus CD-ROM support for Sony CDU531/535
cm206.s	All supported SCSI controllers, plus Philips/LMS cm206 CD-ROM with cm260 adapter card
dtc3280.s	DTC (Data Technology Corp.) 3180/3280 SCSI
eata_dma.s	DPT EATA-DMA SCSI (boards such as PM2011, PM2021, PM2041, PM3021, PM2012B, PM2022, PM2122, PM2322, PM2042, PM3122, PM3222, PM3332, PM2024, PM2124, PM2044, PM2144, PM3224, PM3334)
eata_isa.s	DPT EATA-ISA/EISA SCSI support (boards such as PM2011B/9X, PM2021A/9X, PM2012A, PM2012B, PM2022A/9X, PM2122A/9X, PM2322A/9X)
eata_pio.s	DPT EATA-PIO SCSI (PM2001 and PM2012A)
fdomain.s	Future Domain TMC-16x0 SCSI
goldstar.s	All supported SCSI controllers, plus Goldstar R420 CD-ROM (sometimes sold in a Reveal Multimedia Kit)
in2000.s	Always IN2000 SCSI
iomega.s	IOMEGA PPA3 parallel-port SCSI (also supports parallel-port version of the ZIP drive)
mcd.s	All supported SCSI controllers, plus standard non-IDE Mitsumi CD-ROM
mcdx.s	All supported SCSI controllers, plus enhanced non-IDE Mitsumi CD-ROM
n53c406a.s	NCR 53c406a SCSI
n_5380.s	NCR 5380 and 53c400 SCSI
n_53c7xx.s	NCR 53c7xx, 53c8xx SCSI (most NCR PCI SCSI controllers use this driver)
optics.s	All supported SCSI controllers, plus support for the Optics Storage 8000 AT CD-ROM (the "Dolphin" drive)
pas16.s	Pro Audio Spectrum/Studio 16 SCSI
qlog_fas.s	ISA/VLB/PCMCIA Qlogic FastSCSI! (also supports the Control Concepts SCSI cards based on the Qlogic FASXXX chip)
qlog_isp.s	Supports all Qlogic PCI SCSI controllers, except the PCI-basic, which is supported by the AMD SCSI driver

Filename	Supported Hardware
sanyo.s	All supported SCSI controllers, plus Sanyo CDR-H94A CD-ROM
sbpcd.s	All supported SCSI controllers, plus Matsushita, Kotobuki, Panasonic, Creative Labs (SoundBlaster), Longshine, and TEAC NON-IDE CD-ROMs
scsinet.s	All supported SCSI controllers, plus full Ethernet
seagate.s	Seagate ST01/ST02 and Future Domain TMC-885/950 SCSI
trantor.s	Trantor T128/T128F/T228 SCSI
ultrastr.s	UltraStor 14F, 24F, and 34F SCSI
ustor14f.s	UltraStor 14F and 34F SCSI

You'll need one of these to get Linux started on your system so that you can install it. Because of the possibility of collisions between the various Linux drivers, several bootkernel disk image are provided. Use the one with the least drivers possible to maximize your chances of success. All these disks support UMSDOS.

At first glance, Tables 3.1 and 3.2 can be a little confusing. To clear things up, Table 3.3 contains a handy guide where you can match installation medium and hard-disk format to the preferred image (in **bold**) and the alternative image (in *italics*).

Table 3.3 A Chart for Choosing Bootdisk Images

Installation Medium	IDE Destination	SCSI Destination	MFM Destination
Hard Drive	**bare.i**	Use an SCSI controller bootdisk from the following list	**xt.i**
SCSI CD-ROM	Use an SCSI controller bootdisk from the following list	Use an SCSI controller bootdisk from the following list	
IDE/ATAPI CD-ROM	**bare.i**	Use an SCSI controller bootdisk from the following list	
Aztech, Orchid, Okano, Wearnes, Conrad, CyCDROM non-IDE CD-ROM	**aztech.i**	**aztech.s**	

Table 3.3 A Chart for Choosing Bootdisk Images (continued)

Installation Medium	IDE Destination	SCSI Destination	MFM Destination
Sony CDU31a, Sony CDU33a CD-ROM	cdu31a.i	cdu31a.s	
Sony CDU531, Sony CDU535 CD-ROM	cdu535.i	cdu535.s	
Philips/LMS cm206 CD-ROM	cm206.i	cm206.s	
Goldstar R420 CD-ROM	goldstar.i	goldstar.s	
Mitsumi non-IDE CD-ROM	mcdx.i, mcd.i	mcdx.s, mcd.i	
Optics Storage 8000 AT CD-ROM ("Dolphin")	optics.i	optics.s	
Sanyo CDR-H94A CD-ROM	sanyo.i	sanyo.s	
Matsushita, Kotobuki, Panasonic, Creative Labs (SoundBlaster), Longshine, and TEAC non-IDE CD-ROM	sbpcd.i	sbpcd.s	
NFS	net.i	scsinet.i	
Tape	bare.i (for floppy diskette tape); for SCSI tape, use an SCSI bootdisk from the following list	Use an SCSI controller bootdisk from the following list	xt.i (for floppy diskette tape);

SCSI controller bootdisks: **7000fast.s, advansys.s, aha152x.s, aha1542.s, aha1740.s, aha2x4x.s, am53c974.s, buslogic.s, dtc3280.s, eata_dma.s, eata_isa.s, eata_pio.s, fdomain.s, in2000.s, iomega.s, n53c406a.s, n_5380.s, n_53c7xx.s, pas16.s, qlog_fas.s, qlog_isp.s, seagate.s, trantor.s, ultrastr.s, ustor14f.s.**

Choosing the Proper Rootdisk Image

After selecting the proper bootdisk, you'll need to select the proper rootdisk. The selections are more limited, so you won't have to put too much work into the selection. The rootdisks are stored in the **ROOTDSKS** directory and will work with either 3.5-inch or 5.25-inch high-density diskettes.

Your rootdisk image selections are listed in Table 3.4.

Table 3.4 Rootdisk Selections

Filename	Purpose
COLOR.GZ	This image contains a full-screen color install program and should be considered the "default" rootdisk image. This version of the install system has some known bugs, however—it is, in particular, not forgiving of extra keystrokes entered between screens. By and large, this is probably the file you'll want to use.
UMSDOS.GZ	This is similar to the COLOR disk, but installs using UMSDOS—a filesystem that allows you to install Linux into a directory on an existing MS-DOS partition. This filesystem is not as fast as a native Linux filesystem. For that reason alone, anyone running a Linux Internet server should avoid UMSDOS.
TEXT.GZ	This is a text-based version of the install program derived from scripts used in previous Slackware releases.
TAPE.GZ	This image is designed to support installation from tape. See the section entitled "Installing from Tape" later in this chapter.

NOTE   Notice that these filenames end in the **.GZ** extension, indicating that the files have been compressed with GNU **zip**. Some older distributions of Linux required that the files be decompressed prior to use, but this is not needed anymore. The kernel on the bootdisk will detect that the rootdisk is compressed, and will automatically decompress the disk as it is loaded into RAM. This allows the use of a 1.44MB uncompressed image size for both 1.44MB and 1.2MB floppy drives.

Most users will use the **COLOR.GZ** rootdisk image.

Creating the Diskettes

For this step, you'll need two high-density diskettes. It doesn't matter what's on the diskettes, but they must be formatted—just be warned that this process will completely wipe out anything currently stored on the diskettes. You might also wish to format at this time a third high-density floppy diskette for the installation program to use later when preparing your system bootdisk.

In these examples, we'll be using the **BARE.I** and **COLOR.GZ** images. If you're using a different set of images, just substitute those filenames.

The procedures in this section do not need to be done on the computer you're planning to use as your Linux server. You can create the files on a different PC, or else you could even use a UNIX workstation to create the floppy diskettes. On a UNIX workstation the **dd** command is used to write an image to the floppy diskette drive. When using **dd** on Suns and possibly some other UNIX workstations, you must provide an approximate block size. Here's an example:

```
dd if=bare.i of=/dev/(rdfd0, rdf0c, fd0, or whatever) obs=18k
```

Now it's time to make your bootdisk. First, move into the **bootdisks.144** (or **bootdisks.12** if you use a 1.2-MB floppy diskette drive) on your Slackware CD-ROM.

Assuming that your CD-ROM drive has the drive letter **D:** assigned to it, you'd move into the directory like this:

```
C:\> D:
D:\> CD BOOTDSKS.144
D:\BOOTDSKS.144>
```

Now you'll actually create the bootdisk. Put the eventual bootdisk diskette in drive **A:** and then type the following command:

```
D:\> RAWRITE BARE.I A:
```

This will use the **RAWRITE** command (there's a copy of this in each of the **BOOTDSKS** and **ROOTDSKS** directories) to copy the **BARE.I** disk image to the **A:** floppy diskette drive. As it writes, **RAWRITE** will give you a status report. After it's completed writing the bootdisk, remove it from the drive and put it aside.

Some newer floppy diskette drives have trouble executing this command because of DMA limits. If you have DMA errors, boot DOS instead of Windows 95, and then make your diskettes.

Then insert another formatted high-density floppy diskette and use the same procedure to write out the rootdisk. In this case, you'll need to move into the **ROOTDSKS** directory and write out the **COLOR.GZ** image using **RAWRITE**:

```
D:\BOOTDSKS.144> cd \ROOTDSKS
D:\ROOTDSKS> RAWRITE COLOR.GZ A:
```

There's really not a lot to the **RAWRITE** command; the only things that can go wrong would be if you're not using a high-density diskette or if the diskette is flawed.

Booting Linux with the Bootdisk

Obviously, you boot Linux with the bootdisk you've previously prepared. Put it in your boot drive and restart your PC with either a cold or warm boot (it doesn't matter).

Initially your PC will do the things that it normally does when it boots, such as checking the memory and running through the BIOS. However, soon after the word *LILO* will appear on your screen, followed by a full screen that begins with the line:

```
Welcome to the Slackware Linux bootkernel disk!
```

You'll also see some verbiage about passing parameters along to the kernel. Most users won't need to pass along any additional parameters. Instead, they will be able to press the **Enter** key and proceed to load the Linux RAM disk.

In some cases, *LILO* appears on the screen and the system hangs, or else rows of *0*s and *1*s cascade down the screen. In these cases, you probably are using the wrong bootdisk for your PC. The first thing to do is to create a few alternate bootdisks and try them; if the problem persists, you'll want to scan the Usenet newsgroups and the FTP archives (see Appendix A for details) to make sure that your PC and its peripherals are indeed supported by Linux.

The bootdisk runs through your system hardware, noting which hard drives and peripherals are present as well as scouting out other salient details about your PC. It's at this point that Linux discovers any problems with your PC, and if you have problems installing or using Linux, it's a place you'll want to check. (The same information is displayed and gathered every time you boot.)

If there are no problems, you can put in your rootdisk and press **Enter**. A core of the Linux operating system is then copied to the RAM disk, which then gives you access to some Linux commands, including the important **fdisk** command. The installation process instructs you to login the Linux system as *root*:

```
slackware login : root
```

No password will be required.

Before you proceed, carefully look through the instructions on the screen. There are a few notes that may apply to your specific computing situation.

NOTE

Linux and Hard-Disk Names

After logging in, you'll want to directly run the **fdisk** command (ignoring what the screen instructions say about the **setup** command). The **fdisk** command assumes that the first IDE drive is the default drive. If you plan on installing Linux on another drive, you'll need to specify that on the command line. Table 3.5 lists the hard-disk device names.

Table 3.5 Linux Hard-Disk Device Names

Name	Meaning
/dev/hda	First IDE hard drive
/dev/hdb	Second IDE hard drive
/dev/sda	First SCSI hard drive
/dev/sdb	Second SCSI hard drive
/dev/fd0	First floppy diskette drive (**A:**)
/dev/fd1	Second floppy diskette drive (**B:**)

Note the pattern in Table 3.5? Additionally, Linux allows you to specify the partitions in the device names. For example, the first primary partition on the first IDE drive would be known as **/dev/hda1**, the second primary partition on the first IDE drive would be known as **/dev/hda2**, and so on. If you're installing logical partitions, the first logical partition would appear as **/dev/hda5**, the second logical partition would appear as **/dev/hda6**, and so on.

The files representing these devices will end up in the directory /**dev**.

N O T E

To run **fdisk** on the second SCSI hard drive, you would use the following command line:

```
# fdisk /dev/sdb
```

For most of you (since most PCs are sold with IDE drives), you'll be told that Linux is using the first hard drive as the default. When you press **m** for a list of options, you'll see the following listing:

```
Command action
   a   toggle a bootable flag
   c   toggle the dos compatibility flag
   d   delete a partition
   l   list known partition types
   m   print this menu
   n   add a new partition
   p   print the partition table
   q   quit without saving changes
   t   change a partition's system id
   u   change display/entry units
   v   verify the partition table
   w   write table to disk and exit
   x   extra functionality (experts only)
```

You'll really only use three options, unless you run into some esoteric configurations:

- **d** deletes a current partition. This will work on non-Linux partitions.

- **n** creates a new partition.

- **p** prints a rundown of the current partition table. This will list non-Linux partitions as well.

If you select **p**, you'll see the following:

```
   Device Boot  Begin   Start    End  Blocks   Id  System
/dev/hda1    *      1       1     63   20762+   4  DOS 16-bit (32M)
```

This is the DOS partition created in previous sections.

Before you actually create the Linux partition, you should decide if you want to install a swap partition.

Linux and a Swap Disk

If you are using a PC with 4MB of RAM, you may want to set up a *swap partition*. The system treats this partition as extended RAM; if you run low on memory (and with 4MB of RAM, you're guaranteed to), Linux can treat this hard-disk section as RAM, or *virtual memory*. You'll take a performance hit, as a hard disk will always be slower than real RAM, and you'll have the joy of watching your hard disk churn furiously when you try to use a few applications. However, a swap partition can be used *only* for swap space by Linux; it can't be used for any other storage. Therefore, you need to weigh your RAM needs versus your hard-disk storage needs, keeping in mind that Linux should have as much hard-disk territory for storage as possible, especially if you're running an Internet server.

As far as Internet servers go, it's been our experience that a swap partition doesn't really affect system speed significantly, although there's a certain slowing effect when a site gets busy. In these days of cheap RAM, a serious Internet site would do best to buy some more RAM and not mess with swap disks. Because of the rapid nature of Internet usage—all sorts of processes are created and discarded at a furious pace—most things stay in RAM.

If you want to create a swap partition, read on. If you don't, you can skip to the end of this section and on to the next section, "Creating the Main Linux Partition."

Your first move is to create a swap partition with the **fdisk** command. You'll need to decide how large to make this partition. That will depend on how much free space you think you can give up on your hard drive. For the purposes of this chapter, we'll devote 10 MB to swap space.

Run the **fdisk** command and then choose the **n** option, for creating a new partition. You'll see the following:

```
Command action
   e    extended
   p    primary partition (1-4)
```

Type **p** and enter the partition number. If you've already installed a DOS or OS/2 partition, you'll need to select the number **2**, as partition number 1 is already is use:

```
Partition number (1-4): 2
```

You'll then be asked about where to place the partition and how large to make it. Generally speaking, you'll want to place the partition immediately after the previous partition:

```
First cylinder (64-1010): 64
```

Your numbers will undoubtedly be different. The point here is that **fdisk** automatically lists the first unassigned cylinder (in this case, it was cylinder 64), and you should go with that number.

You'll then be asked how large you want to make the partition:

```
Last cylinder or +size or +sizeM or +sizeK (64-1010): +10M
```

Since we're not into figuring out how many cylinders or how many kilobytes it would take to make up 10 MB, we take the easy way out and specify 10 MB directly as *+10M*.

This won't apply to most users, but Linux doesn't do very well if it's installed as a boot partition on cylinder 1023 or above. (This occurs with very large hard drives—1GB or larger.) This has nothing to do with Linux but rather with the limitations in the PC's BIOS. Subsequently, you should avoid installing the Linux boot partition on a partition containing this cylinder or better.

Fdisk then creates the partition. To make sure that everything went correctly, type **p** to see a list of the current partitions:

```
  Device Boot  Begin   Start   End  Blocks   Id  System
/dev/hda1    *     1       1    63  20762+    4  DOS 16-bit (32M)
/dev/hda2         63      64    95  10560    83  Linux native
```

The number of blocks listed here will be handy when you actually make this partition a swap partition. Jot it down.

Fdisk then gives you its command prompt; type **w** and exit.

You may notice that the hard disk is relatively quiet when you're making these changes to the partition. The **fdisk** command doesn't make its changes until you type the **w** command to exit. You can make all the changes you want and change your mind many times, but until you type **w**, it won't matter.

You'll then want to use the **mkswap** command to make the partition a swap partition. The command line is quite simple: You list the partition you want to make a swap partition (remembering that Linux lists partitions as **/dev/hda1**, **/dev/hda2**, and so on), along with the size of the partition *in blocks*. The command line would look like the following:

```
# mkswap -c /dev/hda2 10560
```

Remember when we told you the number of blocks would come in handy?

The *-c* option checks for bad blocks on the partition. If **mkswap** returns any errors, you can ignore them, as Linux already knows of their existence and will ignore them.

After creating the swap partition, you'll need to activate the swap partition, with a command line like:

```
#  swapon /dev/hda2
```

Finally, you'll need to tell the filesystem that **/dev/hda2** is indeed a swap partition, again using the **fdisk** command. In this instance, you'll need to change the *type* of the partition. When you created this partition, it was set up as a Linux native partition. However, Linux needs to explicitly know that this is a swap partition, so you need to change the type with the **t** command:

```
Partition number (1-4): 2
Hex code (type L to list codes): 82
```

Linux supports a wide range of partition types, as you would see if you typed **L**. However, you can take our word for it regarding 82 as the proper hex code. (You don't need to know every single hex code; there's little reason for you to know that *8* is the hex code for AIX or that *75* is the hex code for PC/IX.)

Quit **fdisk** using **w**, making sure that your changes are written to disk. It will take a few seconds for this to happen.

You're now ready to create your main Linux partition.

Creating the Main Linux Partition

Most of you will want to designate the remainder of the hard drive as the Linux partition, so that's the assumption made in the remainder of this chapter. With *Command (m for help):* on your screen, select **n** for new partition. You'll see the following:

```
Command action
   e   extended
   p   primary partition (1-4)
```

Type **p**, and enter the partition number. If you've already installed a DOS partition, you'll need to select the number **2**, as partition number 1 is already is use:

```
Partition number (1-4): 2
```

If you've already installed a swap partition, you'll need to designate this partition as **3**.

You'll then be asked about where to place the partition and how large to make it. Generally speaking, you'll want to place the partition immediately after the previous partition:

```
First cylinder (64-1010): 64
```

Your numbers will undoubtedly be different. The point here is that **fdisk** automatically lists the first unassigned cylinder here (in this case, it was cylinder 64), and you should go with that number.

You'll then be asked how large you want to make the partition:

```
Last cylinder or +size or +sizeM or +sizeK (64-1010): 1010
```

Since Linux gives us the number of the last cylinder (1010), we'll go with that. There are no advantages to creating more than one Linux partition, unless you're using a *very* large hard drive (larger than 4GB).

Finally, you'll want to make sure that this is a Linux boot partition, so that you can boot from the hard disk in the future via LILO. The **a** command toggles whether or not you want to use a partition as a boot partition. Type **t** and then specify this partition (**2**) as the partition you want to boot from.

Fdisk will then ask you for a command. You'll need to make sure that your changes are recorded, so select **w**, which writes the partition table to disk and exits **fdisk**. After this is done, Linux gives you a command prompt (#) again. It's now time to run the **setup** program.

Installing Linux from the Startup Program

Now comes the fun part—actually installing Linux. For this, you'll run the **setup** command from a command line:

```
# setup
```

You'll then be presented a menu with the following choices:

```
HELP        Read the Slackware Setup Help file
KEYMAP      Remap your keyboard if you're not using a US one
MAKE TAGS   Experts may customize tagfiles to preselect files
ADDSWAP     Set up your swap partition(s)
TARGET      Set up your target partition
SOURCE      Select source media
DISK SETS   Decide which disk sets you wish to install
INSTALL     Install selected disk sets
CONFIGURE   Reconfigure your Linux system
EXIT        Exit Slackware Linux Setup
```

By all means you should first look through the help file, listed first. Some of the steps presented therein may help you in your own Linux installation process.

To move through the selections in this menu, use the cursor (arrow) keys or type the first letter in each line (such as **H** for help).

Basically, the installation from CD-ROM is pretty simple and follows these steps:

1. Set up swap space for Linux.
2. Tell Linux where you want it to be installed.
3. Select the source for the files needed to install Linux (in most cases, this will be the CD-ROM).
4. Select the software you want to install.
5. Install the software.
6. Configure the installed software.

Each of these steps will be covered in its own section.

 Before you get started on these steps, you should know that the Slackware Linux distribution supports many different keymaps for different languages and setups. If you want access to another language—say, German—or another keyboard layout— such as the Dvorak keyboard—you should select **Keymap** from the Setup menu.

N O T E

Setting Up the Swap Space

As you've probably guessed by now, much of the Linux installation involves an actual installation and then additional steps, telling Linux about the installation. This is certainly true if you've installed a swap partition. (If you have not, you can skip this step.) You've already installed the partition, made it active, and changed the partition type to a Linux swap partition. Now you need to tell Linux about this partition again. However, you don't need to format this partition, as you've already done so with the **mkswap** command.

Selecting the Target for Linux

This selection should be rather simple: You'll want to install to the Linux partition you set up earlier in this chapter. When you select **Target** from the Setup menu, you'll automatically be presented with this partition. This section covers the choices you'll make; for the most part, you'll want to go with the default choices.

Formatting the Linux partition is the next step. You'll want to format the Linux partition for a new installation; however, if you're using the **setup** program to upgrade from a previous installation, you won't want to format the Linux partition.

Choosing inode density is next. Again, you'll want to go with the default, unless you have Linux experience and know that the default won't help you.

After the hard disk chugs and formats the Linux partition, you'll be asked if you want to make a DOS partition visible (or, more technically speaking, mounted) from Linux—assuming that you've created such a partition. Making this partition visible won't affect Linux performance, nor will it eat away at the size of the Linux partition. Since you may find it handy to move files via the DOS partition, you'll probably want to make this partition visible. You'll also be asked to provide a name for the drive; the name doesn't really matter, so we use **dos** or **dosc**. When you run the **ls** command later in your Linux usage, you'll see **dos** or **dosc** listed as just another directory, and the files within will appear as Linux files.

Selecting the Source for Linux

You have five choices from which you can install Linux:

- hard-drive partition
- floppy diskettes
- NFS
- premounted directory
- CD-ROM

Since you've bought this book, we'll assume you want to use the accompanying CD-ROM for installation. However, other installation methods will be discussed later in this chapter.

NOTE   There may be cases where DOS sees a CD-ROM drive with no problems, but Linux cannot. In these cases you won't necessarily know about this problem until you install Linux from the CD-ROM and are told that the CD-ROM drive does not exist. In this case, there are two ways to go: Search for a Linux bootkernel that supports your CD-ROM or use DOS to copy the installation files to a hard-drive partition. The first option was discussed earlier in this chapter; the second option will be discussed later in this chapter.

The **setup** program then gives you a set of choices about the CD-ROM from which you're installing. The choices are straightforward; if you're using a Sony or SoundBlaster CD-ROM interface, you certainly would have known about it before now (you would have needed the proper bootdisk to get to this point), so there are no surprises on this menu.

Should You Keep Some Stuff on the CD-ROM?

Slackware Linux gives you the option of doing a partial install, leaving some of the program files on the CD-ROM and running it from there. *Don't*. You don't want to have your Web server tied to running from a CD-ROM. Choose the **slackware** selection.

Choosing the Disk Sets to Install

Now comes the fun part—choosing the software you want to install.

True to its roots as a diskette-based operating system, Linux divides software into *disk sets*. Each disk set uniquely names and corresponds to a specific part of the operating system. For instance, the *A* series contains the core of Linux, and its installation is mandatory.

The **setup** program divides disk sets and the software within into mandatory and optional installations. Some of the elements of Linux, such as the aforementioned A series, are mandatory. Other installations, such as terminal packages, are optional. During the installation process, Linux will automatically install the mandatory packages, while prompting you before installing the optional packages.

There is a way to override this, as will be explained later in this section.

N O T E

During the initial menu entitled Series Selection, you'll be presented with a list of the disk sets as well as a short explanation of what is contained on the disk sets (Table 3.6). Generally speaking, you won't want to install all the disk sets, as there are some disk sets that overlap, and their coexistence on the hard drive is not wise (particularly when it comes to development tools). In addition, you don't want to waste the hard-disk space needed for a full installation—will you really need three or four text editors as well as multiple text-formatting packages and a slew of fonts? Accordingly, choose the software you think you're likely to use. You can always run the **setup** program again and install additional disk sets again in the future.

Technically speaking, all that's needed for a minimal installation of Linux is the A disk set.

N O T E

Table 3.6 A Full Listing of the Linux Disk Sets

Series	Purpose
A	The base system. If you install only this disk set, you'll have enough to get up and running and have **elvis** and **comm** programs available.
AP	Various applications and add-ons, such as the online manual (**man**) pages, **groff**, **ispell**, **joe**, **jed**, **jove**, **ghostscript**, **sc**, **bc**, **ftape** support, and the **quota** utilities.
D	Program development. GCC/G++/Objective C 2.7.2, **make** (GNU and BSD), **byacc** and GNU **bison**, **flex**, the 5.3.12 C libraries, **gdb**, kernel source for Linux 2.0.x. **SVGAlib**, **ncurses**, **clisp**, **f2c**, **p2c**, **m4**, **perl**, **rcs**, and **dll** tools.
E	GNU emacs 19.32. (This might be handy for editing HTML files and configuration scripts.)
F	A collection of FAQs and other documentation. (Always good to have around.)
K	Source code for the Linux 2.0.x kernel. (You'll probably want to install this, if only to possibly recompile a kernel later.)
N	Networking. TCP/IP, UUCP, **mailx**, **dip**, PPP, **deliver**, **elm**, **pine**, BSD **sendmail**, **cnews**, **nn**, **tin**, **trn**, **inn**, and the Apache Web server. (Installation of this disk set should be watched closely, depending on how you want to distribute the news. You should check Chapter 9 for more on the news-retrieval methods.)
T	NTeX Release 1.2.1. NTeX is a very complete TeX distribution for Linux. (Not really necessary for most Linux Internet installations.)
TCL	Tcl, Tk, TclX. A port of the major Tcl packages to Linux, including shared library support. (You'll want this if you plan on using Tcl for server-side scripts.)
X	The base XFree86 3.1.2 system, with **libXpm**, **fvwm** 1.23b, and **xlock** added. (X is handy to have at times.)
XAP	X applications: X11 **ghostscript**, **libgr13**, **seyon**, **workman**, **xfilemanager**, **xv** 3.01, GNU **chess** and **xboard**, **xfm** 1.3, **ghostview**, **gnuplot**, **xpaint**, **xfractint**, **fvwm-95-2**, and various X games. (Most of these applications won't be necessary.)
XD	X11 server link kit, static libraries, and PEX support. (Not really necessary unless you plan on recompiling your X server.)
XV	Xview 3.2p1-X11R6. XView libraries, and the Open Look virtual and nonvirtual window managers for XFree86 3.1.2. (Definitely not needed for most Linux Internet servers.)
Y	Games. The BSD games collection, Tetris for terminals, and Sasteroids. (Perhaps essential for your sanity, but not necessarily needed for the smooth running of your Linux Internet server.)

Mark the disk sets you want to install by pressing the **spacebar**.

You'll then be asked whether you want to use the default tagfiles or create your own. When a piece of software is to be installed, it's said to be *tagged* in this installation process. By using the default tagfiles, you are installing software deemed to be mandatory, while the system prompts you before installing packages that aren't mandatory. Again, your best move is to go with the default, unless you've had experience with custom tagfiles and know exactly what you want to install.

At this point there's an option to install *everything*. Don't do this, unless you've designated a small group of disk sets to be installed and know that you do indeed want to install everything.

WARNING

Linux will begin on the installation. It will tell you what's being installed, even mandatory packages. When it comes to a nonmandatory piece of software, it will stop and ask you if you do indeed want to install the software. An added bonus during this process is that **setup** will tell you how much disk space the nonmandatory software will use (alas, there's no overall reckoning of how much space the entire installation will use). Use the cursor keys to move between the **Yes** and **No** choices, and use **Enter** to move on.

We're not going to list every piece of software that can be installed; you can make most of these decisions on your own. However, there are some things to note as the disk sets are installed:

- Linux will install a kernel best suited for your PC configuration; by and large, most of the precompiled kernels should meet the needs of most users. However, during the installation process, you'll be asked about installing various kernels that are not applicable to your PC configuration. In fact, one of the first disk sets includes support for a Linux kernel lacking SCSI support. Since the **setup** program doesn't know anything about your hardware, it will ask you if you want to install this kernel. In most cases, you'll want to install the kernel from your bootdisk—**setup** gives you this option once all the packages are installed.

- During the installation process you'll be asked whether you want to install a package called **gpm**, which manages the mouse for Linux running in character mode. Don't install this package; it conflicts with the X Window System.

- Many text editors are available in the Linux disk sets, including **emacs** and **vi** clones called **elvis** and **vim**. These disk sets should meet your needs. In addition, the accompanying CD-ROM contains an HTML editor. You shouldn't need any other text editors.

- You'll be asked about alternate shells, including **zsh**, **ash**, and **tcsh**. The default Linux shell is **bash** (Bourne Again SHell), and most users will find that it works well. To save on disk space, don't bother installing others.

- If you install the GNU C compiler, you must also install **binutils**, **libc**, and the **linuxinc** package (this contains the include file from the Linux kernel source). The Linux **setup** program tags some of these packages as mandatory (the warning applies if you use your own tagfiles). This compiler will come in handy if you plan on making changes to or merely compiling the Internet software on the accompanying CD-ROM.

- The version of **emacs** that's initially installed from the CD-ROM was compiled with the assumption that it would be running under the X Window System. If you don't plan on using X, be sure to install the **emac_nox** package, which doesn't contain the X Window support and can be run in character mode. It's also smaller and will save you some disk space.

- Some of the older applications require some older libraries to run, and at some point you'll be asked about including those libraries. You should install the older libraries.

Dealing with Errors

Even though this is a very infrequent occurrence, you may experience an error message or two when installing Linux from the disk sets. One of the errors may be *Device Full*, which means that you've filled your hard drive. Slackware Linux, however, will continue to attempt to install software, even if the disk is full.

To end the installation program, you can either press the **Esc** key a few times or type **Ctrl-C**.

Installing a Kernel

The first Linux configuration task is to install a Linux kernel on your hard drive. It's possible that you've already installed a kernel from the A series (there are two kernels on the A series, an IDE and a SCSI generic kernel), but in most cases it will be preferable to replace this kernel with the one you've used to install. That way, there won't be any surprises when you reboot—you've installed a kernel that you know works on your machine.

To do this, select the **bootdisk** option on the kernel installation menu. You'll be asked to reinsert your installation bootdisk, and the kernel will be copied from it onto your hard drive. Other options on this menu include installing a kernel from a DOS floppy diskette or from the Slackware CD-ROM drive. If you know exactly which kernel you need, you can try one of these options. You should be aware that installing the wrong kernel here can leave Linux unbootable, requiring you to use your bootdisk or **Loadlin** to start the system.

N O T E When you install a kernel from this menu, all it does is put the kernel file onto your root Linux partition as **/vmlinuz**. Until you make a system bootdisk from it or install LILO, your system is still not ready to boot. So, you'll want to make a system bootdisk from the next menu.

Creating a Boot Floppy

Linux will boot from either a floppy drive or hard drive. However, it's recommended that you set up the means to boot either way—if you have hardware problems, you can always boot the system from a floppy diskette drive—hence, the request from the **setup** program to create a boot floppy. This floppy can be used to boot Linux at any point. This will be handy should you experience some hard-disk problems or screw up your hard disk so severely that the system won't load.

Configuring the Modem

If you're planning on using a modem for connecting to the Internet via SLIP or PPP, you need to configure the modem. Essentially, this involves telling Linux exactly what serial port the modem is connected to. The first serial port on a PC is called **com1**, and under Linux parlance this becomes **cua0**; the second serial port on a PC is called **com2**, and under Linux parlance this becomes **cua1**; and so on. (Note the numbering difference; UNIX likes to start things at 0, and PCs prefer to start things at 1.)

After you set up the mouse, you'll be asked to set the speed for the modem. The choices (38400, 19200, and so on) are pretty clear.

N O T E

If you're using a modem and the speed isn't represented on the menu, use the next-fastest speed. For instance, to properly configure a 28800-bps modem, you'd choose **38400**.

Configuring the Mouse

You'll want to use a mouse if you're using the X Window System, and this menu allows you to set up the proper mouse. For newer PCs, setting up a mouse isn't a hassle, since they usually contain a serial port for that purpose. All you need to do is tell Linux what kind of mouse you're using and its location (if you're using a serial mouse, you'll need to specify where the mouse is connected) and then move on from there.

Configuring LILO

LILO is the LInux LOader, and it's used to boot Linux from the hard disk or a floppy disk. Additionally, it can be used to boot additional operating systems (like MS-DOS) from the hard disk. However, LILO isn't the friendliest tool to use; unless you know LILO and how it works, you probably shouldn't use it—especially if you don't plan on booting anything but Linux.

Setting Up the Network Connection

In the installation process, you'll be asked to configure your network. To use Linux as an Internet server, you'll need a connection method (as discussed in Chapters 1 and 2) and the proper networking configuration, as well as networking support in your kernel. At this point, we'll assume that you have TCP/IP support in the kernel; virtually all the precompiled kernels do have it, but if you don't, you'll need to install another kernel or recompile your own kernel.

If you choose not to configure your network at this time, you can always go back and do it using a Slackware Linux called **netconfig**, which guides you through a network configuration. You can run it (when logged in as root) from any command line:

```
netconfig
```

A dialog box appears (much like the Setup dialog box) with the following text:

```
Now we will attempt to configure your mail and TCP/IP. This process
probably won't work on all possible network configurations, but should
give you a good start. You will be able to reconfigure your system at
any time by typing:
```

```
netconfig
```

You'll then be run through a series of questions:

```
Enter hostname:
```

This is the actual host name for your own machine. If you're using a full name for your host name (i.e., *mycomputer.com*), don't enter the trailing *.com*.

```
Enter domain name for $HOSTNAME:
```

where *$HOSTNAME* is the name you entered in the previous question. Here, you would enter the full domain name, such as *kreichard.com*.

If you only plan to use TCP/IP through loopback, then your IP address will be 127.0.0.1 and we can skip a lot of the following questions.

```
Do you plan to ONLY use loopback?
```

Loopback is required for machines that aren't connected to a network. Many Linux and X Window applications assume that there's a network running at all times. These applications need a network, and this question allows you to loop back to your own machine (essentially making your own machine a network). Unless you're planning a one-person intranet, you'll answer **n**.

```
Enter your IP address for the local machine. Example:
111.112.113.114
Enter IP address for $HOSTNAME (aaa.bbb.ccc.ddd):
```

where *$HOSTNAME* is the name you entered in a previous question. This is where you enter the IP address for your machine. If you're working with an ISP for Internet connectivity (as explained in Chapters 1 and 2), this is where you enter the IP address assigned by the ISP. If you enter an incorrect-looking address, you'll receive an error message (*The address you have entered seems to be non-standard. We were expecting $2 groups of numbers separated by dots, like: 127.0.0.1 Are you absolutely sure you want to use the address $1?*).

```
Enter your gateway address, such as 111.112.113.1
If you don't have a gateway on your network, you can enter your own IP
address.
Enter gateway address (aaa.bbb.ccc.ddd):
```

Depending on the networking arrangement you worked out with your ISP, you'll either use the Internet server as a gateway or an ISP address. In either case, you enter the IP address here.

```
Enter your netmask. This will generally look something like this:
255.255.255.0
Enter netmask (aaa.bbb.ccc.ddd):
```

The netmask depends on the IP address you have. Again, this information should have been worked out with your ISP. Reality dictates that there are really only two choices: Class B networks have 255.255.0.0 as a netmask, and Class C networks have 255.255.255.0 as a netmask; most readers of this book will probably have a Class C network. In any case, you must enter the information here.

```
Will you be accessing a nameserver?
```

This is another setting that depends on your ISP. If you're using an ISP's nameserver, then you'll enter **y** and specify the nameserver in a later dialog box. (A *nameserver* is the name of the machine that translates a name like **www.kreichard.com** to its numeric IP address.)

After the question-and-answer process is complete, you'll be told to reboot your machine, so that the proper networking information can be installed.

 It's possible to make these changes to files manually. Later in this chapter we explain how.

N O T E

Other Installation Methods

Linux can't see every CD-ROM drive. In these instances, you'll want to resort to some alternative installation methods. These methods include:

- Installing from hard drive, where you copy all the installation files to a normal (that is, not disk-doubled) DOS partition on your hard disk. This is a pain, as you need to replicate the CD-ROM file structure and its many subdirectories (A1, A2, and so on) on the hard drive. When you run the **setup** program and specify the source of the installation files, you'll choose a hard-disk partition instead of a CD-ROM.

- Installing from 3.25-inch floppy diskette, where you copy the A-series diskettes to DOS-formatted diskette. In the early days of Linux, you could install all of Linux from floppy diskettes, but most of the disk sets have grown too big for this. You'll end up with a core Linux system, but you won't have much software. In this case, you should reinstall after you've mounted the CD-ROM. (This generally isn't a good way to install.)

Booting Linux from DOS Using Loadlin

Loadlin is a handy utility for Linux users that also run MS-DOS or Windows 95. Using **Loadlin**, you can start Linux from a DOS prompt or set up an icon in Windows 95 that allows you to switch to Linux. **Loadlin** is also probably the safest way to launch Linux from your hard drive, since you don't need to mess with the partition table at all—you just boot DOS normally and then use the **LOADLIN.EXE** command to start Linux when you need it.

To use **Loadlin**, you'll need to install it on your DOS drive. To do this, you'll need to use an unzip program, such as **UNZIP.EXE** or **PKUNZIP.EXE**. Most DOS users will already have copies of these. Assuming your Slackware CD is on drive **E:** and you want to put **Loadlin** on drive **C:**, unzip the file like this:

```
C:\> PKUNZIP -d E:\KERNELS\LODLIN16.ZIP
```

The *-d* flag tells the command to preserve the directory structure found in the zip archive—this will create a **C:\LOADLIN** directory on your machine containing a number of files.

The next step is to pick an appropriate kernel from a subdirectory under **\KERNELS** on the CD-ROM. The **\BOOTDSKS.144\WHICH.ONE** document might be helpful in making your selection. The actual kernel file will be named **ZIMAGE** or **BZIMAGE**—this is what you need to copy into your **C:\LOADLIN** directory.

For this example, we'll use the kernel in the **E:\KERNELS\BARE.I** directory:

```
C:\> CD LOADLIN
C:\LOADLIN> COPY E:\KERNELS\BARE.I\ZIMAGE .
```

Now we have everything we need to start a Linux system. To do that, you need to know the following things:

- The device name of the Linux partition you intend to boot (such as **/dev/hda2**).
- The path- and filename of the Linux kernel you plan to use (such as **C:\LOADLIN\ZIMAGE**).
- Whether the partition should be mounted read-only (as in the case of a native Linux partition, so it can do safe file-system checking at boot time) or read-write (needed by UMSDOS, which does not check file systems at boot).

This information is fed to the **LOADLIN.EXE** program, which in turn loads Linux into memory and boots it. Here's an example:

```
C:\LOADLIN> LOADLIN C:\LOADLIN\ZIMAGE ROOT=/dev/hda2 RO
```

This loads the Linux kernel and boots the **/dev/hda2** partition in read-only (RO) mode. If you're using UMSDOS, you'd replace the RO with RW to use read-write mode instead.

N O T E Some DOS drivers interfere with **Loadlin**, in particular the emm386 driver for expanded memory. If this happens, you'll have to remove the driver from your **CONFIG.SYS** and try again. Also, **Loadlin** will not run directly under Windows 95, although you can still set up an icon for it that first switches your computer into DOS mode. (In other words, the process is to start a DOS session under Windows 95 and then launch **Loadlin**.)

If all goes well, your machine should switch to Linux. If you'd like to automate the process further, edit the **LINUX.BAT** file in your **C:\LOADLIN** directory. Then copy **LINUX.BAT** into your **C:\DOS** directory and you'll be able to switch to Linux from DOS by simply typing **LINUX** at a prompt.

Recompiling a Kernel

Most Linux users will find that the precompiled kernels that come on the accompanying CD-ROM will work for them, as PC hardware is becoming reasonable homogenized. However, in the remote chance that you'll need to recompile your kernel (whether directed to in a Linux HOW-TO or through the advice from an expert on the Usenet; these will happen if you're using a nonsupported SCSI CD-ROM, bus mouse, or sound card), here's how to do so.

1.   If you haven't installed the C compiler and kernel source, do that.
2.   Use the bootkernel disk you installed with to start your machine. At the LILO prompt, enter:

```
LILO: mount root=/dev/hda1
```

assuming that **/dev/hda1** is your Linux partition. (This is the assumption made through the rest of this section.) If not, enter your Linux partition instead. After this, ignore any error messages as the system starts up.

3.   Log in as **root**, and recompile the kernel with these steps:

```
cd /usr/src/linux
make config
```

At this point you'll choose your drivers. Repeat this step until you are satisfied with your choices.

If you are using LILO, this will build and install the new kernel:

```
make dep ; make clean ; make zlilo
rdev -R /vmlinuz 1
```

If you are using a bootdisk, these commands will build the kernel and create a new bootdisk for your machine:

```
make dep ; make clean ; make zImage
rdev -R zImage 1
rdev -v zImage -1
rdev zImage /dev/hda1
fdformat /dev/fd0u1440
cat zImage > /dev/fd0
```

You'll need to place a clean floppy disk into your drive before the **fdformat** command.

You should now have a Linux kernel that can make full use of all supported hardware installed in your machine. Reboot and try it out.

Recompiling a kernel to include support for TCP/IP will be covered later in this chapter.

NOTE

Booting the System

After Linux has been installed, you can go ahead and reboot. If you've installed LILO, you'll see it appear after the PC runs through its BIOS check. As Linux boots, you'll see a long Linux-related diagnostic, as Linux checks the system and makes sure everything is where it's supposed to be. For the most part, you can ignore any errors messages you see here (such as a proclamation that the name of the machine *darkstar* does not appear to be supported). After all the diagnostics, you'll finally be presented with a command prompt:

```
Welcome to Linux 2.0.0.
darkstar login:
```

If you're installed networking capabilities when you installed Slackware Linux, you were asked the name of your machine. This name should appear in the place of *darkstar*.

NOTE

Since there are no users on the system, you'll login as the *root user*, so go ahead and type in **root** as the login. There will be no prompting for a password.

NOTE A *root user* is the supreme being on a UNIX system. Most of the traditional security tools within the UNIX operating system don't apply to the root user—when logged in as root, you can do just about anything. It's generally not a good idea to use the UNIX system as the root user, however; the proscribed practice is to set up your own account and then save the root login only for those times when you're performing system administration.

After you're logged in, you'll see the following command prompt:

```
darkstar:~#
```

Your first commands will be to change your machine name and to set up a user account for yourself.

Adding Users

Your first action as the Linux supreme being is to set up an account for your daily usage. To do this, type the following at the command prompt:

```
darkstar:~# adduser

Adding a new user. The username should not exceed 8 character
in length, or you may run into problems later.

Enter login name for new account (^C to quit): kevinr
```

The **adduser** command does exactly what it says: Adds a new user to the system. In the previous example, the user *kevinr* has been added to the system. After specifying the username, you'll be asked additional information about the preferences of user *kevinr*. Unless you're familiar with Linux, you'll want to stick with the defaults for now. (The defaults are listed in brackets. Wherever there's a default, you can go ahead and press the **Enter** key instead of typing in the default selection. In our example, we'll type in the defaults.) The entire sequence will look something like this:

```
Editing information for new user [kevinr]:

Full name: Kevin Reichard
GID[100]:100

Checking for an available UID after 500

First unused uid is 501

UID [501]: 501

Home Directory [/home/kevinr]: /home/kevinr

Shell [/bin/bash]: /bin/bash

Password [kevinr]: newpassword1

Information for newuser [kevinr]:
Home Directory: [/home/kevinr] Shell: [/bin/bash]
Password: [newpassword1] gid: [100] uid: [501]

Is this correct? [y/n]:

Adding login [kevinr] and making directory [/home/kevinr]

Adding the files from the /etc/skel directory:
./.kermrc -> /home/kevin/./.kermrc
./.less -> /home/kevin/./.less
./.lessrc -> /home/kevin/./.lessrc
./.term -> /home/kevin/./.term
./.term/termrc -> /home/kevin/./.term/termrc
./.emacs -> /home/kevin/./.emacs
```

If you're not planning on using Linux for anything but a single-user operating system, you don't need to worry about things like GID (which is short for group ID) and UID (which is short for user ID). And even if you do plan to use Linux on a network, you can change these parameters later.

Additionally, you probably noticed that the name *darkstar* appears as the name of your machine. Since you probably don't want to leave this as the name of your machine, you should change it immediately. This name is contained in the file **/etc/HOSTNAME**, and the default is **darkstar.frop.org**. To change it, you'll use a text editor (in the example, we'll use **vi**) and edit this file. To load the **vi** text editor and the **/etc/HOSTNAME** file, use the following command line:

```
darkstar:~# vi /etc/HOSTNAME
```

You'll want to edit this file, changing *darkstar.frop.org* to whatever you like.

If your system is configured properly, you should have the following directories in your root directory:

```
bin/      dev/    home/        mnt/     sbin/    var/
boot/     dos/    lib/         proc/    tmp/
cdrom/    etc/    lost+found/  root/    usr/
```

If you've installed Slackware Linux from the CD-ROM and the system refuses to see the drive when you reboot, you'll need to install a new kernel, or add the support through loadable kernel modules.

Using Kernel Modules

The kernels used in Slackware Linux are designed to support the hardware needed to get Linux installed. Once you've installed and rebooted your system, you may find that your kernel lacks support for some of your hardware, such as a CD-ROM drive or Ethernet card. In this case, there are a couple of ways you could add this support. The traditional way would be to compile a custom Linux kernel that includes drivers for all your hardware. This requires that you have the Linux source code and C compiler installed and that you know exactly which options need to be compiled into your kernel. In short, compiling a custom kernel can be a rather difficult task for most Linux beginners.

Here come kernel modules to the rescue! If you've installed device drivers before on MS-DOS, you'll probably find this a familiar way of adding support—just think of the module configuration file **/etc/rc.d/rc.modules** as being the Linux counterpart of DOS's **CONFIG.SYS** file. To add support for new hardware, you need to edit the file and uncomment the lines that load the needed support. As an example, let's look at the section of the file used to load CD-ROM support, as shown in Figure 3.4.

```
# These modules add CD-ROM drive support. Most of these drivers will probe
# for the I/O address and IRQ of the drive automatically if the parameters
# to configure them are omitted. Typically the I/O address will be specified
# in hexadecimal, e.g.: cm206=0x300,11
#
#/sbin/modprobe aztcd aztcd=<I/O address>
#/sbin/modprobe cdu31a cdu31a_port=<I/O address> cdu31a_irq=<interrupt>
#/sbin/modprobe cm206 cm206=<I/O address>,<IRQ>
#/sbin/modprobe gscd gscd=<I/O address>
#/sbin/modprobe mcd mcd=<I/O address>,<IRQ>
#/sbin/modprobe mcdx mcdx=<I/O address>,<IRQ>
#/sbin/modprobe optcd optcd=<I/O address>
# Below, this last number is "1" for SoundBlaster Pro card, or "0" for a
clone.
#/sbin/modprobe sbpcd sbpcd=<I/O address>,1
#/sbin/modprobe sonycd535 sonycd535=<I/O address>
#/sbin/modprobe sjcd sjcd=<I/O address>
```

Figure 3.4 A section of the /etc/rc.d/rc.modules file.

Notice that each of the lines starts with #. In most Linux configuration files, any line beginning with # is ignored, much like lines in DOS configuration files that begin with *REM*. To activate support for one of these devices, you'll need to remove the # from the beginning of the line and then edit the line to include any extra information about your hardware needed by the kernel module. For instance, if your machine needs support for a SoundBlaster CD-ROM drive on port 0x300, you need to edit the line for **sbpcd** support so that it looks like this:

```
/sbin/modprobe sbpcd sbpcd=0x300,1
```

Then, the next time you boot your machine, the **sbpcd** module will be loaded, and you'll be able to use your drive. Drivers for nearly every device supported by Linux can be added in a similar fashion.

NOTE If you use kernel modules and decide later to upgrade your kernel, you'll need to upgrade your kernel modules as well. When configuring the kernel, select **M** instead of **Y** to build selected drivers as kernel modules instead of building them into the kernel. Once you've compiled your kernel with:

```
make dep ; make clean ; make zImage
```

you can compile and install the kernel modules with the command

```
make modules ; make modules_install
```

The modules will be installed in a directory named for the running kernel—if you're running Linux 2.0.0, you'll find them under **/lib/modules/2.0.0**.

Looking for Help

Most UNIX systems have an online-manual-page system, and Linux is no exception. You can use the **man** command to summon information about specific commands:

```
darkstar:~# man man
```

Online-manual pages aren't organized by topic; they're organized by specific command.

Shutting Linux Down

Like any good UNIX, Linux responds to the **shutdown** command. You'll need to provide it with a command-like parameter, as well as an amount of time to wait before actually shutting the system down. This may seem odd if you're used to working alone on a PC, but the **shutdown** command is usually saved for serious shutdowns, as most UNIX installations support many users and rarely shutdown. Use the following command line:

```
$ shutdown -r now
```

This shuts down the system immediately.

 Don't just turn off the power to turn off a Linux system. This can cause damage to important files.

WARNING

An alternative method of shutting down Linux is the old tried-and-true PC **Ctrl-Alt-Del** sequence, which is used to reboot a system. When running Linux, this sequence performs the same functions as **shutdown -r now**. When the PC cycles to reboot, simply turn it off. Despite what others may claim, this is a perfectly acceptable way to shut down a Linux system.

What to Do If Things Go Wrong

For the most part, installation of Linux from the accompanying CD-ROM is a relatively straightforward proposition, and you shouldn't have many problems in the installation. However, there may be some cases when you run into problems when you reboot the Linux system after installation. These problems may include:

- **You're told that the system is out of memory.** You'll probably run into this problem if you're operating with 4MB of RAM or less.
- **Your system hangs when you first run Linux.** In this situation, you'll want to watch the screen closely for any error messages. Sometimes Linux will be seeking out a device at a specific address (say, a CD-ROM drive) and instead find a network card. In these situations, Linux will hang. You'll need to tell Linux to look for the device at the address on your system, which requires that you send an option line to Linux upon bootup. This is a situation that's covered in the many documents we included in the CD-ROM.

Other Configuration Procedures

Now that you've got Linux basically installed and running, you can take the time to set up some system peripherals. These include printers, sound cards, and (for laptop users) PCMCIA devices.

Setting Up a Printer

When you installed Slackware Linux, you were asked about the location of your printer. This information was translated into the UNIX equivalent; a printer on the first parallel port is assigned a device name of **/dev/lp0**. Similarly, if you're using a serial printer (they are getting rarer and rarer), it will probably be assigned a device name of **/dev/ttyS1**.

This simple configuration means that you can immediately print ASCII characters, with the Linux system treating your printer like a simple line printer. Printing is actually a more involved process that you might think. Printing in Linux involves the following steps:

1. When your computer boots, the **lpd** daemon runs, looking at the **/etc/printcap** to see what printer you're using; the process continues to run throughout your Linux computing session.
2. When you print a document with **lpr**, the **lpd** command actually handles the print job.
3. To change anything in the printing process (like when you want to kill or suspend print jobs), the **lpc** and **lprm** commands are used to talk with the **lpd** daemon.

Obviously, you'll want to make sure that **/etc/printcap** contains the correct information about your printer. When you look at it in a text editor like **elvis** or **emacs**, you'll see that all the lines are commented out with # characters. Most popular printers are listed in this file (such as HP LaserJets), and if you uncomment out the lines specific to your printer, you should be able to use it.

It's important to get this information correct, since Linux printers that aren't configured properly have a tendency to suffer from the "staircase effect," where lines are staggered at the beginning:

```
We hate the staircase effect.
        It makes our documents look really stupid.
                And it makes it hard for us to do our work properly.
                        In fact, we find that we don't print things out when
our printer is misconfigured.
```

Working with a UPS

Slackware Linux supports uninterruptible power supplies (UPSes). This support is rather easy to implement—first you get a UPS, hook it up to your PC, and then run a Linux daemon called **powerd** that monitors the power situation and shuts down the system if necessary. (It will also halt the shutdown if the power appears in time.)

For more information, check out the **man** page for the **powerd** command.

Installing and Configuring X

Because the Linux Internet server isn't a machine that you're likely to use often as a terminal (you'll want to perform most administrative tasks on other machines), setting up the X Window System (in the form of XFree86) isn't as involved a task as it would normally be. For you, setting up the basic X Window System will be enough.

Before you get started, you'll need to know some things about your server's graphics capabilities, such as the type of graphics card, how much memory the graphics card has, and what sort of mouse is attached to the Linux server. Don't worry if you don't have these facts at hand—you can bluff your way through the installation process. Basically, the information you need to know falls under the following categories:

- **Video card**: what kind of chipset your card uses (such as the ubiquitous S3 chipset), the vendor name and make of your card (such as a Diamond Stealth), and the amount of RAM your card has (such as 1MB). The most important setting here is the kind of chipset. You may need to inspect your video card physically to see what sort of chipset is used. If you're using a machine that has Windows 95 already installed, you can look at the Windows 95 configuration information to see what graphics card is installed.

- **Monitor**: the horizontal synchronization frequencies (something like 30–64 kHz; it should say this somewhere in your monitor documentation), the vertical synchronization frequencies (something like 50–90 Hz; it should say this somewhere in your monitor documentation), and the bandwidth (something like 75 MHz). This information isn't as important as it seems. Most multiscan monitors (like a NEC MultiSync or a Hitachi SuperScan) can be configured with middle-of-the-road setting like the ones mentioned here. If your monitor isn't a multiscanning monitor, you'll need to find the documentation for the specific settings. This is a case where an incorrect setting can cause physical damage to your monitor, so you'll want to make sure that your settings are correct.

- **Mouse**: the type of mouse (Microsoft, Logitech, other) and the connection method (serial, bus, PS/2).

Armed with this information, you're ready to configure the X Window System. Basically, this involves running a script file named **xf86config** to create a file called **XF86Config**, which is the configuration file used by XFree86. If you try to start X without first running **xf86config** or manually editing **XF86Config**, you'll get an error. In their attempt to protect you from yourself, the XFree86 folks did not include a working **XF86Config** file, forcing you to do some configuration work.

Running Xf86config

Most users will do just fine if they run the **xf86config** script. You can run this script at any time:

```
$ xf86config
```

Before you do so, you may want to read through the documentation files found at **/usr/X11/lib/X11/doc**. (These files are covered later in the section called "Looking at Some Documentation Files.") After you read these files, you can run the script. You'll be asked for a good amount of information through this process, so we'll run through it carefully.

You'll first be asked about the PATH environment variables on your Linux system. Unless you've made some changes to the system—and on a virgin Linux installation, there is absolutely no reason to make changes in the PATH environment variables—you'll leave this setting alone. The **xf86config** script will list a PATH containing **/usr/X11R6/bin**, and that's what you want.

The next step is setting up your mouse. You'll be presented with the following list:

```
1. Microsoft compatible (2-button protocol)
2. Mouse Systems (3-button protocol)
3. Bus Mouse
4. PS/2 Mouse
5. Logitech Mouse (serial, old type, Logitech protocol)
6. Logitech MouseMan (Microsoft compatible)
7. MM Series
8. MM HitTablet
```

Here are some tips on choosing a mouse:

- This menu refers to how the mouse is connected, not the brand name. Newer Logitech mouse models are Microsoft compatible, as are most of the new mouse models on the market. If you're using a Microsoft mouse that hooks up to a PS/2 mouse port (called an *auxiliary* port in Linux, although Microsoft uses the term *mouse port* without the modifying PS/2), you should choose **PS/2 Mouse**. **Microsoft compatible** should be chosen when the mouse is connected to a serial port.

- Almost all newer mice are Microsoft compatible. Even newer Logitech mouse models are Microsoft compatible. If your Logitech mouse doesn't require any special drivers from Logitech to load under Windows or Windows 95 and connects to a serial port, then it's probably Microsoft compatible.

- Many newer PCs have PS/2 ports for the mouse, but they aren't labeled as such. For instance, Dell PCs have a dedicated mouse port that's really a PS/2 mouse port. Generally speaking, if your newer PC has a "mouse port," the port is really a PS/2 port.

Select a number and then press **Enter**.

N O T E   Many users install a mouse under X and then discover than X won't load due to conflicts with the mouse setup in Linux. In this case, the **gpm** mouse driver was installed in the **setup** routine. This driver is handy when using Linux in terminal mode, because many programs (such as Midnight Commander and Seyon) use a mouse. However, this driver interferes with the X Window System, and you'll need to disable **gpm** before running X. To see whether you're running **gpm**, use the following command line in terminal mode:

```
ps | grep gpm
```

If **gpm** is indeed running, a line will be returned listing it as well as the PID (process ID). (Actually, if **gpm** is indeed running, you'll have two lines returned—a line for **gpm** and a line for **grep gpm**. You can ignore the **grep gpm** line.) Use the **kill** command to stop **gpm** and then launch X to see if this was indeed the problem.

The X Window System was designed for use with three buttons, but most PC mice don't have three buttons (save most Logitech models; Microsoft models do not). Because most users will be using a Microsoft-compatible mouse, the next step in the **xf86config** process is to ask whether three-button emulation is required (the third mouse button is emulated when both mouse buttons are pressed simultaneously):

```
Please answer the following question with either 'y' or 'n'.
Do you want to enable Emulate3Buttons?
```

Your answer isn't exactly crucial to the performance of an Internet server.

Next, you'll need to tell X where the mouse is connected. If you've spent any time around UNIX, you know that all devices are represented by files in the **/dev** directory. You're presented with the following choices:

- **/dev/mouse** (the standard mouse link, which was created when you installed Linux in the **setup** program)
- **/dev/ttyS0** (serial port 1)
- **/dev/ttyS1** (serial port 2)
- **/dev/ttyS2** (serial port 3)
- **/dev/ttyS3** (serial port 4)
- **/dev/atibm** (ATI bus mouse)
- **/dev/logibm** (Logitech bus mouse)
- **/dev/inportbm** (Microsoft bus mouse)
- **/dev/psaux** (PS/2 auxiliary port)

Enter the name of your mouse. In general, it's better to be specific; if you're using a PS/2 port, then specify **/dev/psaux** and not the more generic **/dev/mouse**.

You can always run this program again to create a new configuration file if you find these settings don't work. In other words, don't be afraid of making a mistake.

NOTE

Special character bindings are also used by X. This requires a longer explanation than is actually merited for a discussion of Linux as an X server, but let's just say that it really doesn't matter if you want to use these bindings or not. Therefore, it doesn't matter how you answer the following question:

```
Please answer the following question with either 'y' or 'n'.
Do you want to enable these bindings for the Alt keys?
```

Crucial Information

The next sections are very important if you expect the X Window System to work. First, you're going to be asked about your monitor: its horizontal synchronization frequency and its the vertical synchronization frequency. You'll be presented with the following menu:

```
   hSync in KHz; monitor type with characteristic modes
1. 31.5; Standard VGA, 640x480 @ 60 Hz
2. 31.5 - 35.1; Super VGA, 800x600 @ 56 Hz
3. 31.5, 35.5; 8514 Compatible, 1024x768 @ 87 Hz interlaced (no 800x600)
4. 31.5, 35.15,35.5 Super VGA, 1024x768 @ 87 Hz interlaced, 800x600 @ 56 Hz
5. 31.5 - 37.9; Extended Super VGA, 800x600 @ 60 Hz, 640x480 @ 72 Hz
6. 31.5 - 48.5; Non-interlaced SVGA, 1024x768 @ 60 Hz, 800x600 @ 72 Hz
7. 31.5 - 57.0; High Frequency SVGA, 1024x768 @ 70 Hz
8. 31.5 - 64.3; Monitor that can do 1280x1024 @ 60 Hz
9. 31.5 - 79.0; Monitor that can do 1280x1024 @ 74 Hz
10. Enter your own horizontal sync range
```

For illustrative purposes, we'll use the Hitachi SuperScan Pro 17. The manual that came with the monitor (yes, the manual was actually saved and not tossed!) says that the horizontal synchronization frequency range for this monitor is 30–64 kHz. So the proper choice here would be **9**. (Why not use choice **10** and enter **30–64**? Because it's really not worth the effort.)

The next menu is for vertical synchronization frequency:

```
1. 50-70
2. 50-90
3. 50-100
4. 40-150
5. Enter your own vertical sync range
```

Again, consulting the manual, we see that the Hitachi's range is officially listed as 50–100, and so we select **3**.

The next batch of information involves text strings that define your monitor settings, the monitor manufacturer, and the model name. These are voluntary.

Next comes the selection of a graphics card. If you like, you can scroll through a listing of 124 graphics cards and try to match your card. This is handy when you know which specific card you have. You'll be asked the following question:

```
Do you want to look at the card database?
```

Press **y** to look at the database; press **n** to skip it. If you select the database, you'll be presented with a series of lines as follows:

```
0   928Movie                        S3-928
1   AGX (generic)                   AGX
2   ALG-5434(E)                     CL-GD5434
3   ATI 8514 Ultra (no VGA)         ATI-Mach8
    . . . .
```

This list fills several screens. Listed are specific cards (such as the AGX) as well as the chipset it uses (AGX). At the bottom of each screen, you're asked to select a card's number, press **Enter** to move to the next page, or **q** to move to the next part of the configuration process, bypassing the remaining card definitions. If you do choose a specific card, you'll be presented with information about the card, including the name of the X server that supports it.

In those cases where you don't know what specific card you own but you do know what sort of chipset you have (such as an S3-based chipset), you shouldn't choose a specific card from this list. Instead, go ahead and press **q** to move to the next menu, where you select a server.

Selecting a server is actually more important than selecting a chipset. All S3-based graphics cards use the S3 X server. This process makes it seem more complicated than it really is to select an X server. The following menu, which you'll receive no matter whether you select a card or not, makes it clear:

```
Now you must determine which server to run. Refer to the manpages
and other documentation. The following servers are available (they
may not be installed on your system):

1. The XF86_Mono server. This is a monochrome server that should work
on any VGA-compatible card, in 640x480 (more on some SVGA chipsets).
2. The XF86_VGA16 server. This is a 16-color VGA server that should
work on any VGA-compatible card.
3. The XF86_SVGA server. This is a 256 color SVGA server that supports
a number of VGA chipsets. It is accelerated on some Cirrus and WD
chipsets; it supports 16/32-bit color on certain Cirrus
configurations.
4. The accelerated servers. These include XF86_S3, XF86_Mach32,
XF86_Mach8, XF86_8514, XF86_P9000, XF86_AGX, XF86_W32 and XF86_Mach64.

These four server types correspond to the four different "Screen"
sections in XF86Config (vga2, vga16, svga, accel).

Which one of these screen types do you intend to run by default (1-4)?
```

If you had chosen a specific card, you would have an additional line in this menu:

```
5. Choose the server from the card definition, XF86_S3.
```

Basically, the X server types match chipsets. Anyone using the S3 chipset would select the **XF86_S3** X server. If you wanted to use an accelerated server and didn't specify a chipset, you should select **4** and then select your chipset from the list of X servers.

You'll then be asked whether you want to create a symbolic link between the **X** program file and the X server. You should do so; follow the defaults and you won't have any problems.

The next question has to do with memory on your video card:

```
How much video memory do you have on your video card?
1 256K
2 512K
3 1024K
4 2048K
5 4096K
6 Other
```

Type in the correct number. If you don't know, select **512K** or **1024K**. Most newer graphics cards have at least 1024 KB of RAM; this is the minimum RAM needed to display a resolution of 1024-by-768 in 256 colors.

The next section deals with identifiers for your card, much like the earlier identifiers for monitors. This information is optional.

If you chose an accelerated server, you will be asked about some technical settings for your graphics card: Clockchip and clock frequencies. This is an area where you can just follow along with the **xf86config** script. If you don't know the clockchip setting, just press **Enter**. If you don't know the clock frequencies for your card, you can let **xf96config** probe the clock values for you, using the X server in probe-only mode. This information is then inserted automatically into the **XF86Config** file. If you're using a card or a chipset that doesn't require this information, then **xf86config** will note this and not probe for clock speeds. This all means that you can sit back and let the **xf86config** script do all the work.

Finally, your last big decision has to do with the resolution you want to run under:

```
For each depth, a list of modes (resolutions) is defined. The default
resolution that the server will start-up with will be the first listed
mode that can be supported by the monitor and card.
```

```
Currently it is set to:

"640x480" "800x600" "1024x768" "1280x1024" for 8bpp
"640x480" "800x600" for 16bpp
"640x480" for 32bpp
```

```
Note that 16bpp and 32bpp are only supported on a  few configurations.
Modes that cannot be supported due to monitor or clock constraints
will automatically be skipped by the server.
```

```
1. Change the modes for 8bpp (256 colors)
2. Change the modes for 16bpp (32K/64K colors)
3. Change the modes for 24bpp (240bit color)
4. The modes are OK, continue.
```

```
Enter your choice:
```

Pay close attention to the first line (*"640x480" "800x600" "1024x768" "1280x1024" for 8bpp*). This is the initial mode for the X server. In this instance, the X server will begin in 640x480 mode. This is VGA mode, and it's rather garish (although perfectly adequate when you stop to consider that you're using the box for an Internet server). You'll want to change the modes so that your X server will begin in the mode you want. In most cases, you can leave well enough alone, but it's not that difficult to change the settings. After you make the changes (or not), select **4** to continue.

The next step asks if you want to write all of this to a file, **/etc/XF86Config**. This is the file that the X server will use upon startup. Unless you have a previous configuration file in this location, you can go ahead and select **y**.

After the **/etc/XF86Config** file is generated in this process, it looks like this:

```
# File generated by xf86config.


#
# Copyright (c) 1994 by The XFree86 Project, Inc.
#
# Permission is hereby granted, free of charge, to any person obtaining a
# copy of this software and associated documentation files (the "Software"),
# to deal in the Software without restriction, including without limitation
```

```
# **********************************************************************
# Refer to the XF86Config(4/5) man page for details about the format of
# this file.
# **********************************************************************


# **********************************************************************
# Files section.  This allows default font and rgb paths to be set
# **********************************************************************


Section "Files"

# The location of the RGB database.  Note, this is the name of the
# file minus the extension (like ".txt" or ".db").  There is normally
# no need to change the default.

    RgbPath    "/usr/X11R6/lib/X11/rgb"

# Multiple FontPath entries are allowed (which are concatenated together),
# as well as specifying multiple comma-separated entries in one FontPath
# command (or a combination of both methods)
#
# If you don't have a floating point coprocessor and emacs, Mosaic or other
# programs take long to start up, try moving the Type1 and Speedo directory
# to the end of this list (or comment them out).
#
```

```
    FontPath    "/usr/X11R6/lib/X11/fonts/misc/"
    FontPath    "/usr/X11R6/lib/X11/fonts/Type1/"
    FontPath    "/usr/X11R6/lib/X11/fonts/Speedo/"
    FontPath    "/usr/X11R6/lib/X11/fonts/75dpi/"
    FontPath    "/usr/X11R6/lib/X11/fonts/100dpi/"


EndSection


# ***********************************************************************
# Server flags section.
# ***********************************************************************


Section "ServerFlags"


# Uncomment this to cause a core dump at the spot where a signal is
# received.  This may leave the console in an unusable state, but may
# provide a better stack trace in the core dump to aid in debugging


#     NoTrapSignals


# Uncomment this to disable the <Ctl><Alt><BS> server abort sequence
# This allows clients to receive this key event.


#     DontZap


# Uncomment this to disable the <Ctl><Alt><KP_+>/<KP_-> mode switching
# sequences.  This allows clients to receive these key events.


#     DontZoom


EndSection


# ***********************************************************************
# Input devices
# ***********************************************************************


# ***********************************************************************
# Keyboard section
# ***********************************************************************


Section "Keyboard"
```

```
    Protocol    "Standard"

# when using XQUEUE, comment out the above line, and uncomment the
# following line

#    Protocol    "Xqueue"

    AutoRepeat    500 5
# Let the server do the NumLock processing.  This should only be required
# when using pre-R6 clients
#    ServerNumLock

# Specify which keyboard LEDs can be user-controlled (eg, with xset(1))
#    Xleds      1 2 3

# To set the LeftAlt to Meta, RightAlt key to ModeShift,
# RightCtl key to Compose, and ScrollLock key to ModeLock:

    LeftAlt     Meta
    RightAlt    ModeShift
#    RightCtl    Compose
#    ScrollLock  ModeLock

EndSection

# **********************************************************************
# Pointer section

**********************************************************************

Section "Pointer"
    Protocol    "PS/2"
    Device      "/dev/psaux"

# When using XQUEUE, comment out the above two lines, and uncomment
# the following line.

#    Protocol    "Xqueue"

# Baudrate and SampleRate are only for some Logitech mice

#    BaudRate    9600
#    SampleRate  150
```

```
# Emulate3Buttons is an option for 2-button Microsoft mice
# Emulate3Timeout is the timeout in milliseconds (default is 50ms)

#       Emulate3Buttons
#       Emulate3Timeout   50

# ChordMiddle is an option for some 3-button Logitech mice

#       ChordMiddle

EndSection

# **********************************************************************
# Monitor section
# **********************************************************************

# Any number of monitor sections may be present

Section "Monitor"

        Identifier   "My Monitor"
        VendorName   "Hitachi"
        ModelName    "SuperScan Pro 17"

# HorizSync is in kHz unless units are specified.
# HorizSync may be a comma separated list of discrete values, or a
# comma separated list of ranges of values.
# NOTE: THE VALUES HERE ARE EXAMPLES ONLY.  REFER TO YOUR MONITOR'S
# USER MANUAL FOR THE CORRECT NUMBERS.

    HorizSync   31.5 - 64.3

#   HorizSync   30-64         # multisync
#   HorizSync   31.5, 35.2    # multiple fixed sync frequencies
#   HorizSync   15-25, 30-50  # multiple ranges of sync frequencies

# VertRefresh is in Hz unless units are specified.
# VertRefresh may be a comma separated list of discrete values, or a
# comma separated list of ranges of values.
# NOTE: THE VALUES HERE ARE EXAMPLES ONLY.  REFER TO YOUR MONITOR'S
# USER MANUAL FOR THE CORRECT NUMBERS.

    VertRefresh 50-100
```

```
# Modes can be specified in two formats.  A compact one-line format, or
# a multi-line format.

# These two are equivalent

#    ModeLine "1024x768i" 45 1024 1048 1208 1264 768 776 784 817 Interlace

#    Mode "1024x768i"
#        DotClock   45
#        HTimings   1024 1048 1208 1264
#        VTimings   768 776 784 817
#        Flags      "Interlace"
#    EndMode

# This is a set of standard mode timings. Modes that are out of monitor spec
# are automatically deleted by the server (provided the HorizSync and
# VertRefresh lines are correct), so there's no immediate need to
# delete mode timings (unless particular mode timings don't work on your
# monitor). With these modes, the best standard mode that your monitor
# and video card can support for a given resolution is automatically
# used.

# 640x400 @ 70 Hz, 31.5 kHz hsync
Modeline "640x400"      25.175 640  664  760  800    400  409  411  450
# 640x480 @ 60 Hz, 31.5 kHz hsync
Modeline "640x480"      25.175 640  664  760  800    480  491  493  525
# 800x600 @ 56 Hz, 35.15 kHz hsync
ModeLine "800x600"      36     800  824  896 1024    600  601  603  625
# 1024x768 @ 87 Hz interlaced, 35.5 kHz hsync
Modeline "1024x768"     44.9  1024 1048 1208 1264    768  776  784  817 Interlace

# 640x480 @ 72 Hz, 36.5 kHz hsync
Modeline "640x480"      31.5   640  680  720  864    480  488  491  521
# 800x600 @ 60 Hz, 37.8 kHz hsync
Modeline "800x600"      40     800  840  968 1056    600  601  605  628 +hsync +vsync

# 800x600 @ 72 Hz, 48.0 kHz hsync
Modeline "800x600"      50     800  856  976 1040    600  637  643  666 +hsync +vsync
# 1024x768 @ 60 Hz, 48.4 kHz hsync
Modeline "1024x768"     65    1024 1032 1176 1344    768  771  777  806 -hsync -vsync

# 1024x768 @ 70 Hz, 56.5 kHz hsync
Modeline "1024x768"     75    1024 1048 1184 1328    768  771  777  806 -hsync -vsync
# 1280x1024 @ 87 Hz interlaced, 51 kHz hsync
Modeline "1280x1024"    80    1280 1296 1512 1568   1024 1025 1037 1165 Interlace
```

```
# 1024x768 @ 76 Hz, 62.5 kHz hsync
Modeline "1024x768"    85    1024 1032 1152 1360   768  784  787  823
# 1280x1024 @ 61 Hz, 64.2 kHz hsync
Modeline "1280x1024"  110    1280 1328 1512 1712  1024 1025 1028 1054

# 1280x1024 @ 74 Hz, 78.85 kHz hsync
Modeline "1280x1024"  135    1280 1312 1456 1712  1024 1027 1030 1064

# 1280x1024 @ 76 Hz, 81.13 kHz hsync
Modeline "1280x1024"  135    1280 1312 1416 1664  1024 1027 1030 1064

# Low-res Doublescan modes
# If your chipset does not support doublescan, you get a 'squashed'
# resolution like 320x400.

# 320x200 @ 70 Hz, 31.5 kHz hsync, 8:5 aspect ratio
Modeline "320x200"     12.588 320  336  384  400   200  204  205  225 Doublescan
# 320x240 @ 60 Hz, 31.5 kHz hsync, 4:3 aspect ratio
Modeline "320x240"     12.588 320  336  384  400   240  245  246  262 Doublescan
# 320x240 @ 72 Hz, 36.5 kHz hsync
Modeline "320x240"     15.750 320  336  384  400   240  244  246  262 Doublescan
# 400x300 @ 56 Hz, 35.2 kHz hsync, 4:3 aspect ratio
ModeLine "400x300"     18     400  416  448  512   300  301  602  312 Doublescan
# 400x300 @ 60 Hz, 37.8 kHz hsync
Modeline "400x300"     20     400  416  480  528   300  301  303  314 Doublescan
# 400x300 @ 72 Hz, 48.0 kHz hsync
Modeline "400x300"     25     400  424  488  520   300  319  322  333 Doublescan
# 480x300 @ 56 Hz, 35.2 kHz hsync, 8:5 aspect ratio
ModeLine "480x300"     21.656 480  496  536  616   300  301  302  312 Doublescan
# 480x300 @ 60 Hz, 37.8 kHz hsync
Modeline "480x300"     23.890 480  496  576  632   300  301  303  314 Doublescan
# 480x300 @ 63 Hz, 39.6 kHz hsync
Modeline "480x300"     25     480  496  576  632   300  301  303  314 Doublescan
# 480x300 @ 72 Hz, 48.0 kHz hsync
Modeline "480x300"     29.952 480  504  584  624   300  319  322  333 Doublescan


EndSection


# ************************************************************************
# Graphics device section
# ************************************************************************

# Any number of graphics device sections may be present
```

```
# Standard VGA Device:

Section "Device"
     Identifier    "Generic VGA"
     VendorName    "Unknown"
     BoardName     "Unknown"
     Chipset       "generic"


#    VideoRam    256


#    Clocks      25.2 28.3


EndSection


# Sample Device for accelerated server:

# Section "Device"
#    Identifier     "Actix GE32+ 2MB"
#    VendorName     "Actix"
#    BoardName      "GE32+"
#    Ramdac         "ATT20C490"
#    Dacspeed       110
#    Option         "dac_8_bit"
#    Clocks       25.0  28.0  40.0   0.0  50.0  77.0  36.0  45.0
#    Clocks       130.0 120.0  80.0  31.0 110.0  65.0  75.0  94.0
# EndSection


# Device configured by xf86config:

Section "Device"
     Identifier  "My Video Card"
     VendorName  "Dell"
     BoardName   "S3"
     #VideoRam    2048
     # Insert Clocks lines here if appropriate
EndSection


# ***********************************************************************
# Screen sections
# ***********************************************************************


# The Colour SVGA server
```

```
Section "Screen"
    Driver      "svga"
    Device      "Generic VGA"
    #Device     "My Video Card"
    Monitor     "My Monitor"
    Subsection "Display"
        Depth       8
        #Modes      "1024x768" "1280x1024" "800x600" "640x480"
        ViewPort    0 0
        Virtual     320 200
        #Virtual    1280 1024
    EndSubsection
EndSection

# The 16-color VGA server

Section "Screen"
    Driver      "vga16"
    Device      "Generic VGA"
    Monitor     "My Monitor"
    Subsection "Display"
        Modes       "640x480" "800x600"
        ViewPort    0 0
        Virtual     800 600
    EndSubsection
EndSection

# The Mono server

Section "Screen"
    Driver      "vga2"
    Device      "Generic VGA"
    Monitor     "My Monitor"
    Subsection "Display"
        Modes       "640x480" "800x600"
        ViewPort    0 0
        Virtual     800 600
    EndSubsection
EndSection

# The accelerated servers (S3, Mach32, Mach8, 8514, P9000, AGX, W32, Mach64)
```

```
Section "Screen"
     Driver        "accel"
     Device        "My Video Card"
     Monitor       "My Monitor"
     Subsection "Display"
        Depth         8
        Modes         "1024x768" "1280x1024" "800x600" "640x480"
        ViewPort      0 0
        Virtual       1280 1024
     EndSubsection
     Subsection "Display"
        Depth         16
        Modes         "640x480" "800x600" "1024x768"
        ViewPort      0 0
        Virtual       1024 768
     EndSubsection
     Subsection "Display"
        Depth         32
        Modes         "640x480" "800x600"
        ViewPort      0 0
        Virtual       800 600
     EndSubsection
EndSection
```

As you scan through this file, you can see where some of the settings came from in the **xf86config** process. You could edit this file manually using an editor like **vi** or **emacs**, but such editing is beyond the scope of this book—our point here is to get you up and running with a working X installation. If you want to fine-tune this installation, check out the online documentation for X or else peruse Appendix A for a listing of books covering the topic.

Looking at Some Documentation Files

If you're not quite sure about what configuration to use when you run the **xf86config** script, you can peruse some of the online documentation for XFree86, which can be found in the **/usr/X11/lib/X11/doc** directory. For convenience' sake, here are some of the files.

You don't need to think that you're reinventing the wheel when you install the X Window System. Many brave pioneers have, through trial and error, configured the X Window System to work with their graphics cards. This information has been compiled into a file called **modeDB.txt**, which can be found in the **/usr/X11/lib/X11/doc** directory. This information was compiled by David Wexelblat (*dwex@xfree86.org*), with contributions from Thomas Roell (*roell@xinside.com*). The information that follows was supplied by volunteers (in other words, it's not been verified by any outside sources). It doesn't cover the more popular accelerated cards (which we will cover later in this section). If you're using an older PC to run Linux, chances are pretty good that you'll find your graphics card somewhere in this file. (Note that some of the cards have more than one entry; you'll need to scrutinize the video card closely to make sure that the card matches the correct entry.)

We're not going to list the entire file here. However, here's a typical entry (in this case, for the OAK Technology OTI-077 card):

```
# Card:      OAK Technology OTI-077
# Contributor:    Pedro R. Benito da Rocha [pedro@luna.gui.uva.es]
# Last Edit Date:   4/27/94
#
# chip    ram    virtual   clocks                         default-mode   flags
  OTI077  1024  1024 768  25.40  28.32  65.40 45.20   "800x600"
                           14.20    18.10  40.30 36.20
```

The point of this information is to cut and paste a section here into your **XF86Config** file.

Of more use with newer PCs will be the **AccelCards** file, which contains information about newer accelerated graphics cards. Again, this information isn't the most up-to-date information about graphics cards (none of the entries are more current than 1994), but it should give you some good insight into configuring your graphics card. As with the other files in this section, the purpose of the **AccelCards** file is to cut and paste the information about the cards in the file into your **XF86Config** file.

```
Card Vendor        : ATI
Card Model         : AX0
Card Bus (ISA/EISA/VLB)  : PCI
Chipset            : Mach32
Video Memory       : 2048k
Memory Type (DRAM/VRAM)  : DRAM
Memory Speed       : 45ns
Clock Chip         : 18811-1
Programmable? (Y/N)     : No
Number of clocks   : 32
Clocks             : 100 126 92 36 51 57 0 44 135 32 110 80 39 45 75 65
Clocks (cont)      : 50 63 46 18 25 28 0 22 67 16 55 40 19 23 37 33
Option Flags       :
RAMDAC             : ATI 68875
Submitter          : Alan Hourihane <alanh@metro.co.uk>
Last Edit Date     : Jan 6, 1994
```

The **Monitors** file lists the settings to use with specific monitors. The point is to cut and paste the information from this file into your completed **XF86Config** file. Be warned that the information in this file isn't as up-to-date as you might like, but that the information is contributed by actual users who made XFree86 work with their monitors. The **Monitors** file is as follows:

```
#From: jos@chopin.muc.de (Jochen Schwenk)
#Date: Sat, 24 Dec 1994 02:59:00 +0100
Section "Monitor"
    Identifier  "AOC-15"
    VendorName  "Unknown"
    ModelName   "Unknown"
   BandWidth    135
    HorizSync   23.5-86
    VertRefresh 50-120
    ModeLine "640x480"    25  640  672  768  800  480  490  492  525
    ModeLine "800x600"    50  800  856  976 1040  600  637  643  666
    ModeLine "1024x768"   85 1024 1032 1152 1360  768  784  787  823
    ModeLine "1152x900"  110 1152 1284 1416 1536  900  902  905  941
    ModeLine "1280x1024" 135 1280 1312 1456 1712 1024 1027 1030 1064
EndSection
```

```
#Date: Fri, 16 Sep 1994 23:16:32 -0700
#From: "Leonard N. Zubkoff" <lnz@dandelion.com>
Section "Monitor"
    Identifier "Apollo 1280x1024-68Hz"
    VendorName "Apollo"
    ModelName "010700-005"
    BandWidth 125
    HorizSync 73.702
    VertRefresh 68.24
    Mode "1280x1024"
    DotClock 124.996
    HTimings 1280 1312 1504 1696 VTimings 1024 1027 1030 1080
    EndMode
EndSection


#Date: Fri, 16 Sep 1994 23:16:32 -0700
#From: "Leonard N. Zubkoff" <lnz@dandelion.com>
Section "Monitor"
    Identifier "Apollo 1280x1024-70Hz"
    VendorName "Apollo"
    ModelName "010700-005"
    BandWidth 125
    HorizSync 75.118
    VertRefresh 70.07
    Mode "1280x1024"
    DotClock 124.996
    HTimings 1280 1312 1472 1664 VTimings 1024 1027 1030 1072
    EndMode
EndSection


#From: peterc@a3.ph.man.ac.uk (Peter Chang)
#Date: Fri, 23 Sep 1994 17:40:40 +0100
Section "Monitor"
    Identifier    "Chuntex CTX CPS-1560/LR"
    VendorName    "Chuntex"
    ModelName     "CTX CPS-1560/LR"
    Bandwidth     75.0
    HorizSync     30.00-60.00
    VertRefresh 50.00-100.00
    Mode "640x480"
        DotClock 25
        HTimings 640 664 760 800 VTimings 480 491 493 525
    EndMode
    Mode "800x600"
```

```
        DotClock 50
        HTimings 800 856 976 1040 VTimings 600 637 643 666
    Flags "+HSync" "+VSync"
    EndMode
    Mode "1024x768"
        DotClock 75
        HTimings 1024 1048 1184 1328 VTimings 768  771  777  806
    Flags "-HSync" "-VSync"
    EndMode
EndSection


#From: dlj0@chern.math.lehigh.edu (DAVID L. JOHNSON)
#Date: Fri, 23 Sep 1994 23:23:18 -0400
Section "Monitor"
    Identifier  "Compudyne KD-1500N"
    VendorName  "Compudyne"
    ModelName   "KD-1500N"
    Bandwidth   74.8
    HorizSync   30.00-66
    VertRefresh 50-90
    Mode "640x480"
        DotClock 25
        HTimings 640 664 760 800 VTimings 480 491 493 525
    EndMode
    Mode "1024x768"
        DotClock 74.8
        HTimings 1024 1056 1256 1328 VTimings 768 776 786 806
    EndMode
EndSection


#From: forsse@meaddata.com (Steve Forsythe)
#Date: Sun, 18 Sep 94 3:27:15 EDT
Section "Monitor"
    Identifier "CTX-1561"
    VendorName "CTX"
    ModelName "CMS-1561"
    BandWidth 100
    HorizSync 30-60
    VertRefresh 50-90
    ModeLine "640x480" 25 640 664 760 800 480 491 493 525
    ModeLine "800x600" 40 800 872 1000 1056 600 601 605 628
    ModeLine "800x600" 50 800 856 976 1040 600 637 643 666
    ModeLine "1024x768" 75 1024 1072 1216 1352 768 769 775 806
EndSection
```

```
#Date: Wed, 21 Sep 1994 14:22:23 -0700 (PDT)
#From: James Dooley <jdooley@ugcs.caltech.edu>
#Updated Date: Date: Mon, 3 Oct 94 22:03:47 EST
#Updated From: "Bill C. Riemers" <bcr@physics.purdue.edu>
Section "Monitor"
    Identifier  "CrystalScan 1572FS"
    VendorName  "CrystalScan"
    ModelName   "1572FS"
    Bandwidth   110
    HorizSync   30.00-60.00
    VertRefresh 50.00-100.00
    Mode "640x480"
        DotClock 25
        HTimings 640 664 760 800 VTimings 480 491 493 525
    EndMode
    Mode "1024x768"
        DotClock 80
        HTimings 1024 1136 1340 1432 VTimings 768 770 774 805
    EndMode
    ModeLine "1024x768i" 45 1024 1048 1208 1264 768 776 784 817 Interlace
    Mode "1280x1024"
        DotClock 80
        HTimings 1280 1296 1512 1568 VTimings 1024 1025 1037 1165
        Flags "Interlace"
    EndMode
EndSection


#Date: Fri, 16 Sep 1994 11:42:19 +0100
#From: Doug Rabson <dfr@render.com>
#Note: Two submissions by the same author? Be careful.
Section "Monitor"
    Identifier "Dell VS17"
    VendorName "Dell"
    ModelName "VS17"
    BandWidth 78.0
    HorizSync 30.0-62.0
    VertRefresh 50-90
    ModeLine "640x480" 28.3 640 680 720 864 480 488 491 521
    ModeLine "1024x768" 60 1024 1128 1240 1344 768 770 775 788
EndSection


#From: Doug Rabson <dfr@render.com>
#Date: Sat, 24 Sep 1994 14:54:58 +0100
#Note: display shifted to the left.
#Note: Two submissions by the same author? Be careful.
```

```
Section "Monitor"
     Identifier  "DELL VS17"
     VendorName  "DELL"
     ModelName   "VS17"
     Bandwidth   25.2 mhz
     HorizSync   30-62
     VertRefresh 50-90
     # Refresh rate = 73.46Hz ; Horizontal Frequency = 59.29KHz
     Mode "1024x768"
          DotClock          81
          HTimings          1024 1120 1272 1368
          VTimings           768  788  801   847
     EndMode
EndSection


#Date: Fri, 16 Sep 1994 12:58:21 +0200 (MET DST)
#From: kiwi@belly.in-berlin.de (Axel Habermann)
Section "Monitor"
     Identifier "EIZO FlexScan T660"
     VendorName "EIZO"
     ModelName "FlexScan T660i-T/TCO"
     BandWidth   135.0
     HorizSync   30.0-82.0
     VertRefresh 55.0-90.0
     ModeLine "1536x1152" 168 1536 1616 1760 2048 1152 1154 1158 1188
     ModeLine "1280x1024" 135 1280 1328 1408 1688 1024 1025 1026 1060
     ModeLine "1024x768" 80 1024 1088 1152 1280 768 770 772 778
EndSection


#Date: Mon, 26 Sep 1994 23:30:00 -1000 (EST)
#From: dawes@XFree86.org (David Dawes)
Section "Monitor"
     Identifier "EIZO FlexScan 9080i"
     VendorName "EIZO"
     ModelName "FlexScan 9080i"
     BandWidth   60.0
     HorizSync   30.0-64.0
     VertRefresh 50.0-90.0
     ModeLine "640x480" 31 640 664 704 832 480 489 492 520
     ModeLine "640x480" 28 640 672 768 800 480 490 492 525
     ModeLine "640x480" 25 640 672 768 800 480 490 492 525
     ModeLine "800x600" 50 800 856 976 1040 600 637 643 666
     ModeLine "800x600" 40 800 864 896 1008 600 600 606 624
     ModeLine "800x600" 36 800 816 952 1056 600 608 610 633
     ModeLine "1024x768i" 45 1024 1064 1224 1264 768 777 783 815 interlace
```

```
    ModeLine "1024x768i" 44 1024 1064 1224 1264 768 777 785 817 interlace
    ModeLine "1024x768" 80 1024 1032 1152 1360 768 784 787 823
    ModeLine "1152x900" 80 1152 1152 1368 1400 900 912 929 945
    ModeLine "1280x1024i" 80 1280 1296 1412 1632 1024 1025 1037 1165 interlace
EndSection


#From: Helmut Geyer <Helmut.Geyer@iwr.uni-heidelberg.de>
#Date: Wed, 21 Sep 1994 23:48:57 +0200 (MET DST)
Section "Monitor"
    Identifier "ELSA GDM-17E40"
    VendorName "ELSA GmbH"
    ModelName "GDM-17E40"
    BandWidth 135
    HorizSync 29-82
    VertRefresh 50-150
    ModeLine "640x480" 25 640 664 760 800 480 491 493 525
    ModeLine "640x480" 31 640 664 704 832 480 489 492 520
    ModeLine "800x600x32" 45 800 820 904 964 600 601 604 621
    ModeLine "1024x768x16" 78.7 1024 1044 1140 1264 768 770 773 796
    ModeLine "1152x875" 135 1152 1416 1456 1664 875 875 877 906
    ModeLine "1152x900" 135 1152 1400 1440 1648  900 901 905 935
    ModeLine "1280x1024i" 80 1280 1296 1512 1568 1024 1025 1037 1165 interlace
    ModeLine "1280x1024" 110 1280 1328 1512 1712 1024 1025 1028 1054
    ModeLine "1280x1024" 135 1280 1312 1456 1712 1024 1027 1030 1064
EndSection


#From: wolff@dutecai.et.tudelft.nl (Rogier Wolff)
#Date: Sat, 24 Sep 1994 17:27:09 +0200 (MET DST)
Section "Monitor"
    Identifier "ESCOM MONO-LCD-screen"
    VendorName "ESCOM"
    ModelName "Unknown"
    BandWidth 28
    HorizSync 30-36
    VertRefresh 43-72
    ModeLine "640x480" 25.175 640 664 760 800 480 491 493 525
EndSection


#From: Alan Hourihane <alanh@fairlite.demon.co.uk>
#Date: Mon, 26 Sep 1994 21:04:34 +0000 (GMT)
Section "Monitor"
    Identifier "Gateway 2000 CrystalScan 1776LE"
    VendorName "Gateway 2000"
    ModelName "CrystalScan 1776LE"
    BandWidth 110
```

```
    HorizSync 30-64
    VertRefresh 50-120
    ModeLine "640x480"  25 640 664 760 800 480 491 493 525
    ModeLine "640x480"  31 640 664 704 832 480 489 492 520
    ModeLine "800x600"  50 800 856 976 1040 600 637 643 666 +hsync +vsync
    ModeLine "1024x768i"  44 1024 1040 1216 1264 768 777 785 817 interlace
    ModeLine "1024x768"  75 1024 1072 1184 1328 768 768 770 800 -hsync -vsync
    ModeLine "1280x1024i"  80 1280 1296 1512 1568 1024 1025 1037 1165 interlace
    ModeLine "1280x1024"  110 1280 1360 1428 1720 1024 1025 1036 1065
EndSection


#From: David Dawes <dawes@XFree86.org>
#Date: Fri, 16 Sep 1994 12:40:08 +1000 (EST)
# GJA — Changed dotclock from 25 to 25.2
Section "Monitor"
    Identifier    "Generic Monitor"
    VendorName    "Unknown"
    ModelName     "Unknown"
    Bandwidth    25.2
    HorizSync    31.5
    VertRefresh 60
    Mode "640x480"
        DotClock 25.2
        HTimings 640 664 760 800 VTimings 480 491 493 525
    EndMode
EndSection


#Date: Fri, 16 Sep 1994 23:16:32 -0700
#From: "Leonard N. Zubkoff" <lnz@dandelion.com>
Section "Monitor"
    Identifier "HP 1280x1024-72Hz"
    VendorName "Hewlett-Packard"
    ModelName "A1097A"
    BandWidth 135
    HorizSync 78.125
    VertRefresh 72.008
    Mode "1280x1024"
    DotClock 135.00
    HTimings 1280 1344 1536 1728 VTimings 1024 1027 1030 1085
    EndMode
EndSection


#From: Gertjan Akkerman <akkerman@dutiba.twi.tudelft.nl>
#Date: Tue, 20 Sep 1994 11:45:21 +0200 (MET DST)
```

```
Section "Monitor"
    Identifier "Highscreen LE 1024"
    VendorName "Vobis"
    ModelName "LE 1024"
    BandWidth 45 # MHz
    HorizSync 31.4-31.6, 35.1-35.2, 35.5-35.6 # KHz
    VertRefresh 50-87 # Hz
    ModeLine "640x480"   25.2 640 664 760 800 480 491 493 525
    ModeLine "800x600"   36.0 800 824 896 1024 600 601 603 625
    ModeLine "1024x768i" 44.9 1024 1040 1216 1264 768 777 785 817 interlace
EndSection

#From: rich@id.slip.bcm.tmc.edu (Rich Murphey)
#Date: Thu, 15 Sep 1994 23:30:52 -0501
Section "Monitor"
    Identifier "Hitachi SuperScan 20S"
    VendorName "Hitachi"
    ModelName "SuperScan 20S model no. CM2095MU"
    BandWidth 100.0
    HorizSync 30-69
    VertRefresh 50-100
    ModeLine "1152x90085" 85 1152 1192 1384 1480 900 905 923 955
EndSection

#From: wolff@dutecai.et.tudelft.nl (Rogier Wolff)
#Date: Sat, 24 Sep 1994 17:27:09 +0200 (MET DST)
# This monitor does the VESA 640x480@60Hz, 800x600@58Hz and 1024x768i@43Hz.
Section "Monitor"
    Identifier "Hyundai hcm-421E"
    VendorName "Hyundai"
    ModelName "421E"
    BandWidth 110
    HorizSync 30-36
    VertRefresh 43-72
    ModeLine "640x480" 25.175 640 664 760 800 480 491 493 525
EndSection

#Date: Thu, 22 Sep 1994 01:38:45 -0400
#From: Chris Mason <mason@mail.csh.rit.edu>
Section "Monitor"
    Identifier "IDEK VisionMaster 17 (1)"
    # was: "IDEK 8617"
    VendorName "IDEK"
    ModelName "8617"
```

```
    BandWidth 135
    HorizSync 31.5-85.0
    VertRefresh 60-80
    ModeLine "800x600" 49 800 816 932 996 600 607 612 635
    ModeLine "1024x768" 85 1024 1028 1196 1348 768 769 775 804
    ModeLine "1280x1024.1" 135 1280 1296 1456 1726 1024 1025 1028 1066
    ModeLine "1280x1128.1" 135 1280 1284 1456 1661 1128 1129 1132 1161
EndSection


#Date: Wed, 21 Sep 1994 22:22:42 +0100
#From: Andrew Dyer <adyer@zarniwoop.chi.il.us>
Section "Monitor"
    Identifier "IDEK VisionMaster 17 (2)"
    # was: "IDEK MF-8617"
    VendorName  "Idek"
    ModelName   "MF-8617"
    Bandwidth   135.0
    HorizSync   23.5-86.0
    VertRefresh 50-120
    Mode "640x480"
        DotClock 25
        HTimings 640 664 760 800 VTimings 480 491 493 525
    EndMode
    Mode "1024x768"
        DotClock 75
        HTimings 1024 1056 1192 1280 VTimings 768  770  776  806
        Flags "-vsync" "-hsync"
    EndMode
EndSection


#Date: Mon, 19 Sep 1994 20:37:05 +0200
#From: eddy@dutecae.et.tudelft.nl (J.G.E. Olk)
Section "Monitor"
    Identifier "IDEK VisionMaster 17 (3)"
    VendorName "IDEK"
    ModelName  "MF-8617"
    BandWidth   135
    HorizSync   23.5-86
    VertRefresh 50-120
    ModeLine "640x480"    25  640  672  768  800  480  490  492  525
    ModeLine "800x600"    50  800  856  976 1040  600  637  643  666
    ModeLine "1024x768"   85 1024 1032 1152 1360  768  784  787  823
    ModeLine "1152x900"  110 1152 1284 1416 1536  900  902  905  941
    ModeLine "1280x1024" 135 1280 1312 1456 1712 1024 1027 1030 1064
EndSection
```

```
#From: Richard Coley <rcoley@pyra.co.uk>
#Date: Thu, 15 Sep 1994 12:29:10 +0100 (BST)
Section "Monitor"
    Identifier "IDEK Vision Master 17 (4)"
    VendorName "LIYAMA"
    ModelName "Vision Master 17 (MF8617)"
    BandWidth 135.0
    HorizSync 23.5-86.0
    VertRefresh 50-120
    ModeLine "1024x768" 80 1024 1032 1216 1344 768 768 773 805
    ModeLine "800x600" 32 800 832 976 1016 600 604 606 634 +hsync +vsync
    ModeLine "640x480" 25 640 672 768 800 480 490 492 525 -hsync -vsync
EndSection


#From: Bob Mende Pie <mende@piecomputer.rutgers.edu>
#Date: Fri, 23 Sep 1994 22:51:51 -0400
Section "Monitor"
    Identifier "IDEK Vision Master 17 (5)"
    #Was: "Idek 8617"
    VendorName "Idek"
    ModelName "8617"
    BandWidth 135.0     # EDIT THIS!
    HorizSync 23.5-86   # EDIT THIS!
    VertRefresh 50-120  # EDIT THIS!

    ModeLine "640x480"   28    640 656 752 792     480 490 492 519
    ModeLine "800x600"   40    800 840 968 1032    600 601 605 625
    ModeLine "1024x768"  75.0  1024 1088 1240 1368 768 770 777 800
    ModeLine "1152x900"  95.0  1152 1232 1384 1528 900 914 917 943
        -hsync -vsync
    ModeLine "1280x1024" 135   1280 1320 1536 1704 1024 1027 1030 1073
        -hsync -vsync
EndSection


#Date: Mon, 19 Sep 1994 13:37:39 +0100
#From: Charles Hawkins <ceh@eng.cam.ac.uk>
Section "Monitor"
    Identifier "Lite-On CM1414E"
    VendorName "Lite-On Technology"
    ModelName "CM1414E"
    BandWidth 45.0
    HorizSync 30-40       # actually 31.5,35.5, but this avoids comma bug
    VertRefresh 40.0-87.0 # actually spec'd at 50.0-87.0
```

```
    ModeLine "640x480" 25 640 672 768 800 480 490 492 509
    ModeLine "800x600" 35 800 824 920 968 600 601 603 624
    Mode "1024x768i"
        DotClock 45
        HTimings 1024 1040 1210 1267 VTimings 768 777 785 817
        Flags "Interlace"
    EndMode
EndSection


#From: Farrell.McKay@nms.otc.com.au (Farrell McKay)
#Date: Mon, 26 Sep 1994 10:05:03 +1000 (EST)
Section "Monitor"
  Identifier "MAG MX15F (1)"
  VendorName "MAG"
  ModelName "MX15F"
  BandWidth 100 MHz
  HorizSync 30-65 KHz
  VertRefresh 50-120 Hz
  ModeLine "800x600"    50  800  856  976 1040  600  637  643  666
    +hsync +vsync
  ModeLine "1024x768"   75 1024 1048 1184 1328  768  771  777  806
    -hsync -vsync
  ModeLine "1280x1024" 110 1280 1320 1480 1728 1024 1029 1036 1077
EndSection


#From: "M{kinen Sami J." <sjm@cs.tut.fi>
#Date: Mon, 19 Sep 1994 23:47:01 +0300
Section "Monitor"
    Identifier      "MAG MX15F (2)"
    VendorName      "MAG"
    ModelName       "MX15F"
    Bandwidth       100.0
    HorizSync       30.00-65.00
    VertRefresh     40.00-120.00
    Mode "640x480"
        DotClock 25
        HTimings 640 664 760 800 VTimings 480 491 493 525
    EndMode
    Mode "1024x768"
        DotClock 80
        HTimings 1024 1128 1300 1400 VTimings 768 770 774 800
    EndMode
EndSection
```

```
#Date: Tue, 20 Sep 94 08:32:45 EDT
#From: bremner@muff.cs.mcgill.ca (David BREMNER)
Section "Monitor"
    Identifier "MegaImage 17"
    VendorName "MegaImage"
    ModelName "S17MGP"
    BandWidth 106
    HorizSync 30-64
    VertRefresh 50-100
    ModeLine "1152x864" 92 1152 1192 1352 1440 864 865 875 895
    ModeLine "1024x768" 85 1024 1032 1152 1360 768 784 787 823
    ModeLine "640x480" 31 640 664 704 832 480 489 492 520
    ModeLine "800x600" 50 800 856 976 1040 600 637 643 666
EndSection


#From: erik@kroete2.freinet.de (Erik Corry)
#Date: Wed, 8 Feb 1995 02:03:20 +0100 (MET)
Section "Monitor"
    Identifier "Miro 20inch CAD Monitor"
    VendorName "Miro"
    ModelName "Unknown-model-name"
    BandWidth 100.0     # Actually about 64
    HorizSync 47-49     # Actually fixed sync at ca. 48KHz
    VertRefresh 58-62   # Actually fixed at ca. 60Hz
    ModeLine "1096x776" 65 1096 1162 1326 1344 776 779 785 806   +vsync -hsync
EndSection


#From: ciotti@nas.nasa.gov (Robert B. Ciotti)
#Date: Fri, 30 Sep 1994 10:34:37 -0700
Section "Monitor"
    Identifier "AUM1371A"
    VendorName "Mitsubishi"
    ModelName "DiamondScan"
    BandWidth 30
    HorizSync 15-38
    VertRefresh 40-90 # monitor Spec
    #VertRefresh 40-92 # pushed from spec to support 1000x750
    ModeLine "1000x750" 45 1000 1040 1208 1248 750 750 756 788 interlace
    ModeLine "800x600"  36 800 851 987  1056  600 608 610 633
    ModeLine "vesa640x480a" 25.175 640 664 760 800 480 491 493 525
    ModeLine "vesa640x480b" 25.175 640 672 768 800 480 490 492 525
    ModeLine "vesa640x480c" 31.5 640 664 704 832 480 489 492 520
EndSection
```

```
#Date: Mon, 26 Sep 1994 23:30:00 -1000 (EST)
#From: dawes@XFree86.org (David Dawes)
Section "Monitor"
    Identifier "NED 3D"
    VendorName "NEC"
    ModelName "MultiSync 3D"
    BandWidth   45.0
    HorizSync   15.5-38.0
    VertRefresh 50.0-90.0
    ModeLine "640x480" 25 640 672 768 800 480 490 492 525
    ModeLine "800x600" 45 800 840 1224 1264 600 600 606 624
    ModeLine "800x600" 36 800 824 896 1024 600 601 603 625
    ModeLine "1024x768i" 46 1024 1064 1224 1264 768 777 785 817 interlace
EndSection


#Date: Sun, 18 Sep 1994 16:00:53 +1000
#From: Stephen Hocking <sysseh@devetir.qld.gov.au>
Section "Monitor"
    Identifier "NEC 4D"
    VendorName "NEC"
    ModelName "4D"
    BandWidth 75
    HorizSync 30-57
    VertRefresh 50-90
    ModeLine "640x480" 25.175 640 672 768 800 480 490 492 525
    ModeLine "800x600" 40 800 840 968 1056 600 601 605 628 +hsync +vsync
    ModeLine "1024x768i" 44.9 1024 1064 1224 1264 768 777 785 817 interlace
    ModeLine "1024x768" 64 1024 1144 1208 1320 768 778 782 808
    ModeLine "1024x768" 75 1024 1048 1184 1328 768 771 777 806 -hsync +vsync
EndSection


#Date: Sat, 17 Sep 1994 00:50:57 -0400
#From: Erik Nygren <nygren@mit.edu>
Section "Monitor"
    Identifier "NEC MultiSync 4FGe"
    VendorName "NEC"
    ModelName "MultiSync 4FGe"
    BandWidth 80Mhz          #\
    HorizSync 27-62KHz        #> from monitor documentation
    VertRefresh 55-90Hz      #/
    ModeLine "640x480"   31  640  680  704  832 480 489 492 520
    ModeLine "800x600"   50  800  864  976 1040 600 637 643 666
    ModeLine "1024x768"  81 1024 1068 1204 1324 768 776 782 807
EndSection
```

```
#From: Hans Nasten <nasten@everyware.se>
#Date: Tue, 27 Sep 1994 10:18:05 +0100 (MET)
Section "Monitor"
    Identifier "NEC 5FG"
    VendorName "NEC"
    ModelName "5FG"
    BandWidth 135.0
    HorizSync 27-79
    VertRefresh 55-90
    ModeLine "640x480"  28 640 664 704 832 480 489 492 520
    ModeLine "640x480"  32 640 664 704 832 480 489 492 520
    ModeLine "800x600"  50 800 856 976 1040 600 637 643 666
    ModeLine "1024x768"  75 1024 1048 1184 1328 768 771 777 806 -hsync -vsync
    ModeLine "1152x900"  90 1152 1176 1234 1464 900 906 914 943 -hsync -vsync
    ModeLine "1280x1024"  115 1280 1276 1372 1664 1024 1028 1035 1062
             -hsync -vsync
EndSection


#From: karlcz@uclink.berkeley.edu (Karl Frederick Czajkowski)
#Date: Thu, 15 Sep 1994 23:14:30 -0700
Section "Monitor"
    Identifier "Nanao F340i-W"
    VendorName "Nanao"
    ModelName "F340i-W"
    BandWidth 75.0
    HorizSync 27-61
    VertRefresh 55-90
    ModeLine "1024x768"  80 1024 1048 1192 1344 768 772 780 821 +hsync +vsync
    ModeLine "1024x768"  72 1024 1056 1129 1280 768 770 776 806 -hsync -vsync
    ModeLine "1024x768"  85 1024 1032 1152 1360 768 784 787 823 +hsync +vsync
    ModeLine "800x600"  50 800 856 976 1040 600 637 643 666 +hsync +vsync
    ModeLine "640x480"  32 640 664 704 832 480 489 492 520
    ModeLine "LowRes"  25 400 416 512 560 300 396 398 498
EndSection


#From: Mark_Weaver@brown.edu (Mark_Weaver@brown.edu)
#Date: Mon, 19 Sep 1994 14:59:09 -0400
Section "Monitor"
    Identifier "Nanao F550i"
    VendorName "Nanao"
    ModelName "F550i"
    BandWidth 100.0      # Just a guess
    HorizSync 30-66      # WARNING: not correct, be careful
    VertRefresh 40-130   # WARNING: not correct, be careful
    ModeLine "640x480"  25 640 664 760 800 480 491 493 525
```

```
    ModeLine "640x480" 31 640 664 704 832 480 489 492 520
    ModeLine "640x480" 40 640 704 832 904 480 530 542 615
    ModeLine "800x600" 45 800 856 976 1040 600 637 643 666
    ModeLine "1024x768s" 65 1024 1032 1176 1344 768 771 777 806
    ModeLine "1024x768" 75 1024 1048 1184 1328 768 771 777 806
    ModeLine "1152x900s" 65 1152 1168 1312 1400 900 901 907 935 Interlace
    ModeLine "1152x900i" 80 1152 1168 1384 1440 900 901 907 945 interlace
    ModeLine "1280x1024i" 110 1280 1328 1482 1682 1024 1025 1035 1085 interlace
  ModeLine "1280x1024" 110 1280 1328 1482 1682 1024 1025 1028 1054
EndSection


#Date: Sun, 18 Sep 1994 22:55:32 -0700 (PDT)
#From: Shyam Subramanyan <shyam@crl.com>
Section "Monitor"
    Identifier "Nanao F550i-w"
    VendorName "Nanao"
    ModelName "F550i-w"
    BandWidth 80
    HorizSync 27-65
    VertRefresh 55-90
    ModeLine "640x480" 31 640 664 704 832 480 489 492 520
    ModeLine "800x600" 45 800 856 976 1040 600 637 643 666
    ModeLine "800x600" 50 800 856 976 1040 600 637 643 666
    ModeLine "1024x768" 75 1024 1048 1184 1328 768 771 777 806
EndSection


#From: Ted.Goldblatt@telematics.com (Ted Goldblatt)
#Date: Fri, 23 Sep 1994 11:52:28 +0500
Section "Monitor"
    Identifier  "Nokia 445X"
    VendorName  "Nokia"
    ModelName   "445X"
    Bandwidth   200
    HorizSync   30-102
    VertRefresh 50-120
    ModeLine "1600x1200"  188.58 1600 1792 1856 2208   1200 1202 1205 1256
    ModeLine "1280x1024"  135    1280 1312 1456 1712   1024 1027 1030 1064
    ModeLine "1152x900"    95    1152 1152 1192 1472    900  900  931  939
EndSection


#From: J Wunsch <joerg_wunsch@uriah.sax.de>
#Date: Fri, 23 Sep 1994 09:28:58 +0200 (MET DST)
Section "Monitor"
    Identifier "Nokia 447B (1)"
    VendorName "Nokia"
```

```
    ModelName "Multigraph 447B"
    BandWidth 110        # MHz
    HorizSync 30-64      # kHz
    VertRefresh 48-100   # Hz
    # "fast" 640x480, 39.17 kHz H, 76 Hz V
    ModeLine "640x480" 31.96    640  684  756  816     480 486 489 515
    # 800 x 600, 40.08 kHz H, 63 Hz V
    ModeLine "800x600" 42        800  868 1008 1048     600 609 613 636
    # 1024 x 768, 61.96 kHz H, 76 Hz V
    ModeLine "1024x768" 80.8    1024 1048 1200 1304     768 777 785 817
    # 1088 x 800, 63.26 kHz H (near limit!), 76 Hz V (still excellent)
    ModeLine "1088x800" 87.04   1088 1120 1264 1376     800 806 816 834
EndSection


#Date: Wed, 21 Sep 94 16:11:47 PDT
#From: eh@c-cube.com (Ernest Hua)
Section "Monitor"
    Identifier   "Nokia 447B (2)"
    VendorName   "Nokia"
    ModelName    "447B"
    Bandwidth    110
    HorizSync    30-64
    VertRefresh 48-100
    Mode "640x480@60Hz" # Horizontal Sync = 31.5kHz
        DotClock 25.175
        HTimings 640  672  768  800 VTimings 480  490  492  525
    EndMode
    Mode "640x480@72Hz" # Horizontal Sync = 37.9kHz
        DotClock 31.5
        HTimings 640  664  704  832 VTimings 480  489  492  520
    EndMode
    Mode "800x600@72Hz" # Horizontal Sync = 48kHz
        DotClock 50
        HTimings 800  856  976 1040 VTimings 600  637  643  666
    EndMode
    Mode "1024x768@76Hz" # Horizontal Sync = 62.5kHz
        DotClock 85
        HTimings 1024 1032 1152 1360 VTimings 768  784  787  823
    EndMode
    Mode "1280x1024@61Hz" # Horizontal Sync = 64.25kHz
        DotClock 110
        HTimings 1280 1328 1512 1712 VTimings 1024 1025 1028 1054
    EndMode
EndSection
```

```
#From: Orest Zborowski  <orestz@eskimo.com>
#Date: Tue, 27 Sep 1994 01:23:59 -0700 (PDT)
Section "Monitor"
    Identifier "Philips 1764DC"
    VendorName "Philips"
    ModelName "1764DC"
    BandWidth 110
    HorizSync 30-66
    VertRefresh 50-100
    ModeLine "640x480" 25 640 664 760 800 480 491 493 525
    ModeLine "800x600" 50 800 856 976 1040 600 637 643 666
    ModeLine "1024x768" 65 1024 1048 1192 1344 768 771 777 806
    ModeLine "1280x1024" 110 1280 1328 1512 1712 1024 1025 1028 1054
EndSection


#Date: Sun, 18 Sep 1994 16:00:53 +1000
#From: Stephen Hocking <sysseh@devetir.qld.gov.au>
Section "Monitor"
    Identifier "PHILIPS 7BM749"
    VendorName "PHILIPS"
    ModelName "7BM749"
    BandWidth 28
    HorizSync 30-33
    VertRefresh 55-70
    ModeLine "704x480m" 28 704 720 832 864 480 480 488 488
    ModeLine "704x504m" 28 704 736 856 888 504 504 542 554
    ModeLine "680x510m" 28 680 688 800 864 510 512 518 542 -hsync -vsync
    ModeLine "688x516m" 28 688 720 832 864 516 516 522 542 -hsync -vsync
    ModeLine "640x350" 25 640 672 768 800 350 387 389 449 +hsync -vsync
    ModeLine "640x400" 25 640 672 768 800 400 412 414 449 -hsync +vsync
    ModeLine "640x480" 25 640 672 768 800 480 480 486 504
EndSection


#From: "william (w.f.) conn" <conn@bnr.ca>
#Date:  Sun, 25 Sep 1994 19:51:00 -0500
Section "Monitor"
    Identifier "Quantex TE1564M, Super View 1280"
    VendorName "Quantex"
    ModelName "TE1564M"
    BandWidth 75
    HorizSync 30-64
    VertRefresh 50-100
    ModeLine "640x480" 25 640 664 760 800 480 491 493 525
    ModeLine "800x600" 36 800 824 896 1024 600 601 603 625
```

```
    ModeLine "1024x768" 65 1024 1032 1176 1344 768 771 777 806
    ModeLine "1280x1024i" 80 1280 1352 1384 1568 1024 1024 1036 1164 interlace
EndSection

#Date: Wed, 21 Sep 1994 19:54:08 -0400 (EDT)
#From: Andrew Robinson <robinson@cnj.digex.net>
Section "Monitor"
    Identifier  "Relisys RE1564"
    VendorName  "Relisys"
    ModelName   "RE1564"
    Bandwidth   80.0
    HorizSync   30-64
    VertRefresh 50-100
    ModeLine "640x480"    31.5     640  664  704  832    480  489  492  520
    ModeLine "800x600"    50       800  856  976 1040    600  637  643  666
    ModeLine "1024x768"   75      1024 1048 1184 1328    768  771  777  806
    ModeLine "1280x1024i" 80      1280 1296 1512 1568   1024 1025 1037 1165
    Interlace
EndSection

#From: matthieu@laas.fr (Matthieu Herrb)
#Date: Tue, 27 Sep 1994 10:05:24 +0100
Section "Monitor"
  Identifier "Sampo alphascan-17"
  ModelName "AlphaScan 17"
  BandWidth 95MHz
  HorizSync 30-77kHz
  VertRefresh 20-105Hz
  ModeLine "640x480"    31.5 640  664  704  832 480  489  492  520
  ModeLine "800x600"    40    800  840  968 1056 600  601  605  628
  ModeLine "1024x768"   80   1024 1056 1096 1374 768  774  776  800
  ModeLine "1024x768i"  40   1024 1064 1224 1264 768  773  781  813 interlace
  ModeLine "1152x900"   94.6 1152 1160 1400 1536 900  906  914  954
  ModeLine "1152x900i"  80   1152 1184 1480 1496 900  912  950 1024 interlace
  ModeLine "1280x1024i" 80   1280 1288 1408 1624 1024 1026 1032 1076 interlace
  ModeLine "1280x1024"  110  1280 1328 1512 1712 1024 1025 1028 1054
EndSection

#Date: Mon, 23 Jan 1995 09:50:44 -0800
#From: "Leonard N. Zubkoff" <lnz@dandelion.com>
Section "Monitor"
    Identifier "Sony CPD-1430"
    VendorName "Sony"
    ModelName "CPD-1430"
    BandWidth 75.0
```

```
    HorizSync 28.0-58.0
    VertRefresh 55.0-110.0
    Mode "640x480-72Hz"
        DotClock 31.150
        HTimings 640 672 712 832
        VTimings 480 488 491 520
    EndMode
    Mode "800x600-72Hz"
        DotClock 50.000
        HTimings 800 864 984 1040
        VTimings 600 637 643 666
    EndMode
    Mode "1024x768i-45Hz"
        DotClock 44.900
        HTimings 1024 1032 1208 1264
        VTimings 768 769 773 817
        Flags "Interlace"
    EndMode
    Mode "1024x768-71Hz"
        DotClock 75.267
        HTimings 1024 1056 1152 1312
        VTimings 768 773 775 808
    EndMode
    Mode "1152x900-60Hz"
        DotClock 80.352
        HTimings 1152 1184 1248 1440
        VTimings 900 900 903 930
    EndMode
EndSection


#From: koenig@nova.tat.physik.uni-tuebingen.de (Harald Koenig)
#Date: Date: Mon, 26 Sep 94 20:33:07 MEZ
Section "Monitor"
    Identifier "Sony Multiscan 15sf"
    VendorName "Sony"
    ModelName "CPD-15SF1"
    BandWidth 110 MHz
    HorizSync 31.5-64 kHz
    VertRefresh 50-120 Hz
#
#    here are some VESA modes to start with
#
    ModeLine   "640x480"    31.5    640 664 704 832    480 489 492 520
    ModeLine   "800x600"    36      800 824 896 1024   600 601 603 625
    ModeLine   "800x600"    40      800 840 968 1056   600 601 605 628 +hsync +vsync
```

```
    ModeLine  "800x600"   50     800  856  976 1040    600  637  643  666  +hsync +vsync
    ModeLine "1024x768"   65    1024 1032 1176 1344    768  771  777  806  -hsync -vsync
    ModeLine "1024x768"   75    1024 1048 1184 1328    768  771  777  806  -hsync -vsync
EndSection


#From: koenig@nova.tat.physik.uni-tuebingen.de (Harald Koenig)
#Date: Date: Mon, 26 Sep 94 20:33:07 MEZ
Section "Monitor"
    Identifier "Sony Multiscan 17se"
    VendorName "Sony"
    ModelName "GDM-17SE1T"
    BandWidth 135 MHz
    HorizSync 31.5-82 kHz
    VertRefresh 50-150 Hz
    ModeLine "640x480" 25 640 672 768 800 480 490 492 525
    ModeLine "1024x768" 76 1024 1024 1088 1168 768 768 779 806
    ModeLine "1280x1024" 110 1280 1340 1444 1582 1024 1024 1048 1070
    ModeLine "1280x1024" 135 1280 1312 1456 1712 1024 1027 1030 1064
#
#   here are some more VESA modes to start with
#
    ModeLine  "640x480"  31.5   640  664  704  832    480  489  492  520
    ModeLine  "800x600"   36     800  824  896 1024    600  601  603  625
    ModeLine  "800x600"   40     800  840  968 1056    600  601  605  628 +hsync +vsync
    ModeLine  "800x600"   50     800  856  976 1040    600  637  643  666  +hsync +vsync
    ModeLine "1024x768"   65    1024 1032 1176 1344    768  771  777  806  -hsync -vsync
    ModeLine "1024x768"   75    1024 1048 1184 1328    768  771  777  806  -hsync -vsync
EndSection


#From: Helmut Geyer <Helmut.Geyer@iwr.uni-heidelberg.de>
#Date: Wed, 21 Sep 1994 23:48:57 +0200 (MET DST)
Section "Monitor"
    Identifier "TARGA TM 1710 D"
        VendorName "TARGA by SONY"
        ModelName "TM 1710 D"
        Bandwidth 100
        HorizSync 30-65
        VertRefresh 50-90
        ModeLine "640x480" 25 640 664 760 800 480 491 493 525
        ModeLine "640x480" 31 640 664 704 832 480 489 492 520
        ModeLine "800x600x32" 45 800 820 904 964 600 601 604 621
        ModeLine "1024x768x16" 78.7 1024 1044 1140 1264 768 770 773 796
        ModeLine "1024x768" 80 1024 1048 1184 1296 768 771 784 797
        ModeLine "1024x768" 85 1024 1032 1152 1336 768 784 800 813
        ModeLine "1152x800" 90 1152 1200 1312 1520 800 805 816 849
```

```
        ModeLine "1152x800" 95 1152 1200 1320 1496 800 805 816 849
        ModeLine "1152x800" 97 1152 1200 1296 1496 800 805 816 849
EndSection


#From: koenig@tat.physik.uni-tuebingen.de (Harald Koenig)
#Date: Sat, 17 Sep 1994 15:46:10 +0200 (MET DST)
Section "Monitor"
    Identifier "TAXAN 875"
    VendorName "TAXAN"
    ModelName "MultiVision 875 PLUS LR"
    BandWidth 130 MHz
    HorizSync 30-78 kHz
    VertRefresh 50-90 Hz
#
#   the TAXAN 875 PLUS LR detects the following factory preset video modes
#   (see App. 2 in the Owner's Guide).  At least for some S3 Vision864 and
#   some other S3 cards you may have to use "800x600x32" instead of "800x600"
#   for 24/32bpp mode.
#
    ModeLine "640x350"    25.175 640 664 688  800 350 395 411 449 +hsync -vsync
    ModeLine "640x400"    25.175 640 664 688  800 400 414 430 449 -hsync +vsync
    ModeLine "640x480"    25.175 640 664 688  800 480 498 500 525 -hsync -vsync
    ModeLine "800x600"    50.350 800 872 920 1048 600 636 642 668 +hsync +vsync
    ModeLine "800x600x32" 49.197 800 856 880 1024 600 636 642 668 +hsync +vsync
    ModeLine "1024x768"   75  1024 1048 1120 1336 768 768 774 804 -hsync -vsync
    ModeLine "1024x768"   75  1024 1048 1120 1296 768 771 777 806 -hsync -vsync
    ModeLine "1024x768"   80  1024 1048 1128 1304 768 783 792 807 +hsync +vsync
    ModeLine "1280x1024" 110 1280 1312 1416 1712 1024 1030 1040 1071
    -hsync -vsync
    ModeLine "1280x1024" 125 1280 1296 1552 1680 1024 1024 1032 1062
    -hsync -vsync
    ModeLine "1152x900"   105 1152 1176 1234 1464 900 906 914 943 -hsync -vsync
#
#   other tested, useful modes:
#
    ModeLine "1024x768@82"   99.8  1024 1124 1288 1512  768  771  786  805
    ModeLine "1024x768@93"  110    1024 1048 1128 1464  768  768  772  809
    ModeLine "1280x1024@71" 135    1280 1488 1544 1824 1024 1029 1030 1042
    ModeLine "1280x1024@74" 135    1280 1488 1544 1744 1024 1029 1030 1042
EndSection


#From: wolff@dutecai.et.tudelft.nl (Rogier Wolff)
#Date: Sat, 24 Sep 1994 17:27:09 +0200 (MET DST)
 # It seems I've been watching a horribly slow-refresh 54Hz screen for
 # quite a while.... The monitor is spec-ed to do 60 Hz. I'll figure out
```

```
# how to adjust these later on.
Section "Monitor"
    Identifier "Unisys-19"
    VendorName "Unisys"
    ModelName "Unknown"
    BandWidth 110
    HorizSync 57-65
    VertRefresh 55-65
    ModeLine "640x480" 25.175 640 664 760 800 480 491 493 525
    ModeLine "1024x768i" 44.9 1024 1048 1208 1264 768 776 784 817 interlace
    ModeLine "1176x1024" 95 1176 1400 1504 1616 1024 1032 1040 1070
    -hsync +vsync
    ModeLine "1176x950" 95 1176 1400 1504 1616 950 958 964 994
    -hsync +vsync
    ModeLine "1280x1024" 110 1280 1584 1704 1872 1024 1032 1040 1070
    -hsync +vsync
    ModeLine "640x1024" 110 640 1584 1704 1872 1024 1032 1040 1070
    -hsync +vsync
EndSection


#Date: Mon, 19 Sep 94 17:50:04 +0200
#From: Didier Poirot <dp@chorus.fr>
Section "Monitor"
    Identifier "ViewSonic 17"
    VendorName "ViewSonic"
    ModelName "17"
    BandWidth 75.0
    HorizSync 30-82
    VertRefresh 50-90
    ModeLine "640x480"    25.175 640 664 760 800 480 491 493 525
    Modeline "1024x768a"  65    1024 1032 1208 1288   768 768 773 798
    Modeline "1024x768b"  65    1024 1080 1224 1344   768 776 778 808
EndSection


#Date: Wed, 21 Sep 1994 22:47:06 -0700
#From: "Brett J. Vickers" <bvickers@rumba.ICS.UCI.EDU>
Section "Monitor"
    Identifier  "ViewSonic 5e"
    VendorName  "ViewSonic"
    ModelName   "5e"
    Bandwidth   25.2 mhz
    HorizSync   30-60
    VertRefresh 50-90
    # Refresh rate = 73.46Hz ; Horizontal Frequency = 59.29KHz
    Mode "1024x768"
```

```
        DotClock 81
        HTimings 1024 1120 1272 1368 VTimings 768  788  801  847
    EndMode
    # Refresh rate = 63.87Hz ; Horizontal Frequency = 57.99KHz
    Mode "1152x864"
        DotClock 90
        HTimings 1152 1248 1472 1552 VTimings 864  864  876  908
    EndMode
    # Refresh rate = 63.87Hz ; Horizontal Frequency = 57.99KHz
    Mode "1152x900"
        DotClock 90
        HTimings 1152 1248 1472 1552 VTimings 900  900  914  946
    EndMode
    # Refresh rate = 59.43Hz ; Horizontal Frequency = 59.91KHz
    Mode "1280x960"
        DotClock 104
        HTimings 1280 1376 1672 1736 VTimings 960  960  973 1008
    EndMode
EndSection


#Date: 22 Sep 1994 10:25:06 -0700 (PDT)
#From: Ken Latta <klatta@pkdla5.syntex.com>
Section "Monitor"
    Identifier  "ViewSonic 6"
    VendorName  "ViewSonic"
    ModelName   "6"
    Bandwidth   80.0
    HorizSync   30.00-57.00
    VertRefresh 43.00-70.04
    Mode "640x480"
        DotClock 25
        HTimings 640 664 760 800 VTimings 480 491 493 525
    EndMode
    Mode "1024x768"
#       DotClock 80
        DotClock 65
        HTimings 1024 1080 1304 1328 VTimings 768 768 776 792
#       HTimings 1024 1136 1340 1432 VTimings 768 770 774 805
    EndMode
EndSection


#From: haw30@eng.amdahl.com (Henry A Worth)
#Date: Tue, 27 Sep 94 22:10:01 PDT
Section "Monitor"
    Identifier "ViewSonic-7"
```

```
        VendorName "ViewSonic"
        ModelName "ViewSonic-7"
        BandWidth 110
        HorizSync 30.0-64.0
        VertRefresh 50.0-90.0
        ModeLine "1152x900" 85 1152 1218 1328 1456 900 902 912 943
        ModeLine "1024x768" 80 1024 1032 1216 1344 768 768 773 805
        ModeLine "1024x768" 75 1024 1048 1184 1328 768 771 777 802
        ModeLine "1024x768" 65 1024 1032 1208 1288 768 768 773 798
        ModeLine "800x600"  45  800  808  920 1000 600 605 615 635
        ModeLine "640x480"  30  640  664  728  800 480 484 490 507
        ModeLine "640x480"  28  640  664  728  792 480 484 490 505
EndSection


# $XFree86: xc/programs/Xserver/hw/xfree86/doc/Monitors,v 3.10 1995/07/13 14:14:42 dawes
Exp $
# $XConsortium: Monitors,v 1.7 95/01/27 15:58:08 kaleb Exp $
```

The **/usr/X11/lib/X11/doc** directory also contains information about specific chipsets. For example, the following file, **README.S3**, contains information about the popular S3 chipset, used by Dell and other large clone makers.

```
Information for S3 Chipset Users
  The XFree86 Project Inc.
  7 July 1995


1.  Supported hardware

The current S3 Server supports the following S3 chipsets: 911, 924, 801/805,
928, 732 (Trio32), 764 (Trio64), 864, 868, 964, and 968. The S3 server will
also recognize the 866, but it has not been tested with this chipset. If you
have any problems or success with these, please report it to us.

Nevertheless, this is not enough to support every board using one of these
chipsets. The following list contains some data points on boards that are
known to work. If your card is similar to one of the described ones, chances
are good it might work for you, too.


S3 801/805, AT&T 20C490 (or similar) RAMDAC


      o  Orchid Fahrenheit 1280+ VLB
      o  Actix GE32
         8 and 15/16 bpp
```

Note: Real AT&T20C490 RAMDACs should be automatically detected by the server. For others which are compatible, you need to provide a `Ramdac "att20c490"' entry in your XF86Config.

Real AT&T 20C490 or 20C491 RAMDACs work with the "dac_8_bit" option. Some clones (like the Winbond 82C490) do not.

S3 805 VLB, S3 GENDAC (RAMDAC + clock synthesizer)

   o MIRO 10SD (available for VLB and PCI) It is not known whether all 10SDs use the S3 GENDAC.
        8 and 15/16 bpp

          ClockChip "s3gendac"
          RamDac   "s3gendac"

S3 801/805, AT&T 20C490 RAMDAC, ICD2061A Clockchip

   o STB PowerGraph X.24 S3 (ISA)
        8 and 15/16 bpp

Note: Real AT&T20C490 RAMDACs should be automatically detected by the server. For others which are compatible, you need to provide a `Ramdac "att20c490"' entry in your XF86Config.

          ClockChip "icd2061a"
          RamDac   "att20c490"
          Option   "dac_8_bit

S3 805, Diamond SS2410 RAMDAC, ICD2061A Clockchip

   o Diamond Stealth 24 VLB
        8 and 15bpp(*) only.

          requires `Option "nolinear"'

(*) The SS2410 RAMDAC is reportedly compatible with the AT&T20C490 in 15bpp mode. To make the server treat it as an AT&T20C490, you need to provide a `Ramdac "att20c490"' entry in your XF86Config.

S3 801/805, Chrontel 8391 Clockchip/Ramdac

   o JAX 8241
   o SPEA Mirage
        8 and 15/16 bpp.

The 8391 is compatible with the AT&T 20C490 RAMDAC

```
ClockChip  "ch8391"
Ramdac     "ch8391"
Option     "dac_8_bit"
```

S3 928, AT&T 20C490 RAMDAC

    o Actix Ultra
       8 and 15/16 bpp

Note: Real AT&T20C490 RAMDACs should be automatically detected by the server. For others which are compatible, you need to provide a `Ramdac "att20c490"' entry in your XF86Config. Also, the server's RAMDAC probe reportedly causes problems with some of these boards, and a RamDac entry should be used to avoid the probe.

Real AT&T 20C490 or 20C491 RAMDACs work with the "dac_8_bit" option. Some clones (like the Winbond 82C490) do not.

S3 928, Sierra SC15025 RAMDAC, ICD2061A Clockchip

    o ELSA Winner 1000 ISA/EISA (``TwinBus'', not Winner1000ISA!!)
    o ELSA Winner 1000 VL
       8, 15/16 and 24(32) bpp

Supports 8bit/pixel RGB in 8bpp and gamma correction for 15/16 and 24bpp modes.

24 bpp might get ``snowy'' if the clock is near the limit of 30MHz. This is not considered dangerous, but limits the usability of 24 bpp.

D-step (or below) chips cannot be used with a line width of 1152; hence the most effective mode for a 1MB board is about 1088x800x8 (similar to 2 MB, 1088x800x16).

```
ClockChip "icd2061a"
```

S3 928, Bt9485 RAMDAC, ICD2061A Clockchip

    o STB Pegasus VL
       8, 15/16 and 24(32) bpp

Supports RGB with sync-on-green if "sync_on_green" option is provided and board jumper is set for BNC outputs.

VLB linear addressing now occurs at 0x7FCxxxxx so that 64MB or more main memory can be supported without losing linear frame buffer access.

```
ClockChip "icd2061a"
Option    "stb_pegasus"
```

S3 928, Bt485 RAMDAC, SC11412 Clockchip

  o SPEA Mercury 2MB VL
     8, 15/16 and 24(32) bpp

```
ClockChip "SC11412"
Option    "SPEA_Mercury"
```

S3 928, Bt485 RAMDAC, ICD2061A Clockchip

  o #9 GXE Level 10, 11, 12
     8, 15/16 and 24(32) bpp

```
ClockChip "icd2061a"
Option    "number_nine"
```

S3 928, Ti3020 RAMDAC, ICD2061A Clockchip

  o #9 GXE Level 14, 16
     8, 15/16 and 24(32) bpp

Supports RGB with sync-on-green.

```
ClockChip "icd2061a"
Option    "number_nine"
```

S3 864, AT&T20C498, ICS2494 Clockchip

  o MIRO 20SD (BIOS 1.xx)

The ICS2494 is a fixed frequency clockchip, you have to use X -probeonly (without a Clocks line in XF86Config) to get the correct clock values.

```
8, 15/16 and 24(32) bpp
```

S3 864, AT&T20C498 or STG1700 RAMDAC, ICD2061A or ICS9161 Clockchip

```
o  Elsa Winner1000PRO VLB
o  Elsa Winner1000PRO PCI
o  MIRO 20SD (BIOS 2.xx)
o  Actix GraphicsENGINE 64 VLB/2MB
   8, 15/16 and 24(32) bpp


   ClockChip "icd2061a"
```

S3 864, 20C498 or 21C498 RAMDAC, ICS2595 Clockchip

```
o  SPEA MirageP64 2MB DRAM  (BIOS 3.xx)
   8, 15/16 and 24(32) bpp
```

Clockchip support is still sometimes flaky and on some machines problems with the first mode after startup of XF86_S3 or after switching back from VT have been seen; switching to next mode with CTRL+ALT+``KP+'' and back seems to solve this problem.

Interlaced modes don't work correctly.

Mirage P64 with BIOS 4.xx uses the S3 SDAC.

```
   ClockChip "ics2595"
```

S3 864, S3 86C716 SDAC RAMDAC and Clockchip

```
o  Elsa Winner1000PRO
o  MIRO 20SD (BIOS 3.xx)
o  SPEA MirageP64 2MB DRAM  (BIOS 4.xx)
o  Diamond Stealth 64 DRAM
   8, 15/16 and 24 bpp
```

S3 864, ICS5342 RAMDAC and Clockchip

```
o  Diamond Stealth 64 DRAM (only some cards)
   8, 15/16 and 24 bpp

   ClockChip "ics5342"
   Ramdac   "ics5342"
```

S3 864, AT&T21C498-13 RAMDAC, ICD2061A Clockchip

    o   #9 GXE64 - PCI
        8, 15/16, 24(32) bpp

            ClockChip "icd2061a"
            Option   "number_nine"

S3 964, AT&T 20C505 RAMDAC, ICD2061A Clockchip

    o   Miro Crystal 20SV
        8, 15/16, 24(32) bpp

            ClockChip "icd2061a"
            Ramdac   "att20c505"

S3 964, Bt485 RAMDAC, ICD2061A Clockchip

    o   Diamond Stealth 64
        8, 15/16, 24(32) bpp

            ClockChip "icd2061a"

S3 964, Bt9485 or AT&T 20C505 RAMDAC, ICS9161a Clockchip

    o   SPEA Mercury 64
        8, 15/16, 24(32) bpp

            ClockChip "ics9161a"
            Option   "SPEA_Mercury"

S3 964, Ti3020 RAMDAC, ICD2061A Clockchip

    o   Elsa Winner2000PRO PCI
        8, 15/16, 24(32) bpp

            ClockChip "icd2061a"

S3 964, Ti3025 RAMDAC, Ti3025 Clockchip

    o   Miro Crystal 40SV
    o   #9 GXE64 Pro VLB
    o   #9 GXE64 Pro PCI
        8 bpp, 15, 16 and 24(32) bpp

There are some known problems with the GXE64 Pro support, including some image shifting/wrapping at 15/16/24 bpp.

We have found that #9 no longer support the GXE64 Pro at 1600x1200. They do however have a new (and more expensive) board called the GXE64Pro-1600 which uses a 220MHz RAMDAC instead of 135MHz part used on the other boards.

S3 764 (Trio64)

- o SPEA Mirage P64 (BIOS 5.xx)
- o Diamond Stealth 64 DRAM
- o #9 GXE64 Trio64
  8/15/16/24 bpp

Note: The Trio64 has a builtin RAMDAC and clockchip, so the server should work with all Trio64 cards, and there is no need to specify the RAMDAC or clockchip in the XF86Config file.

S3 732 (Trio32)

- o Diamond Stealth 64 DRAM SE
  8/15/16/24 bpp

Note: The Trio32 has a builtin RAMDAC and clockchip, so the server should work with all Trio32 cards, and there is no need to specify the RAMDAC or clockchip in the XF86Config file.

S3 868, S3 86C716 SDAC RAMDAC and Clockchip

- o ELSA Winner 1000AVI
  8/15/16/24 bpp

S3 968, Ti3026 RAMDAC, Ti3026 Clockchip

- o Elsa Winner 2000PRO/X
- o Diamond Stealth 64 VIDEO VRAM
  8/15/16/24 bpp

S3 964, IBM RGB 514/524/525/528 RAMDAC & Clockchip

- o Hercules Graphics Terminator 64

```
        s3RefClk    50
        DACspeed   170
        Option  "slow_vram"
```

    8/15/16/24 bpp

S3 968, IBM RGB 514/524/525/528 RAMDAC & Clockchip

    o Genoa Genoa VideoBlitz III AV

```
        s3RefClk    50
        DACspeed   170
```

    o Hercules Graphics Terminator Pro 64

```
        s3RefClk    16
        DACspeed   220
```

This card may require the line:

                Invert_VCLK "*" 0

in each Display subsection.

    o STB Velocity 64

```
        s3RefClk    24
        DACspeed   220
```

    o Number Nine FX Motion 771

```
        s3RefClk    16
        DACspeed   220
```

    8/15/16/24 bpp

2. 16bpp and 32bpp

On 801/805 + AT&T490 Cards (like the Fahrenheit 1280+ VLB) only 15 and 16bpp
are supported. 32bpp isn't available on this type of chips. (There is a 24 bit
mode under MS Windows, but it's not a 32bpp sparse mode but a real 3
bytes/pixel mode).

3. List of Supported Clock Chips

ICD2061A	==> ClockChip "icd2061a"
ICS9161A (ICD2061A compatible)	==> ClockChip "ics9161a"
DCS2824-0 (Diamond, ICD2061A comp.)	==> ClockChip "dcs2824"
S3 86c708 GENDAC	==> ClockChip "s3gendac"
ICS5300 GENDAC (86c708 compatible)	==> ClockChip "ics5300"
S3 86c716 SDAC	==> ClockChip "s3_sdac"
ICS5342 GENDAC	==> ClockChip "ics5342"
STG 1703	==> ClockChip "stg1703"
Sierra SC11412	==> ClockChip "sc11412"
ICS2595	==> ClockChip "ics2595"
TI3025	==> ClockChip "ti3025"
TI3026	==> ClockChip "ti3026"
IBM RGB 5xx	==> ClockChip "ibm_rgb5xx"
Chrontel 8391	==> ClockChip "ch8391"

4. Additional Notes

If you have a RAMDAC that is not listed here, be VERY careful not to overdrive it using XF86_S3. Better contact the XFree86 team first to verify that running XF86_S3 will not damage your board.

If you feel adventurous you could also open up your computer and have a peek at your RAMDAC. The RAMDAC is usually one the larger chips (second or third largest chip that is NOT an EPROM) on the board. The markings on it are usually:

```
<Company logo>
<company identifier><part number>-<speed grade>
<manufacturing week><manufacturing year>
<lot number><other funny numbers>
```

For example:

```
@@
@@ AT&T
ATT20C490-11
9339S ES
9869874
```

This is a AT&T 20C490 with a speed grade of 110 MHz. This would then mean that you put a `DacSpeed 110' line in your XF86Config file. Be advised that some RAMDACs have different modes that have different limits. The manufacturer will always mark the chip naming the higher limits, so you should be careful. The S3 server knows how to handle the limits for most of the RAMDACs it supports providing the DacSpeed is specified correctly.

Chips labeled -80 or -8 should use `DacSpeed 80' in the device section:

```
        S3 86C716-ME SDAC   ==>  DacSpeed 110
        SC15025-8           ==>  DacSpeed  80
        ATT20C490-80        ==>  DacSpeed  80

        IBM 8190429         ==>  DacSpeed 170
        IBM 03H5428         ==>  DacSpeed 170
        IBM 03H6447         ==>  DacSpeed 170
        IBM 03H6448         ==>  DacSpeed 220
        IBM 03H5319         ==>  DacSpeed 220
        IBM 63G9902         ==>  DacSpeed 250

        IBM 37RGB514CF17    ==>  DacSpeed 170
        IBM 37RGB524CF22    ==>  DacSpeed 220
                    ^^
```

Some RAMDACs (like the Ti3025) require some mode timing consideration for their hardware cursor to work correctly. The Ti3025 requires that the mode have a back porch of at least 80 pixel-clock cycles. A symptom of this not being correct is the HW cursor being chopped off when positioned close to the right edge of the screen.

5. Reference clock value for IBM RGB 5xx RAMDACs

Cards with IBM RGB5xx RAMDACs use several different input frequencies for the clock synthesizer which can't be probed without some knowledge of the text mode clocks (which may be a wrong assumption if you're using non-standard text modes). Here is the procedure how you should find out the input frequency:

  First run

            X -probeonly >& outfile

and check the output for the probed clock chip which might look like this:

```
(—) S3: Using IBM RGB52x programmable clock (MCLK 66.000 MHz)
(—) S3: with refclock 16.000 MHz (probed 15.952 & 16.041)
               ^^^^^^        ^^^^^^^^^^^^^^^^^^^^^^^^
```

There will be a "good guessed" value which will be used and two probed values
in brackets based on the 25MHz and 28MHz text clocks. This probing can only
work if you run a normal 80x25 or 80x28 text mode!

The refclock values known so far are:

```
     STB Velocity 64           24 Mhz
     Genoa VideoBlitz II AV  50 MHz
     Hercules S3 964           50 MHz
     Hercules S3 968           16 MHz
     #9 Motion 771             16 MHz
```

depending on the quartz on your card and maybe other features like an
additional clock chip on the Genoa card (which as a 14.3MHz quartz).

If you claim that your card has a 16MHz card but it really uses 50MHz, all
pixel clocks will be tripled and a 640x480 mode with 25MHz will use a 75MHz
pixel clock, so be very careful.

If you found the right refclock, you should set it in the config file (device
section) e.g. with

```
          s3RefClk  16
```

or

```
          s3RefClk  50
```

so that this value will be used even if you use another text mode and probing
fails!

6. How to avoid ``snowing'' display while graphics operations

For cards with S3 Vision864 chip there is a automatic correction that depends
on the pixel clock and the memory clock MCLK at which the S3 chip operates.
For most clock chips this value can't be read (only the S3 SDAC allows reading
the MCLK value so far), so this value has to be estimated and specified by the
user (the default is 60 [MHz]).

With the new `s3MCLK` entry for your XF86Config file now you can specify, e.g.

    s3MCLK 55

for a 55-MHz MCLK, which will reduce snowing. Smaller MCLK values will reduce performance a bit so you shouldn't use a too low value (55 or 50 should be a good guess in most cases).

Below is a small shell script, which might be useful to determine the approximate value for MCLK (about +/- 1-2 MHz error). Before running this script you have to add the line:

    s3MNadjust -31 255

to the device section in your XF86Config file and restart X Window. With this option (which is for testing and debugging only) you'll get lots of disastrous display flickering and snowing, so it should be removed again immediately after running the test script below.

Running this script will use xbench and/or x11perf to run a test to determine the MLCK value, which is printed in MHz. Up to 4 tests are run, so you'll get up to 4 estimates (where the first might be the most accurate one).

```sh
#!/bin/sh

exec 2> /dev/null

scale=2

calc() {
  m=`awk 'BEGIN{printf "%.'$scale'f\n",'"( $1 + $2 ) / $3; exit}" `
  [ -z "$m" ] && m=` echo "scale=$scale; ( $1 + $2 ) / $3" | bc `
  [ -z "$m" ] && m=` echo "$scale $1 $2 + $3 / pq" | dc `
  echo $m
}

run_xbench() {
  r=` ( echo 1; echo 2; echo 3; echo 4 ) | xbench -only $1 | grep rate `
  [ -z "$r" ] && return
  cp="$2 $3"
  set $r
  calc $3 $cp
}
```

```
run_x11perf() {
  r=` x11perf $1 | grep trep | tr '(/)' ' '  ' `
  [ -z "$r" ] && return
  cp="$2 $3"
  set $r
  calc `calc 1000 0 $4` $cp
}
```

```
run_x11perf "-rect500 -rop GXxor"    3.86  5.53  #  0 1  #    4.11    5.52  #
run_xbench invrects500               4.63  5.48  #  0 1  #    4.69    5.48  #


run_x11perf "-rect500 -rop GXcopy"  -16.42 13.90  #  0 1  #  -14.99   13.88  #
run_xbench fillrects500              -7.81 13.57  #  0 1  #   -8.53   13.58  #
```

```
exit
```

What does this file tell us? Well, for starters, it tells us that mucking around with graphics-card settings is not a whole lot of fun, and that unless you're willing to live with the default settings, fine-tuning your X Window setup is not going to be a lot of fun. Perhaps the biggest lesson we can derive from this information is that messing around with graphics-cards setting just isn't worth your while, especially on an Internet server.

Starting X

To start the X Window System, use the following command line:

```
startx
```

This command line actually is a script that launches the commands found in another file, **.xinitrc**, in your home directory This file is to be used to customize X for your own workspace; there's a default copy of the file in **/usr/X11R6/lib/X11/xinit**, but the theory is that you'll copy this file to your home directory and customize it. Since there won't be other people working with X on this terminal, you can go ahead and use the default file.

If your installation was successful, you'll see a screen like the one in Figure 3.5.

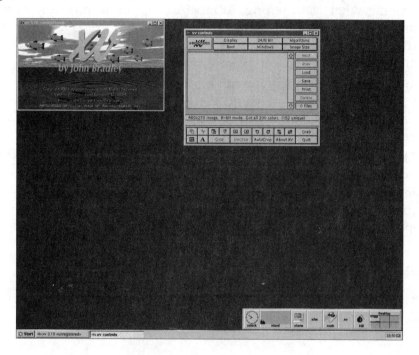

Figure 3.5 The X Window System.

Figure 3.5 may seem a little strange to you if you're used to working with older versions of Linux and XFree86. The default window manager in Slackware Linux is **fvwm-95**, a version of the old **fvwm** window manager. This new version emulates Windows 95; hence, there is the **Start** button on the left bottom of the screen and the clock on the right bottom. In addition, **fvwm-95** is configured with a toolbar that allows access to many popular X tools. You can still call up a menu from anywhere on the screen by pressing the left mouse button. (Actually, your screen won't look exactly like Figure 3.5; the **xv** program was used to create a screen dump; hence, its presence fully demonstrates the power of the Heisenberg Principle.)

If the X Window System fails to launch, pay close attention to the messages displayed. X error messages are usually pretty good at describing what went wrong. In most cases, you're probably dealing with a misaligned mouse connection (when the X server can't connect to the mouse, the entire server is shut down) or the wrong server for your graphics card.

In the case of the latter, you might run into a situation where you get a fuzzy or frozen X display and there's no response to any keyboard input. To get out of X and back to a command-line interface, you'll want to use the **Ctrl-Alt-Backspace** combination to quit X.

There are many things to learn about the X Window System. However, the focus in this book isn't to work with X (since there's very little to do with X, unless you're editing HTML files), and so we'll leave a discussion of X for later in this book. You can also look through Appendix A for a listing of other Linux titles that cover X in more detail.

Stopping X

When you want to shut down the X Window System, just quit the window manager. You'll be presented with a command line.

Setting Up an Internet Connection and Networking

In Chapters 1 and 2, you learned about the specific ways you can connect to the Internet. At this point we'll assume that you have worked out the details (like having a connection method established and an IP address assigned) of the connection.

Now comes the drudge work of the operation: Actually setting up your Internet connection. Before we guide you through this maze, we should explain a little about networking and the Internet. If you're already conversant with networking, you can skip ahead to the next section.

Deep Background on Networking

The Internet, for all the hype and glory, is little more than a giant network that reaches the corners of the earth. Conceptually, the Internet really isn't that much different from a small network that you might be using in your office. Your small network uses network cards and cables to speak to the other computers on the network. When a Linux PC wants to communicate with another computer, it goes through the network card, which then sends the request via the network cabling. Each PC is configured to know exactly where to make the requests.

The same things are true of the Internet; the differences are in scale, not on theory. When you're connected to the Internet, you're using network cards and/or modems to connect to the larger network. When you want to communicate with another computer (perhaps a remote Web server or a news server), you send a request via your network card to the Internet, where the request is then routed to the correct remote computer. Your request is answered, and the results are sent back to you.

This all seems very simple—and conceptually, it is. However, there's a lot going on under the surface in this process. The whole thing is made possible because the Internet world has agreed to a set of standards. These standards are embodied in Transmission Control Protocol/Internet Protocol. Within TCP/IP are a defined set of services. For your computer to talk to other computers on the Internet, it must adhere to TCP/IP and its services.

The Internet was built around TCP/IP as well as the UNIX operating system. TCP/IP was the networking protocol that UNIX used, and when the Internet took off, so did TCP/IP. Being a UNIX workalike (though, technically, not a clone), Linux also has TCP/IP networking built directly into the operating system. And, since TCP/IP defines its services, so does Linux. You can read through the services in the file **/etc/services** (as follows):

```
#
# Network services, Internet style
#
# Note that it is presently the policy of IANA to assign a single well-known
# port number for both TCP and UDP; hence, most entries here have two entries
# even if the protocol doesn't support UDP operations.
# Updated from RFC 1340, ``Assigned Numbers'' (July 1992).  Not all ports
# are included, only the more common ones.
#
#    from: @(#)services    5.8 (Berkeley) 5/9/91
#    $Id: services,v 1.9 1993/11/08 19:49:15 cgd Exp $
#
tcpmux          1/tcp         # TCP port service multiplexer
echo        7/tcp
echo        7/udp
discard         9/tcp         sink null
discard         9/udp         sink null
systat         11/tcp         users
daytime        13/tcp
daytime        13/udp
netstat        15/tcp
qotd        17/tcp         quote
msp         18/tcp         # message send protocol
msp         18/udp         # message send protocol
chargen        19/tcp         ttytst source
chargen        19/udp         ttytst source
ftp         21/tcp
# 22 - unassigned
telnet         23/tcp
# 24 - private
smtp        25/tcp         mail
# 26 - unassigned
time        37/tcp         timserver
time        37/udp         timserver
rlp         39/udp         resource    # resource location
nameserver     42/tcp         name        # IEN 116
whois          43/tcp         nicname
domain         53/tcp         nameserver    # name-domain server
domain         53/udp         nameserver
mtp         57/tcp             # deprecated
bootps         67/tcp         # BOOTP server
bootps         67/udp
bootpc         68/tcp         # BOOTP client
bootpc         68/udp
tftp        69/udp
```

```
gopher        70/tcp        # Internet Gopher
gopher        70/udp
rje           77/tcp        netrjs
finger        79/tcp
www           80/tcp        http    # WorldWideWeb HTTP
www           80/udp          # HyperText Transfer Protocol
link          87/tcp        ttylink
kerberos      88/tcp        krb5    # Kerberos v5
kerberos      88/udp
supdup        95/tcp
# 100 - reserved
hostnames    101/tcp         hostname    # usually from sri-nic
iso-tsap     102/tcp        tsap        # part of ISODE.
csnet-ns     105/tcp        cso-ns     # also used by CSO name server
csnet-ns     105/udp        cso-ns
rtelnet      107/tcp          # Remote Telnet
rtelnet      107/udp
pop2         109/tcp        postoffice   # POP version 2
pop2         109/udp
pop3         110/tcp        # POP version 3
pop3         110/udp
sunrpc       111/tcp
sunrpc       111/udp
auth         113/tcp        tap ident authentication
sftp         115/tcp
uucp-path    117/tcp
nntp         119/tcp        readnews untp    # USENET News Transfer Protocol
ntp          123/tcp
ntp          123/udp            # Network Time Protocol
netbios-ns   137/tcp            # NETBIOS Name Service
netbios-ns   137/udp
netbios-dgm  138/tcp              # NETBIOS Datagram Service
netbios-dgm  138/udp
netbios-ssn  139/tcp              # NETBIOS session service
netbios-ssn  139/udp
imap2        143/tcp            # Interim Mail Access Proto v2
imap2        143/udp
snmp         161/udp          # Simple Net Mgmt Proto
snmp-trap    162/udp        snmptrap    # Traps for SNMP
cmip-man     163/tcp            # ISO mgmt over IP (CMOT)
cmip-man     163/udp
cmip-agent   164/tcp
cmip-agent   164/udp
xdmcp        177/tcp            # X Display Mgr. Control Proto
xdmcp        177/udp
```

```
nextstep    178/tcp     NeXTStep NextStep   # NeXTStep window
nextstep    178/udp     NeXTStep NextStep   # server
bgp         179/tcp                 # Border Gateway Proto.
bgp         179/udp
prospero    191/tcp              # Cliff Neuman's Prospero
prospero    191/udp
irc         194/tcp              # Internet Relay Chat
irc         194/udp
smux        199/tcp               # SNMP Unix Multiplexer
smux        199/udp
at-rtmp       201/tcp               # AppleTalk routing
at-rtmp       201/udp
at-nbp      202/tcp                # AppleTalk name binding
at-nbp      202/udp
at-echo       204/tcp               # AppleTalk echo
at-echo       204/udp
at-zis      206/tcp                # AppleTalk zone information
at-zis      206/udp
z3950       210/tcp     wais        # NISO Z39.50 database
z3950       210/udp     wais
ipx       213/tcp               # IPX
ipx       213/udp
imap3       220/tcp                # Interactive Mail Access
imap3       220/udp                # Protocol v3
ulistserv   372/tcp                # UNIX Listserv
ulistserv   372/udp
#
# UNIX specific services
#
exec        512/tcp
biff        512/udp     comsat
login       513/tcp
who       513/udp     whod
shell       514/tcp     cmd         # no passwords used
syslog      514/udp
printer       515/tcp       spooler        # line printer spooler
talk        517/udp
ntalk       518/udp
route       520/udp     router routed   # RIP
timed       525/udp     timeserver
tempo       526/tcp     newdate
courier       530/tcp      rpc
conference    531/tcp     chat
netnews       532/tcp      readnews
netwall       533/udp              # -for emergency broadcasts
uucp        540/tcp     uucpd       # uucp daemon
```

```
remotefs     556/tcp      rfs_server rfs    # Brunhoff remote filesystem
klogin       543/tcp                  # Kerberized `rlogin' (v5)
kshell       544/tcp                  # Kerberized `rsh' (v5)
kerberos-adm   749/tcp                # Kerberos `kadmin' (v5)
#
webster      765/tcp              # Network dictionary
webster      765/udp
#
# From ``Assigned Numbers'':
#
#> The Registered Ports are not controlled by the IANA and on most systems
#> can be used by ordinary user processes or programs executed by ordinary
#> users.
#
#> Ports are used in the TCP [45,106] to name the ends of logical
#> connections which carry long term conversations.  For the purpose of
#> providing services to unknown callers, a service contact port is
#> defined.  This list specifies the port used by the server process as its
#> contact port.  While the IANA can not control uses of these ports it
#> does register or list uses of these ports as a convenience to the
#> community.
#
ingreslock   1524/tcp
ingreslock   1524/udp
prospero-np   1525/tcp       # Prospero non-privileged
prospero-np   1525/udp
rfe          5002/tcp       # Radio Free Ethernet
rfe          5002/udp       # Actually uses UDP only
#
#
# Kerberos (Project Athena/MIT) services
# Note that these are for Kerberos v4, and are unofficial.  Sites running
# v4 should uncomment these and comment out the v5 entries above.
#
#kerberos     750/udp      kdc    # Kerberos (server) udp
#kerberos     750/tcp      kdc    # Kerberos (server) tcp
krbupdate     760/tcp      kreg   # Kerberos registration
kpasswd       761/tcp      kpwd    # Kerberos "passwd"
#klogin       543/tcp            # Kerberos rlogin
eklogin       2105/tcp      # Kerberos encrypted rlogin
#kshell       544/tcp      krcmd   # Kerberos remote shell
#
# Unofficial but necessary (for NetBSD) services
#
supfilesrv    871/tcp            # SUP server
supfiledbg    1127/tcp      # SUP debugging
```

Not all these services are relevant to a discussion of using Linux as an Internet server. However, it's important to know how TCP/IP networking and services are set up, if only to reassure you that Linux is quite capable of being a full-featured Internet server.

N O T E Some of the services in the **/etc/services** file will be discussed throughout the course of this book. For example, a discussion of ports and World Wide Web servers will take place in Chapter 4. For now, you don't need to commit the contents of **/etc/services** to memory, but you should note its presence here for future reference.

Recompiling a Kernel to Include TCP/IP

There's always the chance that you didn't install a kernel that supported TCP/IP. If you didn't, then you'll need to recompile your kernel. (If you don't, you can skip ahead to the next section.)

This isn't a hard task (we covered it earlier in this chapter), but it's one where some guidance is helpful. As you'll recall from earlier in this chapter, you begin the recompilation process with the following command lines:

```
cd /usr/src/linux
make config
```

There will be a series of questions, dealing with all aspects of the Linux operating system. Some aren't really relevant to the networking task at hand; two sections, however, deal with networking. (They begin with *** *Networking options* and *** *It is safe to leave these untouched*.) Here's an explanation of the questions that require some special attention, specifically in dealing with TCP/IP networking (the default values are in brackets; if you just press **Enter** without entering a **y** or **n**, the default value will be entered):

```
TCP/IP networking (CONFIG_INET) [y]
```

Answer **y**. This is the big Kahuna—whether or not you want TCP/IP networking to be installed.

```
IP forwarding/gatewaying (CONFIG_IP_FORWARD) [n]
```

Answer **y**, contrary to the default. This allows you to forward TCP/IP packets to another network, and this tends to be the definition of the Internet, after all.

```
IP multicasting (CONFIG_IP_MULTICAST) [n]
```

This poses a tricky issue. On the one hand, you probably won't have much occasion to use multicasting if you're running a vanilla Web server or an intranet. On the other hand, many newer Web services that require bells and whistles (like chat and audio) do require multicasting. It's best to prepare for the future and answer **y**.

```
IP firewalling (CONFIG_IP_FIREWALL) [n]
```

Answer **y**, because firewalls allow a greater level of security on Web server and other Web services.

```
IP accounting (CONFIG_IP_ACCT) [n]
```

This feature tracks IP traffic on a per-address and per-port basis, both incoming and outgoing. It might be good to track if your system is overloaded, but generally this information falls to the arcane side of thing.

```
PC/TCP compatibility mode (CONFIG_INET_PCTCP) [n]
```

This setting allows Linux to coexist with other networked PCs that run PC/TCP networking software. Unless your intranet has users with this software, you can leave the default setting.

```
Reverse ARP [CONFIG_INET_RARP) [n]
```

This is an obscure setting. If you don't know what RARP is, you don't need it. Leave the default setting.

```
Assumes subnets are local (CONFIG_INET_SNARL) [y]
```

You might be running subnets though your Linux box, but this isn't a condition of being on the Internet. You can leave the default and then override the settings elsewhere if needed.

```
Disable NAGLE algorithm (normally enabled) (CONFIG_TCP_NAGLE_OFF) [n]
```

The Nagle algorithm is a small tool that actually has a big impact: It prevents small packets from being sent separately and instead halts things until a larger packet is sent. For a typical Web server installation, your packets will be large enough so that packet size isn't an issue. But for other installations, such as **telnet**, you can end up with a lot of small packets, which is where the Nagle algorithm is handy. Since there's no reason to disable the Nagle algorithm, you can leave the default setting.

```
The IPX protocol [n]
```

The IPX protocol isn't part of Internet connectivity—it's a tool used in Novell networks. Leave the default setting.

Editing Network Files

Earlier in this chapter, in the section entitled "Setting Up the Network Connection," you ran through the **netconfig** script, which sets up your system for TCP/IP networking.

There might be occasions to change your networking setup. As you might expect, Slackware Linux stores this information in text configuration files. These files are stored in the **/etc** directory and can be edited with any text editor (**vi** or **emacs** will work fine). We'll run down the important files here.

/etc/hosts

This file stores the server hostname and IP address.

```
#
# hosts         This file describes a number of hostname-to-address
#         mappings for the TCP/IP subsystem.  It is mostly
#         used at boot time, when no name servers are running.
#         On small systems, this file can be used instead of a
#         "named" name server.  Just add the names, addresses
#         and any aliases to this file...
```

```
#
# By the way, Arnt Gulbrandsen <agulbra@nvg.unit.no> says that 127.0.0.1
# should NEVER be named with the name of the machine.  It causes problems
# for some (stupid) programs, irc and reputedly talk. :^)
#

# For loopbacking.
127.0.0.1     localhost

#Other hosts on the LAN
245.330.210.123         kevin.kreichard kevin

# End of hosts.
```

/etc/HOSTNAME

The file stores the hostname for your machine. It's a one-line file:

```
kreichard.com
```

This file is mandatory, so if you don't install a network and use the default setting, you'll be assigned a hostname of *darkstar.frop.org*.

/etc/rc.d/rc.inet1

This file stores several important addresses:

- Your IP address
- Your netmask
- Your network address
- Your broadcast address (if you have one)
- Your gateway address (if you have one)

The file is as follows:

```
#!/bin/sh
#
# rc.inet1    This shell script boots up the base INET system.
#
# Version:    @(#)/etc/rc.d/rc.inet1   1.01    05/27/93
#
```

```
HOSTNAME=`hostname`

# Attach the loopback device.
/sbin/ifconfig lo 127.0.0.1
/sbin/route add -net 127.0.0.0

# IF YOU HAVE AN ETHERNET CONNECTION, use these lines below to configure the
# eth0 interface. If you're only using loopback or SLIP, don't include the
# rest of the lines in this file.

# Edit for your setup.
#IPADDR="128.253.154.32"   # REPLACE with YOUR IP address!
#NETMASK="255.255.255.0"   # REPLACE with YOUR netmask!
#NETWORK="128.253.154.0"   # REPLACE with YOUR network address!
#BROADCAST="128.253.154.255"  # REPLACE with YOUR broadcast address, if you
# have one. If not, leave blank and edit below.
#GATEWAY="128.253.154.1"   # REPLACE with YOUR gateway address!

# Uncomment the line below to initialize the ethernet device.
# /sbin/ifconfig eth0 ${IPADDR} broadcast ${BROADCAST} netmask ${NETMASK}

# Uncomment these to set up your IP routing table.
#/sbin/route add -net ${NETWORK} netmask ${NETMASK}
#/sbin/route add default gw ${GATEWAY} metric 1

# End of rc.inet1
```

These settings were all set if you ran the **netconfig** script, as described earlier in this chapter.

/etc/rc.d/rc.inet2

This file is used to boot up your Internet system. Its contents are as follows:

```
#!/bin/sh
#
# rc.inet2    This shell script boots up the entire INET system.
#       Note, that when this script is used to also fire
#       up any important remote NFS disks (like the /usr
#       distribution), care must be taken to actually
#       have all the needed binaries online _now_ ...
#
# Author:   Fred N. van Kempen, <waltje@uwalt.nl.mugnet.org>
#
```

```
# Constants.
NET="/usr/sbin"
IN_SERV="lpd"
LPSPOOL="/var/spool/lpd"

# At this point, we are ready to talk to The World...
echo "Mounting remote file systems..."
/sbin/mount -a -t nfs          # This may be our /usr runtime!!!

echo -n "Starting daemons:"

# Start the SYSLOGD/Klogd daemons.  These must come first.
if [ -f ${NET}/syslogd ]; then
  echo -n " syslogd"
  ${NET}/syslogd
  echo -n " klogd"
  ${NET}/klogd
fi

# Start the SUN RPC Portmapper.
if [ -f ${NET}/rpc.portmap ]; then
    echo -n " portmap"
    ${NET}/rpc.portmap
fi

# Start the INET SuperServer
if [ -f ${NET}/inetd ]; then
  echo -n " inetd"
  ${NET}/inetd
else
  echo "no INETD found.  INET canceled!"
  exit 1
fi

# # Start the NAMED/BIND name server.
# if [ -f ${NET}/named ]; then
#   echo -n " named"
#   ${NET}/named
# fi

# # Start the ROUTEd server.
# if [ -f ${NET}/routed ]; then
#   echo -n " routed"
#   ${NET}/routed -g -s
# fi
```

```
# # Start the RWHO server.
# if [ -f ${NET}/rwhod ]; then
#    echo -n " rwhod"
#    ${NET}/rwhod -t -s
# fi


# Start the various INET servers.
for server in ${IN_SERV} ; do
  if [ -f ${NET}/${server} ]; then
    echo -n " ${server}"
    ${NET}/${server}
  fi
done


# # Start the various SUN RPC servers.
if [ -f ${NET}/rpc.portmap ]; then
  # Start the NFS server daemons.
  if [ -f ${NET}/rpc.mountd ]; then
    echo -n " mountd"
    ${NET}/rpc.mountd
  fi
  if [ -f ${NET}/rpc.nfsd ]; then
    echo -n " nfsd"
    ${NET}/rpc.nfsd
  fi
#   # Fire up the PC-NFS daemon(s).
#   if [ -f ${NET}/rpc.pcnfsd ]; then
#     echo -n " pcnfsd"
#     ${NET}/rpc.pcnfsd ${LPSPOOL}
#   fi
#   if [ -f ${NET}/rpc.bwnfsd ]; then
#     echo -n " bwnfsd"
#     ${NET}/rpc.bwnfsd ${LPSPOOL}
#   fi
fi # Done starting various SUN RPC servers.


# The 'echo' below will put a carriage return at the end
# of the list of started servers.
echo


# # Setting up NIS:
# # (NOTE: For detailed information about setting up NIS, see the
# #   documentation in /usr/doc/yp-clients and /usr/doc/ypserv)
# #
```

```
# # First, we must set the NIS domainname.  NOTE: this is not
# # necessarily the same as your DNS domainname, set in
# # /etc/resolv.conf!  The NIS domainname is the name of a domain
# # served by your NIS server.
#
# if [ -r /etc/defaultdomain ]; then
#    domainname `cat /etc/defaultdomain`
# fi
#
# # Then, we start up ypbind.  It will use broadcast to find a server.
#
# if [ -d /var/yp ] ; then
#    echo "Running ypbind..."
#    /usr/sbin/ypbind
# fi


# Done!
```

/etc/host.conf

This short file is used to specify how hostnames are resolved. Typically, it will look something like this:

```
order hosts, bind
multi on
```

There's not a lot to this file. The first line uses *order* to tell Slackware Linux what order to use when resolving names—the **hosts** file (described earlier) and then a nameserver. The second line merely tells Slackware Linux that the host system can have multiple IP addresses (in a multihomed situation), a rather common occurrence.

These settings were all set if you ran the **netconfig** script, as described earlier in this chapter.

/etc/networks

This file is used to specify a network in the case where there's no other way for the Linux system to know what IP address of a network is available. This is used mostly when a system is booted. Its contents are as follows:

```
#
# networks     This file describes a number of netname-to-address
#        mappings for the TCP/IP subsystem.  It is mostly
#        used at boot time, when no name servers are running.
#

loopback     127.0.0.0
localnet     245.330.210.123

# End of networks.
```

These settings were all set if you ran the **netconfig** script, as described earlier in this chapter.

/etc/resolv.conf

This short file tells Slackware Linux how to resolve IP addresses. Its contents are as follows.

```
domain kreichard.com
nameserver 139.245.7.145
```

These settings were all set if you ran the **netconfig** script, as described earlier in this chapter.

Some Networking Diagnostics

To see if your network is up and running, use the **ping** command in conjunction with an known IP address:

```
ping 137.192.19.254
```

If the **ping** command is successful, you'll receive text saying that data was received back from the IP address you specify. If the **ping** command is not successful, you'll know that your network connection has failed.

Summary

This chapter covered the long and arduous process of installing Slackware Linux from beginning to networked end, covering such topics as:

- Preparing your system for installation by setting up a Linux partition
- Running the **setup** script to install the desired disk components
- Running the **netconfig** script to set up your network configuration
- Running the **xf86config** script to fine-tune your X Window configuration
- Looking at the files that configure your Slackware Linux system on a network

In the next chapter, you'll learn about setting up a Web server.

SECTION II

Setting Up Internet Services

With your Slackware Linux Internet server set up and ready to roll, it's time to set up the services.

Chapter 4 covers the most important service of all: a Web server for the World Wide Web. Slackware Linux ships with several Web servers, but the most important of them all is the Apache Web server, the most popular Web server on the Internet. Subsequently, most of the coverage in Chapter 4 concerns the Apache Web server, ranging from installation and configuration, to modifying the Apache Web server for specific circumstances. Also covered are other Web servers, including Apache-SSL and WN.

Chapter 5 covers Gopher and setting up a Gopher server on your Linux Internet server. Although Gopher is considered to be an antiquated service by some, it can still be a handy tool for any Internet server. No Gopher server ships by default with Slackware Linux, but the accompanying CD-ROM contains GN, a useful and stable Gopher server, which is covered in some depth in the chapter.

Chapter 6 covers Glimpse and Harvest, two tools for indexing the information on your Internet server.

Chapter 7 covers the WU-FTP server, which allows outside users to login a Slackware Linux Internet server using the File Transfer Protocol.

Chapter 8 describes how to set up and maintain the **sendmail** and **smail** mail server.

Chapter 9 briefly covers news servers and if you should set up one on your Slackware Linux Internet server.

Chapter 10 covers some miscellaneous services, including Whiteboard Software and the Squid cache.

SETTING UP A WEB SERVER

This chapter covers:

- Spinning on the World Wide Web
- The Apache Web server
- File locations for the Apache Web serve
- Editing configuration files
- Testing your installation
- Optional modules
- Installing optional modules
- The WN Web server
- Other Web servers on the accompanying CD-ROM
- Other Web servers not on the accompanying CD-ROM

Spinning Your Web Worldwide

Many people equate the Web with the Internet. The two aren't interchangeable; the Web refers to the World Wide Web, which is a specific service of the greater Internet.

The Web is an incredibly important part of the Internet, though, and much of your impetus in setting up an Internet site is undoubtedly in setting up a Web server. A Web server is a remarkably simple piece of software (conceptually, anyway). A Web server answers requests from Web browsers (like Netscape Navigator or Arena), sending files along via the HyperText Transfer Protocol. Along the way, the server can run a program or script on behalf of the user and then send the results of the program or script to the user.

This chapter covers the installation and configuration of Web servers. During the course of this book, you'll learn how to manipulate and use the Web server to your advantage; for instance, later in this book you'll learn how to edit HTML pages and install programs for your users to run. This chapter won't cover everything to do with Web servers, but it will allow you to get a server up and running.

In this chapter, several Web servers will be covered. The majority of the time will be spent on the Apache Web server, which ships as part of Slackware Linux and should have been automatically installed when you installed Slackware Linux as part of the setup process in Chapter 3. However, in the interest of full disclosure and complete information, several other Web servers will be discussed. You may find that these Web servers are better suited for your needs (for instance, the WN Web server has many features that aren't found in the Apache Web server). But, to be totally honest, you'll want to spend the majority of your time studying the Apache Web server.

The Apache Web Server

The Apache Web Server ships with Slackware Linux. If you're unfamiliar with the world of Web servers, you should be quite elated to find such a powerful and popular Web server available at no charge in conjunctions with an operating system like Slackware Linux. As a matter of fact, the

Apache Web server is the most popular Web server in the world, according to research organizations like Server Watch (*http://techweb.cmp.com*) and Netcraft (*http://www.netcraft.co.uk/Survey/Reports/*). As a matter of fact, in the most recent poll as this book was written (November 1996), over 38 percent of all Web sites and domains were running off of Apache Web servers. This was more than double the next popular Web server (NCSA, upon which Apache was based, polled almost 15 percent of all Web sites and domains), while the most popular commercial Web server, the Microsoft Internet Information Server, rolled in at around 10 percent.

There's a lot to like about the Apache Web server. Following is a listing of the major features of the Apache Web server:

- DBM databases for authentication allow you to easily set up password-protected pages with enormous numbers of authorized users, without bogging down the server.
- Customized responses to errors and problems.
- Files or CGI scripts can be returned by the server in response to errors and problems, such as a script to intercept 500 Server Errors and perform on-the-fly diagnostics for both users and yourself.
- Multiple *DirectoryIndex* directives allow you to say *DirectoryIndex index.html index.cgi*, which instructs the server to either send **index.html** or run **index.cgi** when a directory URL is requested, whichever it finds in the directory.
- Unlimited numbers of Alias and Redirect directives.
- Content negotiation: the ability to automatically serve clients of varying sophistication and HTML level compliance, with documents that offer the best representation of information that the client is capable of accepting.
- Multihomed servers (sometimes known as the "APB" patches), which allows the server to distinguish between requests made to different IP addresses mapped to the same machine.

The Apache Web server is a product of the Apache HTTP Server Project, which is a dedicated bunch of volunteers who took the original NCSA Web server as the basis for their efforts in an attempt to keep a high-performance Web server in the public domain, forever free of charge.

The name *Apache* doesn't refer to anything remotely Native American—it's a reference to patch files from the NCSA Web server. After the files were applied to version 1.3, it was A PAtCHy server.

However, the Apache Web server isn't the only Web server available to Linux users. Because of Apache's popularity and widespread usage on the Internet, it's the Web server that will be explained in the most detail in this chapter. Other Web servers (most of them on the accompanying CD-ROM) will be covered later in this chapter.

Working with the Apache Web Server

When you installed Slackware Linux from the CD-ROM, you were prompted whether you wanted to install the Apache Web server (it's in the N series of disk sets). In Chapter 3, you were advised to do so. If you did, you'll find a file called **httpd** in the **/usr/sbin** directory. This is the actual Apache Web server.

You'll note that it ends in *d*, which is Internet shorthand for *daemon*. You should be far enough into your Linux education to know that a daemon is a process that's running on the surface, waiting to be called before springing into action. When an incoming request comes in from a Web browser, the **httpd** daemon springs into action.

The Apache files are in a few different places on the Slackware Linux file system. The locations are listed in Table 4.1.

Table 4.1 Apache Web Server File Locations

File/Directory	Purpose
/usr/sbin/httpd	The server daemon
/var/lib/httpd/cgi-bin	CGI programs
/var/lib/httpd/conf	Configuration files
/var/lib/httpd/icons	Bitmap icons used by the Web server to denote different things
/var/lib/httpd/html	HTML pages
/var/lib/httpd/log	Log files

If you've worked with the Apache Web server before, you know that the file locations listed in Table 4.1 aren't consistent with a normal Apache Web-server installation. The locations of files and directories really don't matter as far as the actual usage of the Web server goes, but you may want to change the file locations and such if you've installed Apache as downloaded from the Apache Web server and are using it on other Web servers (the purpose being to maintain consistency among filesystems). The default file locations are listed in Table 4.2.

Table 4.2 Default File Locations for the Apache Web Server Straight from Apache

File/Directory	Purpose
/home/httpd/cgi-bin	CGI programs
/etc/httpd/conf	Configuration files
/home/httpd/icons	Bit-mapped icons used by the Web server to denote different things
/home/httpd/html	HTML pages
/var/log/httpd	Log files

In the following sections, we'll cover how to set up the Web server straight out of the box—i.e., as installed in the basic Slackware Linux installation. Later in this chapter we'll cover how to make changes to the Apache Web server.

Before You Run the Server: Configuration Files

If you try to launch the **httpd** daemon, you'll get an error message, stating that a file location is inaccurate. Before you can actually use the Web server, you'll need to configure it. There's not a lot to configuring the Apache Web server, and it's really a matter of going through three files—all stored in the **/var/lib/httpd/conf** directory—and adapting the configuration files to your particular setup. The three files are **httpd.conf**, **srm.conf**, and **access.conf**.

Basically, these three files are used by the Apache Web server for all configuration work. It's a slightly weird situation; any directive can be placed in any of these files. The server reads in these three files for directives. How does the server know where to look for those files?

Because the files are assumed to be in the server-root directory, which is set with the *ServerRoot* directive. So before the Apache Web server can be launched, it needs to know where to find the configuration files.

The three files are:

- **httpd.conf,** which contains directives that directly control the server. You can actually override this with the *-f* command-line flag.
- **srm.conf**, which contains directives that control the specification of documents provided by the server to clients. You can override this filename with the *ResourceConfig* directive in the **httpd.conf** file.
- **access.conf**, which contains directives that control access to documents. The filename may be overridden with the *AccessConfig* directive in the **httpd.conf** file.

Another lesser configuration file, **mime.types**, is also read by the server. It contains MIME document types.

A lot of weirdness and confusion surrounds these configuration files. Basically, any directive can appear in any configuration file. Even though some general usage guidelines are associated with each configuration file, you're not required to place all document-management information in the **srm.conf** file; it could just as well appear in the **httpd.conf** file. However, if you do this, you'll soon find out that your configuration tasks are made much too difficult because you much search through three configuration files each time you want to make a change. Therefore, it's best to stick to the general principles associated with each file.

Editing the Httpd.Conf File

To get the Web server up and running, your first chore will be to make a small change to the **httpd.conf** file, using **emacs** or **elvis**. Here is the entire file:

```
# This is the main server configuration file. See URL http://www.apache.org/
# for instructions.

# Do NOT simply read the instructions in here without understanding
# what they do, if you are unsure consult the online docs. You have been
# warned.
```

```
# Originally by Rob McCool

# ServerType is either inetd, or standalone.

ServerType standalone

# If you are running from inetd, go to "ServerAdmin".

# Port: The port the standalone listens to. For ports < 1023, you will
# need httpd to be run as root initially.

Port 80

# If you wish httpd to run as a different user or group, you must run
# httpd as root initially and it will switch.

# User/Group: The name (or #number) of the user/group to run httpd as.
#  On SCO (ODT 3) use User nouser and Group nogroup
User nobody
Group #-1

# ServerAdmin: Your address, where problems with the server should be
# e-mailed.

ServerAdmin you@your.address

# ServerRoot: The directory the server's config, error, and log files
# are kept in

ServerRoot /usr/lib/httpd

# BindAddress: You can support virtual hosts with this option. This option
# is used to tell the server which IP address to listen to. It can either
# contain "*", an IP address, or a fully qualified Internet domain name.
# See also the VirtualHost directive.

#BindAddress *

# ErrorLog: The location of the error log file. If this does not start
# with /, ServerRoot is prepended to it.

ErrorLog logs/error_log
```

```
# TransferLog: The location of the transfer log file. If this does not
# start with /, ServerRoot is prepended to it.

TransferLog logs/access_log

# PidFile: The file the server should log its pid to
PidFile logs/httpd.pid

# ServerName allows you to set a host name which is sent back to clients for
# your server if it's different than the one the program would get (i.e. use
# "www" instead of the host's real name).
#
# Note: You cannot just invent host names and hope they work. The name you
# define here must be a valid DNS name for your host. If you don't understand
# this, ask your network administrator.

#ServerName new.host.name

# CacheNegotiatedDocs: By default, Apache sends Pragma: no-cache with each
# document that was negotiated on the basis of content. This asks proxy
# servers not to cache the document. Uncommenting the following line disables
# this behavior, and proxies will be allowed to cache the documents.

#CacheNegotiatedDocs

# Timeout: The number of seconds before receives and sends time out
#   n.b. the compiled default is 1200 (20 minutes !)

Timeout 400

# Server-pool size regulation.  Rather than making you guess how many
# server processes you need, Apache dynamically adapts to the load it
# sees -- that is, it tries to maintain enough server processes to
# handle the current load, plus a few spare servers to handle transient
# load spikes (e.g., multiple simultaneous requests from a single
# Netscape browser).

# It does this by periodically checking how many servers are waiting
# for a request.  If there are fewer than MinSpareServers, it creates
# a new spare.  If there are more than MaxSpareServers, some of the
# spares die off.  These values are probably OK for most sites --

MinSpareServers 5
MaxSpareServers 10
```

```
# Number of servers to start -- should be a reasonable ballpark figure.

StartServers 5

# Limit on total number of servers running, i.e., limit on the number
# of clients who can simultaneously connect -- if this limit is ever
# reached, clients will be LOCKED OUT, so it should NOT BE SET TOO LOW.
# It is intended mainly as a brake to keep a runaway server from taking
# Unix with it as it spirals down...

MaxClients 150

# MaxRequestsPerChild: the number of requests each child process is
#  allowed to process before the child dies.
#  The child will exit so as to avoid problems after prolonged use when
#  Apache (and maybe the libraries it uses) leak.  On most systems, this
#  isn't really needed, but a few (such as Solaris) do have notable leaks
#  in the libraries.

MaxRequestsPerChild 30

# VirtualHost: Allows the daemon to respond to requests for more than one
# server address, if your server machine is configured to accept IP packets
# for multiple addresses. This can be accomplished with the ifconfig
# alias flag, or through kernel patches like VIF.

# Any httpd.conf or srm.conf directive may go into a VirtualHost command.
# See alto the BindAddress entry.

#<VirtualHost host.foo.com>
#ServerAdmin webmaster@host.foo.com
#DocumentRoot /www/docs/host.foo.com
#ServerName host.foo.com
#ErrorLog logs/host.foo.com-error_log
#TransferLog logs/host.foo.com-access_log
#</VirtualHost>
```

Like many shells scripts in the UNIX world, this configuration file uses the # symbol to comment out lines—that is, make it so that those particular lines are not acted upon by a program or shell. In addition, some of the lines here are not commented but rather contain dummy information, and it's these lines that you'll need to edit. We'll run down each one of the lines, explaining what it means, and if you really need to pay much attention to it.

ServerType

ServerType standalone refers to whether the server runs in *standalone* mode (where the server responds directly to incoming Web requests) or in *inetd* mode, where the Web server responds to the **intetd** daemon, which is essentially a clearinghouse for incoming Internet server requests. If you run in inetd mode, then the command to launch the server will be automatically inserted into the **/etc/inetd.conf** file after the **httpd** daemon is launched for the first time. When running **httpd** in standalone mode (the default), the command to launch this daemon every time Linux boots is inserted in the proper startup file (usually **/etc/rc.local** or **/etc/rc3.d**). You'll have better performance if you leave the server in standalone mode, since inetd mode means that a new server will need to start from scratch every time there's a request, while standalone mode just handles all the incoming requests on its own. In fact, if you expect a lot of traffic, you'll be forced to run in standalone mode, unless you want a lot of angry users complaining about Web requests that get timed out. However, an **httpd** daemon executed in inetd mode will be less vulnerable to attacks from the outside world.

Port

Port 80 refers to the port that the server listens to. The number 80 is the default, but this number can be any number between 0 and 65535. Linux (as well as UNIX in general) defines a number of ports (actually, all ports numbered below 1024) as being reserved for specific purposes (there's a list of these in **/etc/services**, a list that you first encountered in Chapter 3). In most circumstances, you'll want to leave the port as 80, since this seems to be the default in the Web-server world.

This port setting has one side effect that you'll want to note if security is an issue: Because of the low number, you must start the server logged in as root. After binding to the port and before accepting requests, Apache will change to a low privileged user as set by the User directive. If you run the server as root while handling connections, your site may be open to a major security attack.

However, you can use any unused port for the Web server. If you allow users other than root to launch the **httpd** daemon, then they must use a port higher than 1023 (8080 is a popular alternative).

Users and Groups

When you launch the Web server, it must have permissions to access files on the filesystem and have something to change to from root, since generally speaking it's not a good idea to have the Web server run as root for security reasons (if someone brings down the Web server, they could have access to your entire filesystem). Therefore, you need to assign it a username and groupname for permissions. The default is *User nobody* and *Group #-1*.

ServerAdmin

ServerAdmin you@your.address is the mail address of the server administrator, and this is also the address returned by the server in error messages to users. Many Webmasters set up a dedicated e-mail account (such as *webmaster@largecorp.com*) to handle these situations, because many users send vague messages and don't mention that they're complaining specifically about the Web server, as opposed to the Gopher server or mail server. The *you@your.address* portion needs to be changed before the Web server can launch.

ServerRoot

ServerRoot /usr/lib/httpd refers to the directory containing the **httpd** support files. In the configuration files, this is an incorrect location for the Slackware Linux installation; it's the file location for the default Apache Web-server installation, not the one that's part of the general Slackware installation. You'll want to change this to /**var/lib/httpd** (assuming that you made no changes to Apache file locations). This needs to be changed before the Apache Web server will launch under Slackware Linux.

Also, the Slackware Linux distribution also changes the location of the **conf** and **logs** directories. In a typical Apache installation, these directories would reside in **/usr/lib/httpd**; instead, these directories reside in /**var/lib/httpd**.

BindAddress

BindAddress * is used to specify which IP addresses to listen to for HTTP requests. When this setting is a wildcard (*), then the server will listen for connections to every IP address or a Internet domain name. You can change this to a specific IP address. This option can be used as an alternative method for supporting virtual hosts instead of using VirtualHost sections (covered later in this chapter).

ErrorLog

ErrorLog logs/error_log lists the location of the error logs, which can be very handy in finding out problems that users might encounter. The location listed here is actually prepended to the *ServerRoot* value (if there were a leading slash [/], then it would be an absolute pathname); the actual file location is **/var/lib/httpd/logs/error_log**. You could comment out this line, but the documentation (curiously enough) recommends using the following entry to turn off error logging:

```
ErrorLog /dev/null
```

TransferLog

TransferLog logs/access_log lists the location of the transfer log, which tells you what's being grabbed from your Web server. The location listed here is actually prepended to the *ServerRoot* value; the actual file location is **/var/lib/httpd/logs/access_log**.

PidFile

PidFile logs/httpd.pid lists the location of the PID file, which is where the server records the process ID of the **httpd** daemon. The location listed here is actually prepended to the *ServerRoot* value (if there were a leading slash [/], then it would be an absolute pathname); the actual file location is **/var/lib/httpd/logs/httpd.pid**. If you're running the Web server in inetd mode, then there will be no PidFile generated.

Why would this possibly be useful? You may want to make changes to configuration or log files and want to take the server down. The easiest way to do so is to send a SIGHUP signal (or **kill -1**) to the process ID listed in the PidFile.

ServerName

ServerName new.host.name is used to return an Internet host other than the one that the server would normally return. The trick here is that it has to be a legitimate DNS name for your host (this is more useful when you're running multiple hosts on the same machine, of course). This is handy when there's a discrepancy between the machine name and what you want the world to see as the server. For instance, many larger sites have machine names that have an individual string listed before the domain name. In a situation like this, you don't want the world to see that the server name is (for example) *kevin.kreichard.com*—you want the world to see a server name of *www.kreichard.com*.

CacheNegotiatedDocs

#CacheNegotiatedDocs allows proxy servers to cache documents called from your Web server. This is handy if you're running an intranet and know that your documents won't change often. However, since this isn't usually the case, this line is commented out.

TimeOut

TimeOut 400 refers to the time (in seconds) between a request and a time-out if the request can't be handled.

SpareServers

MinSpareServers 5 and *MaxSpareServers 10* refer to the amount of spare servers that Apache maintains. Remember that a new process is started for each new user that connects to a Web server; all new users are said to have their own servers running. Most Web servers require that you fill in a specific number of servers that are always maintained. Apache, however, adjusts to the workload; if there's a need for a lot of servers, Apache will create extra servers at a rate of one per second (or spare servers, in the parlance of this configuration file). These settings should be adequate for all but the busiest Web sites; having too high a number of *MinSpareServers* and/or *MaxSpareServers* is a waste of system resources.

StartServers

StartServers 5 is the number of servers Apache starts when launched. Since Apache will dynamically create servers in times of high demand, this figure isn't that important.

MaxClients

MaxClients 150 refers to the number of users that can be connected simultaneously. If you've got more RAM than average you can probably jack up this number a little if you find that your Web server is turning away a lot of users.

MaxRequestsPerChild

MaxRequestsPerChild 30 is the number of additional requests each client can make before the process is eliminated. A setting of **0** makes all processes permanent. This is done for memory-management reasons (it reduces the damage caused by memory leakage, as well as reducing the number of processes when the server load reduces), not because of any real need to limit users.

Virtual Hosts

#<VirtualHost host.foo.com>, *#ServerAdmin webmaster@host.foo.com*, *#DocumentRoot /www/docs/host.foo.com*, *#ServerName host.foo.com*, *#ErrorLog logs/host.foo.com-error_log*, *#TransferLog logs/host.foo.com-access_log*, and *#</VirtualHost>* are all used when running virtual hosts. Slackware Linux and the Apache Web server aren't set up to do this right out of the box.

After you make your changes (as shown previously, all you really need to change are two lines), you can move on to the next configuration file, **access.conf**.

Editing the Access.conf File

The **access.conf** file controls who can and cannot connect to your Web server. It's listed as the following:

```
# access.conf: Global access configuration
# Online docs at http://www.apache.org/
```

```
# This file defines server settings which affect which types of services
# are allowed, and in what circumstances.

# Each directory to which Apache has access, can be configured with respect
# to which services and features are allowed and/or disabled in that
# directory (and its subdirectories).

# Originally by Rob McCool

# /usr/local/etc/httpd/ should be changed to whatever you set ServerRoot to.
<Directory /usr/lib/httpd/cgi-bin>
Options Indexes FollowSymLinks
</Directory>

# This should be changed to whatever you set DocumentRoot to.

<Directory /usr/lib/httpd/htdocs>

# This may also be "None", "All", or any combination of "Indexes",
# "Includes", "FollowSymLinks", "ExecCGI", or "MultiViews".

# Note that "MultiViews" must be named *explicitly* -- "Options All"
# doesn't give it to you (or at least, not yet).

Options Indexes FollowSymLinks

# This option allows you to turn on the XBitHack behavior, which allows you
# to make text/html server-parsed by activating the owner x bit with chmod.
# This directive may be used wherever Options may, and has three
# possible arguments: Off, On or Full. If set to full, Apache will also
# add a Last-Modified header to the document if the group x bit is set.

# Unless the server has been compiled with -DXBITHACK, this function is
# off by default. To use, uncomment the following line:

#XBitHack Full

# This controls which options the .htaccess files in directories can
# override. Can also be "None", or any combination of "Options", "FileInfo",
# "AuthConfig", and "Limit"

AllowOverride All
```

```
# Controls who can get stuff from this server.

<Limit GET>
order allow,deny
allow from all
</Limit>

</Directory>

# You may place any other directories you wish to have access
# information for after this one.
```

Even though this file seems long, there's really only a few things you need to pay attention to for a basic Web configuration. However, there are a few things you should note about this file. It uses a slightly different syntax than the other configuration files. For instance, it uses bracketing statements to indicate settings. To change the directory for CGI files, this file uses bracketing statements of *<Directory></Directory>* to essentially turn off and on the settings. (This actually mimics HTML editing, which you'll learn about in Chapter 11.)

One area of changes will cover the file locations, which should mirror the file locations you changed in the **httpd.conf** file earlier in this chapter. For instance, you'll want to change the following settings:

```
<Directory /usr/lib/httpd/cgi-bin>
Options Indexes FollowSymLinks
</Directory>
```

to match the location of the **cgi-bin** directory on your own Web server (the Slackware Linux default is **/var/lib/httpd**), so unless you've made some changes in file locations, your section should look like the following:

```
<Directory /var/lib/httpd/cgi-bin>
Options Indexes FollowSymLinks
</Directory>
```

Similarly, this line needs to be changed in the same manner:

```
<Directory /usr/lib/httpd/htdocs>
```

to match the location of the **htdocs** directory on your own Web server (the Slackware Linux default is **/var/lib/httpd**), so unless you've made some changes in file locations, your line should look like the following:

```
<Directory /var/lib/httpd/htdocs>
```

This file also controls whether or not you can place a *Last Modified* header on every file that's been set with the *x* bit using the **chmod** command; the setting is in the following line:

```
#XBitHack Full
```

This is handy for letting users know when documents have last been changed. The line is commented out, but you may want to turn it on and mark your main files with the *x* bit (sometimes called the *sticky bit*).

This section controls who has access to your server:

```
<Limit GET>
order allow,deny
allow from all
</Limit>
```

The default is to let all users have access to the server. However, you could deny users from a specific domain—say, from America Online—with the following changes in the section:

```
<Limit GET>
order allow,deny
allow from all
deny from aol.com
</Limit>
```

You could add other lines, such as the domain name of your dreaded competitor, Spacely Sprockets:

```
<Limit GET>
order allow,deny
```

```
allow from all
deny from aol.com
deny from spacely.com
</Limit>
```

You could also change the settings to deny access to everyone save employees of your corporation (we'll use *kreichard.com* as the domain name, although you'll want to use your own corporate domain name on your server), as in the following:

```
<Limit GET>
order deny,allow
deny from all
allow from kreichard.com
</Limit>
```

This setting can come in handy if you're running an intranet.

Notice that a few different things were changed in this example. The second line, beginning with *order*, was changed to *order deny,allow*. This changes the logical order used to determine who has access to the server.

The Srm.conf File

There is one additional file that can be used to configure the Apache Web server: **srm.conf**, which specifies the documents that the server provides to clients. The default **srm.conf** file is as follows:

```
# With this document, you define the name space that users see of your http
# server. This file also defines server settings which affect how requests are
# serviced, and how results should be formatted.

# See the tutorials at http://www.apache.org/ for
# more information.

# Originally by Rob McCool; Adapted for Apache

# DocumentRoot: The directory out of which you will serve your
# documents. By default, all requests are taken from this directory, but
# symbolic links and aliases may be used to point to other locations.
```

```
DocumentRoot /usr/lib/httpd/htdocs

# UserDir: The name of the directory which is appended onto a user's home
# directory if a ~user request is received.

UserDir public_html

# DirectoryIndex: Name of the file or files to use as a pre-written HTML
# directory index.  Separate multiple entries with spaces.

DirectoryIndex index.html

# FancyIndexing is whether you want fancy directory indexing or standard

FancyIndexing on

# AddIcon tells the server which icon to show for different files or filename
# extensions

AddIconByEncoding (CMP,/icons/compressed.gif) x-compress x-gzip
AddIconByType (TXT,/icons/text.gif) text/*
AddIconByType (IMG,/icons/image2.gif) image/*
AddIconByType (SND,/icons/sound2.gif) audio/*
AddIconByType (VID,/icons/movie.gif) video/*
AddIcon /icons/text.gif .ps .shtml
AddIcon /icons/movie.gif .mpg .qt
AddIcon /icons/binary.gif .bin
AddIcon /icons/burst.gif .wrl
AddIcon /icons/binhex.gif .hqx .sit
AddIcon /icons/uu.gif .uu
AddIcon /icons/tar.gif .tar  .tar
AddIcon /icons/back.gif ..
AddIcon /icons/dir.gif ^^DIRECTORY^^
AddIcon /icons/blank.gif ^^BLANKICON^^

# DefaultIcon is which icon to show for files which do not have an icon
# explicitly set.

DefaultIcon /icons/unknown.gif

# AddDescription allows you to place a short description after a file in
# server-generated indexes.
# Format: AddDescription "description" filename
```

```
# ReadmeName is the name of the README file the server will look for by
# default. Format: ReadmeName name
#
# The server will first look for name.html, include it if found, and it will
# then look for name and include it as plaintext if found.
#
# HeaderName is the name of a file which should be prepended to
# directory indexes.

ReadmeName README
HeaderName HEADER


# IndexIgnore is a set of filenames which directory indexing should ignore
# Format: IndexIgnore name1 name2...

IndexIgnore */.??* *~ *# */HEADER* */README* */RCS


# AccessFileName: The name of the file to look for in each directory
# for access control information.

AccessFileName .htaccess


# DefaultType is the default MIME type for documents which the server
# cannot find the type of from filename extensions.

DefaultType text/plain


# AddEncoding allows you to have certain browsers (Mosaic/X 2.1+) uncompress
# information on the fly. Note: Not all browsers support this.

AddEncoding x-compress Z
AddEncoding x-gzip gz


# AddLanguage allows you to specify the language of a document. You can
# then use content negotiation to give a browser a file in a language
# it can understand.  Note that the suffix does not have to be the same
# as the language keyword -- those with documents in Polish (whose
# net-standard language code is pl) may wish to use "AddLanguage pl .po"
# to avoid the ambiguity with the common suffix for perl scripts.

AddLanguage en .en
AddLanguage fr .fr
AddLanguage de .de
```

```
AddLanguage da .da
AddLanguage el .el
AddLanguage it .it

# LanguagePriority allows you to give precedence to some languages
# in case of a tie during content negotiation.
# Just list the languages in decreasing order of preference.

LanguagePriority en fr de

# Redirect allows you to tell clients about documents which used to exist in
# your server's namespace, but do not anymore. This allows you to tell the
# clients where to look for the relocated document.
# Format: Redirect fakename url

# Aliases: Add here as many aliases as you need (with no limit). The format is
# Alias fakename realname

Alias /icons/ /usr/lib/httpd/icons/

# ScriptAlias: This controls which directories contain server scripts.
# Format: ScriptAlias fakename realname

ScriptAlias /cgi-bin/ /usr/lib/httpd/cgi-bin/

# If you want to use server side includes, or CGI outside
# ScriptAliased directories, uncomment the following lines.

# AddType allows you to tweak mime.types without actually editing it, or to
# make certain files to be certain types.
# Format: AddType type/subtype ext1

#AddType text/x-server-parsed-html .shtml
#AddType application/x-httpd-cgi .cgi

# For server-side includes which will be treated as HTML3
# for purposes of content negotiation, use

#AddType text/x-server-parsed-html3 .shtml3

# Uncomment the following line to enable Apache's send-asis HTTP file
# feature
```

```
#AddType httpd/send-as-is asis

# To enable type maps, you might want to use

#AddType application/x-type-map var

# If you wish to use server-parsed imagemap files, use

#AddType application/x-httpd-imap map

# Customizable error response (Apache style)
#  these come in three flavors
#
#    1) plain text
#ErrorDocument 500 "The server made a boo boo.
#  n.b.  the (") marks it as text, it does not get output
#
#    2) local redirects
#ErrorDocument 404 /missing.html
#  to redirect to local url /missing.html
#ErrorDocument 404 /cgi-bin/missing_handler.pl
#  n.b. can redirect to a script or a document using server-side-includes.
#
#    3) external redirects
#ErrorDocument 402 http://other.server.com/subscription_info.html
#
```

There are a number of settings to review here. The first two settings covered here must be changed before you can use the Web server; the rest can be changed at your leisure.

DocumentRoot

This is the directory where your documents are stored; the default is **/usr/lib/httpd/htdocs** in Apache, although the default Linux installation places them in **/var/lib/httpd/htdocs**. Slackware Linux already did you the favor of moving the documents away from the server files, which is the recommended course of action. The location of this file isn't a big deal. Some Webmasters recommend that it be moved to a shorter name, like **/www** or something similar, but experience shows that this really isn't a big issue.

The point here is that you must have an existing directory to store documents before the Web server can be put online. The easiest thing to do is to change the line in the **srm.conf** file to

```
DocumentRoot /var/lib/httpd/htdocs
```

ScriptAlias

This setting controls where your CGI programs are stored; the default is **/usr/lib/httpd/cgi-bin/**. In normal Internet parlance, a call to a CGI program runs along the lines of

```
http://www.kreichard.com/cgi-bin/program
```

Normally you don't throw CGI programs in the document root for security and access reasons. Instead, you install them somewhere else in the filesystem that's more secure. (We'll learn more about CGI files and such in Chapter 11.)

If you look at the default Linux Apache installation, you'll see that there's a directory called **cgi-bin** in the **/var/lib/httpd** directory. Inside of it are several CGI programs. These can be quite handy, and in Chapter 11 we'll cover these programs as well as additional programs that can make your life easier.

ScriptAlias and *DocumentRoot* are the two settings that must be changed or reviewed before the Web server can be launched. However, you might want to review a number of other settings in this file. In the following sections, we'll review these settings. If you're impatient to get a server up and running, you can skip ahead to the section entitled "Starting Apache."

Working with MIME

The Multipurpose Internet Mail Extensions (MIME) are used by Web browsers and Web servers to dictate the type of file that's being sent from server to browser. The Internet world has standardized on a set of

MIME types, and most of them are already built into the Apache Web server, in the **mime.types** files.

How MIME works is pretty simple. A Web browser will ask a Web server for a file. This could be a Web page (with a file extension of **.html** or **.htm**), a text file (with a file extension of **.txt**), a GIF graphics files (with a file extension of **.gif**), and so on. The Web server heeds the request and then adds a *Content-Type* header to the file. When the Web browser receives the file and the header, it has enough information to know what to do with the file. For instance, if a Web browser received a document with a header that says that the file is a Web page (HTML), then the browser will display the page. However, if a Web browser received a file with a header like:

```
Content-type: audio/x-wav
```

it will know that the file is a sound file in the WAV format and, depending how the browser is set up, will either play the sound itself or launch an external application to play the sound file. In addition, browsers can be set up to save files directly to disk; it's pretty common to set up a browser to save all compressed files ending in **.zip** to disk. In those cases where the browser hasn't been configured to deal with a MIME type, the browser will prompt the user for a course of action: view the file with the browser, launch an external application, save the file to disk, or cancel the transaction.

For MIME types to work, a few important things need to be happening online:

- Everyone must use the correct file extension within filenames. The MIME format is a fairly "dumb" format, in that it keys off of filenames and extensions, rather than the actual content of the files. If someone decided to add a **.wave** extension to all their sound-oriented filenames, the Web server wouldn't know what to do with the resulting files.

- A Web server must be configured to recognize the MIME type. As you can tell from the **mime.types** file listing from earlier in this chapter, almost all popular MIME types are listed. As new MIME types are added to the Internet world, it's up to you to add support for them to your Apache Web server.

Adding MIME Types

Contrary to what you might think, the recommended course of action when adding MIME types to a server isn't to add a line to the **mime.types** file. Instead, it's recommended that you use the *AddType* directive to add a line to your **srm.conf** file. For instance, to add support for the virtual-reality MIME type, which is rapidly becoming more and more popular, you would add the following line to your **srm.conf** file:

```
AddType x-world/x-vrml .wrl
```

When a user requests a file ending in **.wrl**, the following header will be sent along with the file:

```
Content-type x-world/x-vrml
```

The browser will then take that information and either launch an external viewer when the file arrives or, as in the case with virtual-reality browsers, display with file within the browser itself.

You can also use the *AddType* directive to play games with CGI programs. In the old days, it was typical to store all your CGI programs in a single directory (**cgi-bin**) and give that one directory the proper permissions to execute programs. You can get around this by uncommenting the following MIME type in the **srm.conf** file:

```
AddType application/x-httpd-cgi .cgi
```

When a browser requests a CGI script from a directory outside of **cgi-bin**, the server will then run the application and return its output to the browser, instead of sending a Web page. This allows CGI scripts to be executed wherever they're stored.

If the Apache Web server can't find an application type, it uses the type specified using the *DefaultType* directive. The default setting for this directive is *text/plain*.

There's not much else to note regarding the *AddType* directive. You can add multiple file extensions to a MIME type; for instance, the extensions **.jpeg**, **.jpg**, and **.jpe** are all specified as relating to the JPEG MIME type. However, you cannot have file extensions that are linked to multiple MIME types.

After you have edited this file with **emacs** or **elvis**, go ahead and save the changes to disk. The Apache Web server should be ready to run.

Starting Apache

It's rather easy to launch the daemon. Use the following command line:

```
httpd
```

You don't need to launch the **httpd** daemon every time you want to use the Web server; it will be launched automatically every time your Linux system is booted.

When someone connects to your Web server, they'll be served a file called **index.html** initially if they didn't specify a URL. When someone connects to *http://www.kreichard.com*, they'll actually be returned the following URL (which will be what shows up on their Web browser's URL line): *http://www.kreichard.com/index.html*. The Apache installation that ships with Slackware Linux contains a dummy **index.html** page that you'll want to change. (In Chapter 11 we'll cover creating and editing Web pages, as well as where you'll want to store the Web pages.)

To see whether the server is running, use the Arena Web browser (which ships as part of Slackware Linux) to see if you can read the default **index.html** page used in the Web server:

```
arena http://localhost/
```

You could also launch **arena** with no HTTP address and then use the following URL:

```
http://www.myhost.com
```

If you were successful, you'll see Arena with the file shown in Figure 4.1.

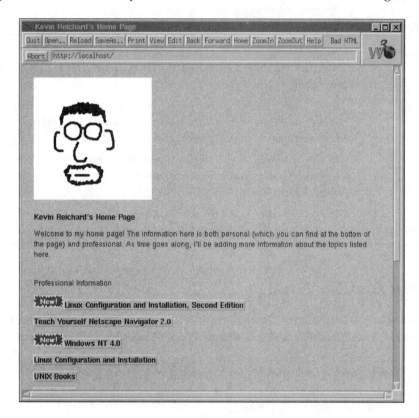

Figure 4.1 The Arena Web browser displaying the index.html file.

Command-Line Options

There are a number of command-line options to the **httpd** command, as listed in Table 4.3.

Table 4.3 Command-Line Options to the Httpd Command

Option	Explanation
-d *serverroot*	This sets the initial value for the *ServerRoot* variable to *serverroot*. This can be overridden by the *ServerRoot* command in the configuration file (as explained earlier in this chapter).
-f *config*	This executes the commands in the file *config* on startup. If *config* does not begin with a slash (/), then it is taken to be a path relative to the *ServerRoot*. The default is **conf/httpd.conf**.
-X	This launches the Web server in single-process mode; the **httpd** daemon doesn't create any children or detach from the terminal. This should be used for internal debugging purposes only.
-v	This prints the **httpd** version before exiting.
-?	This prints a list of options before exiting.

What Can Go Wrong

A number of things can go wrong when you launch the Web server. Here are some of the more common error messages and how you can fix your problems.

```
httpd: could not bind to port port
bind: Operation not permitted
```

This error message occurs when you change the *Port* setting in the **httpd.conf** to a port that's not available to the server, usually due to incorrect permissions. Remember that most ports under 1024 are already claimed by the Linux system and are thus available only to the root user. Try logging in as the root user and launching the **httpd** service to see if this is indeed the case.

```
httpd: could not bind to port
bind: Address already in use
```

This error message occurs when the port is already in use. Port 80 is usually reserved for Web servers, so there's the chance that another Web server is running. No Linux system has a Web server installed and running automatically, especially not Slackware Linux. Unfortunately, no program or routine will allow you to see a list of ports in use and what they're running. The **/etc/services** file does list the ports and how they're assigned, but they don't list what's actually in use. You could peruse through the listings returned by **ps** or **netstat** to see what processes or net services are actually running and try to extrapolate from that.

```
httpd: could not open document config file
fopen: No such file or directory
```

This error message usually occurs when you've improperly configured the location of the **httpd.conf** file. Try using the **httpd** command with the *-f* option again.

```
403 Access Forbidden
```

This error message will be returned after a Web browser has actually connected to your Web server. This usually means that you've improperly configured your **access.conf** file to keep everyone away.

```
500 Server Error
```

This error message usually means that some software is failing, usually a CGI script.

Other Directives in Srm.conf

The **srm.conf** file, which was covered earlier in this chapter, contains a number of settings that can help you fine-tune your Linux Internet server. We'll cover the major directives here.

Setting Directory Indexing

If a user tries to connect to a directory without specifying a file, there needs to a way to tell the Web server what page to send to the user. The default setting is to use a file called **index.html** placed in each directory. The default setting in the **srm.conf** file that controls this is as follows:

```
DirectoryIndex index.html
```

Therefore, when someone connects to *http://www.kreichard.com*, by default they are sent the **index.html** file that resides in the *DocumentRoot* directory, with the resulting URL:

> *http://www.kreichard.com/index.html*

Like everything else in the Apache Web server (and Linux, for that matter), you can go overboard customizing this setting. You could place a CGI program in the **srm.conf** *DirectoryIndex* setting:

```
DirectoryIndex file.cgi index.html
```

In this case, the Apache Web server will look for a file named **file.cgi**. If it fails to find this file, it will then look for **index.html**. These files are assumed to be in the *DocumentRoot* directory, but you could specify a file or path either relative to the *DocumentRoot* location or an absolute pathname.

If Apache doesn't find either **file.cgi** or **index.html**, it will return a list of files in the directory.

If you're running a large Web site, you may have reason to have multiple files for indices, which can be changed easily on the fly. However, if you're running a relatively straightforward Web site, there's no reason to make your *DirectoryIndex* too elaborate.

Fancy Indexing

Another feature that ends up smacking of overkill is the *FancyIndexing* feature. When Apache sends a list of files in the directory, there is the option—*FancyIndexing*—of sending along information about the file (such as the last time it was modified) and an icon, representing the file type (based on the filename extension).

However, this really isn't overkill. There will be times when you want to allow users the ability to download files from a Web server, in lieu of an FTP connection. In these instances, you'll want to give information about the files available past just a filename. In fact, you can set up an FTP alternative by creating a directory that has nothing but files available for downloading. When a user selects that file, it's then sent to the Web browser, which is prompted as to what action should be taken on the file. (A smart user will select saving the file to disk.) In these situations, *FancyIndexing* can be quite useful.

Adding Icons

In situations where *FancyIndexing* is used, you'll need some sort of mechanism for selecting the icons to place next to files. The directives *AddIcon*, *AddIconByEncoding*, and *AddIconByType* do this. Here are the defaults for these setting from the **srm.conf** file:

```
AddIconByEncoding (CMP,/icons/compressed.gif) x-compress x-gzip
AddIconByType (TXT,/icons/text.gif) text/*
AddIconByType (IMG,/icons/image2.gif) image/*
AddIconByType (SND,/icons/sound2.gif) audio/*
AddIconByType (VID,/icons/movie.gif) video/*
AddIcon /icons/text.gif .ps .shtml
AddIcon /icons/movie.gif .mpg .qt
AddIcon /icons/binary.gif .bin
AddIcon /icons/burst.gif .wrl
AddIcon /icons/binhex.gif .hqx .sit
AddIcon /icons/uu.gif .uu
AddIcon /icons/tar.gif .tar  .tar
AddIcon /icons/back.gif ..
AddIcon /icons/dir.gif ^^DIRECTORY^^
AddIcon /icons/blank.gif ^^BLANKICON^^
```

These directives are self-explanatory. When the Apache Web server returns an encoded file directory listing ending in **.Z** or **.gz**, it will place an icon (**compressed.gif**) next to the filename. When the Apache Web server sends out any MIME type of text, image, audio, and video in a directory listing, it will send along the appropriate icons (**text.gif**, **image2.gif**, **sound2.gif**, and **movie.gif**, respectively). When the Apache Web server sends out a directory listing containing specific types of files (such as an MPEG movie file), it will send along a specific icon in the directory listing (in this case, **movie.gif**). The GIF files listed here ship with the Apache Web server, by the way, and are stored in the **/icons** directory.

You're free to add more specific MIME types and icons. You'll notice that the files listed here are all GIF files, which can be created by pretty much any graphics editor.

The final two entries are used to specify what to use for a subdirectory (the **dir.gif** icon) and a blank line (the **blank.gif** icon).

Unless you really have a need to play a lot of games with these icons, it's easiest to add icons by type, rather than by specific file type. Then again, the vast majority of filenames will be covered by the default settings in the **srm.conf** file, so your easiest course of action would be to just leave well enough alone.

You can add a description to a directory listing using the *AddDescription* directive. You can either use a description for a specific filename:

```
AddDescription "He is not a crook." nixon.gif
```

or a description for a range of filenames, specified using wildcards:

```
AddDescription "C source-code file." *.c
```

The *AddDescription* directive is commented out in the default **srm.conf** file.

In those cases where the Apache Web server can't come up with an appropriate icon for a file, it uses the *DefaultIcon* icon. The default in **srm.conf** is **/icons/unknown.gif**.

HeaderName and ReadmeName

You can add text to a directory listing by specifying text files using the *ReaderName* and *HeaderName* directives. The *HeaderName* directive inserts a specified text file (the default being **HEADER**) to the beginning of a directory listing. The *ReadmeName* directive adds a text file (the default being **README**) to the end of a directory listing. This can come in handy if you want some text to describe the type of files in the directory, or other information that you feel the user should know.

The IndexIgnore Directive

You don't always want to make every file in a directory visible to users—that's why the Linux operating system comes with hidden files.

In this case, you'll want to use the *IndexIgnore* directive to make sure that system files and other files are hidden.

The default for this directive in the **srm.conf** file is

```
IndexIgnore */.??* *~ *# */HEADER* */README* */RCS
```

This line blocks six types of files:

- **/.??** blocks out system hidden files (that is, files that begin with a period), while letting through the parent directory (which is specified with two periods).

- **~* blocks out backup files created by **emacs**. Many Web developers use **emacs** to edit HTML pages.

- **#* blocks out backup files created by **emacs**. Many Web developers use **emacs** to edit HTML pages.

- **/HEADER** blocks out the **HEADER** file used by the *HeaderName* directive.

- **/README** blocks out the **README** file used by the *ReadmeName* directive.

- **/RCS* blocks out the **RCS** directory, which is created by the Revision Control System, a software-development tool that ships as part of the Linux operating system.

You can add more options for this directive.

Adding Encoding

Similar to the *AddType* directive is the *AddEncoding* directive, which is used by the server to tell the browser how a file is encoded. There are several types of encoding in the Internet world. Basically, the encoded refers to how a file is archived or compressed.

No file within Apache specifies encoding types, so this task falls to the **srm.conf** file. If you go back and skim through this file, you'll see the following two lines within:

```
AddEncoding x-compress Z
AddEncoding x-gzip gz
```

They tell the server to send along a *Content-Encoding* header along with the actual file. These two cases are from the UNIX world, specifying that files ending in **.Z** are compressed using the **compress** command and that files ending in **.gz** are compressed using the GNU **gzip** command. For instance, when a server sends out a file named **file.Z**, it also sends along a header like the following:

```
Content-Encoding: x-gzip
```

When a browser runs across this header, it launches a command line and uncompresses or unzips the file before viewing it in the browser or launching an external application to view the file.

NOTE Perhaps the most common compression format is the PKWare ZIP format, supported by both PKZip and WinZip. You might be tempted to add support for content encoding for this popular format, but don't—many different software packages support this format. In addition, support for ZIP files isn't built in the operating system as it is in the UNIX operating system.

The Alias and Redirect Directives

You reviewed the *ScriptAlias* directive earlier in this chapter. This directive has two cousins that are also set in the **srm.conf** file: *Alias* and *Redirect*. These commands, along with *ScriptAlias*, allow you to remap portions of the Web server across your entire Linux file system.

Alias is exactly what it sounds like: It allows you to set up an alias for a subdirectory. Remember that it's usually best to keep URLs short and sweet; a URL of *http://www.kreichard.com/personal/hobbies/cigars/don_tomas/ index.html* probably won't be typed in accurately by most folks, but a URL of *http://www.kreichard.com/don_tomas* certainly would. In this case, you could set up an alias for that directory. In this case, you might want to set up an alias like the following:

```
Alias /don_tomas/ /usr/local/personal/hobbies/cigars/don_tomas/
```

This tells the Web server to go to */usr/local/personal/hobbies/cigars/ don_tomas/* when the URL is *http://www.kreichard.com/don_tomas/*. The same would apply to requests for specific files: A URL of *http://www.kreichard.com/don_tomas/summary.html* would return the file

/usr/local/personal/hobbies/cigars/don_tomas/summary.html. The user won't see the longer pathname.

There's really only one thing to watch out for: Make sure that you're not using an alias that sits somewhere in the *DocumentRoot*.

Redirect works similarly. It just redirects the request from the Web browser to another location, either another file on the local filesystem or the Internet. (*Alias*, on the other hand, is meant for use on the local file system.) For instance, you might want to redirect all requests for *microsoft* to *linux*. For instance, someone requesting a URL of *http://www.kreichard.com/microsoft* would be redirected to *http://www.linux.org* with the following line in the **srm.conf** file:

```
Redirect /microsoft http://www.linux.org
```

This is handy when working with Internet resources that have shifted to other locations; for instance, when your hot Internet software company is swallowed by Microsoft or IBM, you can use the *Redirect* directive to route requests to the new owners.

The IndexOptions Directive

Many of these directives can be set under one meta-directive, *IndexOptions*. Its options follow:

- *FancyIndexing* turns on fancy indexing of directories.
- *IconsAreLinks* makes the icons part of the anchor for the filename, for fancy indexing.
- *ScanHTMLTitles* enables the extraction of the title from HTML documents for fancy indexing. If the file does not have a description given by **AddDescription**, then **httpd** reads the document for the value of the *TITLE* tag. Be warned that this is CPU- and disk-intensive.
- *SuppressLastModified* suppresses the display of the last modification date, in fancy-indexing listings.
- *SuppressSize* suppresses the file size in fancy-indexing listings.
- *SuppressDescription* suppresses the file description in fancy-indexing listings.

The Mime.types File

The **mime.types** file follows:

```
application/activemessage
application/andrew-inset
application/applefile
application/atomicmail
application/dca-rft
application/dec-dx
application/mac-binhex40
application/macwriteii
application/msword
application/news-message-id
application/news-transmission
application/octet-stream       bin
application/oda                oda
application/pdf                pdf
application/postscript         ai eps ps
application/remote-printing
application/rtf                rtf
application/slate
application/x-mif        mif
application/wita
application/wordperfect5.1
application/x-csh              csh
application/x-dvi              dvi
application/x-hdf              hdf
application/x-latex            latex
application/x-netcdf           nc cdf
application/x-sh               sh
application/x-tcl              tcl
application/x-tex              tex
application/x-texinfo          texinfo texi
application/x-troff            t tr roff
application/x-troff-man        man
application/x-troff-me         me
application/x-troff-ms         ms
application/x-wais-source      src
application/zip                zip
application/x-bcpio            bcpio
application/x-cpio             cpio
application/x-gtar             gtar
application/x-shar             shar
```

```
application/x-sv4cpio          sv4cpio
application/x-sv4crc           sv4crc
application/x-tar              tar
application/x-ustar            ustar
audio/basic                   au snd
audio/x-aiff                  aif aiff aifc
audio/x-wav                   wav
image/gif                     gif
image/ief                     ief
image/jpeg                    jpeg jpg jpe
image/tiff                    tiff tif
image/x-cmu-raster            ras
image/x-portable-anymap       pnm
image/x-portable-bitmap       pbm
image/x-portable-graymap      pgm
image/x-portable-pixmap       ppm
image/x-rgb                   rgb
image/x-xbitmap               xbm
image/x-xpixmap               xpm
image/x-xwindowdump           xwd
message/external-body
message/news
message/partial
message/rfc822
multipart/alternative
multipart/appledouble
multipart/digest
multipart/mixed
multipart/parallel
text/html                     html
text/plain                    txt
text/richtext                 rtx
text/tab-separated-values     tsv
text/x-setext                 etx
video/mpeg                    mpeg mpg mpe
video/quicktime               qt mov
video/x-msvideo               avi
video/x-sgi-movie             movie
```

Normally you don't want to mess with the contents of this file. Instead, you should use some of the directives discussed earlier in this chapter to add MIME types to this list.

Log Files

The Apache Web server uses a number of files to track usage of all sorts. They are

- **httpd.pid**, which saves the process ID (pid) of the parent **httpd** process to the file **logs/httpd.pid**. This file location is saved with the *PidFile* directive, which by default is set in the **httpd.conf** file. Most of the time this information isn't of much use, unless you actually want to shut down the server (which we'll cover later in this chapter).

- **error_log**, which is used to log error messages. You can change the filename by changing the *ErrorLog* directive. This can come in handy when you're setting different error logs for different virtual hosts.

- **access_log**, which is used to log each HTTP request. You can change the filename by changing the *TransferLog* directive. This can come in handy when you're setting different logs for different virtual hosts.

Resetting Log Files

There's one rule about log files: They grow and grow and grow. (Well, the **access_log** and **error_log** files grow, anyway. As a matter of fact, the **access.log** file grows by 1MB for each 10,000 requests.) At some point, they'll become too large to be manageable, and you'll want to begin new files.

The temptation is to move or delete the logfile, but don't do it. Basically, the Web server continues writing to the logfile at the same offset as before the logfile moved. This results in a new logfile being created which is just as big as the old one, but it now contains thousands (or millions) of null characters.

Here's what to do: Move the logfile and then tell Apache to tell it to reopen the logfiles using the *SIGHUP (-1)* signal:

```
mv access_log access_log.old ; kill -1 `cat access.conf`
```

You could set up a **cron** task to backup and replace your logfiles on a regular basis.

Shutting Down the Web Server

To shut down the Web server, send a HUP signal, which causes the program to reread its configuration files, and a TERM signal, which causes it to die gracefully. If the process dies (or is killed) abnormally, then it will be necessary to kill the children **httpd** processes.

Virtual Host Support

So far in this chapter we've discussed a model where you have one domain on one machine. However, you have the potential to have multiple domains on a single machine. This can come in handy if you're planning on being some sort of Internet server provider, where you provide Web pages and access to multiple persons and corporations.

For instance, your machine may have a domain name of *www.kreichard.com*, and you want to add your family members' own domain names for their usage: *www.jreichard.com* and *www.sreichard.com*. It might be easier just to give them their own locations on the file system (like *www.kreichard.com/julie* and *www.kreichard.com/steve*), but familial pride dictates that they have their own domain names. (Companies will want to have their own domain name for more mundane and capitalistic reasons: identification and mind share.) Since many small companies and family members won't want to go through the fuss of setting up their own servers and Internet connections, you jump in to solve the problem.

The answer here to set up virtual hosts. You go ahead and register *www.jreichard.com* and *www.sreichard.com* with InterNIC, but those names are actually housed on your Linux server. Because of some technical issues in the basic HTTP protocol, a Web server cannot answer to different domain-name requests with the same IP address, so each virtual host must have a different IP address.

Before you do this, you'll need to recompile your Linux kernel to allow Apache virtual hosts. The source code and any modules for doing so are on the accompanying CD-ROM (under **/usr/source**). It's actually a fairly easy thing to do, as you saw in Chapter 3. Aram Mirzadeh (*awm@qosina.com*) has compiled the following instructions for setting up virtual hosts on a Linux system:

1. Recompile the kernel, with the *IP Aliasing* and *IP Routing* options.

2. Use the following lines to add new IPs to your system:

```
insmod /usr/src/linux/modules/ip_alias.o
ifconfig eth0:0 www.foo.com
route add -host www.foo.com dev eth0:0
```

substituting your hostname for *www.foo.com*, of course.

3. Add *<virtual host 200.200.200.50>* ... *</virtualhost>* to your **httpd.conf** file. Here is an example:

```
<VirtualHost www.virtual.com>
ServerAdmin webmaster@real.com
DocumentRoot /usr/local/etc/httpd/virtual
ServerName www.virtual.com
ScriptAlias /cgi-bin/ /usr/local/etc/httpd/cgi-virtual
ErrorLog logs/virtual-error_log
TransferLog logs/virtual-access_log
</VirtualHost>
```

Configuring DNS to Run Apache Virtual Hosts

You'll then need to set up a DNS system for multiple domains. Again, these instructions are from Aram Mirzadeh (*awm@qosina.com*). It really doesn't have to be virtual, but it's the same procedure.

Here is my **/etc/named.boot** file, which is read in by **bind** to set up the location of the files:

```
directory        /var/named

; type           domain                      source host/file    backup

cache            .                           root.cache

primary          0.0.127.IN-ADDR.ARPA        db.127.0.0
primary          qosina.com                  db.qosina
primary          187.64.206.IN-ADDR.ARPA     db.206.64.187
primary          qosmedix.com                db.qosmedix   <<- virtual
primary          qosinet.com                 db.qosinet
primary          .                           db.cache

secondary        mis.qosina.com              db.mis
```

The cache file (**root.cache**) is the output of the following command:

```
dig @ns.internic.net ns > /var/named/db.cache
```

It should look something like the following:

```
; <<>> DiG 2.1 <<>> @ns.internic.net ns
; (1 server found)
;; res options: init recurs defnam dnsrch
;; got answer:
;; ->>HEADER<<- opcode: QUERY, status: NOERROR, id: 10
;; flags: qr aa rd; Ques: 1, Ans: 9, Auth: 0, Addit: 9
;; QUESTIONS:
;;       ., type = NS, class = IN

;; ANSWERS:
.       518400  NS      D.ROOT-SERVERS.NET.
.       518400  NS      E.ROOT-SERVERS.NET.
.       518400  NS      I.ROOT-SERVERS.NET.
.       518400  NS      F.ROOT-SERVERS.NET.
.       518400  NS      G.ROOT-SERVERS.NET.
.       518400  NS      A.ROOT-SERVERS.NET.
.       518400  NS      H.ROOT-SERVERS.NET.
.       518400  NS      B.ROOT-SERVERS.NET.
.       518400  NS      C.ROOT-SERVERS.NET.
```

```
;; ADDITIONAL RECORDS:
D.ROOT-SERVERS.NET.        518400    A        128.8.10.90
E.ROOT-SERVERS.NET.        518400    A        192.203.230.10
I.ROOT-SERVERS.NET.        518400    A        192.36.148.17
F.ROOT-SERVERS.NET.        518400    A        192.5.5.241
G.ROOT-SERVERS.NET.        518400    A        192.112.36.4
A.ROOT-SERVERS.NET.        518400    A        198.41.0.4
H.ROOT-SERVERS.NET.        518400    A        128.63.2.53
B.ROOT-SERVERS.NET.        518400    A        128.9.0.107
C.ROOT-SERVERS.NET.        518400    A        192.33.4.12


;; Total query time: 118 msec
;; FROM: luers.qosina.com to SERVER: ns.internic.net  198.41.0.4
;; WHEN: Mon Nov 27 18:55:12 1995
;; MSG SIZE   sent: 17  rcvd: 312
```

Next, let's look at the real domain:

```
/var/named/qosina.com:

@ IN SOA luers.qosina.com. hostmaster.qosina.com. (
                              96031801        ; Serial  <<- (*)
                              10800           ; Refresh
                              3600            ; Retry
                              604800          ; Expire
                              86400)          ; Minimum TTL
; - * - This is the serial number of the file.  Whenever a change is made
; you need to update this number to a higher number, and restart your bind
; program for the changes to become effective.  This number is also used
; by your secondary servers to update their records.   It is very important
; to keep good track of this number, I use YYMMDD## as my serial number.
;
; Name Servers
;
                IN NS    ns.qosina.com.
                IN NS    auth00.NS.UU.NET.
                IN NS    auth01.NS.UU.NET.

;
; Just to keep sendmail happy
localhost       IN A     127.0.0.1
```

```
;
; Addresses for the canonical names
luers           IN A    206.64.187.10
                IN MX   10 luers.qosina.com.
                IN MX   15 mail.qosina.com.
                IN MX   20 mail.uu.net.
mail            IN A    206.64.187.11
                IN MX   15 mail.qosina.com.
                IN MX   20 mail.uu.net.
machines1       IN A    206.64.187.40
                IN MX   10 luers.qosina.com.
                IN MX   15 mail.qosina.com.
                IN MX   20 mail.uu.net.
...
machines20      IN MX   206.64.187.60
                IN MX   10 luers.qosina.com.
                IN MX   15 mail.qosina.com.
                IN MX   20 mail.uu.net.
;
; Aliases and CNAMES
qosina.com.     IN A          206.64.187.10
ftp             IN CNAME      qosina.com.
www             IN CNAME      qosina.com.
```

Now the other domain (in this case the virtual domain) is

```
/var/named/virtual.com:
```

Remember that we now have 2 IPs on the same machine. Our real IP is 206.65.187.10. We're not inventing another machine with a different IP, but because we set up the *dummy0* routing as well as *arp*, the requests for the virutal IP *206.64.187.25* will also arrive at this machine:

```
@ IN  SOA virtual.qosmedix.com. hostmaster.qosmedix.com. ( <<-
                        95110501        ; Serial
                        10800           ; Refresh after 3 hours
                        3600            ; Retry after 1 hour
                        604800          ; Expire after 1 week
                        86400)          ; Minimum TTL of 1 day
;
```

```
; Name Servers
;
                IN NS   luers.qosina.com.
                IN NS   auth00.ns.uu.net.
                IN NS   auth01.ns.uu.net.
;
; Addresses for the canonical names
;
virtual         IN A    206.64.187.25              <<—
                IN MX   10 luers.qosina.com.
                IN MX   15 mail.qosina.com.
                IN MX   20 mail.uu.net.
;
; Just to make sure sendmail is happy
localhost       IN A    127.0.0.1


;
; Aliases, and CNAMES
;
qosmedix.com    IN A         206.64.187.25         <<—
ftp             IN CNAME     qosmedix.com.         <<—
www             IN CNAME     qosmedix.com.         <<—
```

And lastly we need to do the reverse lookups for all our domains since they're on the same C-class network. Using the following command:

```
/var/named/db.206.64.187
```

we get something like the following:

```
@ IN SOA luers.qosina.com. hostmaster.qosina.com. (
                96031501        ; Serial
                10800           ; Refresh
                3600            ; Retry
                604800          ; Expire
                86400 )         ; Minimum TTL
        IN      NS      luers.qosina.com.
        IN      NS      auth00.NS.UU.NET.
        IN      NS      auth01.NS.UU.NET.
10      IN      PTR     luers.qosina.com.
11      IN      PTR     mail.qosina.com.
25      IN      PTR     virtual.qosmedix.com.     <<—
40      IN      PTR     machine1.qosina.com.
...
60      IN      PTR     machine20.qosina.com.
```

The remaining local.host file looks like the following: (no changes needed for multiple domains):
/var/named/db.127.0.0:

```
@       IN      SOA     luers.qosina.com. hostmaster.qosina.com. (
                        95110801        ; Serial
                        10800           ; Refresh
                        3600            ; Retry
                        604800          ; Expire
                        86400 )         ; Minimum
        IN      NS      luers.qosina.com.
        IN      NS      auth00.NS.UU.NET.
        IN      NS      auth01.NS.UU.NET.
1       IN      PTR     localhost.
```

Here is just another sidenote. The preceding domains are getting to Internet via **UUNET/Alternet**, hence the secondary NS records for UU.NET, as well as MX records for mail.UU.NET. If you're not dealing with UUNET then these must also change.

If you had multiple domains as well as multiple C-class addresses, then you would break up the reverse lookups for each domain depending on their C-class address. You'll also need another line in the named boot file with the reverse lookup of the particular address (in arpa format *c.b.a.in-addr.arpa*).

Setting Up Apache

Now that Slackware Linux is set up to support multiple hosts, it's time to configure Apache to support multiple hosts: by running a separate **httpd** program for each hostname or by running a single **httpd** that services all the hostnames.

The Apache group suggests that multiple **httpd** daemons be run when the different virtual hosts need very different **httpd** configurations, such as different values for *ServerType, User, Group, TypesConfig,* or *ServerRoot,* and the machine does not process a very high request rate. Conversely, the Apache group suggests using a single daemon when sharing the **httpd** configuration between virtual hosts is acceptable (which will probably be the case when you're an ISP and are servicing many different clients or when the machine services a large number of requests), and so the performance loss in running separate daemons may be significant.

The following instructions are part of the Apache documentation.

Setting Up Multiple Daemons

Begin by creating a separate **httpd** installation for each virtual host. For each installation, use the *BindAddress* directive in the configuration file to select which IP address (or virtual host) that daemon services, such as:

```
BindAddress www.smallco.com
```

This hostname can also be given as an IP address.

Setting Up a Single Daemon

For this case, a single **httpd** will service requests for all the virtual hosts. The *VirtualHost* directive in the configuration file is used to set the values of *ServerAdmin*, *ServerName*, *DocumentRoot*, *ErrorLog*, and *TransferLog* configuration directives to different values for each virtual host. These would set up virtual hosts *www.smallco.com* and *www.baygroup.org*:

```
<VirtualHost www.smallco.com>
ServerAdmin webmaster@mail.smallco.com
DocumentRoot /groups/smallco/www
ServerName www.smallco.com
ErrorLog /groups/smallco/logs/error_log
TransferLog /groups/smallco/logs/access_log
</VirtualHost>

<VirtualHost www.baygroup.org>
ServerAdmin webmaster@mail.baygroup.org
DocumentRoot /groups/baygroup/www
ServerName www.baygroup.org
ErrorLog /groups/baygroup/logs/error_log
TransferLog /groups/baygroup/logs/access_log
</VirtualHost>
```

This *VirtualHost* hostnames can also be given as IP addresses.

Almost any configuration directive can be put in the *VirtualHost* directive, with the exception of *ServerType*, *User*, *Group*, *StartServers*, *MaxSpareServers*, *MinSpareServers*, *MaxRequestsPerChild*, *BindAddress*, *PidFile*, *TypesConfig*, and *ServerRoot*.

File Handle/Resource Limits

When using a large number of virtual hosts, Apache may run out of available file descriptors if each virtual host specifies different log files. The total number of file descriptors used by Apache is one for each distinct error log file, one for every other log file directive, plus 10-20 for internal use. UNIX operating systems limit the number of file descriptors that may be used by a process; the limit is typically 64 and may usually be increased up to a large hard-limit.

Although Apache attempts to increase the limit as required, this may not work if the number of file descriptors required exceeds the hard limit. In the event of problems you can reduce the number of log files by not specifying log files in the *VirtualHost* sections and logging everything to the main log files. In this case, increase the file descriptor limit before starting Apache, using a script like:

```
#!/bin/sh
ulimit -S -n 100
exec httpd
```

There have been reports that Apache may start running out of resources allocated for the root process. This will exhibit itself as errors in the error log like *unable to fork*. There are two ways you can bump this up:

1. Have a **csh** script wrapper around **httpd** that sets the *rlimit* to some large number, like 512.

2. Edit **http_main.c** to add calls to *setrlimit()* from *main()*, along the lines of:

```
struct rlimit rlp;

rlp.rlim_cur = rlp.rlim_max = 512;
    if (setrlimit(RLIMIT_NPROC, &rlp)) {
    fprintf(stderr, "setrlimit(RLIMIT_NPROC) failed.\n");
exit(1);
}
```

Configuring Sendmail to Run Apache Virtual Hosts

With virtual hosts come virtual mailboxes. You'll need to set up **sendmail** (provided you're actually using **sendmail**, of course; there's more on this in Chapter 8) to accept virtual hosts. The following solution was posted to the Usenet newsgroup *comp.mail.sendmail* by *johan@josnet.se.*

WARNING Playing with **sendmail** files is pretty evil. If you're not quite sure about this solution, don't be mucking around in **sendmail** configuration files.

First, let's create the file that is going to tell **sendmail** which e-mails to accept and where to send them:

```
/etc/maildb/domainaliases:      ( a text file )
fake@virtual.com        real@realdomain.com
dude@mydomain.com       dude@realdomain.com
dudett@otherdom.edu     aaa@other.provider.com
root@virtual.org        awm
root@virtual.com        awm
root@mydomain.com       awm
hostmaster@mydomain.com awm
```

Compile **makemap** with the following options:

```
# cd /usr/src/sendmail-8.7.x/makemap
# rm Makefile makemap
# make CFLAGS='-m486 -O2 -I../src -DNDBM -DNEWDB' LDFLAGS='-s -lgdbm -ldb' makemap
# cp makemap /usr/bin
```

Let's let **sendmail** know that extra domains are coming:

```
Cw mydomain.com virtual.com
```

Compile the domainaliases to a database format:

```
# cd /usr/maildb
# makemap hash domainaliases < domainaliases
# makemap dbm domainaliases < domainaliases
# makemap btree domainaliases < domainalisaes
```

If you see a message like *not supported*, then go back a step and recompile the **makemap** program as instructed. Also remember which database type you used, as you have to tell **sendmail** which one it is.

Now let's tell **sendmail** about the file. In **/etc/sendmail.cf** add the following line, right after the DM entry. Pick one, whichever db you used above.

```
Kdomainaliases hash /etc/maildb/domainaliases.db
Kdomainaliases dbm -o /etc/maildb/domainaliases
Kdomainaliases btree /etc/maildb/domainaliases
```

Now for the rule-set—make sure you type it exactly. The entries are separated by a tab field, not spaces. These are to be inserted inside the S98 Ruleset:

```
PRE 8.7.1

R$+   < @ $+ . >          $: $1 < @ $2 > .
R$+   < @ $+ . > $*       $: (domainaliases $1@$2 $: $1 < @ $2 > $3 $)
R$+   < @ $+ . > $*       $: (domainaliases $2 $: $1 < @ $2 > $3 $)
R$+   < @ $+ > .          $: $1 < @ $2 . >


 POST 8.7.1

R$+< $+. >                $1< $2 >
R$+< $+ >                 $: < > $(domainaliases $1$2 $)
R< > $+ @ $*              $: < $1 > $(domainaliases * @ $2 $)
R< $+ > * $*              $: < > $1 $2
R< > $*                   $: $>3 $1
```

Now, you have to restart your **sendmail** daemon to grab the new configuration. Lastly, you need to test the new configuration files (be sure to check your **/var/log/maillog** file for any messages):

```
# sendmail -bt
ADDRESS TEST MODE (ruleset 3 NOT automatically invoked)
Enter <ruleset> <address>
> 0 fake@virtual.com
rewrite: ruleset  0    input: fake @ virtual . com
rewrite: ruleset 98    input: fake @ virtual . com
rewrite: ruleset 98  returns: fake @ virtual . com
rewrite: ruleset 97    input: fake @ virtual . com
rewrite: ruleset  3    input: fake @ virtual . com
rewrite: ruleset 96    input: real < @ virtual . com >
rewrite: ruleset 96  returns: real < @ virtual . com . >
rewrite: ruleset  3  returns: real < @ virtual . com . >
rewrite: ruleset  0    input: real < @ virtual . com . >
rewrite: ruleset 98    input: real < @ virtual . com . >
rewrite: ruleset 98  returns: fake @ realdomain . com
rewrite: ruleset 97    input: fake @ realdomain . com
rewrite: ruleset  3    input: fake @ realdomain . com
rewrite: ruleset 96    input: real < @ realdomain . com >
rewrite: ruleset 96  returns: real < @ realdomain . com . >
rewrite: ruleset  3  returns: real < @ realdomain . com . >
rewrite: ruleset  0    input: real < @ realdomain . com . >
rewrite: ruleset 98    input: real < @ realdomain . com . >
rewrite: ruleset 98  returns: real < @ realdomain . com . >
rewrite: ruleset  0  returns: $# local $: @ real
rewrite: ruleset 97  returns: $# local $: @ real
rewrite: ruleset  0  returns: $# local $: @ real
rewrite: ruleset 97  returns: $# local $: @ real
rewrite: ruleset  0  returns: $# local $: @ real
```

This has been tested on **sendmail** 8.7.1 to 8.7.3.

Non-IP Virtual Hosting

Apache has always supported using multiple IPs on the same server, and by and large this approach works fairly well. However, reports of a shortage of IP addresses on the Internet have become a little too prevalent to be dismissed out of hand, and some solutions have been implemented in the Internet world. For instance, the HTTP 1.1 protocol allows a server to identify what hostname is being addressed (this wasn't true in the old days). The version of the Apache Web server that ships as Slackware Linux addresses the issue by supporting the HTTP 1.1 protocol, as well as the older (and still perfectly satisfactory) IP-address-per-hostname method.

Of course, not all Internet software supports HTTP 1.1 standards. Most newer Web browsers do, such as Netscape Navigator 2.0 and better, and by and large these server make up the majority of Web browsers on the market. (The version of Arena on the accompanying CD-ROM meets HTTP 1.1 standards.) Users of older browsers and nongraphical browsers do not meet HTTP 1.1 standards, but there are some ways to work around it.

 NOTE You must already have your DNS and Sendmail issues resolved, before you can continue with this section. There is no Ethernet section because you don't need routing. Your main server will take care of it. Please consult those pages on the cookbook examples. The only difference is that in your DNS table, you need to use the same IP for your virtual domain as your main server, instead of giving it a new IP.

The first step is to make sure you're running Apache 1.1b1 or later. You can either send a HEAD request to your **httpd** process or type **httpd -v** at a command line to get the version number of your server. After you have verified this information, you continue. Make sure that you have full access to your configuration files (in **/var/local/etc/httpd/conf/**).

First, you need to add the name of the host to your DNS table. If you're going to do virtual hosting, it is very important to run a local primary DNS for those domains. Your goal is to make the IP of your new domain the same IP as your main server. Also make sure InterNIC knows about your domain.

Next we need to let the **httpd** server know which hosts to answer and with which files to answer the requests with. In your **httpd.conf** file add the following lines:

```
ServerName www.virtual.com
ServerAlias virtual.com *.virtual.com
DocumentRoot /usr/local/etc/httpd/web/virtual/
...
```

Now you can add other variables/directives in this section to create a **cgi-bin** directory for the virtual hosts' use. Now let's make sure that all the browsers out there can get to our new site. Add the following to your **httpd.conf** file (outside of the virtual host section) usually in the top of the file. This will allow our site to be viewed either as *http://www.virtual.com* or as *http://www.virtual.com/virtual/*:

```
Alias /virtual /usr/local/etc/httpd/web/virtual/
```

With respect to creating links and/or anchors when doing HTML programming for the new host, you could either use relative links or have the **/virtual/** as the first path before addressing anything.

Here is an example of a full section in **httpd.conf**:

```
<VirtualHost www.qosmedix.com>
ServerAdmin webmaster@qosmedix.com
DocumentRoot /usr/local/etc/httpd/qosmedix
ServerName www.qosmedix.com
ScriptAlias /cgi-bin/ /usr/local/etc/httpd/cgi-qox
ErrorLog logs/qosmedix-error_log
AddType application/x-httpd-cgi .cgi
TransferLog logs/qosmedix-access_log
</VirtualHost>
```

Here's what you need to add to **access.conf**:

```
<Directory /usr/local/etc/httpd/qosmedix>
    Options Indexes FollowSymLinks Includes
    AllowOverride All
    <Limit GET>
        order allow,deny
        allow from all
    </Limit>
</Directory>
```

Other Versions of Apache

You do have the option of compiling and installing a different version of the Apache Web server. There's always the chance that the latest version will be better suited to your needs. If you want to check for a newer version, simply point your Web browser to *http://www.apache.org/*, where the latest versions are available for download. There are directions at the Apache Web site for recompiling the Web server. It's actually rather simple.

You can install the Apache Web server after grabbing it from the Internet. Begin by moving the file from where you download it.

```
cd /cdrom/internet
```

You can move the file with the following command line:

```
cp apache_1_1.tar /usr/local/etc
```

In this example we're moving the file to **/usr/local/etc**. You can substitute your own location.

> You may have a different archive filename if you grabbed the source code directly from the Apache Web site.

N O T E

You'll then unarchive the file using the **tar** command and the appropriate options:

```
tar -xvf apache_1_1.tar
```

The **tar** command will tell you what it's doing (the purpose of the *v*, or verbose, option), setting up directories and unarchiving files. It will create a main Apache directory called **apache_1_1**. Within this directory there's a directory containing source code, entitled **/src**. Make this directory your current directory.

Like most UNIX software there days, Apache uses a **makefile** to configure settings for specific hardware and software settings. This means that you'll need to edit a file called **Configure** to make the installation specific to Linux. There really aren't many lines to edit. You'll need to make sure that you're using the GNU C compiler by editing the *CC* line as follows:

```
CC=gcc
```

You'll also need to change the defaults to Linux instead of Solaris.

There are also some other things in the **Configure** file that you'll need to change, depending on what modules you are using. For a basic installation, you can go ahead with the **Configure** file you have. Later in this chapter you'll learn about modules and adding functionality to the Apache Web server.

With these simple tasks completed, you can run the **configure** script and then run **make**:

```
configure
make
```

 The compiled Apache Web server on the accompanying CD-ROM is the basic and most recent version. The more recent Apache versions have included optional modules, which add functionality to the Web server. However, you may find that the optional modules can better suit your needs. Check the Apache Web site (*http://www.apache.org/*) for a listing of the optional modules. In addition, we'll revisit the topic later in this chapter.

If you reinstall the Apache Web server, you'll notice that there are different file locations set up for most functions. If you're installing over an existing installation, you'll need to either edit your configuration files to match the new file locations or move the files to the old file locations. Or you could just alias the old locations to the new locations (the simplest solution of all, although you shouldn't have too many aliases on your Linux system).

Apache API Notes

The following is of interest to those who want to add functionality to the Apache Web server through the addition of specific modules. The information should also be of interest to anyone who wants to delve into the depths of the Apache Web server. It's taken from the Apache online documentation.

These are some notes on the Apache API and the data structures you have to deal with. They are not yet nearly complete, but they will help you get your bearings. Keep in mind that the API is still subject to change as we gain experience with it. (See the **TODO** file for what might be coming). However, it will be easy to adapt modules to any changes that are made. (We have more modules to adapt than you do.)

Here are a few notes on general pedagogical style. In the interest of conciseness, all structure declarations here are incomplete—the real ones have more slots. For the most part, these are reserved to one component of the server core or another and should be altered by modules with caution.

Basic Concepts

We begin with an overview of the basic concepts behind the API and how they are manifested in the code.

Handlers, Modules, and Requests

Apache breaks down request handling into a series of steps, more or less the same way the Netscape server API does (although this API has a few more stages than NetSite does, as hooks for stuff that might be useful in the future). These are:

- URI -> filename translation
- *Auth* id checking (Is the user who he says he is?)
- *Auth* access checking (Is the user authorized here?)
- Access checking other than *auth*
- Determining MIME type of the object requested
- Fixups—there aren't any of these yet, but the phase is intended as a hook for possible extensions like *SetEnv*, which don't really fit well elsewhere.
- Actually sending a response back to the client
- Logging the request

These phases are handled by looking at each of a succession of modules, looking to see if each of them has a handler for the phase, and attempting to invoke it if so. The handler can typically do one of three things:

- Handle the request and indicate that it has done so by returning the magic constant OK.
- Decline to handle the request, by returning the magic integer constant *DECLINED*. In this case, the server behaves in all respects as if the handler simply hadn't been there.

- Signal an error by returning one of the HTTP error codes. This terminates normal handling of the request, although an *ErrorDocument* may be invoked to try to mop up, and it will be logged in any case.

Most phases are terminated by the first module that handles them; however, for logging, fixups, and nonaccess authentication checking, all handlers always run (barring an error). Also, the response phase is unique in that modules may declare multiple handlers for it, via a dispatch table keyed on the MIME type of the requested object. Modules may declare a response-phase handler that can handle any request, by giving it the key */* (i.e., a wildcard MIME type specification). However, wildcard handlers are only invoked if the server has already tried and failed to find a more specific response handler for the MIME type of the requested object (either none existed, or they all declined).

The handlers themselves are functions of one argument (like a *request_rec* structure), which returns an integer, as mentioned previously.

A Brief Tour of a Module

At this point, we need to explain the structure of a module. Our candidate will be one of the messier ones, the CGI module—this handles both CGI scripts and the *ScriptAlias* config file command. It's actually a great deal more complicated than most modules, but if we're going to have only one example, it might as well be the one with its fingers everywhere.

Let's begin with handlers. In order to handle the CGI scripts, the module declares a response handler for them. Because of *ScriptAlias*, it also has handlers for the name translation phase (to recognize *ScriptAlias*ed URIs) and the type-checking phase (any *ScriptAlias*ed request is typed as a CGI script).

The module needs to maintain some per (virtual) server information, namely, the *ScriptAlias*es in effect; the module structure therefore contains pointers to a function that builds these structures and to another that combines two of them (in case the main server and a virtual server both have *ScriptAlias*es declared).

Finally, this module contains code to handle the *ScriptAlias* command itself. This particular module declares only one command, but there could be more, so modules have command tables which declare their commands, and describe where they are permitted, and how they are to be invoked.

Here is a final note on the declared types of the arguments of some of these commands. A pool is a pointer to a resource pool structure; these are used by the server to keep track of the memory which has been allocated, files opened, etc., either to service a particular request or to handle the process of configuring itself. That way, when the request is over (or, for the configuration pool, when the server is restarting), the memory can be freed, and the files closed, en masse, without anyone having to write explicit code to track them all down and dispose of them. Also, a *cmd_parms* structure contains various information about the config file being read, and other status information, which is sometimes of use to the function that processes a config file command (such as *ScriptAlias*). With no further ado, here is the module itself:

```
/* Declarations of handlers. */

int translate_scriptalias (request_rec *);
int type_scriptalias (request_rec *);
int cgi_handler (request_rec *);


/* Subsidiary dispatch table for response-phase handlers, by MIME type
 */

handler_rec cgi_handlers[] = {
{ "application/x-httpd-cgi", cgi_handler },
{ NULL }
};


/* Declarations of routines to manipulate the module's configuration
 * info.  Note that these are returned, and passed in, as void *'s;
 * the server core keeps track of them, but it doesn't, and can't,
 * know their internal structure.
 */

void *make_cgi_server_config (pool *);
void *merge_cgi_server_config (pool *, void *, void *);
```

```
/* Declarations of routines to handle config file commands */

extern char *script_alias(cmd_parms *, void *per_dir_config, char
*fake,
                          char *real);

command_rec cgi_cmds[] = {
{ "ScriptAlias", script_alias, NULL, RSRC_CONF, TAKE2,
    "a fakename and a realname"},
{ NULL }
};

module cgi_module = {
    STANDARD_MODULE_STUFF,
    NULL,                       /* initializer */
    NULL,                       /* dir config creator */
    NULL,                       /* dir merger -- default is to override
*/
    make_cgi_server_config,     /* server config */
    merge_cgi_server_config,    /* merge server config */
    cgi_cmds,                   /* command table */
    cgi_handlers,               /* handlers */
    translate_scriptalias,      /* filename translation */
    NULL,                       /* check_user_id */
    NULL,                       /* check auth */
    NULL,                       /* check access */
    type_scriptalias,           /* type_checker */
    NULL,                       /* fixups */
    NULL                        /* logger */
};
```

How Handlers Work

The sole argument to handlers is a *request_rec* structure. This structure
describes a particular request that has been made to the server on behalf
of a client. In most cases, each connection to the client generates only
one *request_rec* structure.

A Brief Tour of the Request_rec

The *request_rec* contains pointers to a resource pool that will be cleared
when the server is finished handling the request; to structures

containing per-server and per-connection information, and most importantly, to information on the request itself.

The most important such information is a small set of character strings describing attributes of the object being requested, including its URI, filename, content-type and content-encoding (these being filled in by the translation and type-check handlers that handle the request, respectively).

Other commonly used data items are tables giving the MIME headers on the client's original request, MIME headers to be sent back with the response (which modules can add to at will), and environment variables for any subprocesses that are spawned off in the course of servicing the request. These tables are manipulated using the *table_get* and *table_set* routines.

Finally, there are pointers to two data structures which, in turn, point to per-module configuration structures. Specifically, these hold pointers to the data structures that the module has built to describe the way it has been configured to operate in a given directory (via **.htaccess** files or *<Directory>* sections), for private data it has built in the course of servicing the request (so modules' handlers for one phase can pass notes to their handlers for other phases). There is another such configuration vector in the *server_rec* data structure pointed to by the *request_rec*, which contains per (virtual) server configuration data.

Here is an abridged declaration, giving the fields most commonly used:

```
struct request_rec {

  pool *pool;
  conn_rec *connection;
  server_rec *server;

  /* What object is being requested */

  char *uri;
  char *filename;
  char *path_info;
  char *args;          /* QUERY_ARGS, if any */
  struct stat finfo;   /* Set by server core;
                        * st_mode set to zero if no such file */
```

```
char *content_type;
char *content_encoding;

/* MIME header environments, in and out.  Also, an array containing
 * environment variables to be passed to subprocesses, so people can
 * write modules to add to that environment.
 *
 * The difference between headers_out and err_headers_out is that
 * the latter are printed even on error and persist across internal
 * redirects (so the headers printed for ErrorDocument handlers will
 * have them).
 */

table *headers_in;
table *headers_out;
table *err_headers_out;
table *subprocess_env;

/* Info about the request itself... */

int header_only;      /* HEAD request, as opposed to GET */
char *protocol;       /* Protocol, as given to us, or HTTP/0.9 */
char *method;         /* GET, HEAD, POST, etc. */
int method_number;    /* M_GET, M_POST, etc. */

/* Info for logging */

char *the_request;
int bytes_sent;

/* A flag that modules can set, to indicate that the data being
 * returned are volatile, and clients should be told not to cache
it.
 */

int no_cache;

/* Various other config info which may change with .htaccess files
 * These are config vectors, with one void* pointer for each module
 * (the thing pointed to being the module's business).
 */

void *per_dir_config;    /* Options set in config files, etc. */
void *request_config;    /* Notes on *this* request */

};
```

Where Request_rec Structures Come from

Most *request_rec* structures are built by reading an HTTP request from a client and filling in the fields. However, there are a few exceptions:

- If the request is to an imagemap, a type map (i.e., a ***.var** file), or a CGI script which returned a local *Location:*, then the resource that the user requested is going to be ultimately located by some URI other than what the client originally supplied. In this case, the server does an internal redirect, constructing a new *request_rec* for the new URI, and processing it almost exactly as if the client had requested the new URI directly.

- If some handler signaled an error and an *ErrorDocument* is in scope, the same internal redirect machinery comes into play.

Finally, a handler occasionally needs to investigate what would happen if some other request were run. For instance, the directory indexing module needs to know what MIME type would be assigned to a request for each directory entry, in order to figure out what icon to use.

Such handlers can construct a subrequest, using the functions *sub_req_lookup_file* and *sub_req_lookup_uri*; this constructs a new *request_rec* structure and processes it as you would expect, up to but not including the point of actually sending a response. (These functions skip over the access checks if the subrequest is for a file in the same directory as the original request.)

(Server-side includes work by building subrequests and then actually invoking the response handler for them, via the function *run_sub_request*).

Handling Requests, Declining, and Returning Error Codes

As already discussed, each handler, when invoked to handle a particular *request_rec*, has to return an *int* to indicate what happened. That can be *OK* (the request was handled successfully; this may or may not terminate the phase), *DECLINED* (no erroneous condition exists, but the module declines to handle the phase; the server tries to find another), or an HTTP error code, which aborts handling of the request.

Note that if the error code returned is *REDIRECT*, then the module should put a *Location* in the request's *headers_out* to indicate where the client should be redirected to.

Special Considerations for Response Handlers

Handlers for most phases do their work by simply setting a few fields in the *request_rec* structure (or, in the case of access checkers, simply by returning the correct error code). However, response handlers have to actually send a request back to the client.

They should begin by sending an HTTP response header, using the function *send_http_header*. (You don't have to do anything special to skip sending the header for HTTP/0.9 requests; the function figures out on its own that it shouldn't do anything.) If the request is marked *header_only*, that's all they should do; they should return after that, without attempting any further output.

Otherwise, they should produce a request body that responds to the client as appropriate. The primitives for this are *rputc* and *rprintf* for internally generated output, and *send_fd* to copy the contents of some *FILE ** straight to the client.

At this point, you should more or less understand the following piece of code, which is the handler that handles GET requests that have no more specific handler; it also shows how conditional GETs can be handled, if it's desirable to do so in a particular response handler—*set_last_modified* checks against the *If-modified-since* value supplied by the client, if any, and returns an appropriate code (which will, if nonzero, be *USE_LOCAL_COPY*). No similar considerations apply for *set_content_length*, but it returns an error code for symmetry:

```
int default_handler (request_rec *r)
{
    int errstatus;
    FILE *f;

    if (r->method_number != M_GET) return DECLINED;
    if (r->finfo.st_mode == 0) return NOT_FOUND;
```

```
    if ((errstatus = set_content_length (r, r->finfo.st_size))
        || (errstatus = set_last_modified (r, r->finfo.st_mtime)))
        return errstatus;

    f = fopen (r->filename, "r");

    if (f == NULL) {
        log_reason("file permissions deny server access",
                   r->filename, r);
        return FORBIDDEN;
    }

    register_timeout ("send", r);
    send_http_header (r);

    if (!r->header_only) send_fd (f, r);
    pfclose (r->pool, f);
    return OK;
}
```

Finally, if all this is too much of a challenge, there are a few ways out of it. First off, as shown previously, a response handler that has not yet produced any output can simply return an error code, in which case the server will automatically produce an error response. Secondly, it can punt to some other handler by invoking *internal_redirect*, which is how the internal redirection machinery already discussed is invoked. A response handler that has internally redirected should always return OK.

(Invoking *internal_redirect* from handlers that are not response handlers will lead to serious confusion.)

Special Considerations for Logging Handlers

When a request has internally redirected, there is the question of what to log. Apache handles this by bundling the entire chain of redirects into a list of *request_rec* structures that are threaded through the *r->prev* and *r->next* pointers. The *request_rec* passed to the logging handlers in such cases is the one that was originally built for the initial request from the client; note that the *bytes_sent* field will only be correct in the last request in the chain (the one for which a response was actually sent).

Resource Allocation and Resource Pools

One of the problems of writing and designing a server-pool server is that of preventing leakage, that is, allocating resources (memory, open files, etc.) without subsequently releasing them. The resource pool machinery is designed to make it easy to prevent this from happening, by allowing resource to be allocated in such a way that they are automatically released when the server is done with them.

This works in the following way: the memory which is allocated, file opened, and the like, to deal with a particular request are tied to a resource pool which is allocated for the request. The pool is a data structure which itself tracks the resources in question.

When the request has been processed, the pool is cleared. At that point, all the memory associated with it is released for reuse, all files associated with it are closed, and any other clean-up functions associated with the pool are run. When this is over, we can be confident that all the resource tied to the pool have been released and that none of them have leaked.

Server restarts, and allocation of memory and resources for per-server configuration, are handled in a similar way. A configuration pool keeps track of resources allocated while reading the server configuration files and handling the commands therein (for instance, the memory that was allocated for per-server module configuration, log files, and other files that were opened). When the server restarts and has to reread the configuration files, the configuration pool is cleared, and so the memory and file descriptors that were taken up by reading them the last time are made available for reuse.

It should be noted that use of the pool machinery isn't generally obligatory, except for situations like logging handlers, where you really need to register cleanups to make sure that the log file gets closed when the server restarts (this is most easily done by using the function *pfopen*, which also arranges for the underlying file descriptor to be closed before any child processes, such as for CGI scripts, are exceeded), or in case you are using the timeout machinery (which isn't documented here). However, there are two benefits to using it: Resources allocated to a pool never leak (even if you allocate a scratch string, and just forget about it), and for memory allocation, *palloc* is generally faster than *malloc*.

We begin here by describing how memory is allocated to pools and then discuss how other resources are tracked by the resource pool machinery.

Allocation of Memory in Pools

Memory is allocated to pools by calling the function *palloc*, which takes two arguments, one being a pointer to a resource pool structure and the other being the amount of memory to allocate (in chars). Within handlers for handling requests, the most common way of getting a resource pool structure is by looking at the pool slot of the relevant *request_rec*; hence, the repeated appearance of the following idiom in module code:

```
int my_handler(request_rec *r)
{
    struct my_structure *foo;
    ...

    foo = (foo *)palloc (r->pool, sizeof(my_structure));
}
```

Note that there is no *pfree*—palloced memory is freed only when the associated resource pool is cleared. This means that *palloc* does not have to do as much accounting as *malloc()*; all it does in the typical case is to round up the size, bump a pointer, and do a range check.

It also raises the possibility that heavy use of *palloc* could cause a server process to grow excessively large. The two ways to deal with this are dealt with later; briefly, you can use *malloc* and try to be sure that all the memory gets explicitly freed, or you can allocate a subpool of the main pool, allocate your memory in the subpool, and clear it out periodically. The latter technique is discussed in the following section on subpools and is used in the directory-indexing code, in order to avoid excessive storage allocation when listing directories with thousands of files.

Allocating Initialized Memory

There are functions that allocate initialized memory and are frequently useful. The function *pcalloc* has the same interface as *palloc* but clears out the memory it allocates before it returns it. The function *pstrdup* takes a resource pool and a *char* * as arguments and allocates memory for a copy of the string the pointer points to, returning a pointer to the copy. Finally, *pstrcat* is a *varargs*-style function, which takes a pointer to a resource pool, and at least two *char* * arguments, the last of which must be NULL. It allocates enough memory to fit copies of each of the strings, as a unit; for instance,

```
pstrcat (r->pool, "foo", "/", "bar", NULL);
```

returns a pointer to 8 bytes worth of memory, initialized to **foo/bar**.

Tracking Open Files

As indicated previously, resource pools are also used to track other sorts of resources besides memory. The most common are open files. The routine which is typically used for this is *pfopen*, which takes a resource pool and two strings as arguments; the strings are the same as the typical arguments to *fopen*, like the following:

```
...
FILE *f = pfopen (r->pool, r->filename, "r");

if (f == NULL) { ... } else { ... }
```

There is also a *popenf* routine, which parallels the lower-level open system call. Both of these routines arrange for the file to be closed when the resource pool in question is cleared.

Unlike the case for memory, there are functions to close files allocated with *pfopen* and *popenf*, namely *pfclose* and *pclosef*. (This is because on many systems the number of files that a single process can have open is quite limited.) It is important to use these functions to close files allocated with *pfopen* and *popenf*, since to do otherwise could cause fatal errors on systems such as Linux, which react badly if the same *FILE** is closed more than once.

(Using the close functions is not mandatory, since the file will eventually be closed regardless, but you should consider it in cases where your module is opening, or could open, a lot of files).

Other Sorts of Resources—Cleanup Functions

On rare occasions, too-free use of *palloc()* and the associated primitives may result in undesirably profligate resource allocation. You can deal with such a case by creating a subpool, allocating within the subpool rather than the main pool and clearing or destroying the subpool, which releases the resources associated with it. (This really is a rare situation; the only case in which it comes up in the standard module set is in the case of listing directories, and then only with very large directories. Unnecessary use of the primitives discussed here can hair up your code quite a bit, with very little gain.)

The primitive for creating a subpool is *make_sub_pool*, which takes another pool (the parent pool) as an argument. When the main pool is cleared, the subpool will be destroyed. The subpool may also be cleared or destroyed at any time, by calling the functions *clear_pool* and *destroy_pool*, respectively. (The difference is that *clear_pool* frees resources associated with the pool, while *destroy_pool* also deallocates the pool itself. In the former case, you can allocate new resources within the pool, and clear it again, and so forth; in the latter case, it is simply gone.)

As a final note, subrequests have their own resource pools, which are subpools of the resource pool for the main request. The polite way to reclaim the resources associated with a subrequest that you have allocated (using the *sub_req_lookup_...* functions) is *destroy_sub_request*, which frees the resource pool. Before calling this function, be sure to copy anything that you care about which might be allocated in the subrequest's resource pool into someplace a little less volatile (for instance, the filename in its *request_rec* structure).

Again, under most circumstances, you shouldn't feel obliged to call this function; only 2 KB of memory or so are allocated for a typical subrequest, and it will be freed anyway when the main request pool is cleared. It is only when you are allocating many, many subrequests for a single main request that you should seriously consider the *destroy...* functions.

Configuration, Commands, and the Like

One of the design goals for this server was to maintain external compatibility with the NCSA 1.3 server—that is, to read the same configuration files, to process all the directives therein correctly, and in general to be a drop-in replacement for NCSA. On the other hand, another design goal was to move as much of the server's functionality into modules that have as little as possible to do with the monolithic server core. The only way to reconcile these goals is to move the handling of most commands from the central server into the modules.

However, just giving the modules command tables is not enough to divorce them completely from the server core. The server has to remember the commands in order to act on them later. That involves maintaining data private to the modules, either per-server or per-directory. Most things are per-directory, including in particular access control and authorization information, but also information on how to determine file types from suffixes, which can be modified by *AddType* and *DefaultType* directives, and so forth. In general, the governing philosophy is that anything that can be made configurable by directory should be; per-server information is generally used in the standard set of modules for information like *Alias*es and *Redirect*s, which come into play before the request is tied to a particular place in the underlying file system.

Another requirement for emulating the NCSA server is being able to handle the per-directory configuration files, generally called **.htaccess** files, even though in the NCSA server they can contain directives which have nothing at all to do with access control. Accordingly, after URI -> filename translation, but before performing any other phase, the server walks down the directory hierarchy of the underlying file system, following the translated pathname, to read any **.htaccess** files that might be present. The information which is read in then has to be merged with the applicable information from the server's own config files (either from the *<Directory>* sections in **access.conf** or from defaults in **srm.conf**, which actually behaves for most purposes almost exactly like *<Directory />*).

Finally, after having served a request involving reading **.htaccess** files, we need to discard the storage allocated for handling them. That is solved the same way it is solved wherever else similar problems come up, by tying those structures to the per-transaction resource pool.

Per-Directory Configuration Structures

Let's look out how all this plays out in *mod_mime.c*, which defines the file typing handler which emulates the NCSA server's behavior of determining file types from suffixes. What we'll be looking at, here, is the code that implements the *AddType* and *AddEncoding* commands. These commands can appear in **.htaccess** files, so they must be handled in the module's private per-directory data, which in fact consists of two separate tables for MIME types and encoding information, and is declared as follows:

```
typedef struct {
    table *forced_types;       /* Additional AddTyped stuff */
    table *encoding_types;     /* Added with AddEncoding... */
} mime_dir_config;
```

When the server is reading a configuration file or *<Directory>* section, which includes one of the MIME module's commands, it needs to create a *mime_dir_config* structure, so those commands have something to act on. It does this by invoking the function it finds in the module's *create per-dir config slot*, with two arguments: the name of the directory to which this configuration information applies (or NULL for **srm.conf**) and a pointer to a resource pool in which the allocation should happen.

If we are reading a **.htaccess** file, that resource pool is the per-request resource pool for the request; otherwise, it is a resource pool used for configuration data and cleared on restarts. Either way, it is important for the structure being created to vanish when the pool is cleared, by registering a cleanup on the pool if necessary.

For the MIME module, the *per-dir config creation* function just pallocs the structure above and creates a couple of tables to fill it. That looks like this:

```
void *create_mime_dir_config (pool *p, char *dummy)
{
    mime_dir_config *new =
      (mime_dir_config *) palloc (p, sizeof(mime_dir_config));

    new->forced_types = make_table (p, 4);
    new->encoding_types = make_table (p, 4);

    return new;
}
```

Now, suppose we've just read in a **.htaccess** file. We already have the per-directory configuration structure for the next directory up in the hierarchy. If the **.htaccess** file we just read in didn't have any *AddType* or *AddEncoding* commands, its per-directory config structure for the MIME module is still valid, and we can just use it. Otherwise, we need to merge the two structures.

To do that, the server invokes the module's per-directory config merge function, if one is present. That function takes three arguments:

the two structures being merged, and a resource pool in which to allocate the result. For the MIME module, all that needs to be done is overlay the tables from the new per-directory config structure with those from the parent:

```
void *merge_mime_dir_configs (pool *p, void *parent_dirv, void *subdirv)
{
    mime_dir_config *parent_dir = (mime_dir_config *)parent_dirv;
    mime_dir_config *subdir = (mime_dir_config *)subdirv;
    mime_dir_config *new =
      (mime_dir_config *)palloc (p, sizeof(mime_dir_config));

    new->forced_types = overlay_tables (p, subdir->forced_types,
                                        parent_dir->forced_types);
    new->encoding_types = overlay_tables (p, subdir->encoding_types,
                                          parent_dir->encoding_types);

    return new;
}
```

Note that if there is no per-directory merge function present, the server will just use the subdirectory's configuration info and ignore the parent's. For some modules, that works just fine (for the includes module, whose per-directory configuration information consists solely of the state of the XBITHACK), and for those modules, you can just not declare one and leave the corresponding structure slot in the module itself NULL.

Command Handling

Now that we have these structures, we need to be able to figure out how to fill them. That involves processing the actual *AddType* and *AddEncoding* commands. To find commands, the server looks in the module's command table. That table contains information on how many arguments the commands take, in what formats, where it is permitted, and so forth. That information is sufficient to allow the server to invoke most command-handling functions with preparsed arguments. Without further ado, let's look at the *AddType* command handler, which looks like this (the *AddEncoding* command looks basically the same, and won't be shown here):

```
char *add_type(cmd_parms *cmd, mime_dir_config *m, char *ct, char
*ext)
{
    if (*ext == '.') ++ext;
    table_set (m->forced_types, ext, ct);
    return NULL;
}
```

This command handler is unusually simple. As you can see, it takes four arguments, two of which are preparsed arguments, the third being the per-directory configuration structure for the module in question, and the fourth being a pointer to a *cmd_parms* structure. That structure contains many arguments that are frequently of use to some, but not all, commands, including a resource pool (from which memory can be allocated, and to which cleanups should be tied), and the (virtual) server being configured, from which the module's per-server configuration data can be obtained if required.

Another way in which this particular command handler is unusually simple is that there are no error conditions that it can encounter. If there were, it could return an error message instead of NULL; this causes an error to be printed out on the server's **stderr**, followed by a quick exit, if it is in the main config files; for a **.htaccess** file, the syntax error is logged in the server error log (along with an indication of where it came from), and the request is bounced with a server-error response (HTTP error status, code 500).

The MIME module's command table has entries for these commands, which look like this:

```
command_rec mime_cmds[] = {
{ "AddType", add_type, NULL, OR_FILEINFO, TAKE2,
    "a mime type followed by a file extension" },
{ "AddEncoding", add_encoding, NULL, OR_FILEINFO, TAKE2,
    "an encoding (e.g., gzip), followed by a file extension" },
{ NULL }
};
```

The entries in these tables are:

- The name of the command
- The function that handles it
- A (void *) pointer, which is passed in the *cmd_parms* structure to the command handler—this is useful in cases where many similar commands are handled by the same function.
- A bit mask indicating where the command may appear—there are mask bits corresponding to each *AllowOverride* option and an additional mask bit, *RSRC_CONF*, indicating that the command may appear in the server's own config files, but not in any **.htaccess** file.
- A flag indicating how many arguments the command handler wants preparsed and how they should be passed in

TAKE2 indicates two preparsed arguments. Other options are TAKE1, which indicates one preparsed argument; FLAG, which indicates that the argument should be *On* or *Off* and is passed in as a boolean flag; and RAW_ARGS, which causes the server to give the command the raw, unparsed arguments (everything but the command name itself). There is also ITERATE, which means that the handler looks the same as TAKE1, but that if multiple arguments are present, it should be called multiple times, and finally ITERATE2, which indicates that the command handler looks like a TAKE2, but if more arguments are present, then it should be called multiple times, holding the first argument constant.

Finally, we have a string that describes the arguments that should be present. If the arguments in the actual config file are not as required, this string will be used to help give a more specific error message. (You can safely leave this NULL).

Finally, having set this all up, we have to use it. This is ultimately done in the module's handlers, specifically for its file-typing handler, which looks more or less like this; note that the per-directory configuration structure is extracted from the *request_rec*'s per-directory configuration vector by using the *get_module_config* function:

```
int find_ct(request_rec *r)
{
    int i;
    char *fn = pstrdup (r->pool, r->filename);
    mime_dir_config *conf = (mime_dir_config *)
            get_module_config(r->per_dir_config, &mime_module);
    char *type;

    if (S_ISDIR(r->finfo.st_mode)) {
        r->content_type = DIR_MAGIC_TYPE;
        return OK;
    }

    if((i=rind(fn,'.')) < 0) return DECLINED;
    ++i;

    if ((type = table_get (conf->encoding_types, &fn[i])))
    {
        r->content_encoding = type;

        /* go back to previous extension to try to use it as a type */

        fn[i-1] = '\0';
        if((i=rind(fn,'.')) < 0) return OK;
        ++i;
    }

    if ((type = table_get (conf->forced_types, &fn[i])))
    {
        r->content_type = type;
    }

    return OK;
}
```

Side Notes—Per-Server Configuration, Virtual Servers, etc.

The basic ideas behind per-server module configuration are basically the same as those for per-directory configuration; there is a creation function and a merge function, the latter being invoked where a virtual server has partially overridden the base server configuration and a combined structure must be computed. As with the per-directory configuration, the default, if no merge function is specified, and a module is configured in some virtual server, is that the base configuration is simply ignored.

The only substantial difference is that when a command needs to configure the per-server private module data, it needs to go to the *cmd_parms* data to get at it. Here's an example, from the *alias* module, which also indicates how a syntax error can be returned (note that the per-directory configuration argument to the command handler is declared as a dummy, since the module doesn't actually have per-directory config data):

```
char *add_redirect(cmd_parms *cmd, void *dummy, char *f, char *url)
{
    server_rec *s = cmd->server;
    alias_server_conf *conf = (alias_server_conf *)
            get_module_config(s->module_config,&alias_module);
    alias_entry *new = push_array (conf->redirects);

    if (!is_url (url)) return "Redirect to non-URL";

    new->fake = f; new->real = url;
    return NULL;
}
```

Apache Core Features

These configuration parameters control the core Apache features and are always available: *AccessConfig, AccessFileName, AllowOverride, AuthName, AuthType, BindAddress, DefaultType, <Directory>, DocumentRoot, ErrorDocument, ErrorLog, Group, KeepAlive, KeepAliveTimeout, <Limit>, listen, <Location>, MaxClients, MaxRequestsPerChild, MaxSpareServers, MinSpareServers, Options, PidFile, Port, require, ResourceConfig, ServerAdmin, ServerAlias, ServerName, ServerPath, ServerRoot, ServerType, StartServers, TimeOut, User,* and *<VirtualHost>*.

Each one of these directives and parameters will be covered in the following sections. This information comes directly from the Apache online documentation. Some of the directives have already been covered in this chapter.

AccessConfig

Syntax:	*AccessConfig filename*
Default:	*AccessConfig* **conf/access.conf**
Context:	server config, virtual host
Status:	core

The server will read this file for more directives after reading the **ResourceConfig** file. The filename is relative to the *ServerRoot*. This feature can be disabled using:

```
AccessConfig /dev/null
```

Historically, this file only contained *<Directory>* sections; it can now contain any server directive allowed in the server-configuration context.

AccessFileName

Syntax:	*AccessFileName filename*
Default:	*AccessFileName* **.htaccess**
Context:	server config, virtual host
Status:	core

When returning a document to the client, the server looks for an access-control file with this name in every directory of the path to the document, if access control files are enabled for that directory. For example,

```
AccessFileName .acl
```

before returning the document **/usr/local/web/index.html**, the server will read **/.acl**, **/usr/.acl**, **/usr/local/.acl**, and **/usr/local/web/.acl** for directives, unless they have been disabled with the following:

```
<Directory />
AllowOverride None
</Directory>
```

AllowOverride

Syntax:	*AllowOverride override override ...*
Default:	*AllowOverride All*
Context:	directory
Status:	core

When the server finds an **.htaccess** file (as specified by *AccessFileName*) it needs to know which directives declared in that file can override earlier access information.

Override can be set to *None,* in which case the server will not read the file but will allow all the directives, or one or more of the following:

- *AuthConfig* allows use of the authorization directives (*AuthDBMGroupFile, AuthDBMUserFile, AuthGroupFile, AuthName, AuthType, AuthUserFile,* and *require.*
- *FileInfo* allows use of the *AddEncoding, AddLanguage, AddType, DefaultType,* and *LanguagePriority* directives, which control document types.
- Indexes allows use of the *AddDescription, AddIcon, AddIconByEncoding, AddIconByType, DefaultIcon, DirectoryIndex, FancyIndexing, HeaderName, IndexIgnore, IndexOptions,* and *ReadmeName directives*, which control directory indexing.
- *Limit* allows use of the directives controlling host access—*allow, deny,* and *order.*
- *Options* allows use of the directives controlling specific directory features—*Options* and *XBitHack.*

AuthName

Syntax:	*AuthName auth-domain*
Context:	directory, **.htaccess**
Override:	*AuthConfig*
Status:	core

This directive sets the name of the authorization realm for a directory. This realm is given to the client so that the user knows which username and password to send. It must be accompanied by *AuthType* and requires directives, such as *AuthUserFile* and *AuthGroupFile*, to work.

AuthType

Syntax:	*AuthType type*
Context:	directory, **.htaccess**
Override:	*AuthConfig*
Status:	core

This directive selects the type of user authentication for a directory. Only basic authentication is currently implemented. It must be accompanied by *AuthName* and require directives, such as *AuthUserFile* and *AuthGroupFile*, to work.

BindAddress

Syntax:	*BindAddress saddr*
Default:	*BindAddress ***
Context:	server config
Status:	core

A UNIX HTTP server can either listen on for connections to every IP address of the server machine or just one IP address of the server machine. *Saddr* can be the wildcard (*), an IP address, or a fully qualified Internet domain name. If the value is *, then the server will listen for connections on every IP address; otherwise, it will listen only on the IP address specified.

This option can be used as an alternative method for supporting virtual hosts instead of using *<VirtualHost>* sections.

DefaultType

Syntax:	*DefaultType mime-type*
Default:	*DefaultType text/html*
Context:	server config, virtual host, directory, **.htaccess**
Override:	*FileInfo*
Status:	core

There will be times when the server is asked to provide a document whose type cannot be determined by its MIME mappings. The server must inform the client of the content-type of the document, so in the event of an unknown type it uses the *DefaultType*. For example,

```
DefaultType image/gif
```

would be appropriate for a directory that contained many GIF images with filenames missing the **.gif** extension.

<Directory>

Syntax: *<Directory directory> ... </Directory>*
Context: server config, virtual host
Status: core

<Directory> and *</Directory>* are used to enclose a group of directives that apply only to the named directory and subdirectories of that directory. Any directive allowed in a directory context may be used. The directory is either the full path to a directory or a wildcard string. In a wildcard string, ? matches any single character, and * matches any sequences of characters. For example,

```
<Directory /usr/local/httpd/htdocs>
Options Indexes FollowSymLinks
</Directory>
```

If multiple directory sections match the directory (or its parents) containing a document, then the directives are applied in the order of shortest match first, interspersed with the directives from the **.htaccess** files. For example,

```
<Directory />
AllowOverride None
</Directory>

<Directory /home/*>
AllowOverride FileInfo
</Directory>
```

For access to the document **/home/web/dir/doc.html** the steps follow:

1. Apply directive *AllowOverride None* (disabling **.htaccess** files).
2. Apply directive *AllowOverride FileInfo* (for directory **/home/web**).
3. Apply any *FileInfo* directives in **/home/web/.htaccess**.

The directory sections typically occur in the **access.conf** file, but they may appear in any configuration file. *<Directory>* directives cannot nest or appear in a *<Limit>* section.

DocumentRoot

Syntax: *DocumentRoot directory-filename*
Default: *DocumentRoot* **/usr/local/etc/httpd/htdocs**
Context: server config, virtual host
Status: core

This directive sets the directory holding the document files. Unless matched by a directive like *Alias*, the server appends the path from the requested URL to the document root to make the path to the document. For example,

```
DocumentRoot /usr/web
```

an access to *http://www.my.host.com/index.html* refers to **/usr/web/index.html**.

There appears to be a bug in *mod_dir* that causes problems when the *DocumentRoot* has a trailing slash (like *DocumentRoot /usr/web/*), so avoid that.

ErrorDocument

Syntax: *ErrorDocument error-code document*
Context: server config, virtual host, directory, **.htaccess**
Status: core

In the event of a problem or error, Apache can be configured to do one of four things:

- Behave like NCSA **httpd** 1.3.
- Output a customized message.
- Redirect to a local URL to handle the problem/error.
- Redirect to an external URL to handle the problem/error.

The last three options are configured using *ErrorDocument*, which is followed by the HTTP response code and a message or URL. Messages in this context begin with an opening quotation mark ("), which does not form part of the message itself. Apache will sometime offer additional information regarding the problem/error. This can be embedded into the message using %s.

URLs will begin with a slash (/) for local URLs or will be a full URL that the client can resolve. Here are some examples:

```
ErrorDocument 500 /cgi-bin/tester
ErrorDocument 404 /cgi-bin/bad_urls.pl
ErrorDocument 401 http://www2.foo.bar/subscription_info.html
ErrorDocument 403 "Sorry can't allow you access today
```

ErrorLog

Syntax: *ErrorLog filename*

Default: *ErrorLog* **logs/error_log**

Context: server config, virtual host

Status: core

The error-log directive sets the name of the file where the server will log any errors it encounters. If the filename does not begin with a slash (/), then it is assumed to be relative to the *ServerRoot*. For example,

```
ErrorLog /dev/null
```

effectively turns off error logging.

Group

Syntax:	*Group unix-group*
Default:	*Group #-1*
Context:	server config
Status:	core

The *Group* directive sets the group under which the server will answer requests. In order to use this directive, the standalone server must be run initially as root. *Unix-group* is either a group name or a group number (which must begin with #).

It is recommended that you set up a new group specifically for running the server. Some system administrators use user *nobody*, but this is not always possible or desirable. If you start the server as a non-root user, it will fail to change to the specified and will instead continue to run as the group of the original user.

IdentityCheck

Syntax:	*IdentityCheck boolean*
Default:	*IdentityCheck off*
Context:	server config, virtual host, directory, .htaccess
Status:	core

This directive enables RFC931-compliant logging of the remote username for each connection, where the client machine runs **identd** or something similar. This information is logged in the access log. Boolean is either *on* or *off*.

The information should not trusted in any way except for rudimentary usage tracking.

KeepAlive

Syntax:	*KeepAlive max-requests*
Default:	*KeepAlive 5*
Context:	server config
Status:	core

This directive enables Keep-Alive support. Set *max-requests* to the maximum number of requests you want Apache to entertain per request. A limit is imposed to prevent a client from hogging your server resources. Set this to **0** to disable support.

The Keep-Alive extenstion to HTTP, as defined by the HTTP/1.1 draft, allows persistent connections. These long-lived HTTP sessions allow multiple requests to be send over the same TCP connection, and in some cases have been shown to result in an almost 50 percent speedup in latency times for HTML documents with lots of images.

Apache 1.1 comes with Keep-Alive support on by default. The *KeepAlive* and *KeepAliveTimeout* directives (*KeepAliveTimeout* is covered in the following section) are used to modify Apache's behavior.

In order for Keep-Alive support to be used, first the browser must support it. Many current browsers, including Netscape Navigator, Microsoft Internet Explorer, and Spyglass Mosaic-based browsers, do. Some Windows 95–based browsers misbehave with Keep-Alive-supporting servers; they may occasionally hang on a connect. This has been observed with several Windows browsers and occurs when connecting to any Keep-Alive server, not just Apache. Netscape 3.0b5 and later versions are known to work around this problem.

However, Keep-Alive support is active only with files where the length is known beforehand. This means that most CGI scripts, server-side included files, and directory listings will not use the Keep-Alive protocol. While this should be completely transparent to the end user, it is something the Webmaster may want to keep in mind.

KeepAliveTimeout

Syntax:	*KeepAliveTimeout seconds*
Default:	*KeepAliveTimeout 15*
Context:	server config
Status:	core

This specifies the number of seconds Apache will wait for a subsequent request before closing the connection. Once a request has been received, the timeout value specified by the *Timeout* directive applies.

Listen

Syntax:	*Listen [IP address:]port number*
Context:	server config
Status:	core

The *Listen* directive instructs Apache to listen to more than one IP address or port; by default it responds to requests on all IP interfaces, but only on the port given by the *Port* directive.

<Limit>

Syntax:	*<Limit method method ... > ... </Limit>*
Context:	any
Status:	core

<Limit> and *</Limit>* are used to enclose a group of access-control directives that apply only to the specified access methods, where method is any valid HTTP method. Any directive except another *<Limit>* or *<Directory>* may be used; the majority will be unaffected by the *<Limit>*. An example,

```
<Limit GET POST>
require valid-user
</Limit>
```

If an access-control directive appears outside a *<Limit>* directive, then it applies to all access methods.

<Location>

Syntax:	*<Location URL prefix>*
Context:	server config, virtual host
Status:	core

The *<Location>* directive provides for access control by URL. It is comparable to the *<Directory>* directive and should be matched with a *</Location>* directive. Directives that apply to the URL given should be

Listen within. *<Location>* sections are processed in the order they appear in the configuration file, after the *<Directory>* sections and **.htaccess** files are read.

Due to the way HTTP functions, the URL prefix should (save for proxy requests) be of the form */path/*, and should not include the *http://servername*. It doesn't necessarily have to protect a directory (it can be an individual file or a number of files) and can include wildcards. In a wildcard string, *?* matches any single character, and * matches any sequences of characters.

This functionality is especially useful when combined with the *SetHandler* directive. For example, to enable status requests, but allow them only from browsers at *foo.com*, you might use:

```
<Location /status>
SetHandler server-status

order deny,allow
deny from all
allow from .foo.com

</Location>
```

MaxClients

Syntax:	*MaxClients number*
Default:	*MaxClients 150*
Context:	server config
Status:	core

The *MaxClients* directive sets the limit on the number of simultaneous requests that can be supported; not more than this number of child server processes will be created.

MaxRequestsPerChild

Syntax:	*MaxRequestsPerChild number*
Default:	*MaxRequestsPerChild 0*
Context:	server config
Status:	core

The *MaxRequestsPerChild* directive sets the limit on the number of requests that an individual child server process will handle. After *MaxRequestsPerChild* requests, the child process will die. If *MaxRequestsPerChild* is **0**, then the process will never expire.

Setting *MaxRequestsPerChild* to a nonzero limit has two beneficial effects: It limits the amount of memory the process can consume by (accidental) memory leakage, and by giving processes a finite lifetime, it helps reduce the number of processes when the server load reduces.

MaxSpareServers

Syntax: *MaxSpareServers number*

Default: *MaxSpareServers 10*

Context: server config

Status: core

The *MaxSpareServers* directive sets the desired maximum number of idle child server processes. An idle process is one not handling a request. If there are more than *MaxSpareServers* idle, then the parent process will kill off the excess processes.

Tuning of this parameter should be necessary only on very busy sites. Setting this parameter to a large number is almost always a bad idea.

MinSpareServers

Syntax: *MinSpareServers number*

Default: *MinSpareServers 5*

Context: server config

Status: core

The *MinSpareServers* directive sets the desired minimum number of idle child server processes. An idle process is one not handling a request. If there are fewer than *MinSpareServers* idle, then the parent process creates new children at a maximum rate of one per second.

Tuning this parameter should be necessary only on very busy sites. Setting this parameter to a large number is almost always a bad idea.

Options

Syntax:	*Options option option …*
Context:	server config, virtual host, directory, **.htaccess**
Override:	*Options*
Status:	core

The *Options* directive controls which server features are available in a particular directory. *Option* can be set to *None*, in which case none of the extra features are enabled, or one or more of the following:

- *All* (All options are included except for MultiViews.)
- *ExecCGI* (Execution of CGI scripts is permitted.)
- *FollowSymLinks* (The server will follow symbolic links in this directory.)
- *Includes* (Server-side includes are permitted.)
- *IncludesNOEXEC* (Server-side includes are permitted, but the **#exec** command and **#include** of CGI scripts are disabled.)
- *Indexes* (If a URL that maps to a directory is requested and there is no **index.html** in that directory, then the server will return a formatted listing of the directory.)
- *MultiViews* (Content-negotiated MultiViews are allowed.)
- *SymLinksIfOwnerMatch* (The server will follow only symbolic links for which the target file or directory is owned by the same user ID as the link.)

If multiple options could apply to a directory, then the most specific one is taken complete; the options are not merged. In this example

```
<Directory /web/docs>
Options Indexes FollowSymLinks
</Directory>
<Directory /web/docs/spec>
Options Includes
</Directory>
```

only *Includes* will be set for the **/web/docs/spec** directory.

PidFile

Syntax:	*PidFile filename*
Default:	*PidFile* **logs/httpd.pid**
Context:	server config
Status:	core

The *PidFile* directive sets the file where the process ID of the daemon is stored. If the filename does not begin with a slash (/), then it is assumed to be relative to the *ServerRoot*. The *PidFile* is used only in standalone mode.

It is often useful to be able to send the server a signal, so that it closes and then reopens its *ErrorLog* and *TransferLog* and rereads its configuration files. This is done by sending a **SIGHUP (kill -1)** signal to the process ID listed in the *PidFile*.

Port

Syntax:	*Port num*
Default:	*Port 80*
Context:	server config
Status:	core

The server needs to listen to a network port, which is set with the *Port* directive. *Num* is a number from 0 to 65535; some port numbers (especially below 1024) are reserved for particular protocols. See **/etc/services** for a list of some defined ports; the standard port for the HTTP protocol is 80.

Port 80 is one of UNIX's special ports. All ports numbered below 1024 are reserved for system use, which means that non-root users cannot make use of them; instead, they can only use higher port numbers.

To use port 80, you must start the server from the root account. After binding to the port and before accepting requests, Apache will change to a low privileged user as set by the *User* directive.

If you cannot use port 80, choose any other unused port. Non-root users will have to choose a port number higher than 1023, such as 8000.

require

Syntax:	*require entity-name entity entity...*
Context:	directory, **.htaccess**
Override:	*AuthConfig*
Status:	core

This directive specifies which authenticated users can access a directory. The allowed syntaxes are

```
require user userid userid …
```

In this instance, only the named users can access the directory. In another case,

```
require group group-name group-name …
```

In this instance, only users in the named groups can access the directory. In this case,

```
require valid-user
```

All valid users can access the directory.

If *require* appears in a *<Limit>* section, then it restricts access to the named methods; otherwise, it restricts access for all methods. For example,

```
AuthType Basic
AuthName somedomain
AuthUserFile /web/users
AuthGroupFile /web/groups
Limit <GET POST>
require group admin
</Limit>
```

Require must be accompanied by *AuthName* and *AuthType* directives, and directives like *AuthUserFile* and *AuthGroupFile* (to define users and groups) in order to work correctly.

ResourceConfig

Syntax:	*ResourceConfig filename*
Default:	*ResourceConfig* **conf/srm.conf**
Context:	server config, virtual host
Status:	core

The server reads this file specified by *ResourceConfig* for more directives after reading the **httpd.conf** file. *Filename* is relative to the *ServerRoot*. This feature can be disabled using:

```
ResourceConfig /dev/null
```

Historically, this file contained most directives except for server configuration directives and *<Directory>* sections; it can now contain any server directive allowed in the server-config context.

ServerAdmin

Syntax:	*ServerAdmin email-address*
Context:	server config, virtual host
Status:	core

The *ServerAdmin* sets the e-mail address that the server includes in any error messages it returns to the client.

ServerAlias

Syntax:	*ServerAlias host1 host2 ...*
Context:	virtual host
Status:	core

The *ServerAlias* directive sets the alternate names for a host, for use with Host-header-based virtual hosts.

ServerName

Syntax:	*ServerName fully-qualified domain name*
Context:	server config, virtual host
Status:	core

The *ServerName* directive sets the hostname of the server. This is used only when creating redirection URLs. If it is not specified, then the server attempts to deduce it from its own IP address; however, this may not work reliably, or may not return the preferred hostname. For example,

```
ServerName www.wibble.com
```

would be used if the canonical (main) name of the actual machine were *monster.wibble.com*.

ServerPath

Syntax:	*ServerPath pathname*
Context:	virtual host
Status:	core

The *ServerAlias* directive sets the legacy URL pathname for a host, for use with Host-header-based virtual hosts.

ServerRoot

Syntax:	*ServerRoot directory-filename*
Default:	*ServerRoot* **/usr/local/etc/httpd**
Context:	server config
Status:	core

The *ServerRoot* directive sets the directory where the server file live. Typically it will contain the subdirectories **conf/** and **logs/**. Relative paths for other configuration files are taken as relative to this directory.

ServerType

Syntax:	*ServerType type*
Default:	*ServerType standalone*
Context:	server config
Status:	core

The *ServerType* directive sets how the server is executed by the system. *Type* is one of

- *inetd* (The server will be run from the system process **inetd**; the command to start the server is added to **/etc/inetd.conf**.)
- *standalone* (The server will run as a daemon process; the command to start the server is added to the system startup scripts, such as **/etc/rc.local** or **/etc/rc3.d/....**)

Inetd is the lesser used of the two options. For each HTTP connection received, a new copy of the server is started from scratch; after the connection is complete, this program exits. There is a high price to pay per connection, but for security reasons, some administrators prefer this option.

Standalone is the most common setting for ServerType since it is far more efficient. The server is started once and services all subsequent connections. If you intend running Apache to serve a busy site, *Standalone* will probably be your only option.

If you are paranoid about security, run in *inetd* mode. Security cannot be guaranteed in either, but even though most people are happy to use *standalone*, *inetd* is probably least prone to attack.

StartServers

Syntax:	*StartServers number*
Default:	*StartServers 5*
Context:	server config
Status:	core

The *StartServers* directive sets the number of child server processes created on startup. As the number of processes is dynamically controlled depending on the load, there is usually little reason to adjust this parameter.

TimeOut

Syntax:	*TimeOut num*
Default:	*TimeOut 1200*
Context:	server config
Status:	core

The *TimeOut* directive sets the maximum time that the server will wait for the receipt of a request and the completion of a request, in seconds. So if it takes more than *TimeOut* seconds for a client to send a request or receive a response, the server will break off the connection. Thus *TimeOut* limits the maximum a transfer can take; for large files and slow networks, transfer times can be large.

User

Syntax:	*User unix-userid*
Default:	*User #-1*
Context:	server config
Status:	core

The *User* directive sets userid, specifying which server will answer requests. In order to use this directive, the standalone server must be run initially as root. *Unix-userid* is either a username (referring to the given user by name) or a user number (referring to a user by their number; this number must begin with #).

The user should have no privileges that result in being able to access files that are not intended to be visible to the outside world; similarly, the user should not be able to execute code that is not meant for HTTPD requests. It is recommended that you set up a new user and group specifically for running the server. Some admins use user *nobody*, but this is not always possible or desirable.

If you start the server as a non-root user, it will fail to change to the lesser privileged user and will instead continue to run as that original user. If you do start the server as root, then it is normal for the parent process to remain running as root.

Don't set *User* (or *Group*) to root unless you know exactly what you are doing and what the dangers are.

<VirtualHost>

Syntax: *<VirtualHost addr[:port]> ... </VirtualHost>*

Context: server config

Status: core

<VirtualHost> and *</VirtualHost>* are used to enclose a group of directives that apply only to a particular virtual host. Any directive that is allowed in a virtual host context may be used. When the server receives a request for a document on a particular virtual host, it uses the configuration directives enclosed in the *<VirtualHost>* section. *Addr* can be the IP address of the virtual host or a fully qualified domain name for the IP address of the virtual host. For example,

```
<VirtualHost host.foo.com>
ServerAdmin webmaster@host.foo.com
DocumentRoot /www/docs/host.foo.com
ServerName host.foo.com
ErrorLog logs/host.foo.com-error_log
TransferLog logs/host.foo.com-access_log
</VirtualHost>
```

Currently, each *VirtualHost* must correspond to a different IP address for the server, so the server machine must be configured to accept IP packets for multiple addresses. If the machine does not have multiple network interfaces, then this can be accomplished with the **ifconfig alias** command.

Apache Modules: Adding Functionality to the Web Server

Apache uses modules, made up of C-language files, that add functionality to the Web server. Many of these modules were compiled in the **httpd** file that ships as part of Slackware Linux. Other modules were not, which means that if you want the functionality found in the module, you'll need to recompile the Web server using the instructions found earlier in this chapter.

Why should you pay attention to these modules? Because if the module has been compiled in the Web server, you'll have access to the commands (or, in Apache parlance, *directives*) listed in the summaries of the modules. These commands can be included in configuration scripts.

The following sections will cover the modules already compiled into Apache. Later on, optional modules will be covered. These optional modules can be found on the Internet at *http://www.apache.org*. The descriptions of the modules are based directly on the Apache documentation, also viewable at *http://www.apache.org*. After a description of these modules, there will be instructions on how to add modules to the Apache Web server.

Mod_access Module

This module is contained in the **mod_access.c** file and is compiled in by default. It provides access control based on client hostname or IP address. There are three possible directives: *allow*, *deny*, and *order*.

allow

Syntax:	*allow from host host ...*
Context:	directory, **.htaccess**
Override:	limit
Status:	base

The *allow* directive affects which hosts can access a given directory; it is typically used within a *<Limit>* section. *Host* is one of the following:

- All (all hosts are allowed access.)
- A (partial) domain-name (A host whose name is, or ends in, this string is allowed access.)
- A full IP address (An IP address of a host is allowed access.)
- A partial IP address (The first 1 to 3 bytes of an IP address, for subnet restriction, is allowed access.)

For example,

```
allow from .ncsa.uiuc.edu
```

allows all hosts in the specified domain.

This directive compares whole components; *bar.edu* would not match *foobar.edu*.

deny

Syntax: *deny from host host ...*

Context: directory, **.htaccess**

The *deny* directive affects which hosts can access a given directory; it is typically used within a *<Limit>* section. *Host* is one of the following:

- All (All hosts are allowed access.)
- A (partial) domain-name (A host whose name is, or ends in, this string is allowed access.)
- A full IP address (An IP address of a host is allowed access.)
- A partial IP address (The first 1 to 3 bytes of an IP address, for subnet restriction, is allowed access.)

For example,

```
deny from 16
```

denies access to all hosts in the specified network.

This compares whole components; *bar.edu* would not match *foobar.edu*.

order

Syntax:	*order ordering*
Default:	*order deny,allow*
Context:	directory, **.htaccess**

The *order* directive controls the order in which *allow* and *deny* directives are evaluated. Ordering is one of:

- *deny,allow* (The *deny* directives are evaluated before the *allow* directives.)
- *allow,deny* (The *allow* directives are evaluated before the *deny* directives.)
- *mutual-failure* (Only those hosts that appear on the *allow* list and do not appear on the *deny* list are granted access.)

For example,

```
order deny,allow deny from all allow from .ncsa.uiuc.edu
```

Hosts in the *ncsa.uiuc.edu* domain are allowed access; all other hosts are denied access.

Mod_actions Module

This module is contained in the **mod_actions.c** file and is compiled in by default. It provides for executing CGI scripts based on media type or request method.

This module lets you run CGI scripts whenever a file of a certain type is requested. This makes it much easier to execute scripts that process files.

There are two directives: *Action* and *Script*.

Action

Syntax: *Action mime-type cgi-script*

Context: server config, virutal host, directory, **.htaccess**

Override: fileInfo

Status: base

This directive adds an action, which will activate the specified *cgi-script* when a file of content type *mime-type* is requested. It sends the URL and file path of the requested document using the standard CGI *PATH_INFO* and *PATH_TRANSLATED* environment variables.

Script

Syntax: *Script method cgi-script*

Context: server config, virutal host, directory

Status: base

This directive adds an action, which will activate the specified *cgi-script* when a file is requested using the method of HTTP *method*, which can be one of GET, POST, PUT, or DELETE. It sends the URL and file path of the requested document using the standard *CGI PATH_INFO* and *PATH_TRANSLATED* environment variables.

The *Script* command defines default actions only. If a CGI script is called, or some other resource that is capable of handling the requested method internally, it will do so. Also note that script with a method of GET will only be called if there are query arguments present (like *foo.html?hi*). Otherwise, the request will proceed normally. For example,

```
Script GET /cgi-bin/search    #e.g. for <ISINDEX>-style searching
Script PUT /~bob/put.cgi
```

Mod_alias Module

This module is contained in the **mod_alias.c** file and is compiled in by default. It provides for mapping different parts of the host filesystem in the document tree and also for URL redirection.

The following directives are supported: *Alias*, *Redirect*, and *ScriptAlias*.

Alias

Syntax: *Alias url-path directory-filename*

Context: server config, virtual host

Status: base

The *Alias* directive allows documents to be stored in the local filesystem other than under the *DocumentRoot*. URLs with a (%-decoded) path beginning with *url-path* will be mapped to local files beginning with *directory-filename*. For example,

```
Alias /image /ftp/pub/image
```

A request for *http://myserver/image/foo.gif* would cause the server to return the file */ftp/pub/image/foo.gif*.

Redirect

Syntax: *Redirect url-path url*

Context: server config, virtual host, directory, **.htaccess**

Status: base

The *Redirect* directive maps an old URL into a new one. The new URL is returned to the client which attempts to fetch it again with the new address. *Url-path* is a (%-decoded) path; any requests for documents beginning with this path will be returned a redirect error to a new (%-encoded) URL beginning with *url*. For example:

```
Redirect /service http://foo2.bar.com/service
```

If the client requests *http://myserver/service/foo.txt*, it will be told to access *http://foo2.bar.com/service/foo.txt* instead.

Redirect directives take precedence over *Alias* and *ScriptAlias* directives, irrespective of their ordering in the configuration file.

ScriptAlias

Syntax: *ScriptAlias url-path directory-filename*

Context: server config, virtual host

Status: base

The *ScriptAlias* directive has the same behavior as the *Alias* directive, except that in addition it marks the target directory as containing CGI scripts. URLs with a (%-decoded) path beginning with *url-path* will be mapped to scripts beginning with *directory-filename*. For example:

```
ScriptAlias /cgi-bin/ /web/cgi-bin/
```

A request for *http://myserver/cgi-bin/foo* would cause the server to run the script */web/cgi-bin/foo*.

Mod_asis Module

This module is contained in the **mod_asis.c** file and is compiled in by default. It provides for **.asis** files. Any document with MIME type *httpd/send-as-is* will be processed by this module.

The purpose is to allow file types to be defined such that Apache sends them without adding HTTP headers. This can be used to send any kind of data from the server, including redirects and other special HTTP responses, without requiring a *cgi-script* or an *nph* script.

In the server configuration file, define a new MIME type called *httpd/send-as-is*:

```
AddType httpd/send-as-is asis
```

This defines the **.asis** file extension as being of the new *httpd/send-as-is* MIME type. The contents of any file with a **.asis** extension will then be sent by Apache to the client with almost no changes. Clients will need HTTP headers to be attached, so do not forget them. A *Status:* header is also required; the data should be the three-digit HTTP response code followed by a textual message.

Here's an example of a file whose contents are sent as is so as to tell the client that a file has redirected.

```
Status: 302 Now where did I leave that URL
Location: http://xyz.abc.com/foo/bar.html
Content-type: text/html

<HTML>
<HEAD>
<TITLE>Lame excuses'R'us</TITLE>
</HEAD>
<BODY>
<H1>Fred's exceptionally wonderful page has moved to
<A HREF="http://xyz.abc.com/foo/bar.html">Joe's</A> site.
</H1>
</BODY>
</HTML>
```

The server always adds a *Date:* and *Server:* header to the data returned to the client, so these should not be included in the file. The server does not add a *Last-Modified* header; it probably should.

Mod_auth Module

This module is contained in the **mod_auth.c** file and is compiled in by default. It provides for user authentication using textual files. The directives made possible by this module are *AuthGroupFile* and *AuthUserFile*.

AuthGroupFile

Syntax: *AuthGroupFile* filename

Context: directory, **.htaccess**

Override: *AuthConfig*

Status: base

The *AuthGroupFile* directive sets the name of a textual file containing the list of user groups for user authentication. *Filename* is the absolute path to the group file.

Each line of the group file contains a groupname followed by a colon, followed by the member usernames separated by spaces. For example,

```
mygroup: bob joe anne
```

would place *bob*, *joe*, and *anne* in *mygroup*. Searching large groups files is very inefficient; *AuthDBMGroupFile* should be used instead.

Make sure that the *AuthGroupFile* is stored outside the document tree of the Web server; do not put it in the directory that it protects. Otherwise, clients will be able to download the *AuthGroupFile*.

AuthUserFile

Syntax: *AuthUserFile filename*

Context: directory, **.htaccess**

Override: *AuthConfig*

Status: base

The *AuthUserFile* directive sets the name of a textual file containing the list of users and passwords for user authentication. *Filename* is the absolute path to the user file.

Each line of the user file contains a username followed by a colon, followed by the *crypt()* encrypted password. The behavior of multiple occurrences of the same user is undefined.

Searching user groups files is inefficient; *AuthDBMUserFile* should be used instead.

Make sure that the *AuthUserFile* is stored outside the document tree of the Web server; do not put it in the directory that it protects. Otherwise, clients will be able to download the *AuthUserFile*.

Mod_auth_anon Module

This module is contained in the **mod_auth_anon.c** file and is compiled in by default. It performs access control in a manner similar to anonymous-ftp sites, like having a user ID of *anonymous*, and the e-mail address as a password. These e-mail addresses can be logged.

Combined with other (database) access control methods, this allows for effective user tracking and customization according to a user profile while still keeping the site open for unregistered users. One advantage of using *Auth*-based user tracking is that, unlike magic cookies and funny URL pre/postfixes, it is completely browser-independent and allows users to share URLs.

Check the online documentation for a full description of this module.

Mod_auth_msql Module

This module is contained in the **mod_auth_msql.c** file and is compiled in by default. It allows access control using the public domain mSQL database (*ftp://ftp.bond.edu.au/pub/Minerva/msql*), a fast but limited SQL engine that can be contacted over an internal UNIX domain protocol as well as over normal TCP/IP socket communication.

There are a number of tokens available via this module.

```
Auth_MSQLhost < FQHN | IP Address | localhost >
```

This is the hostname of the machine running the mSQL demon. The effective uid of the server should be allowed access. If not given or if it is the magic name *localhost*, it is passed to the mSQL library as a NULL pointer. This effectively forces it to use **/dev/msql** rather than the (slower) socket communication.

```
Auth_MSQLdatabase < mSQL database name >
```

This is the name of the database where the following table(s) are contained. Use the mSQL command *relshow [<hostname> dbase]* to verify the spelling of the database name.

```
Auth_MSQLpwd_table < mSQL table name >
```

This token contains at least the fields with the username and the (encrypted) password. Each uid should occur only once in this table and for performance reasons should be a primary key. Normally this table is compulsory, but it is possible to use a fall-through to other methods and use the mSQL module for group control only. See the *Auth_MSQL_Authorative* directive, which follows.

```
Auth_MSQLgrp_table < mSQL table name in the above database >
```

This contains at least the fields with the username and the groupname. Therefore, a user that is in multiple groups has multiple entries. There might be some performance problems associated with this, and one might consider having separate tables for each group (rather than all groups in one table) if your directory structure allows for it. One only needs to specify this table when doing group control.

```
Auth_MSQLuid_field < mSQL field name >
```

This is the name of the field containing the username in the *Auth_MSQLpwd_table* and optionally in the *Auth_MSQLgrp_table* tables.

```
Auth_MSQLpwd_field < mSQL field name >
```

This is the fieldname for the passwords in the *Auth_MSQLpwd_table* table.

```
Auth_MSQLgrp_field < mSQL field name >
```

This is the fieldname for the groupname. Only the fields used need to be specified. When this module is compiled with the *BACKWARD_VITEK* option, the *uid* and *pwd* field names default to *user* and *password*. However, you are strongly encouraged to always specify these values explicitly given the security issues involved.

```
Auth_MSQL_nopasswd < on | off >
```

This skips password comparison if the *passwd* field is empty (i.e., it allows any password). This is *off* by default to ensure that an empty field in the mSQL table does not allow people in by default with a random password.

```
Auth_MSQL_Authorative < on | off >
```

The default is *on*. When set *on*, there is no fall-through to other authorization methods. So if a user is not in the mSQL dbase table (and perhaps not in the right group) or has the password wrong, then he or she is denied access. When this directive is set to *off*, control is passed on to any other authorization modules, such as the basic *Auth* module with the **htpasswd** file or the *Unix-(g)dbm* modules. The default is *on* to avoid nasty fall-through surprises. Be sure you know what you are doing when you decide to switch it off.

```
Auth_MSQL_EncryptedPasswords < on | off >
```

The default is *on*. When set *on*, the values in the *pwd_field* are assumed to be crypted using your machine's *crypt()* function and the incoming password is crypted before comparison. When this function is *off*, the comparison is done directly with the plaintext-entered password. (Yes, *http-basic-auth* does send the password as plaintext over the wire.) The default is a sensible *on*, but a multivendor or international environment (which sometimes leads to different crypts functions) might force you to change this.

An example mSQL table could be created with the following commands:

```
% msqladmin create www
% msql www
-> create table user_records (
->    User_id   char(32) primary key,
->    Cpasswd   char(32),
->    Xgroup    char(32)
->    ) \g
query OK
-> \q
%
```

The *User_id* can be as long as desired. However, some of the popular Web browsers truncate names at or stop the user from entering names longer than 32 characters. Furthermore, the *crypt* function on your platform might impose further limits. Also, use of the *require users uid [uid..]* directive in the **access.conf** file where the uid's are separated by spaces can possibly prohibit the use of spaces in your usernames. Also, please note the *MAX_FIELD_LEN* directive elsewhere in this section.

To use the preceding set of directives, the following example could be in your **access.conf** file. Also, there is a more elaborate description following this example.

```
<directory /web/docs/private>
Auth_MSQLhost localhost
```

or

```
Auth_MSQLhost datab.machine.your.org
```

If this directive is omitted or set to *localhost*, it is assumed that Apache and the mSQL database run on the same (physical) machine and the faster **/dev/msql** communication channel will be used. Otherwise, it is the machine to contact by TCP/IP. Consult the mSQL documentation for more information.

```
Auth_MSQLdatabase www
```

This is the name of the database on the previously mentioned machine, which contains both the tables for group and for user/passwords. Currently it is not possible to have these split over two databases. Make sure that the **msql.acl** (access-control file) of mSQL does indeed allow the effective uid of the Web server read access to this database. Check the **httpd.conf** file for this uid.

```
Auth_MSQLpwd_table user_records
```

This is the table that contains the specified uid/password combination.

```
Auth_MSQLuid_field User_id
Auth_MSQLpwd_field Cpasswd
```

These two directive specify the field names in the *user_record* table. If this module is compiled with the *BACKWARD_VITEK* compatibility switch, the default user and password are assumed if you do not specify them. Currently the *user_id* field must be a primary key or one must ensure that each user only occurs once in the table. If a uid occurs twice, access is denied by default; but see the *ONLY_ONCE* compiler directive for more information.

```
Auth_MSQLgrp_table user_records
Auth_MSQLgrp_field Xgroup
```

Optionally one can also specify a table that contains the user/group combinations. This can be the same table that also contains the username/password combinations. However, if a user belongs to two or more groups, one will have to use a different table with multiple entries.

```
Auth_MSQL_nopasswd off
Auth_MSQL_Authorative on
Auth_MSQL_EncryptedPasswords on
```

These three optional fields (all set to the sensible defaults so that you really do not have to enter them) are described in more detail later. If you choose to set these fields to any other values, be very sure that you understand the security implications and do verify that Apache does what you expect it to do.

```
AuthName example mSQL realm
AuthType basic
```

These are normal Apache/NCSA tokens for access control.

Some Compile-Time Options

A number of compile-time options are made possible by this module.

```
#define ONLY_ONCE 1
```

If the mSQL table containing the uid/passwd combination does not have the uid field as a primary key, it is possible for the uid to occur more than once in the table with possibly different passwords. When this module is compiled with the *ONLY_ONCE* directive set, access is denied if the uid occurs more than once in the uid/passwd table. If you choose not to set it, the software takes the first pair returned and ignores any further pairs. The SQL statement used for this is:

```
select password form pwd_table where user='uid'
```

even though this might lead to unpredictable results. For this reason as well as for performance reasons, you are strongly advised to make the *uid* field a primary key.

```
#define KEEP_MSQL_CONNECTION_OPEN
```

Normally the TCP/IP connection with the database is opened and closed for each SQL query. When the Apache Web server and the database are on the same machine and **/dev/msql** is used, this does not cause a serious overhead problem. However, when your platform does not support this (see the mSQL documentation) or when the Web server and the database are on different machines, the overhead can be considerable. When the preceding directive is set *defined*, the server leaves the connection open (i.e., no call to *msqlClose()*). If an error occurs, an attempt is made to reopen the connection for the next HTTP request.

This has a number of very serious drawbacks:

- It costs two already-rare file descriptors for each child.
- It costs msql connections, typically one per child. The (compiled in) number of connections mSQL can handle is low, typically 6 or 12. which might prohibit access to the mSQL database for later processes.
- When a child dies, it might not free that connection properly or quickly enough.
- When errors start to occur, connection/file-descriptor resources might become exhausted very quickly.

In short, use this at your own peril and only in a highly controlled and monitored environment.

```
#define BACKWARD_VITEK
#define VITEK_uid_name user
#define VITEK_gid_name passwd
```

A second mSQL *auth* module for Apache has also been developed by Vitek Khera (*khera@kciLink.com*) and was subsequently distributed with some early versions of Apache. It can be obtained from *ftp://ftp.kcilink.com/pub/mod_auth_msql.c**. Older "vitek" versions had the field/table names compiled in. Newer versions of Apache have more **access.conf** configuration options. However, these were chosen not to be in the line of the *ewse* version of this module. Also, the *vitek* module does not give group control or empty password control.

The Apache version you have should be backward compatible with the *vitek* module by

- Adding support for the *Auth_MSQL_EncryptedPasswords* on/off functionality.
- Adding support for the different spelling of the four configuration tokens for *user-table-name*, *user/password-field-name*, and *dbase-name*.
- Setting some field names to a default that used to be hard-coded in older *vitek* modules.

If this troubles you, remove the *BACKWARD_VITEK* define:

```
#define MAX_FIELD_LEN (64)
#define MAX_QUERY_LEN
(32+24+MAX_FIELD_LEN*2+3*MSQL_FIELD_NAME_LEN+1*MSQL_TABLE_NAME_LEN)
```

In order to avoid using the very large *HUGE_STRING_LENGTH*, the preceding two compile-time directives are supplied. The *MAX_FIELD_LEN* contains the maximum number of characters in your user, password, and group fields. The maximum query length is derived from those values.

Mod_cgi Module

This module is contained in the **mod_cgi.c** file and is compiled in by default. It provides for execution of CGI scripts. Any file with MIME type *application/x-httpd-cgi* will be processed by this module.

Any file that has the MIME type *application/x-httpd-cgi* will be treated as a CGI script and run by the server, with its output being returned to the client. Files acquire this type either by having a name ending in an extension defined by the *AddType* directive or by being in a *ScriptAlias* directory.

When the server invokes a CGI script, it will add a variable called *DOCUMENT_ROOT* to the environment. This variable contains the value of the *DocumentRoot* configuration variable.

The server will set the CGI environment variables as described in the CGI specification, with the following provisos:

- *REMOTE_HOST* will only be set if the server has not been compiled with *MINIMAL_DNS*.
- *REMOTE_IDENT* will only be set if *IdentityCheck* is set to *on*.
- *REMOTE_USER* will only be set if the CGI script is subject to authentication.

Mod_dir Module

This module is contained in the **mod_dir.c** file and is compiled in by default. It provides for directory indexing.

This module controls the directory indexing. The index of a directory can come from one of two sources:

- A file written by the user, typically called **index.html**. The *DirectoryIndex* directive sets the name of this file.
- A listing generated by the server. The other directives control the format of this listing. The *AddIcon, AddIconByEncoding,* and *AddIconByType* are used to set a list of icons to display for various file types; for each file listed, the first icon listed that matches the file is displayed.

This module adds the following directives: *AddDescription*, *AddIcon*, *AddIconByEncoding*, *AddIconByType*, *DefaultIcon*, *DirectoryIndex*, *FancyIndexing*, *HeaderName*, *IndexIgnore*, *IndexOptions*, and *ReadmeName*.

AddDescription

Syntax:	*AddDescription string file file…*
Context:	server config, virtual host, directory, **.htaccess**
Override:	indexes
Status:	base

This sets the description to *display* for a file, for *FancyIndexing*. *file* is a file extension, partial filename, wildcard expression, or full filename for files to describe. String is enclosed in quotation marks ("). For example,

```
AddDescription "The planet Mars" /web/pics/mars.gif
```

AddIcon

Syntax:	*AddIcon icon name name …*
Context:	server config, virtual host, directory, **.htaccess**
Override:	indexes
Status:	base

This sets the icon to display next to a file ending in *name* for *FancyIndexing*. *icon* is either a (%-escaped) relative URL to the icon or of the format (*alttext,url*) where *alttext* is the text tag given for an icon for nongraphical browsers.

Name is ^^DIRECTORY^^ for directories, ^^BLANKICON^^ for blank lines (to format the list correctly), a file extension, a wildcard expression, a partial filename, or a complete filename. Examples include

```
AddIcon (IMG,/icons/image.xbm) .gif .jpg .xbm
AddIcon /icons/dir.xbm ^^DIRECTORY^^
AddIcon /icons/backup.xbm *~
```

AddIconByType should be used in preference to *AddIcon*, when possible.

AddIconByEncoding

Syntax: *AddIconByEncoding icon mime-encoding mime-encoding …*
Context: server config, virtual host, directory, **.htaccess**
Override: indexes
Status: base

This sets the icon to display next to files with *mime-encoding* for *FancyIndexing. icon* is either a (%-escaped) relative URL to the icon or of the format (*alttext,url*) where *alttext* is the text tag given for an icon for nongraphical browsers.

   mime-encoding is a wildcard expression matching required the content-encoding. An example is

```
AddIconByEncoding /icons/compress.xbm x-compress
```

AddIconByType

Syntax: *AddIconByType icon mime-type mime-type …*
Context: server config, virtual host, directory, **.htaccess**
Override: indexes
Status: base

This sets the icon to display next to files of type *mime-type* for *FancyIndexing. icon* is either a (%-escaped) relative URL to the icon or of the format (*alttext,url*) where *alttext* is the text tag given for an icon for nongraphical browsers.

   Mime-type is a wildcard expression matching the required MIME types. An example is

```
AddIconByType (IMG,/icons/image.xbm) image/*
```

DefaultIcon

Syntax:	*DefaultIcon url*
Context:	server config, virtual host, directory, **.htaccess**
Override:	indexes
Status:	base

The *DefaultIcon* directive sets the icon to display for files when no specific icon is known, for *FancyIndexing*. *Url* is a (%-escaped) relative URL to the icon. An example is

```
DefaultIcon /icon/unknown.xbm
```

DirectoryIndex

Syntax:	*DirectoryIndex local-url local-url ...*
Default:	*DirectoryIndex* **index.html**
Context:	server config, virtual host, directory, .htaccess
Override:	indexes
Status:	base

The *DirectoryIndex* directive sets the list of resources to look for when the client requests an index of the directory by specifying a NULL file at the end of the a directory name. *Local-url* is the (%-encoded) URL of a document on the server relative to the requested directory; it is usually the name of a file in the directory. Several URLs may be given; the server will return the first one that it finds. If none of the resources exist, then the server will generate its own listing of the directory. An example is:

```
DirectoryIndex index.html
```

A request for *http://myserver/docs/* would return *http://myserver/docs/index.html* if it exists or would list the directory if it does not.

The documents do not need to be relative to the directory, as in the following:

```
DirectoryIndex index.html index.txt /cgi-bin/index.pl
```

would cause the CGI script **/cgi-bin/index.pl** to be executed if neither **index.html** or **index.txt** exists in a directory.

FancyIndexing

Syntax:	*FancyIndexing boolean*
Context:	server config, virtual host, directory, **.htaccess**
Override:	indexes
Status:	base

The *FancyIndexing* directive sets the *FancyIndexing* option for a directory. Boolean can be *on* or *off*. The *IndexOptions* directive should be used in preference.

HeaderName

Syntax:	*HeaderName filename*
Context:	server config, virtual host, directory, **.htaccess**
Override:	indexes
Status:	base

The *HeaderName* directive sets the name of the file that will be inserted at the top of the index listing. *Filename* is the name of the file to include and is taken to be relative to the directory being indexed. The server first attempts to include **filename.html** as an HTML document; otherwise, it will include *filename* as plain text. For example,

```
HeaderName HEADER
```

When indexing the directory **/web**, the server will first look for the HTML file **/web/HEADER.html** and include it if found; otherwise, it will include the plain text file **/web/HEADER**, if it exists.

IndexIgnore

Syntax:	*IndexIgnore file file ...*
Context:	server config, virtual host, directory, **.htaccess**
Override:	indexes
Status:	base

The *IndexIgnore* directive adds to the list of files to hide when listing a directory. *file* is a file extension, partial filename, wildcard expression, or full filename for files to ignore. Multiple *IndexIgnore* directives add to the list, rather than replacing the list of ignored files. By default, the list contains '.'. For example,

```
IndexIgnore README .htaccess *~
```

IndexOptions

Syntax: *IndexOptions option option ...*

Context: server config, virtual host, directory, **.htaccess**

Override: indexes

Status: base

The *IndexOptions* directive specifies the behavior of the directory indexing. *Option* can be one of the following:

- *FancyIndexing* (This turns on fancy indexing of directories.)
- *IconsAreLinks* (This makes the icons part of the anchor for the filename, for fancy indexing.)
- *ScanHTMLTitles* (This enables the extraction of the title from HTML documents for fancy indexing; if the file does not have a description given by *AddDescription*, then **httpd** will read the document for the value of the *TITLE* tag, but be warned that this is CPU- and disk-intensive.)
- *SuppressLastModified* (This suppresses the display of the last modification date, in fancy indexing listings.)
- *SuppressSize* (This suppresses the file size in fancy indexing listings.)
- *SuppressDescription* (This suppresses the file description in fancy indexing listings.)

The default is that no options are enabled. If multiple *IndexOptions* could apply to a directory, then the most specific one is taken complete; the options are not merged. For example,

```
<Directory /web/docs>
IndexOptions FancyIndexing
</Directory>
<Directory /web/docs/spec>
IndexOptions ScanHTMLTitles
</Directory>
```

Only *ScanHTMLTitles* will be set for the **/web/docs/spec** directory.

ReadmeName

Syntax:	*ReadmeName filename*
Context:	server config, virtual host, directory, **.htaccess**
Override:	indexes
Status:	base

The *ReadmeName* directive sets the name of the file that will be appended to the end of the index listing. *Filename* is the name of the file to include and is taken to be relative to the directory being indexed. The server first attempts to include **filename.html** as an HTML document; otherwise, it will include filename as plain text. In this example,

```
ReadmeName README
```

When indexing the directory **/web**, the server will first look for the HTML file **/web/README.html** and include it if found; otherwise, it will include the plain text file **/web/README**, if it exists.

Mod_imap Module

This module is contained in the **mod_imap.c** file and is compiled in by default. It provides for **.map** files, replacing the functionality of the *imagemap* CGI program. Any directory or document type configured to use the handler *imap-file* (using either *AddHandler* or *SetHandler*) will be processed by this module.

The following directive activates files ending with **.map** as *imagemap* files:

```
AddHandler imap-file map
```

Note that the following is still supported:

```
AddType application/x-httpd-imap map
```

The imagemap module adds some new features that were not possible with previously distributed imagemap programs:

- URL references relative to the *Referer:* information.
- Default *<BASE>* assignment through a new map directive base.
- No need for **imagemap.conf** file.
- Point references.
- Configurable generation of imagemap menus.

There are three directives made possible with this module: *ImapMenu, ImapDefault,* and *ImapBase.*

ImapMenu

Syntax: *ImapMenu {none, formatted, semiformatted, unformatted}*
Context: server config, virtual host, directory, **.htaccess**
Override: indexes

The *ImapMenu* directive determines the action taken if an imagemap file is called without valid coordinates. It has the following options:

- *none* (If ImapMenu is none, no menu is generated, and the default action is performed.)
- *formatted* (A formatted menu is the simplest menu, as comments in the imagemap file are ignored; a level-one header, a rule, and then the links each on a separate line are printed—the menu has a consistent, plain look close to that of a directory listing.)
- *semiformatted* (Comments are printed where they occur in the imagemap file. Blank lines are turned into HTML breaks; no header or hrule is printed; otherwise, the menu is the same as a formatted menu.)

- *unformatted* (Comments are printed, and blank lines are ignored. Nothing is printed that does not appear in the imagemap file, and all breaks and headers must be included as comments in the imagemap file. This gives you the most flexibility over the appearance of your menus but requires you to treat your map files as HTML instead of plain text.)

ImapDefault

Syntax: *ImapDefault {error, nocontent, map, referer, URL}*

Context: server config, virtual host, directory, **.htaccess**

Override: indexes

The *ImapDefault* directive sets the default used in the imagemap files. Its value is overridden by a default directive within the imagemap file. If not present, the default action is nocontent, which means that a *204 NoContent* message is sent to the client. In this case, the client should continue to display the original page.

ImapBase

Syntax: *ImapBase {map, referer, URL}*

Context: server config, virtual host, directory, **.htaccess**

Override: indexes

The *ImapBase* directive sets the default base used in the imagemap files. Its value is overridden by a base directive within the imagemap file. If not present, the base defaults to *http://servername/*.

Mod_include Module

This module is contained in the **mod_include.c** file and is compiled in by default. It provides for server-parsed HTML documents, known as SPML documents. Any document with MIME type *text/x-server-parsed-html* or *text/x-server-parsed-html3* will be parsed by this module, with the resulting output given the MIME type *text/html*.

The document is parsed as an HTML document, with special commands embedded as SGML comments. A command has the syntax:

```
<!-#element attribute=value attribute=value ... ->
```

The value will often be enclosed in quotation marks; many commands only allow a single attribute-value pair. The allowed elements follow:

- *config* (This command controls various aspects of the parsing; the valid attributes are *errmsg* for error messages, *sizefmt* for setting the format when displaying the size of a file, and *timefmt*, which is a string used by the *strftime(3)* library routine when printing dates.)
- *echo* (This command prints one of the *include* variables; *var* is the value is the name of the variable to print.)
- *exec* (This command executes a given shell command or CGI script. The *IncludesNOEXEC* option disables this command completely, and the valid attributes are *cgi* for CGI scripts and *cmd* for server commands.)
- *fsize* (This command prints the size of the specified file, subject to the *sizefmt* format specification. It has these potential attributes: *file* for a relative file path and *virtual* for URL paths.)
- *flastmod* (This command prints the last modification date of the specified file, subject to the *timefmt* format specification, with the same attributes as the *fsize* command.)
- *include* (This command inserts the text of another document or file into the parsed file. Any included file is subject to the usual access control, and if the directory containing the parsed file has the *Option IncludesNOEXEC* set and including the document would cause a program to be executed, then it will not be included, preventing the execution of CGI scripts.)

An attribute defines the location of the document; the inclusion is done for each attribute given to the **include** command. The valid attributes are *file* (the value is a path relative to the directory containing the current document being parsed) and *virtual* (a URL relative to the current document being parsed).

There are a number of **include** variables for the **echo** command and to any program invoked by the document:

- *DATE_GMT* (the current date in Greenwich Mean Time)
- *DATE_LOCAL* (the current date in the local time zone)
- *DOCUMENT_NAME* (the filename, excluding directories, of the document requested by the user)
- *DOCUMENT_URL* (the %-decoded URL path of the document requested by the user; in the case of nested include files, this is not then URL for the current document)
- *LAST_MODIFIED* (the last modification date of the document requested by the user)

There is one directive made possible by this module: *XBitHack*.

XBitHack

Syntax: *XBitHack status*
Default: *XBitHack off*
Context: server config, virtual host, directory, **.htaccess**
Override: options
Status: base

The *XBitHack* directive controls the parsing of ordinary HTML documents. *Status* can have the following values:

- *off* (There is no special treatment of executable files.)
- *on* (Any file that has the user-execute bit set will be treated as a server-parsed HTML document.)
- *full* (It is like *on*, except that the group-execute bit is tested. If it's set, then set the last-modified date of the returned file to be the last modified time of the file, and it it's not set, then no last-modified date is sent. Setting this bit allows clients and proxies to cache the result of the request.)

Mod_log_common Module

This module is contained in the **mod_log_common.c** file and is compiled in by default. It provides for logging of the requests made to the server using the Common Logfile Format.

The log file contains a separate line for each request. A line is composed of several tokens separated by spaces:

```
host ident authuser date request status bytes
```

If a token does not have a value, then it is represented by a hyphen (-). The meanings and values of these tokens follow:

- *host*: The fully qualified domain name of the client, or its IP number if the name is not available.
- *ident*: If *IdentityCheck* is enabled and the client machine runs **identd**, then this is the identity information reported by the client.
- *authuser*: If the request was for an password-protected document, then this is the userid used in the request.
- *date*: The date and time of the request, in the following format:

```
date = [day/month/year:hour:minute:second zone]
day = 2*digit
month = 3*letter
year = 4*digit
hour = 2*digit
minute = 2*digit
second = 2*digit
zone = (`+' | `-') 4*digit
```

- *request*: The request line from the client, enclosed in quotation marks (").
- *status*: The three-digit status code returned to the client.
- *bytes*: The number of bytes in the object returned to the client, not including any headers.

There is one directive supplied by this module: *TransferLog*.

TransferLog

Syntax: *TransferLog file-pipe*

Default: *TransferLog* **logs/transfer_log**

Context: server config, virtual host

Status: base

The *TransferLog* directive sets the name of the file where the server will log the incoming requests. *File-pipe* is either a filename (relative to the *ServerRoot*) or | followed by a command (a program to receive the agent log information on its standard input; a new program will not be started for a *VirtualHost* if it inherits the *TransferLog* from the main server).

If a program is used, then it will be run under the user who started **httpd**. This will be root if the server was started by root; be sure that the program is secure.

Mod_mime Module

This module is contained in the **mod_mime.c** file and is compiled in by default. It provides for determining the types of files from the filename.

This module is used to determine the MIME types of documents. Some MIME types indicate special processing to be performed by the server; otherwise, the type is returned to the client so that the browser can deal with the document appropriately.

The filename of a document is treated as being composed of a basename followed by some extensions, in the following order:

```
base.type.language.enc
```

The *type* extension sets the type of the document; types are defined in the *TypesConfig* file and by the *AddType* directive. The *language* extension sets the language of the document, as defined by the *AddLanguage* directive. Finally, the *enc* directive sets the encoding of the document, as defined by the *AddEncoding* directive.

Supported directives are *AddEncoding, AddHandler, AddLanguage, AddType, ForceType, SetHandler,* and *TypesConfig.*

AddEncoding

Syntax: *AddEncoding mime-enc extension extension...*

Context: server config, virtual host, directory, **.htaccess**

Override: *FileInfo*

Status: base

The *AddEncoding* directive adds to the list of filename extensions. *Mime-enc* is the MIME encoding to use for documents ending in extension. For example,

```
AddEncoding x-gzip gz
AddEncoding x-compress Z
```

This will cause files ending in **.gz** to be marked as encoded using the x-gzip encoding, and **.Z** files to be marked as encoded with x-compress.

AddHandler

Syntax: *<AddHandler handler-name extension>*

Context: server config, virtual host, directory, **.htaccess**

Status: base

AddHandler maps the filename extension *extension* to the handler *handler-name*. For example, to activate CGI scripts with the file extension **.cgi**, you might use

```
AddHandler cgi-script cgi
```

Once that has been put into your **srm.conf** or **httpd.conf** file, any file ending with **.cgi** will be treated as a CGI program.

AddLanguage

Syntax: *AddLanguage mime-lang extension extension...*

Context: server config, virtual host, directory, **.htaccess**

Override: *FileInfo*

Status: base

The *AddLanguage* directive adds to the list of filename extensions that may end in for the specified content language. *Mime-lang* is the MIME language of files with names ending with *extension*, after any content encoding extensions have been removed. For example,

```
AddEncoding x-compress Z
AddLanguage en .en
AddLanguage fr .fr
```

The document **xxxx.en.Z** will be treated as being a compressed English document. Although the content language is reported to the client, the browser is unlikely to use this information. The *AddLanguage* directive is more useful for content negotiation, where the server returns one from several documents based on the client's language preference.

AddType

Syntax: *AddType mime-type extension extension...*

Context: server config, virtual host, directory, **.htaccess**

Override: *FileInfo*

Status: base

The *AddType* directive adds to the list of filename extensions that may end in for the specified content type. *Mime-type* is the MIME type to use for documents ending in *extension* after content-encoding and language extensions have been removed. For example,

```
AddType image/gif GIF
```

It is recommended that new MIME types be added using the *AddType* directive rather than changing the *TypesConfig* file.

Unlike the NCSA **httpd**, this directive cannot be used to set the type of particular files.

ForceType

Syntax: *<ForceType media type>*

Context: directory, **.htaccess**

Status: base

When placed into an **.htaccess** file or a *<Directory>* or *<Location>* section, this directive forces all matching files to be served as the content type given by media type. For example, if you had a directory of GIF files but did not want to label them all with **.gif**, you might want to use:

```
ForceType image/gif
```

This will override any filename extensions.

SetHandler

Syntax:	*<SetHandler handler-name>*
Context:	directory, **.htaccess**
Status:	base

When placed into an **.htaccess** file or a *<Directory>* or *<Location>* section, this directive forces all matching files to be parsed through the handler given by *handler-name*. For example, if you had a directory you wanted to be parsed entirely as imagemap rule files, regardless of extension, you might put the following into an **.htaccess** file in that directory:

```
SetHandler imap-file
```

Here is another example. If you wanted to have the server display a status report whenever a URL of *http://servername/status* was called, you might put the following into **access.conf**:

```
<Location /status>
SetHandler server-status
</Location>
```

TypesConfig

Syntax:	*TypesConfig filename*
Default:	*TypesConfig* **conf/mime.types**
Context:	server config
Status:	base

The *TypesConfig* directive sets the location of the MIME types configuration file. *Filename* is relative to the *ServerRoot*. This file sets the default list of mappings from filename extensions to content types; changing this file is not recommended. Use the *AddType* directive instead. The file contains lines in the format of the arguments to an *AddType* command:

```
mime-type extension extension …
```

The extensions are lowercased. Blank lines and lines beginning with a hash character (#) are ignored.

Mod_negotiation Module

This module is contained in the **mod_negotiation.c** file and is compiled in by default. It provides for content negotiation. Any document with MIME type *application/x-type-map* will be processed by this module.

The HTTP standard allows clients (browsers like Mosaic or Netscape) to specify what data formats they are prepared to accept. The intention is that when information is available in multiple variants (e.g., in different data formats), servers can use this information to decide which variant to send. This feature has been supported in the CERN server for a while, and even though it is not yet supported in the NCSA server, it is likely to assume a new importance in light of the emergence of HTML-capable browsers.

The Apache module *mod_negotiation* handles content negotiation in two different ways: special treatment for the pseudo-MIME-type *application/x-type-map* and the MultiViews per-directory option (which can be set in **srm.conf** or in **.htaccess** files, as usual). These features are alternate user interfaces to what amounts to the same piece of code (in the new file **http_mime_db.c**) that implements the content negotiation portion of the HTTP protocol.

Each of these features allows one of several files to satisfy a request based on what the client says it's willing to accept; the differences are in the way the files are identified. A type map (like a ***.var** file) names the files containing the variants explicitly, while in a MultiViews search, the server does an implicit filename pattern match and chooses from among the results.

Apache also supports a new pseudo-MIME type, *text/x-server-parsed-html3*, which is treated as *text/html;level=3* for purposes of content negotiation and as server-side-included HTML elsewhere.

A type map is a document that is typed by the server (using its normal suffix-based mechanisms) as *application/x-type-map*. To use this feature, you must have an *AddType* someplace that defines a file suffix as *application/x-type-map*; the easiest thing may be to stick:

```
AddType application/x-type-map var
```

in **srm.conf**.

Type-map files have an entry for each available variant; these entries consist of contiguous RFC822-format header lines. Entries for different variants are separated by blank lines. Blank lines are illegal within an entry. It is conventional to begin a map file with an entry for the combined entity as a whole, like

```
URI: foo; vary="type,language"

URI: foo.en.html
Content-type: text/html; level=2
Content-language: en

URI: foo.fr.html
Content-type: text/html; level=2
Content-language: fr
```

If the variants have different qualities, that may be indicated by the *qs* parameter, as in this picture (available as JPEG, GIF, or ASCII-art):

```
URI: foo; vary="type,language"

URI: foo.jpeg
Content-type: image/jpeg; qs=0.8

URI: foo.gif
Content-type: image/gif; qs=0.5

URI: foo.txt
Content-type: text/plain; qs=0.01
```

There are a number of recognized headers. *URI* is the uri of the file containing the variant (of the given media type, encoded with the given content encoding). These are interpreted as URLs relative to the map file; they must be on the same server, and they must refer to files to which the client would be granted access if they were to be requested directly. *Content-type* is the media type; the level may be specified, along with *qs*. These are often referred to as MIME types; typical media types are *image/gif*, *text/plain*, or *text/html*; *level=3*. The *content-language* is the language of the variant, specified as an Internet standard language code (*en* for English, *kr* for Korean, and so on). *Content-encoding* defines the encoding. If the file is compressed or otherwise encoded, rather than containing the actual raw data, this says how that was done. For compressed files (the only case where this generally comes up), content encoding should be *x-compress* or *gzip*, as appropriate. The *content-length* is the size of the file. Clients can ask to receive a given media type only if the variant isn't too big; specifying a content length in the map allows the server to compare against these thresholds without checking the actual file.

Multiviews is a per-directory option, meaning that it can be set with an *Options* directive within a *<Directory>* section in **access.conf** or (if *AllowOverride* is properly set) in **.htaccess** files. *Options All* does not set Multiviews; you have to ask for it by name. (Fixing this is a one-line change to **httpd.h**.)

The effect of Multiviews follows: If the server receives a request for **/some/dir/foo**, if **/some/dir** has Multiviews enabled, and if **/some/dir/foo** does *not* exist, then the server reads the directory looking for files named *foo.* and effectively fakes up a type map that names all those files, assigning them the same media types and content-encodings it would have if the client had asked for one of them by name. It then chooses the best match to the client's requirements and forwards them.

This applies to searches for the file named by the *DirectoryIndex* directive, if the server is trying to index a directory; if the configuration files specify:

```
DirectoryIndex index
```

then the server will arbitrate between **index.html** and **index.html3** if both are present. If neither is present and **index.cgi** is there, the server will run it.

If one of the files found by the globbing is a CGI script, it's not obvious what should happen. That case gets special treatment—if the request was a POST or a GET with *QUERY_ARGS* or *PATH_INFO*, the script is given an extremely high quality rating and is generally invoked; otherwise, it is given an extremely low quality rating, which generally causes one of the other views (if any) to be retrieved. This is the only jiggering of quality ratings done by the MultiViews code; aside from that, all *Qualities* in the synthesized type maps are 1.0.

Documents in multiple languages can also be resolved through the use of the *AddLanguage* and *LanguagePriority* directives:

```
AddLanguage en  .en
AddLanguage fr  .fr
AddLanguage de  .de
AddLanguage da  .da
AddLanguage el  .el
AddLanguage it  .it


# LanguagePriority allows you to give precedence to some languages
# in case of a tie during content negotiation.
# Just list the languages in decreasing order of preference.

LanguagePriority en fr de
```

Here, a request for **foo.html** matched against **foo.html.en** and **foo.html.fr** would return a French document to a browser that indicated a preference for French and an English document otherwise. In fact, a request for *foo* matched against **foo.html.en**, **foo.html.fr**, **foo.ps.en**, **foo.pdf.de**, and **foo.txt.it** would do just what you expect—treat those suffices as a database and compare the request to it, returning the best match. The languages and data types share the same suffix name space.

This machinery comes into play only if the file the user attempted to retrieve does not exist by that name; if it does, it is simply retrieved as usual. (So, someone who actually asks for **foo.jpeg**, as opposed to *foo*, never gets **foo.gif**).

The two directives made possible with this module are *CacheNegotiatedDocs* and *LanguagePriority*.

CacheNegotiatedDocs

Syntax: *CacheNegotiatedDocs*

Context: server config

Status: base

If set, this directive allows content-negotiated documents to be cached by proxy servers. This could mean that clients behind those proxys could retrieve versions of the documents that are not the best match for their abilities, but it will make caching more efficient.

LanguagePriority

Syntax: *LanguagePriority mime-lang mime-lang…*

Context: server config, virtual host, directory, **.htaccess**

Override: *FileInfo*

Status: base

The *LanguagePriority* sets the precedence of language variants for the case where the client does not express a preference, when handling a Multiviews request. The list of *mime-lang* are in order of decreasing preference. For example,

```
LanguagePriority en fr de
```

For a request for **foo.html**, where **foo.html.fr** and **foo.html.de** both exist but the browser did not express a language preference, then **foo.html.fr** would be returned.

Mod_userdir Module

This module is contained in the **mod_userdir.c** file and is compiled in by default. It provides for user-specific directories.

There is one directive supplied by this module: *UserDir*.

UserDir

Syntax:	*UserDir directory/filename*
Default:	*UserDir public_html*
Context:	server config, virtual host
Status:	base

The *UserDir* directive sets the real directory in a user's home directory to use when a request for a document for a user is received. *Directory* is either *disabled,* to disable this feature, or the name of a directory, using one of the following patterns, is disabled. If not disabled, then a request for *http://www.foo.com/~bar/one/two.html* will be translated to:

```
UserDir public_html     -> ~bar/public_html/one/two.html
UserDir /usr/web        -> /usr/web/bar/one/two.html
UserDir /home/*/www     -> /home/bar/www/one/two.html
```

The following directives will send redirects to the client:

```
UserDir http://www.x.com/users   ->
http//www.x.com/users/bar/one/two.html
UserDir http://www.x.com/*/y     -> http://www.x.com/y/one/two.html
```

Optional Modules

The following modules have not been compiled in the Apache Web server that ships with Slackware Linux. Information here comes from the Apache Web site.

Use them at your own risk; some are experimental and have not been heavily tested.

Mod_auth_db Module

This module is contained in the **mod_auth_db.c** file and is not compiled in by default. It provides for user authentication using Berkeley DB files. It is an alternative to DBM files for those systems supporting DB and not DBM.

There are two directives supplied with this module: *AuthDBGroupFile* and *AuthDBUserFile*.

AuthDBGroupFile

Syntax: *AuthDBGroupFile filename*

Context: directory, **.htaccess**

Override: *AuthConfig*

Status: extension

The *AuthDBGroupFile* directive sets the name of a DB file containing the list of user groups for user authentication. *Filename* is the absolute path to the group file.

The group file is keyed on the username. The value for a user is a comma-separated list of the groups to which the users belongs. There must be no whitespace within the value, and it must never contain any colons.

Make sure that the *AuthDBGroupFile* is stored outside the document tree of the Web server. Do not put it in the directory that it protects; otherwise, clients will be able to download the *AuthDBGroupFile*.

AuthDBUserFile

Syntax: *AuthDBUserFile filename*

Context: directory, **.htaccess**

Override: *AuthConfig*

Status: extension

The *AuthDBUserFile* directive sets the name of a DB file containing the list of users and passwords for user authentication. *Filename* is the absolute path to the user file.

The user file is keyed on the username. The value for a user is the *crypt()* encrypted password, optionally followed by a colon and arbitrary data. The colon and the data following it will be ignored by the server.

Make sure that the *AuthDBUserFile* is stored outside the document tree of the Web server. Do not put it in the directory that it protects; otherwise, clients will be able to download the *AuthDBUserFile*.

Mod_auth_dbm Module

This module is contained in the **mod_auth_dbm.c** file and is not compiled in by default. It provides for user authentication using DBM files (which will be covered later in this chapter). The directives provided by this module are *AuthDBMGroupFile* and *AuthDBMUserFile*.

AuthDbmGroupFile

Syntax: *AuthGroupFile filename*

Context: directory, **.htaccess**

Override: *AuthConfig*

Status: extension

The *AuthDBMGroupFile* directive sets the name of a DBM file containing the list of user groups for user authentication. *Filename* is the absolute path to the group file.

The group file is keyed on the username. The value for a user is a comma-separated list of the groups to which the users belongs. There must be no whitespace within the value, and it must never contain any colons.

Make sure that the *AuthDBMGroupFile* is stored outside the document tree of the Web server. Do not put it in the directory that it protects; otherwise, clients will be able to download the *AuthDBMGroupFile*.

AuthDBMUserFile

Syntax: *AuthDBMUserFile filename*

Context: directory, **.htaccess**

Override: *AuthConfig*

Status: extension

The *AuthDBMUserFile* directive sets the name of a DBM file containing the list of users and passwords for user authentication. *filename* is the absolute path to the user file.

The user file is keyed on the username. The value for a user is the *crypt()* encrypted password, optionally followed by a colon and arbitrary data. The colon and the data following it will be ignored by the server.

Make sure that the *AuthDBMUserFile* is stored outside the document tree of the Web server. Do not put it in the directory that it protects; otherwise, clients will be able to download the *AuthDBMUserFile*.

Mod_cern_meta Module

This module is contained in the **mod_cern_meta.c** file and is not compiled in by default. It provides for CERN HTTPD metafile semantics.

This module emulate the CERN HTTPD metafile semantics. Meta files are HTTP headers that can be output in addition to the normal range of headers for each file accessed. They appear rather like the Apache **.asis** files and are able to provide a crude way of influencing the *Expires:* header, as well as providing other curiosities. There are many ways to manage meta information; this one was chosen because there is already a large number of CERN users who can exploit this module.

More information on the CERN metafile semantics is available at *http://www.w3.org/pub/WWW/Daemon/User/Config/General.html*.

There are two directives supplied with this module: *MetaDir* and *MetaSuffix*.

MetaDir

Syntax: *MetaDir directory name*
Default: *MetaDir .web*
Context: server config
Status: base

This specifies the name of the directory in which Apache can find meta information files. The directory is usually a hidden subdirectory of the directory that contains the file being accessed. It is set to look in the same directory as the file.

MetaSuffix

Syntax: *MetaSuffix suffix*
Default: *MetaSuffix .meta*
Context: server config
Status: base

This specifies the filename suffix for the file containing the meta information. For example, the default values for the two directives will cause a request to *DOCUMENT_ROOT/somedir/index.html* to look in *DOCUMENT_ROOT/somedir/.web/index.html.meta* and will use its contents to generate additional MIME header information.

Mod_cookies Module

This module is contained in the **mod_cookies.c** file and is not compiled in by default. It provides for Netscape cookies. There is no documentation available for this module. One directive is made possible by this module: *CookieLog*.

CookieLog

Syntax:	*CookieLog filename*
Context:	server config, virtual host
Status:	experimental

The *CookieLog* directive sets the filename for logging of cookies. The filename is relative to the *ServerRoot*.

Mod_digest Module

This module is contained in the **mod_digest.c** file and is not compiled in by default. It provides for user authentication using MD5 Digest Authentication.

The directive made possible with this module is *AuthDigestFile*.

AuthDigestFile

Syntax:	*AuthDigestFile filename*
Context:	directory, **.htaccess**
Override:	*AuthConfig*
Status:	base

The *AuthDigestFile* directive sets the name of a textual file containing the list of users and encoded passwords for digest authentication. *Filename* is the absolute path to the user file.

The digest file uses a special format. Files in this format can be created using the **htdigest** utility found in the **support/** subdirectory of the Apache distribution.

Using MD5 Digest Authentication is very simple. Simply set up authentication normally. However, use *AuthType Digest* and *AuthDigestFile* instead of the normal *AuthType Basic* and *AuthUserFile*. Everything else should remain the same.

MD5 Digest Authentication provides a more secure password system but works only with supporting browsers. Most browsers do not support digest authentication, however; for personal and intranet use, where browser users can be controlled, it is ideal.

Mod_dld Module

This module is contained in the **mod_dld.c** file and is not compiled in by default. It provides for loading of executable code and modules into the server at startup time, using the GNU **dld** library.

The optional *dld* module is a proof-of-concept piece of code that loads other modules into the server as it is configuring itself (the first time only; for now, rereading the config files cannot affect the state of loaded modules), using the GNU dynamic linking library (DLD).

LoadFile **/lib/libc.a** seems to be required for just about everything. DLD needs to read the symbol table out of the server binary when starting up; these commands will fail if the server can't find its own binary when it starts up or if that binary is stripped.

There are two directives made possible with this module: *LoadFile* and *LoadModule*.

LoadFile

Syntax: *LoadFile filename filename …*

Context: server config

Status: experimental

The *LoadFile* directive links in the named object files or libraries when the server is started; this is used to load additional code that may be required for some module to work. *Filename* is relative to *ServerRoot*.

LoadModule

Syntax: *LoadModule module filename*

Context: server config

Status: experimental

The *LoadModule* directive links in the object file or library filename and adds the module structure named *Module* to the list of active modules. *module* is the name of the external variable of type module in the file. For example,

```
LoadModule ai_backcompat_module modules/mod_ai_backcompat.o
LoadFile /lib/libc.a
```

loads the *module* in the **modules** subdirectory of the *ServerRoot*.

Mod_env Module

This module is contained in the **mod_env.c** file and is not compiled in by default. It provides for passing environment variables to CGI/SSI scripts.

This module allows Apache's CGI and SSI environment to inherit environment variables from the shell that invoked the **httpd** process. CERN Web servers are able to do this, so this module is especially useful to Web administrators who wish to migrate from CERN to Apache without rewriting all their scripts.

The two directives made possible with this module are *PassEnv* and *SetEnv*.

PassEnv

Syntax: *PassEnv variable*

Context: server config, virtual host

Status: base

This directive passes an environment variable to CGI scripts from the server's own environment. For example,

```
PassEnv LD_LIBRARY_PATH
```

takes the LD_LIBRARY_PATH from the server's environment.

SetEnv

Syntax: *SetEnv variable value*

Context: server config, virtual host

Status: base

This sets an environment variable, which is then passed on to CGI scripts. For example,

```
SetEnv SPECIAL_PATH /foo/bin
```

sets the *SPECIAL_PATH* environment variable.

Mod_fastcgi Module

This module is contained in the **mod_fastcgi.c** file. It provides for startup of and communication with FastCGI applications. This module is not compiled into the server by default. To use this module you must copy **src/mod_fastcgi.c** from this kit into your Apache server's source directory. Then you have to add the following line to the server build Configuration file:

```
Module fastcgi_module   mod_fastcgi.o
```

Any file with the MIME type *application/x-httpd-fcgi* will be processed by this module. Note that the *ScriptAlias* directive takes priority over the *AddType* directive; a file located in a directory that is the target of *ScriptAlias* directive will have type *application/x-httpd-cgi* and be handled by *mod_cgi*, regardless of its name. So don't put FastCGI applications in your **/cgi-bin/** directory—they won't work properly.

FastCGI is a faster alternative to CGI. FastCGI gets its speed by having the Web server keep the application processes running between requests. So, unlike CGI, you do not have the overhead of starting up a new process and doing application initialization each time somebody requests a document. The processes start up with the Web server and keep on running.

FastCGI applications communicate with a Web server using a simple communications protocol. A single full-duplex connection communicates the environment variables and *stdin* data to the application, and *stdout* and *stderr* data to the Web server.

For more information on FastCGI including freely available FastCGI server modules and application libraries, go to the FastCGI home page (*http://www.fastcgi.com*).

Any file that has a MIME type of *application/x-httpd-fcgi* and that has an Application Class associated with it will be treated as a FastCGI script. A file gets this MIME type by not residing in a *ScriptAlias* directory and having a name ending in an extension defined by an *AddType application/x-httpd-fcgi* directive. An Application Class is established by the *AppClass* directive.

There is one directive made possible with this module: *AppClass*.

AppClass

Syntax:	*AppClass exec-path [-processes N] [-listen-queue-depth N] [-restart-delay N] [-priority N] [-initial-env name=value]*
Context:	**srm.conf**

The *AppClass* directive starts one or more FastCGI application processes, using the executable file **exec-path**. This file must have MIME type *application/x-httpd-fcgi*. The server is responsible for restarting these processes should they die. All the FastCGI application processes started by a given *AppClass* directive share a common UNIX domain listening socket.

When a client request comes in for the file **exec-path**, the request is handled by the *mod_fastcgi* module. The FastCGI module connects the requests to a processes belonging to the corresponding application class.

The optional parameters to the *AppClass* directive are as follows:

- **Processes**: number of FastCGI processes that the server will spawn, default value is 1.

- **Listen-queue-depth**: depth of listening queue shared by the processes, default value is 5.

- **Restart-delay**: number of seconds before the Web server restarts a dead FastCGI process. The server will restart dead processes no more often than one every restart-delay seconds.

- **Priority**: priority of FastCGI processes, default value is same priority as the HTTP server.

- **Initial-env**: a name-value pair in the initial environment passed to the application processes. Several name-value pairs can be specified by using this option several times. The default initial environment is empty (no name-value pairs).

If there are any errors in processing the FastCGI directive *AppClass*, the server will exit with appropriate error messages. Errors include syntax errors, **exec-path** has incorrect MIME-type, and **exec-path** does not exist.

An example from the **srm.conf** file:

```
AddType application/x-httpd-fcgi .fcgi
Alias /fcgi-bin/ /usr/local/etc/httpd/fcgi-devel-kit/examples/
AppClass /usr/local/etc/httpd/fcgi-devel-kit/examples/tiny-fcgi.fcgi
-processes 2
```

In this example if a request comes in for */fcgi-bin/tiny-fcgi.fcgi*, it'll be bound to the application class defined here, and the request will be sent to one of the two *tiny-fcgi.fcgi* processes.

NOTE To try this configuration example with the FastCGI Developer's Kit, you need to make a link from the name **examples/tiny-fcgi.fcgi** to the existing file **examples/tiny-fcgi**.

Mod_info Module

This module is contained in the **mod_info.c** file and is not compiled in by default. It provides a comprehensive overview of the current server configuration including all installed modules. To enable it, add the following line to the server build **Configuration** file, and rebuild the server:

```
Module info_module    mod_info.o
```

To configure it, add the following to your **access.conf** file:

```
<Location /server-info>
SetHandler server-info
</Location>
```

You may wish to add a limit clause inside the location directive to limit access to your server configuration information. Once configured, the server information is obtained by accessing *http://your.host.dom/server-info*.

Mod_log_agent Module

This module is contained in the **mod_log_agent.c** file and is not compiled in by default. It provides for logging of the client user agents. There is only one directive: *AgentLog*.

AgentLog

Syntax:	*AgentLog file-pipe*
Default:	*AgentLog* **logs/agent_log**
Context:	server config, virtual host
Status:	extension

The *AgentLog* directive sets the name of the file where the server will log the *UserAgent* header of incoming requests. *File-pipe* is one of either a filename relative to the *ServerRoot* or | followed by a command, which launches a program to receive the agent log information on its standard input. A new program will not be started for a *VirtualHost* if it inherits the *AgentLog* from the main server.

If a program is used as a response to the agent, then it will be run under the user who started **httpd**. This will be root if the server was started by root; be sure that the program is secure.

This directive is provided for compatibility with NCSA 1.4.

Mod_log_config Module

This module is contained in the **mod_log_config.c** file and is not compiled in by default. It provides for logging of the requests made to the server, using a user-specified format.

This is an experimental module, which implements the *TransferLog* directive (same as the common log module) and an additional directive, *LogFormat*. The argument to the *LogFormat* is a string, which can include literal characters copied into the log files, and % directives as follows:

%...h	Remote host
%...l	Remote logname (from *identd*, if supplied)
%...u	Remote user (from auth; may be bogus if return status (%s) is 401)
%...t	Time, in common log format time format
%...r	First line of request
%...s	Status—For requests that got internally redirected, this is status of the original request—%...>s for the last
%...b	Bytes sent
%...{Foobar}i	The contents of *Foobar:* header line(s) in the request sent to the client
%...{Foobar}o	The contents of *Foobar:* header line(s) in the reply

The trailing periods (...) can be nothing at all (*%h %u %r %s %b*), or it can indicate conditions for inclusion of the item (which will cause it to be replaced with, if the condition is not met). Note that there is no escaping performed on the strings from *%r, %...i,* and *%...o*.

The forms of condition are a list of HTTP status codes, which may or may not be preceded by *!*. Thus, `%400,501{User-agent}i`' logs User-agent on 400 errors and 501 errors (Bad Request, Not Implemented) only; `%!200,304,302{Referer}i`' logs Referer on all requests that did not return some sort of normal status.

The default *LogFormat* reproduces CLF, which is discussed later.

The way this is supposed to work with virtual hosts is as follows: A virtual host can have its own *LogFormat* or its own *TransferLog*. If it doesn't have its own *LogFormat*, it inherits from the main server. If it doesn't have its own *TransferLog*, it writes to the same descriptor (meaning the same process for | ...).

That means that you can do things like:

```
<VirtualHost hosta.com>
LogFormat "hosta ..."
...
</VirtualHost>

<VirtualHost hosta.com>
LogFormat "hostb ..."
...
</VirtualHost>
```

to have different virtual servers write into the same log file, but have some indication which host they came from, even though a *%v* directive may well be a better way to handle this.

There are two directives with this module: *LogFormat* and *TransferLog*.

LogFormat

Syntax:	*LogFormat string*
Default:	*LogFormat "%h %l %u %t \"%r\" %s %b"*
Context:	server config, virtual host
Status:	experimental

This sets the format of the logfile.

TransferLog

Syntax:	*TransferLog file-pipe*
Default:	*TransferLog* **logs/transfer_log**
Context:	server config, virtual host
Status:	experimental

The *TransferLog* directive sets the name of the file to which the server will log the incoming requests. *File-pipe* is one of *filename* (a filename relative to the *ServerRoot*) or | followed by a command (a program to receive the agent log information on its standard input; a new program will not be started for a *VirtualHost* if it inherits the *TransferLog* from the main server).

If a program is used, then it will be run under the user who started **httpd**. This will be root if the server was started by root; be sure that the program is secure.

Mod_log_referer Module

This module is contained in the **mod_log_referer.c** file and is not compiled in by default. It provides for logging of the documents that reference documents on the server.

The log file contains a separate line for each refer. Each line has the format:

```
uri -> document
```

where *uri* is the (%-escaped) URI for the document that references the one requested by the client, and *document* is the (%-decoded) local URL to the document being referred to.

There are two directives supplied by this module: *RefererIgnore* and *RefererLog*.

RefererIgnore

Syntax: *RefererIgnore string string ...*
Context: server config, virtual host
Status: extension

The *RefererIgnore* directive adds to the list of strings to ignore in *Referer* headers. If any of the strings in the list is contained in the *Referer* header, then no referer information will be logged for the request. For example,

```
RefererIgnore www.ncsa.uiuc.edu
```

This avoids logging references from *www.ncsa.uiuc.edu*.

RefererLog

Syntax: *RefererLog file-pipe*

Default: *RefererLog* **logs/referer_log**

Context: server config, virtual host

Status: extension

The *RefererLog* directive sets the name of the file where the server will log the *Referer* header of incoming requests. *File-pipe* is either *filename* (a filename relative to the *ServerRoot*) or | followed by a command (this launches a program to receive the referrer log information on its standard input; a new program will not be started for a *VirtualHost* if it inherits the *RefererLog* from the main server).

If a program is used, then it will be run under the user who started **httpd**. This will be root if the server was started by root; be sure that the program is secure.

This directive is provided for compatibility with NCSA 1.4.

Apache's Handler Use

A *handler* is an internal Apache representation of the action to be performed when a file is called. Generally, files have implicit handlers, based on the file type. Normally, all files are simply served by the server, but certain file typed are handled separately. For example, you may use a type of *application/x-httpd-cgi* to invoke CGI scripts.

Apache 1.1 adds the additional ability to use handlers explicitly. Either based on filename extensions or on location, these handlers are unrelated to file type. This is advantageous because it is both a more elegant solution, and it also allows for both a type and a handler to be associated with a file.

Handlers can either be built into the server or a module, or they can be added with the *Action* directive. The built-in handlers in the standard distribution are as follows:

- *send-as-is*: Send file with HTTP headers as is (*mod_asis*).
- *cgi-script*: Treat the file as a CGI script (*mod_cgi*).
- *imap-file*: Imagemap rule file (*mod_imap*).
- *server-info*: Get the server's configuration information (*mod_info*).
- *server-parsed*: Parse for server-side includes (*mod_include*).
- *server-status*: Get the server's status report (*mod_status*).
- *type-map*: Parse as a type map file for content negotiation (*mod_negotiation*).

There are two directives associated with handlers: *AddHandler* and *SetHandler*.

AddHandler

Syntax: *<AddHandler handler-name extension>*

Context: server config, virtual host, directory, **.htaccess**

Status: base

AddHandler maps the filename extension *extension* to the handler *handler-name*. For example, to activate CGI scripts with the file extension **.cgi**, you might use

```
AddHandler cgi-script cgi
```

Once that has been put into your **srm.conf** or **httpd.conf** file, any file ending with **.cgi** will be treated as a CGI program.

SetHandler

Syntax: *<SetHandler handler-name>*

Context: directory, **.htaccess**

Status: base

When placed into an **.htaccess** file or a *<Directory>* or *<Location>* section, this directive forces all matching files to be parsed through the handler given by *handler-name*. For example, if you had a directory you wanted to be parsed entirely as imagemap rule files, regardless of extension, you might put the following into an **.htaccess** file in that directory:

```
SetHandler imap-file
```

Here is another example: If you wanted to have the server display a status report whenever a URL of *http://servername/status* was called, you might put the following into **access.conf**:

```
<Location /status>
SetHandler server-status
</Location>
```

In order to implement the handler features, an addition has been made to the Apache API that you may wish to use. Specifically, a new record has been added to the *request_rec* structure:

```
char *handler
```

If you wish to have your module engage a handler, you need only to set *r->handler* to the name of the handler at any time prior to the *invoke_handler* stage of the request. Handlers are implemented as they were before, albeit using the handler name instead of a content type. While it is not necessary, the naming convention for handlers is to use a dash-separated word, with no slashes, so as to not invade the media type name space.

DBM Files for User Authentication

Using DBM files for user authentication dramatically reduces the lookup time for a password for areas under user authentication, where the user database is larger than a couple hundred entries. This is what HotWired uses for its 150,000+ user database.

You can use new directives to replace a password file with a DBM. You can also replace a group file with DBM or combine the two. You can use other fields in the DBM to store other user details.

DBM files, native to most UNIX platforms, are an implementation of a self-maintaining hash table, where a given key maps to a stored value. DBM files are not ASCII and not portable between operating systems, but there is a Perl tool called **dbmmanage** in the **/support** directory included with the Apache distribution to modify and view (and even add a user, automatically encrypting their password) DBM files. Apache's version uses the **ndbm** library—there are other libraries, but this was chosen as the one implemented on most systems and the one Perl uses by default when binding a DBM file to an associative array. Be sure you are using **ndbm** and not GNU's **gdbm** if you run into trouble.

On some systems, when you open a DBM file named **filename**, it will actually create two files, **filename.dir** and **filename.pag**. Other systems will create a **filename.db**. For the purposes of this documentation, when we refer to a DBM filename, it's to the root name, i.e., **filename**. The keys of the DBM file are the user names, and the values mapped to those keys are the encrypted passwords.

To activate DBM authentication, you might have to compile the Apache server with *-lndbm* set in the *EXTRA_LIBS* variable in the **Configuration** file. You also need to uncomment the line in the **Configuration** file:

```
Module dbm_auth_module mod_auth_dbm.o
```

This module creates a new directive, *AuthDBMUserFile*, which can be dropped in place of *AuthUserFile* in your configuration file or **.htaccess** files. The argument to that directive is the DBM filename, such as:

```
AuthDBMUserFile /www/passwords
```

These passwords are encrypted using standard UNIX *crypt()*, which the utility **dbmmanage** can handle with the *adduser* option.

Each entry in a DBM file has a key and a value. For the password file the key is the username. The value is the standard UNIX *crypt()* password. The value field can also contain other data that are ignored during password checks; these data must be separated from the password with a colon character (:). The **dbmmanage** utility supplied with Apache can be used to add and remove users and encrypt passwords.

A new keyword, *AuthDBMGroupFile*, can be dropped in place of *AuthGroupFile* in your configuration or **.htaccess** files. The argument to that keyword is the DBM filename, such as:

```
AuthDBMGroupFile /www/groups
```

Each entry in a DBM file has a key and a value. For the group file the key is the username. The value is a list of groupnames of which the user is a member; they are separated from each other with commas (,). Note that there must be no whitespace within the value and that the value must never contain any colon characters (:).

In some cases it is easier to manage a single database that contains both the password and group details for each user. This simplifies any support programs that need to be written: they now only have to deal with writing to and locking a single DBM file. This can be accomplished by first setting the group and password files to point to the same DBM:

```
AuthDBMGroupFile /www/userbase
AuthDBMUserFile /www/userbase
```

The key for the single DBM is the username. The value consists of:

```
Unix Crypted Password : List of Groups [ : (ignored) ]
```

The password section contains the UNIX *crypt()* password as before. This is followed by a colon and the comma-separated list of groups. Other data may optionally be left in the DBM file after another colon; it is ignored by the authentication module. This is what **telescope.org** uses for its combined password and group database.

The implementation of **dbmopen** in the Apache modules reads the string length of the hashed values from the DBM data structures rather than relying upon the string being NULL-appended. Some applications, such as the Netscape Web server, rely upon the string being NULL-appended, so if you are having trouble using DBM files interchangeably between applications, this may be a part of the problem.

The Status Module

The *Status* module allows a server administrator to find out how well their server is performing. An HTML page is presented that gives the current server statistics in an easily readable form. If required, this page can be made to automatically refresh (given a compatible browser). Another page gives a simple machine-readable list of the current server state.

The details given are:

- The number of children serving requests
- The number of idle children
- *The status of each child, the number of requests that child has performed, and the total number of bytes served by the child*
- *A total number of accesses and byte count served*
- The time the server was started/restarted and the time it has been running for
- *Averages giving the number of requests per second, the number of bytes served per second, and the average number of bytes per request*
- *The current percentage CPU used by each child and in total by Apache*
- *The current hosts and requests being processed*

A compile-time option must be used to display the details listed in *italic*, as the instrumentation required for obtaining these statistics does not exist within standard Apache.

To enable status reports only for browsers from the **foo.com** domain add this code to your **access.conf** configuration file:

```
<Location /server-status>
SetHandler server-status

<Limit GET POST>
order deny,allow
deny from all
allow from .foo.com
</Limit>
</Location>
```

You can now access server statistics by using a Web browser to access the page *http://your.server.name/server-status*.

You can get the status page to update itself automatically if you have a browser that supports a refresh function (as most new browsers do). Access the page *http://your.server.name/server-status?refresh=N* to refresh the page every *N* seconds.

A machine-readable version of the status file is available by accessing the page *http://your.server.name/server-status?auto*. This is useful when automatically run; see the Perl program in the **/support** directory of Apache, **log_server_status**.

To obtain full statistics you must compile Apache with a special directive. On some machines there may be a small performance loss if you do this. Try full statistics and see if you notice any difference. Do this by adding the following to the *AUX_CFLAGS* line in the Configuration file and then recompiling as usual:

```
AUX_CFLAGS= (something) -DSTATUS
```

Additional Modules

There are additional modules available at the Apache Web site. They are listed in Table 4.4.

Table 4.4 Optional Modules at the Apache Web Site

Module Name	Purpose
mod_access	Host-based access control
mod_actions	File type/method-based script execution
mod_alias	Aliases and redirects
mod_asis	The **.asis** file handler
mod_auth	User authentication using text files
mod_auth_anon	Anonymous user authentication, FTP-style
mod_auth_db	User authentication using Berkeley DB files
mod_auth_dbm	User authentication using DBM files
mod_auth_external	User authentication using the USER and PASS environment variables
mod_auth_msql	User authentication using mSQL files
mod_auth_pg95	User authentication in Postgres95
mod_block	Blocks access from specific URL referrals
mod_cern_meta	Support for HTTP header metafiles

Table 4.4 Optional Modules at the Apache Web Site (continued)

Module Name	Purpose
mod_cgi	Invoking CGI scripts
mod_cookies	Support for Netscape-like cookies
mod_counter	Crude, unsupported user counter
mod_digest	MD5 authentication
mod_dir	Automatic directory listings
mod_env	Passing of environments to CGI scripts
mod_dld	Start-time linking with the GNU libdld
mod_imap	The image-map file handler
mod_include	Server-parsed documents
mod_info	Server configuration information
mod_limit	Sets limits on daily usage by users
mod_log_agent	Logging of user agents
mod_log_common	Standard logging in the Common Logfile Format
mod_log_config	User-configurable logging replacement for **mod_log_common**
mod_log_referer	Logging of document references
mod_mime	Determining document types
mod_negotiation	Content negotation
mod_proxy	Caching proxy abilities
mod_simultaneous	Limit the number of simultaneous accesses to files in a directory
mod_sp	Server-push implementation
mod_speling	URL spelling corrections
mod_status	Server status display
mod_trailer	Adds a trailer to specific files
mod_uri_remap	One-to-one mapping on entry URI level
mod_userdir	Adds user home directories

Table 4.5 lists the contributed modules found at *http://www.zyzzyva.com/ server/module_registry/*.

Table 4.5 Contributed Modules

Module Name	Purpose
mod_auth_dbi	Authentication via Perl DBI, Oracle, Informix, and more
mod_auth_cookie	Fake basic authentication using cookies
mod_auth_cookie_file	Cookie-based authentication, with a **.htpasswd**-like file
mod_auth_cookie_msql.c	Cookie-based authentication with mSQL database
mod_auth_external	Authenticates using another program
mod_auth_kerb	Kerberos authentication
mod_auth_msql	An mSQL authentication package
mod_auth_nis	NIS/passwd-based authentication; using normal user IDs
mod_auth_pg95	User authentication with the Postgres95 database
mod_auth_sys	Basic authentication using system accounts
mod_auth_sys2	Uses both system files and **.htaccess** for authentication
mod_auth_uid	Disallows serving Web pages based on uid/gid
mod_beza	Module and patch converting national characters
mod_blob_pg95	URI to Postgres95 Large Object mapping
mod_cgi_sugid	Sets user/group ID for CGI execution (like CERN)
mod_cntr	Dynamically count Web-page access
mod_conv	Viewing FTP archive using WWW, conversions
mod_fontxlate	Configurable national character set translator
mod_log_dir	Implements per-directory logging
mod_log_elf	Extended log format logger
mod_neoinclude	NeoWebScript Tcl scripting extension
mod_pagescript	SSI extensions
mod_perl	Embed Perl interpreters to avoid CGI overhead
mod_perl_fast	Embed Perl interpreters to avoid CGI overhead
mod_php	Server-parsed scripting language with RDBMS support
mod_rcs	Russian documents support in various charsets
mod_rewrite	URI on-the-fly rewriting via regular expressions
mod_sucgi	Handles userdir CGI requests as that user
mod_uri_rewrite	Rewriting/mapping of local URIs
mod_userpath	A different method of mapping user URLs
mod_xssi	Server-side include extensions

Some of these modules are experimental and in development; some are established. The aforementioned module Web site has more information about each module.

Adding Modules

As you can tell from the previous listing of modules, there's a lot of functionality that you can add to your Web server via additional modules. There are listings of modules at the Apache Web site (*http://www.apache.org/dist/contrib/modules/*), and a registry of Apache modules is maintained at *http://www.zyzzyva.com/server/module_registry/*.

The instructions for adding modules comes from Aran Mirzadeh (awm@gosina.com). To add a module to the Apache server, you need to edit the Configuration file in the source directory. There are two things to consider:

- **Does the extension need any extra libraries to be linked in?** If yes, then add the name of these libraries to the *EXTRA_LIBS* variable in the file. For example, to link the mSQL authentication package, you need to add *-lmsql* to the list. If your library is in a nonstandard location, you will also need to specify the path using the *-L/path/to/lib/dir* option before the *-l* option.

- **Does the extension need any extra include paths to find header files?** If the include files needed by the module are in a nonstandard place, then chances are you will need to add the path to those files to the compile command. For example, if the header files for the mSQL authorization package are in **/usr/local/Minerva/include**, then you will probably need to add *-I/usr/local/Minerva/include* to the *CFLAGS* variable in the Configuration file. Next, copy the source file for the module to the Apache **src** directory. Now you must add the module to the list of modules. This is as simple as adding a line like this to the Configuration file:

```
Module module_name module_code.o
```

where the tag *Module* tells the **Configure** program this is a line describing a module, and the *module_name* is as defined in the source code. Look for a line that is something like this:

```
module msql_auth_module = {
```

followed by some definitions. This is the name of that module. The **module_code.o** tells the build process the name of the object file containing the code to implement the module. This is the same as the name of the source file with the *.c* replaced by *.o*.

Run **Configure** followed by a **make** and the new module will be added into the **httpd** program.

A Secure Server: Apache-SSL

Security is a hot topic in the Internet world. Users are worried— sometimes with reason, sometimes without—that their online transactions are subject to snooping by unscrupulous hackers.

We're not going to get into the merits of online security here; that topic alone could fill a good-sized book. Our purpose here is to pointout the availability of a secure Apache server, Apache-SSL. Basically, this is a version of the Apache Web server that has an implementation of the Secure Sockets Layer (SSL) compiled in. This is in the form of SSLeay, a freely available implementation of Netscape's Secure Socket Layer. The current version of SSLeay implements version 2 of SSL.

Because of weirdness surrounding United States export laws (remember, the government classifies encryption tools as munitions and subjects them to heavy scrutiny), we decided against including the tools to implement SSL on the accompanying CD-ROM. As a private citizen, you can download the file yourself from the Oxford University FTP server, *ftp://ftp.ox.ac.uk/pub/crypto/SSL*. The filename is **apache_1.1.1+1.3.ssl.tar.gz**, and it's a small file—20KB or so.

Inside this compressed file is a set of patches for Apache (for version 1.1.1), extra source files, some documentation, and some example configuration files. All you need to do is merge the patches with the

Apache source code and then compile and link the resulting code with SSLeay (version 0.5.1b+ or 0.6.1+). The modified source can still be used to compile a standard Apache. You can grab SSLeay from *ftp://ftp.psy.uq.oz.au/pub/Crypto/SSL/*.

There are many weird issues surround Apache-SSL, and you had best be warned that you're walking through a minefield (yes, the inevitable munitions reference) in trying to implement it. The terms for using and implementing Apache-SSL have been shifting in recent months, so you're best off checking the Apache Web site (*http://www.apache.org*) and seeing what new information is available there. You might also need to contact RSA Data Security (*http://www.rsa.com*) for information about using RSA security technology, especially in a commercial setting.

Digital certificates are available for Apache-SSL from Thawte Consulting. You can find full instructions and a fill-in application form at *http://www.thawte.com/certs/server/request.html*. You cannot arrange digital certificates from VeriSign, unfortunately.

The WN Web Server

If you find that Apache for some reason or another doesn't meet your needs, there are some alternative Web servers on the accompanying CD-ROM in the **internet** directory. One such worthy alternative is the WN Web server, from John Franks of Northwestern University (*john@math.nwu.edu*).

The following WN sections on installation and usage are taken from the online documentation by permission of the author. You can read through the entire online guide at *http://hopf.math.nwu.edu/docs/manual.html*.

How WN Works

Files served by an HTTP server may have many attributes relevant to their serving. These attributes include content-type, optional title, optional expiration date, optional keywords, whether the file should be parsed for server-side includes, access restrictions, etc. Some servers try to encode this information in ad hoc ways, in a filename suffix, or in a global "configuration file." The approach of WN is to keep this information in small databases, one for each directory in the document hierarchy.

The WN maintainer never needs to understand the format of these database files (named **index.cache** by default), but this format is very simple and a brief description will indicate how WN works. When the server receives a request, say for **/dir/foo.html**, it looks in the file **/dir/index.cache**, which contains lines like:

```
file=foo.html&content=text/html&title=whatever…
```

If the server finds a line starting with *file=foo.html* then the file will be served. If such a line does not exist, the file will not be served (unless special permission to serve all files in the directory has been granted). This is the basis of WN security. Unlike other servers, the default action for WN is to deny access to a file. A file can be served only if explicit permission to do so has been granted by entering it in the **index.cache** database or if explicit permission to serve all files in **/dir** has been given in **index.cache**. This database also provides other security functions. For example, restricting the execution of CGI scripts can be done on the basis of the ownership (or group ownership) of their **index.cache** files. There is no need to limit execution to scripts located in particular designated directories. The location of a file in the data hierarchy should be orthogonal to security restrictions on it, and this is the case with the WN server.

The **index.cache** database file has a number of other functions beyond its security role. Attributes of **foo.html** that can be computed before it is served and don't often change are stored in the fields of the line starting *file=foo.html*. For example, the MIME content type *text/html* must be deduced from the filename suffix **.html**. This is done once at the time **index.cache** is created and need not be done every time the file is served.

The title of a file is another example. With the WN server every file served has a title (even binaries) and optionally has a list of keywords, an expiration date, and other fields associated with it. For an HTML document the title and the keywords are automatically extracted from the header of the document and stored in fields of that file's line in its **index.cache** file. These are used for the built-in keyword and title searches the server supports. The maintainer also has the option of adding his own fields to this database file. They could contain such things as document author, document ID number, etc. These user-defined fields can be searched with the built-in WN searches, or their contents can be inserted into the document, on the fly, as it is served.

So how are the **index.cache** databases created? Their format is quite simple and a maintainer is free to create them any way she chooses, but normally they are created by the utility **WNdex** (pronounced *windex*). This program, which is part of the WN distribution, is designed to produce the **index.cache** file from a file with a friendlier format with the default name index. A very simple index file might look like

```
File=foo.html

File=clap.au
Title=Sound of one hand clapping

File=hand
Title=Picture of one hand clapping
Content-type=text/gif
```

Of course if the file hand were named **hand.gif** the content-type line would not be necessary as **wndex** could deduce the type from the **.gif** suffix. Likewise it is not necessary to give a title for **foo.html** because **wndex** will read the HTML header from that file and extract the title and perhaps other things like keywords and expiration date.

WN Features

The WN server has several features not available with other servers or only available through the use of CGI scripts.

Searching

One of the design goals of WN is to provide the maintainer with tools to create extensive navigational aids for the server. A variety of search mechanisms are available.

Title Searches

In response to the URL *http://host/dir/search=title* the server will provide an HTML form (automatically generated or prepared by the maintainer) asking for a regular expression search term. When supplied the server will search the **index.cache** files in **/dir** and designated subdirectories for a items whose titles contain a match for the search term. An HTML document with a menu of these items is returned.

Keyword Searches

This is like title searches except that matches are sought in keywords instead of titles. Keywords for HTML documents are automatically obtained from headers. For other documents (or HTML documents) they can be manually supplied in the index file.

Title/Keyword Search

This is like keyword searches except that the match can be either in the keyword or the title.

User-Supplied Field Searches

This is like keyword searches except that matches are sought in user-supplied fields. The user-supplied fields can contain any text and are attached to a document by entering them in that document's record in the index file. Their purpose is to include items like a document Id number, or document author in the **index.cache** database. A field search could then produce all documents by a given author for example. Or using regular expressions in the search term produces a list of all documents whose ID number satisfies certain criteria.

Context Searches

Unlike the title and keyword searches, this is a full text search of all text/* documents in one directory (not subdirectories). The returned HTML document contains a list of all the titles of documents containing a match together with a sublist of the lines from those documents containing the match. This provides one line of context for the match. For HTML documents the matched expression in each of these lines will be a highlighted anchor.

Selecting one takes you to the document with your viewer focused on the matching location. The primary intent of this feature is to provide full-text searching for an HTML document that might consist of a substantial number of files.

File-Context and Grep Searches

A file-context search is just like a context search except that it is limited to a single file. The file grep search returns a *text/html* document containing the lines in the file matching the regular expression.

List Searches

The server will search an HTML document looking for an unordered list of anchors linking to WWW objects. The contents of each anchor will be searched for a match to the supplied regular expression. The search returns an HTML document containing an unordered list of those anchors with a match. This is quite useful with the digest utility, which creates HTML documents to be searched in this way from files with internal structure like mail or news digests, mailing lists, etc.

Index Searches

This is a mechanism by which arbitrary search engines can be linked to WN through a search module. The server will provide the search term to the search module and expects an HTML list of links to matching items to be returned.

All the searching methods listed previously except the index searches are built into the server and require no additional effort for the maintainer. They are simply referenced with URLs like *http://host/dir/search=context*, where **/dir** is any directory containing files to be served and an **index.cache** listing them. Of course search permission can be denied for any directory or any file contained in that directory.

Parsed Text, Server-Side Includes, and Wrappers

The WN server has extensive capabilities for automatically including files in one that is being served or wrapping a served file with another (i.e., pre-pending and post-pending information to a file being served).

This latter is useful if you wish to place a standard message at the beginning or end (or both) of a large collection of files. For security all files included in a file or used as a wrapper for it are listed in that file's **index.cache** file. This combined with various available security options, like requiring that a served file and all its includes and wrappers have the same owner (or group owner) as the **index.cache** file listing them, provide a safe and productive Web environment.

One important application of wrappers is to customize the HTML documents returned listing the successful search matches. If a search item is given a wrapper, the server assumes that it contains text describing the search, and it merely inserts an unordered list of links to the matching items.

In addition to including files the output of programs may be inserted and the value of any user-defined field in the **index.cache** database entry for a file may be inserted.

Also parsed text may conditionally insert items with a simple if-else-endif construct based on *Accept* headers, *User-Agent* headers, *Referer* headers, and the like.

Filters

An arbitrary filter can be assigned to any file to be served. A filter is a program that reads the file and has the program output served rather than the content of the file. The name of the filter is another field in the file's line in its **index.cache** file. One common use of this feature is for on-the-fly decompression. For example, a file can be stored in its compressed form and assigned a filter like **zcat**, which uncompresses it. Then the client is served the uncompressed file, but only the compressed version is stored on disk. As another example, you might use **nroff -man** as a filter to process UNIX **man** files before serving. There are many other interesting uses of filters. Be creative!

Ranges

If the server is accessed via a URL like *http://host/dir/foo;lines=20-30* and file is any *text/** document it will return a *text/plain* document consisting of lines 20 through 30 of file **foo**. This is very useful for structured text files like address lists or digests of mail and news. A WN utility called **digest** will produce an HTML document with a list of links to separate sections (line ranges) of the structured file. The **digest** utility is executed with two regular expressions as arguments: one to match the section separator and the other to match the section title. For a mail digest, for example, these could be ^*From* and ^*Subject:*, respectively. Then the sections of the virtual documents would be delimited by a line starting with *From* and would have the message subject as their title. A similar mechanism provides byte ranges from files.

Installing the Software

Transfer the file **wn.tar.gz** from the CD-ROM and uncompress it and untar it to make the WN source directory hierarchy. (This file is also available via anonymous ftp from *ftp.acns.nwu.edu* in the directory **/pub/wn**.) The file must be uncompressed with the GNU compression utility **gzip** (or **gunzip**). The resulting file **wn.tar** should be unpacked with this UNIX command:

```
tar -xvf wn.tar
```

The top level of the directory created by untarring this file contains several directories, including: **wn**, **wndex**, **authwn**, and **docs**.

You can also use the Perl script **configure**, which is in the main source directory. Do this with the command:

```
perl configure
```

This script will ask you various questions, like what version of UNIX you are using and the path to the directory you want to be the root of your data hierarchy.

Default answers are printed in square brackets [ ], so you can simply press **Enter** to enter that value. You can quit at any time by pressing **Ctrl-C**, and nothing should be changed. If you want to try it once to see what the questions are, that is fine.

This script creates two files, **config.h** and **Makefile**, which are customized based on the answers you gave. You may rerun this script as many times as you like. The first time you run the script the default values are those in the file **config.h.dist**. Subsequent times the default values are taken from the most recent **config.h** you have produced (if it still exists).

An alternative to running this script is to copy the files **Makefile.dist** and **config.h.dist** to **Makefile** and **config.h**, respectively, and to edit them manually. If you want to use some of the features that are not turned on by default like multiple IP interfaces, you will have to edit at least **config.h**. I recommend starting with the Perl script and getting your server up and running. Then you can go back and browse through **config.h** to see if there are things you want to change. If there are, you will have to recompile, but that takes only a few minutes.

Here are some of the questions you will be asked when you run **configure**. You will be given a list of supported operating systems and asked to pick the one you are using (you'll obviously choose Linux). You will be asked the complete pathname of your data directory. You will also have to enter the names of the access logfile and the error log file you wish to use (they can be the same file). If you don't want logging or you want to use the system **syslog** facility (i.e., the -S option), then these should both be defined to be the empty string (i.e., a pair of quotation marks with nothing between them, like ""). If you specify the names of these log files, then you must make sure that either these two files exist and are writable by the server or that they are files in a directory where the server has permission to create them.

Additional customizations in **config.h** are possible but should not be needed. These customizations require that you manually edit the **config.h** file. For example, there is a *#define DEFAULT_URI* line in the **config.h** file. It is set to */index.html*. This is the document returned in response to a request with only the hostname (something like *http://hostname.edu/* with no filename at the end). You would need to change it if, for example, you wanted to have the default server response be to run a CGI script.

There is also a *#define NO_DNS_HOSTNAMES* line in **config.h**, which is commented out by default. Uncommenting this line will mean that there will be no hostnames in your log file, just IP addresses. This will reduce the load on your server (but probably not speed up responses since the lookups usually take place after the transaction is complete). Keep in mind that uncommenting this will mean that none of your CGI scripts will get the hostname and also that your access files cannot have hostnames in them, just IP addresses.

You may also customize the file **Makefile** in the top-level directory. In particular, you should do this if you wish to specify a C compiler other than **cc** (e.g., **gcc** should be used for compiling). Also some systems require that special libraries for sockets, or whatever, be mentioned in the **compile** command.

In the top-level directory do a **make** to produce the server **wn**, the standalone version **swn**, and the utility **wndex**. This utility is used to produce **index.cache** files for use by the server (it is described later). If the **make** proceeds without problem, you should next do a **make install**. This will strip the binaries and place them in the top level bin directory or whatever directory you specified when you ran the **configure** script.

If you specified a log file name or error-log-file name when you ran the configuration script or edited **config.h**, you will need to make sure that these files exist and that they are writable by the user ID under which the server will run. The best way to do this is to create the files as root (**touch wn.log**), change their ownership to the appropriate user (**chown nobody wn.log**), and finally set the permissions appropriately (**chmod 644 wn.log**). An alternative is to create a directory in which these files will reside and make sure that the user *nobody* has permission to create files in this directory. Then the server will create the files with proper ownership and permissions.

Running the Server as a Standalone Daemon

You can now either run the server as a standalone daemon, the **swn** executable, or run it under **inetd**, the **wn** executable. We first describe the standalone version. Run this with this command:

```
swn -p port [other options] /path/to/wnroot
```

where *port* is the number of the port on which you wish the server to run. If this is a nonprivileged port (i.e., > 1024), then **swn** can be run as an ordinary user. However, for privileged ports like 80, you must run this command as root. If **swn** is run without the *-p* option it will use port 80 by default. If **swn** is run by root, then when it starts up it will change its user ID to the one set when running the configuration script or by editing the **config.h** file line where *USERID* is *#defined*. Otherwise, it will have all the permissions of the user who runs it.

The safest practice is to use the numeric UID of *nobody* for the *USERID* set in **config.h** (this is the default) and then start the server as root. The server needs to have root permissions to connect to a socket on a privileged port and listen for requests. But immediately after doing so it will change its user ID to that of *nobody* and have minimal access permissions. In this situation the user *nobody* needs to have only read permission to your server data and should not own or have write permission. In particular *nobody* should not have ownership or write access of the **index.cache** database file.

Running the Server under Inetd

The other way to run the server is to use it under **inetd**. This is an efficient way to run a server if the load on it is relatively light (a few thousand hits per day) and the host on which it runs is used for other purposes. There are variations on how **inetd** works from system to system so you may need to look at the **man** page for **inetd.conf(5)**.

Edit the file **/etc/services** and create the line:

```
wn 80/tcp
```

(or replace 80 by the port you wish to use). Then edit the file **/etc/inetd.conf** and insert the line:

```
wn stream tcp nowait nobody /full/path/for/wn wn
```

After the last *wn* you can have optional arguments to turn on logging or use a different data directory. Some **inetd**s limit the number of arguments you may use, so you may want to use a small script in place of **wn** here.

It is important to run **wn** as *nobody* (the fifth field in the preceding **inetd.conf** line) or some other user with no special access privileges. It should never be necessary to run **wn** under **inetd** as root; to do so would be a serious mistake for maintaining security. Every attempt has been made to make **wn** as secure as possible, even if it is run as root; however, no program accessible to remote users on the internet can be assumed perfectly secure.

After editing the **inetd.conf** and services files, you should find the process ID number of the **inetd** process and do the command **kill -HUP process_id#**. This must be done as root. You find the *process_id#* using the Linux command **ps**. If you have never done this before, get someone who has to help you.

Your Hostname: What's in a Name?

If the fully qualified domain name of your server is *abc.com*, you might like to have your server known as *www.abc.com* or some other vanity name. For most purposes this is simply a matter of properly setting up domain name service (DNS) on your system so that the system responds to the desired name.

 To use multiple vanity names for different IP addresses on a single server, see the section on multihomed servers.

NOTE

There are a few instances, however, where the WN server does use its own hostname. Ideally, the server should do nothing with its hostname and not even need to know it. This is not possible for two reasons. First, the CGI protocol requires the server to pass its hostname to CGI scripts in an environmental variable whenever those scripts are run. Secondly clients often implement redirection so that it cannot handle relative URLs but only complete URLs. When a server redirects to another local document, it must supply its own hostname. These are the only places WN uses a hostname.

For most cases then, WN only uses it hostname when a redirection is done. This happens in several circumstances. The most common is when a request is made for a directory and the trailing / is left off of the URL.

So how does WN know its hostname? When you run the **configure** program you are queried for the value you want or you have the option of using a system call at the time the server is run. This value is placed into the **config.h** header file and compiled into your server. In the file **config.h** the *WN_HOSTNAME* value is set by default to the empty string. If this is not changed the server will get its name from the *gethostaddr()* system call. If this is set to another string, that string will be used. If you are using WN as a multihomed server, then you need to set different names for the different IP addresses. This is done in the file **wn/vhost.h**, which you edit to set up the correspondence between IP addresses and root directories.

Testing Your Setup

After compiling and setting up the software, you can test it on a sample directory provided with the distribution. To do this first make a symbolic link in your root data directory to the **docs** directory in the source distribution. The command:

```
ln -s /your/src/dir/docs docs
```

executed in the root directory should do this.

Now you are ready to test your server installation on this directory. Try it with your favorite HTTP client. The URL should be:

http://YourHost/docs/index.html

Shutting Down Your Server

If your are running under **inetd** as already described, then to shut down the server first remove or comment out the line you created in the file **inetd.conf**. Then you should again find the process ID number of the **inetd** process and do the command

```
kill -HUP pocess_id#
```

just as you did to start WN.

If you are running **swn**, the standalone version of WN, you will have to use the Linux **ps** command to find the process ID of the running **swn** daemon. Then as root you run the command

```
kill -9 process_id#
```

where, of course, *process_id#* is the process ID of **swn**.

Managing Log Files

There are two ways to log WN transactions—using dedicated log files or using the standard UNIX **syslog** facility. We first describe dedicated log files. Normally when you use WN you will keep two log files. The first is a log of all normal transactions, and the second records error conditions or items that might require your attention. For example, if the server cannot find a file that your index file indicates should be served, it will log an error. There are two ways to tell the server the names of these files. The first is by supplying the file names when you run the configure script and then compiling these into your server. And the second is by supplying the file names on the command line when you execute the server.

For example, executing the command:

```
swn -L /path2/logfile -l /path2/error.log   /path/wnroot
```

will cause the server to use **logfile** and **error.log** as the log file and error log, respectively. Of course, it is necessary for the server to have write permission to these files and execute permission on the directory containing them.

A good way to achieve this if the server is running as *nobody* is to create the files yourself and change their ownership to the user *nobody*. This can be done, for example, with the commands:

```
touch logfile
/usr/etc/chown   nobody   logfile
chmod 600   logfile
```

executed as root in the directory where the log file is to reside. The first of these commands creates the file **logfile**. The second makes *nobody* the owner, and the third gives *nobody* (and no one else except root) permission to read and write this file. You might want to allow others to read, but not write to the log file, if security of the log file is not a concern.

Thus a script executed by **cron** to rotate log files might look like:

```
cd /logfile/dir
mv logfile    logfile.old
touch    logfile
/usr/etc/chown    nobody    logfile
chmod 600    logfile
kill -HUP `/bin/cat    wn.pid`
/usr/etc/chown    maintainer    logfile.old
chmod 600    logfile.old
```

where **wn.pid** is a file containing the process ID of the server created by using the *-q* option or by specifying this filename when the **configure** script is run. If neither of these has been done, the standalone server **swn** will print its process ID on standard output when it is run. If you are using **wn** under **inetd**, there is no need to send the *-HUP* signal as the server must close this file after each transaction.

There are three formats that the server can use in writing its log files. The two most common are verbose and common log format. The verbose mode is essentially the common log format but with the user-agent, referrer, and HTTP cookie of a transaction appended to the line for that transaction as well as better transaction error messages if necessary. You can chose between these two by answering the relevant question when running the **configure** script before compilation (or by editing **config.h**). For the third format possibility, you need to use the *-v* command-line option, which we describe next.

When the server is invoked with the *-v* option, it will write a log file in the format specified by the value of this option. The legal values for this option are *common*, *verbose*, and *ncsa*. They cause the log file to be written in the so-called common log format, or WN's verbose format including user agent, referer, and cookies, or in the NCSA extended format, which includes just referer and user agent. The NCSA format will likely be of interest only if you want to use log-processing tools that expect this format. If the *-v* option is not specified, the server will default to either the common log format or the WN verbose format depending on which was selected when the **configure** script was run.

The utility **V2C** can convert verbose log files to log files in the shorter common log format.

Troubleshooting

If things are not working as they should, here are some tips to help you isolate the problems.

If the compilation was successful you can check the server itself by executing it from the command line. If you use the command:

```
wn /full/path/of/root/dir
```

it should run and pause for input. Type the line:

```
GET /<ret>
```

and in response **wn** should print the raw HTML of the **index.html** file in your top level directory (perhaps along with a message about not being able to open a log file). If instead you type:

```
GET /docs/overview.html<ret>
```

(and you still have the **/docs** subdirectory in your top-level directory), the overview document should be sent to your screen. If this doesn't happen, there should be an error message, which may be helpful. Better error messages are placed in the log file, so you may want run **wn** again with the additional arguments *-L logfile* and then examine the contents of the log file. Or if you run **wn -L /dev/tty** the log entries will be printed to your screen instead of being put in a file. If the server can't open a file, for example, the name of that file will be recorded in the log file. Check its permissions.

Remember that all files that **wn** serves must be world readable. More serious errors are put in a separate error log. So you might want to try the command **wn -L file -l file2** and then type the GET requests described previously.

If this succeeds you should run the server for real, either under **inetd** (as already described) or standalone (with an **swn** command). In order to use port 80, the server must be started by root. It will then switch to user *nobody*. It does this immediately after connecting to port 80, before it does anything else including opening its log file. If you get a message stating that the server cannot open its logfile, then either you have specified putting the log file in a directory where user *nobody* does not have permission to create files or you have specified an existing file that the server does not have permission to write. After starting the server a useful test is to **telnet** to your server at port on which you are running. You should get a connection message and a pause for input. If you get a *Connection refused* message and you are running under **inetd**, it is likely that there is a problem with your **inetd** setup or for some reason your system can't find or can't execute the **wn** binary. If you are using **swn**, this message means that **swn** is not in fact running.

Creating Your Data Hierarchy

In each directory of your data hierarchy, you create a file called **index** with information about each file you want to serve. This simplest **index** file might contain the single line:

```
Attribute=serveall
```

which when properly processed will grant the server permission to serve any file in the directory (but not in subdirectories). For more information about this directive, see the following section on the serveall attribute. A more elaborate **index** file might look like the following:

```
Owner=mailto:webmistress@host.edu

File=file.txt
Title=This is a descriptive title for file.txt

# This is a comment
File=file2.html
```

```
File=soundfile
Title=This plays some sounds
Content-type=audio/basic
```

The file contains four groups of lines called *records*. The first record (the single line starting *Owner=* in this example) describes properties of the directory and is called the *directory record*. It can be empty, but in general it is a good idea for the directory record to contain an owner line, like the preceding, referring to the maintainer of the directory.

The remainder of this **index** file has three file directives describing three files, **file.txt**, **file2.html**, and **soundfile**, in the directory that we wish to serve. The line starting with # is a comment. Wherever a # occurs, the remainder of that line is treated as a comment (i.e., ignored).

The **index** file is processed with the **wndex** utility to produce a small database called **index.cache** containing information about this directory and its contents. Detailed information on the **wndex** utility follows, but simply running it with no arguments in a directory containing an index file will produce the **index.cache** file for that directory. This file contains all the information in the index file plus additional information gathered automatically about the files to be served. In particular the **index.cache** file will list the names of the files given in the *File=* lines of the index file. Any file on the server whose name is not listed in an **index.cache** file will not be served. This is the basis of WN security. For security reasons the server will refuse to use any **index.cache** file, which is in reality a symbolic link to another file.

The **index.cache** database has a number of other functions beyond its security role. Attributes of the files listed in the index file that can be computed before they are served and that don't often change are stored in the **index.cache** file. For example, the MIME content type of **soundfile** is read from the *Content-type=* line. The other files do not need such a line, since **wndex** can deduce from the filename extensions that **file.txt** has *type text/plain* and **file2.html** has *type text/html*. This is done once at the time **index.cache** is created and need not be done every time the file is served. By the way, if the sound file were named **soundfile.au** it wouldn't need a Content-type line.

The title of a file is another example of information stored in the **index.cache** file. With the WN server every file served has a title (even binaries) and optionally has a list of keywords associated with it. For an HTML document the title and the keywords are automatically extracted by **wndex** from the header of the document and stored in fields of that file's line in **index.cache**. These are used for the built-in keyword and title searches that the server supports.

File Ownership and Permissions

The files that you wish to serve should be owned by you or by their creator or by whoever is in charge of maintaining them. They should not be owned by *nobody* or whatever user ID the server runs under (as set in **config.h**). This because the *nobody* ID should have the minimum permissions possible. It needs to have read access to the files to be served, but it has no need to be able to write to those files or alter them in any way.

Thus normally the files served might be owned by the maintainer and have their permissions set to be world readable but writable only by the maintainer (or by no one).

Likewise the **index.cache** file which controls access to everything in a directory should be owned by the maintainer of that directory and the only permission *nobody* should have for this file is read permission. In fact, for security reasons if the server was started as root (and then switched to a safer user like *nobody*), **wn** or **swn** will refuse to use any **index.cache** file that is owned by the user ID (e.g., *nobody*) under which the server is running. This restriction does not apply if **swn** is run on an unprivileged port by an ordinary user, because such a user might not be able to make **index.cache** files owned by someone else.

There is one exception to the rule of having nothing owned by *nobody* (and that's not a double negative). The exception is the log files. These files must be writable by the server, and it generally seems sensible to have them owned by the user *nobody* under whose identity the server runs. The log file and the error log file can be specified on the command line when the server is run or can be defined in **config.h**.

Using the Wndex Utility

Before describing the index file in greater detail, we briefly explain the use of the program that reads this file and produces the **index.cache** database file. Simply running **wndex** with no arguments in a directory containing a file named **index** causes that file to be read and a file called **index.cache** to be created in that directory.

There are several command-line arguments for **wndex**. The -*r* option causes **wndex** to recursively descend your data hierarchy using all subdirectories listed in the *Subdirs=* line of the directory record in the index file (see the following discussion).

The -*i* and -*c* options specify an alternate name for the index file and the **index.cache** file, respectively. For example, the command **wndex -i foo -c bar** will attempt to use **foo** as the index file and produce the file **bar** instead of **index.cache**.

The -*d* option specifies a directory other than the current directory in which to find the index file and in which to create the **index.cache** and **index.html** files.

Finally, the -*q* option (for quiet) suppresses the printing of any warning or informational messages by wndex.

The Directory Record

The first group of lines in an index file provides information about the directory itself and the collection of files it contains rather than about any single file in the directory. It is called the *directory record*. This beginning collection of lines might look like:

```
Owner=mailto:you@host.edu
SearchWrapper=dir_search_wrap
Accessfile=/dir/access
Subdirs=dir1,dir2,directory3
```

This specifies the owner of items in the directory (which is used in the HTTP headers sent by the server). It also specifies a "wrapper" for the various searches of the directory (i.e., an HTML document that provides a customized response listing the matching items in one of the various searches of the directory; for more details see the section on server-side wrappers and includes). The *Accessfile=* line specifies the name of the file that controls access (by IP address) to this directory. If this item is omitted, then items in the directory may be served to anyone. For more information on using the access mechanism, see the section of this document on access. Finally the line starting with *Subdirs=* specifies the subdirectories of this directory, which you wish to have recursively searched when a title or keyword search is done on this directory.

After the directory record line group an index file will typically have groups of lines called *file records* describing a particular file. A file record can be as simple as a single line like the line *File=file2.html* in the preceding example, or it can contain several lines describing the file.

Your Default Page

When someone sends a request to your server with only the server name and no filename like:

```
http://hopf.math.nwu.edu/
```

the WN server automatically translates this to:

```
http://hopf.math.nwu.edu/index.html
```

adding the filename **index.html**. More generally, if a request is made for a directory, say with the URL *http://host/dir1/dir2/*, this will be translated to a request for *http://host/dir1/dir2/index.html*.

If you wish the default filename in a particular directory to be something other than **index.html**, you can use the *Default-Document=* directive in the directory record of your index file to change it. If you wish to change the default filename for all directories on the server, you can change the *#define INDEXFILE_NAME* line in the **config.h** file and recompile.

Serving Files Not Listed in an Index File

WN is also able to serve files without explicitly listing them in an index or **index.cache** file. This is done by putting the line:

```
Attributes=serveall
```

in the directory record of the index file for a directory. It specifies that any file in this directory, which does not start with the period character . (as in Linux hidden files) or end with ~ (as in backup files created by emacs), may be served, not just those listed in the index file. The files **index** and **index.cache** will also not be served. The server will attempt to set the content type correctly based on the filename suffix using the same default correspondences between type and suffix that **wndex** uses. If the *Attributes=serveall* line (and the corresponding entry it creates in the **index.cache** file) are not present, then only the files explicitly listed will be served.

It is fine to have file records in an index file that also has the *Attributes=serveall* directive. In this case the file directives take precedence. Thus if you had an index file consisting of:

```
Attributes=serveall

File=foo.html
Content-type=application/postscript
```

the server would consult the file record for **foo.html** first and see that it is of type application/postscript (it would be silly to actually do this, of course) and use that type. But another file **bar.html** in the directory would also be served with the type indicated by its suffix. Files with no file record in the index file and no recognized suffix will be given the default content type, which can set with the *Default-content* directive.

When **wndex** is run on an index file with the serveall attribute, all the files currently in that directory which can be served are given entries in the **index.cache** file. Title and keyword searches only see files listed in an **index.cache** file. Likewise, context and grep searches only seek matches in files listed in the **index.cache** file. Thus if a file is added to a directory with the *serveall* attribute, it will not be visible to searches unless **wndex** is rerun in that directory. If it has not been rerun, the file will still be served, however. Still, it is good practice to rerun **wndex** every time you add or delete a file in a directory with the *serveall* attribute. (Of course, it is required to do this for a directory without the *serveall* directive.) There is no need to rerun **wndex** if you only change an existing file, unless you change its title or keywords.

There is no way to use wrappers or includes for files not listed in the index file. So generally, the few seconds it takes to add a document's name and a descriptive title to your index file and then to run **wndex** will pay off.

If you do not wish the *Attributes=serveall* directive to be allowed on your server, you can disable it by uncommenting the *#define NO_SERVEALL* line in the **config.h** file. This does not affect the ability of **wndex** to write **index.cache** entries for all files in a directory with the serveall attribute, but it does mean that the server will only serve files listed in an **index.cache** file.

Customized Error Messages

There are three situations when the client request will be denied but for which you can supply customized error messages. These are requests for nonexistent files, requests for files that require a password but for which no valid password was given, and requests from an invalid host for files limited to certain hosts. The lines:

```
No-Such-File-URL=http://host/dir/nosuch.html
Access-denied-URL=http://host/dir/noaccess.html
Auth-denied-file=~/dir/nopassword.html
```

in a directory record of an index file specify URLs to which clients are redirected when a nonexistent file is requested and when a document protected by an access control file is requested from an invalid host. The last line specifies a file to be sent when a password-protected file is requested without a password or with an invalid password. For technical reasons it wouldn't work to have this be a redirection. In the first two lines (specifying redirection), the URLs given can be relative URLs, so the lines:

```
No-Such-File-URL=/dir/nosuch.html
Access-denied-URL=noaccess.html
```

are valid. Default values for these three directives may be specified by editing the **config.h** file and recompiling the server.

WN Security

A great deal of effort has gone into attempting to make WN as secure as possible. Security has received the highest priority in all design decisions. This is not grounds for WN maintainers to feel that they can lessen their vigilance, however. The first thing you should be aware of is that there is a trade-off between security and functionality. You can have high security and restricted functionality or lower security with greater functionality or something in between. WN is designed to let the maintainer choose the point on this continuum he or she is comfortable with. This section tries to discuss the various options you as a maintainer will have and what the implications of your choices are.

First, it is important to understand possible threats to the integrity of a system running the WN server. There are two types of threat that this document addresses separately: (1) external, from a client or purported client on a remote host, and (2) local, from a user with an account on the server host.

After reading this section you may wish to look at the section on file ownership and permissions.

External Threats

The maintainer's objective is to prevent any unauthorized access to (or alteration of) files on the host system. Scripts or programs run on the server with the CGI protocols cause special problems and are discussed separately later. If you do not need to use any executable scripts, you should run the server with the -e option. The -e option disallows any attempt to execute a command on your server and does not allow any data sent by a client even to be written to a temporary disk file. In this situation the key to WN security is twofold: No document is served without explicit permission from the maintainer, and nothing is written to disk on the server except the log file.

The basic philosophy of WN security is that by default no client requests are granted. Permission to serve a document must be explicitly granted by the maintainer. The WN server keeps a small database in each directory of its data hierarchy, which contains information about files to be served from that directory. In particular no document can be served unless explicit permission to serve it is given in such a database.

Despite this strong security foundation, several additional steps are prudent. The most important is that the maintainer must ensure that no untrusted person has write access to any part of the WN hierarchy. For example, an incoming anonymous FTP directory should never be part of a WN hierarchy (better yet don't have one at all), because an attacker might be able to put a database there granting illicit access to some documents on the server system for which the user ID running the server has read permission. There are several defenses against such a counterfeit database, and we discuss them next.

Protecting your Index.cache Files

All security control for the WN server resides in the per-directory database files (these files have the default name **index.cache**). Consequently, it is extremely important to guarantee their integrity. There are several command-line options for the server that help protect against counterfeit **index.cache** files.

The -*t* and -*T* options allow you to specify a trusted owner or group owner (not both) for **index.cache** files. To do this use the -*t uid#* or -*T gid#* options to **wn** or **swn**. When invoked with only the -*t* argument (or the -*T* argument), **wn** or **swn** will not serve a document unless the **index.cache** file listing it has the prescribed owner or gid. This uid# or gid# should be that of the maintainer, not the user ID under which **wn** or **swn** runs. Indeed, for security reasons if the server has been started as root and changed to another uid, it will refuse to use an **index.cache** file whose owner is the uid under which it is running. If on your server all **index.cache** files are created by a single user or a single group, I strongly recommend using the -*t* or -*T* option.

This added security is weakened somewhat if you use the -*u* option, which allows **index.cache** files owned by untrusted users, but only permits them to grant access to files owned by the same user as the **index.cache** file. This option might be appropriate if you permit users to have their own home page on your server. It would allow users to serve documents that they own but no others. If both the -*u* and the -*t* argument are used, the -*u* takes effect, except the trusted user specified with the -*t* option is exempt from its restrictions.

When the server is run, it must assume the permissions of some user on the host. Which user is determined when you run the **configure** Perl script or by defining *USER_ID* in **config.h**. It is important that this *USER_ID* have as few permissions as possible. On many systems there is a user called *nobody* with minimal permissions. The numeric user_id of *nobody* is a good choice and is the default choice of the WN configure script. Of course the server must have read permission on all the files served, but it should not have write permission for any directory or file other than its log files. If the *syslog* option for logging is enabled, there is no need for write permission on a log file. A good practice is to have all the files in your hierarchy that you intend to serve be owned by the maintainer or their creator. They should be world readable (assuming they are for general consumption) but with restricted write permission. The files in your hierarchy should not be owned by the user ID under which WN will run.

WN does not by default use the **chroot** system call to further restrict the files which the server can access. Doing so would enhance security at the expense of extra work for the maintainer. The effect of this is to prevent the server from even internally accessing any file that is not in your data directory. If you are especially concerned about security, you may wish to run one of the public domain TCP wrappers in conjunction with WN which will allow you to use the **chroot** system call. This can simultaneously enhance security for other TCP services like anonymous FTP.

Internal Threats

Whenever untrusted users have accounts on a system, there is risk involved. The objective of WN is to ensure that running the server does not increase this risk. If the server is wisely managed, I believe this goal can be achieved. Here are some guidelines.

If it is possible, make sure that no untrusted user has write access to any part of your WN hierarchy. As already mentioned, an attacker with write access to your hierarchy can create an **index.cache** file that will give access to anything on your server that is readable by the user ID under which WN runs. Even worse, she can create a shell script and an **index.cache** file permitting it to be executed, so it can be executed with all the permissions of that user ID. A good rule of thumb is

Always assume that everyone with write access to any part of your data hierarchy has all the permissions of the user Id under which your server runs!

This should not be true if you are using some of the command-line options described previously, but it is good practice to behave as if it were true.

Sometimes it is not possible or desirable to deny write access to your WN hierarchy. For example, you may need to allow all users to have a home page in their home directory or in some other designated place. There are two important things to do in this case.

The first of these is to run the server with the *-u* option. This has the effect of requiring that every file served (including wrappers and includes) have the same owner as the **index.cache** file that grants it permission to be served. This means that untrusted users can only serve files that they own. This will prevent a user from serving **/etc/passwd** but will not prevent him from making his own copy of **/etc/passwd** and serving that. If the *-t* or *-T* option is also used, then **index.cache** files owned by the trusted user or trusted group are exempt from this requirement, and they may grant permission to serve any file the server can read. For security reasons the server will refuse to use an **index.cache** file, which is a symbolic link to another file.

The *-e* or *-E* command-line options mentioned previously are also a good idea in this case, to prevent any execution of scripts or at least restrict their execution to trusted **index.cache** files.

You should note that when run in its default configuration there is no way to use password authentication to prevent users on your system, who can create **index.cache** files, from gaining access to files you are serving. They can simply make a symbolic link in their part of the hierarchy to the file you want to restrict and a **index.cache** file permitting it to be served. Since the server has access to the restricted file, it will serve it if it is listed in an **index.cache** file. This simple threat can be avoided by using the *-u* option described previously, but the number of potential threats is quite large. For example, if the *-e* or *-E* option is not used, a hostile user could write a CGI script that reads the sensitive files and mails them to himself. In general I would strongly advise against trying to have sensitive documents (protected by password or **.access** files) and potentially hostile users on the same server. I would also strongly advise against allowing potentially hostile CGI scripts, executed includes, or external modules. They can be disallowed through the use of the *-E* or *-e* command-line options. If they are not disallowed, a CGI script can alter or destroy log files. A hostile authorization module could collect user passwords.

The *-u* and *-E* options greatly enhance security, but it is important to keep the following principle in mind. You should assume that any permissions you grant to the userid under which WN runs are also granted to every user who can create an **index.cache** file in your data hierarchy.

Some Recommended Security Configurations

This a list of possible ways you might configure your server by setting values in **config.h** and using command-line arguments. It assumes that you are running either **swn** or **wn** on the privileged port 80 and that the default value of *USERID* and *GROUPID* defined in **config.h** have not been changed. This will mean that **swn** will be started as root but will almost immediately switch its privileges to those of the unprivileged user *nobody*. Likewise if **wn** is running under **inetd**, we assume that it is set to run with the privileges of *nobody*. The following list of configurations is in decreasing order of security.

Forbid CGI and Only Maintainer Trusted

This strongest level of security is achieved by running either **swn** (or **wn** under **inetd**) with the *-t* or *-T* option, the *-e* option, and no other options. (For the really paranoid, uncommenting the *#define FORBID_CGI* line in the file **config.h** and recompiling removes the CGI code from the binary.)

With these options no CGI programs or filters or script output includes are permitted. Also the POST method is not accepted (an error is returned for a POST request). Furthermore only **index.cache** files owned by the user specified in the *-t* option are used. The server should be run as *nobody* (the default), and the numeric user ID specified with *-t* should be the maintainer's.

Only Maintainer or Maintainer Group Trusted

This is the strongest level of security if you need the functionality of CGI scripts or filters or script output as server includes. This security configuration does not allow any user home pages (unless the maintainer produces the **index.cache** file for them). To use this level, run **swn** (or **wn** under **inetd**) with the *-t* or *-T* option and no other options. This places all control in the hands of a single maintainer or a maintainer group. No document or script output may be served unless the maintainer has authorized it by explicit mention in one of the **index.cache** database files. The server will not recognize any **index.cache** file unless it is owned by the maintainer specified with the -*t* option or the group specified with the -*T* option. Only one of -*t* or -*T* can be used.

Restricted User Serving Privileges

This permits users on the server host to have and control their own home pages and documents, but with a number of limitations. They will not be permitted to run CGI scripts, filters, or include scripts. Also the server will require that every file served (including wrappers and includes) have the same owner as the **index.cache** file that grants it permission to be served. This means that users can only serve files that they own.

This configuration is obtained by running with the -*E* option and the -*u* option. The -*E* option is similar to the -*e* option, except that **index.cache** files owned by a trusted user Id or trusted group Id (set with the -*t* or -*T* option) are exempt from the restrictions. The -*u* option requires that, in order to be served, a file must be owned by the owner of the **index.cache** file that lists it. Trusted users as specified with -*t* or -*T* are exempt from this restriction also.

Other WN Search Features

There are a number of other WN features that are more fully explained in the documentation:

- Title searches allow the server to provide an HTML form (automatically generated or prepared by the maintainer) asking for a regular expression search term. When supplied the server will search the **index.cache** files in **/dir** and designated subdirectories for items whose titles contain a match for the search term. An HTML document with a menu of these items is returned.

- Keyword searches are like title searches except that matches are sought in keywords instead of titles. Keywords for HTML documents are automatically obtained from headers. For other documents (or HTML documents), they can be manually supplied in the index file.

- Title/keyword searches combine the two previous methods.

- Fielded searches for user-supplied fields allows up to 20 additional field values associated with a document. These are used for searching purposes in the same way that keywords are. This is intended to give some additional keyword like fields, for example, document author or document ID number.

- Context searches allow for full text searches of all text documents in one directory. The returned HTML document contains a list of titles of documents containing a match, each with a sublist of the lines from those documents containing the match.

- Grep searches are like context searches, except that only a list of anchors pointing to files containing a match is returned. There are no lines of context showing the match.

- Line searches are like context searches, except that only one list of all matching lines is returned, instead of the matching lines being sublists of a list of files containing a match. That is, all the items in sublists of a context search are concatenated in one large list of lines containing matches.

- File context and grep searches are just like a context search, except that they are limited to a single file. The file grep search returns a text/html document containing the lines in the file matching the regular expression.

- A list search searches an HTML document looking for an unordered list of anchors linking to WWW objects. The contents of each anchor will be searched for a match to the supplied regular expression. The search returns an HTML document containing an unordered list of those anchors with a match.

- Indexed searches are supported in WN by auxiliary modules. Two such modules are provided as examples.

Other Web Servers on the CD-ROM

The accompanying CD-ROM contains a number of other Web servers, located in the **/internet/web_servers** directory. We're not going to spend a lot of time discussing these Web servers, since they're not as good or functional as the Apache and WN Web servers already discussed in this chapter.

The NCSA Web Server

The NCSA Web server is from the National Center for Supercomputing Applications (NCSA), the same outfit that gave the world the Mosaic Web browser. The NCSA Web server is still a popular Web server, according to those firms that track server installations. However, since the Apache Web server was designed as a replacement for the NCSA Web server and is built with NCSA code (to the point of using most of the same file and directory names, a situation that you'll need to be aware of, as explained later in this section), you're generally giving up some features and stability if you decide to go with an NCSA Web server instead of the Apache Web server.

That's enough sermonizing; if you want to use the NCSA Web server, the copy on the accompanying CD-ROM is **httpd_1_5_2a-export_linux2_0_0_tar.Z**, a precompiled version for Linux. It contains the NCSA Web server binary as well as support files.

Installation is simple. First, move the file from the CD-ROM to your hard drive with a command line like:

```
mv /cdrom/internet/web_servers/httpd_1_5_2a-export_linux2_0_0_tar.Z
/usr/local/etc
```

assuming that your CD-ROM drive uses **/cdrom,** or:

```
mv httpd_1_5_2a-export_linux2_0_0_tar.Z /usr/local/etc
```

assuming that your current directory is **internet/web_servers** on your CD-ROM drive.

Then you'll uncompress the compressed file using the following commands:

```
cd /usr/local/etc
uncompress httpd_1_5_2a-export_linux2_0_0_tar.Z
```

resulting in a file named **httpd_1_5_2a-export_linux2_0_0_tar**.

Your next step is to unarchive this file using the following command line:

```
tar xvf httpd_1_5_2a-export_linux2_0_0_tar
```

You'll end up with a very long list of files in a directory called **/usr/local/etc/httpd_1_5_2**. Change this directory to **/usr/local/etc/httpd**, and you're in business. There are a number of files to configure— **access.conf**, **httpd.conf**, and **srm.conf**—and to be honest you can follow along with the directions for the Apache Web server earlier in this chapter to see what needs to be configured.

WARNING   Don't uncompress and install the NCSA Web server if you have the Apache Web server running and want to continue using Apache. Since Apache is really an update of the NCSA Web server, there are some file conflicts—Apache kept a lot of filenames and locations from the original NCSA installation, and so you might find that important Apache files, especially configuration files, will be overwritten by the NCSA Web server.

The CERN Web Server

The CERN Web Server (also known as W3C httpd) is a generic public-domain full-featured hypertext server, which can be used as a regular HTTP server. The server is typically running on port 80 to serve hypertext and other documents, but it can also serve as a proxy—a server on a firewall machine—that provides access for people inside a firewall to the outside world. When running as proxy, **httpd** may be configured to do caching of documents resulting in faster response times.

This was the original Web server, but it's also a defunct Web server. The final version is 3.0A, and it was released on July 15, 1996. Because the CERN server can be used quite adequately as a proxy server (a topic you'll learn about later in this book), it's included here.

The archive is **w3c-httpd-3.0A.tar.gz**, and it's found on the CD-ROM in the **internet/web_servers** directory. You'll want to first uncompress and untar the distribution tar files:

```
uncompress w3c-httpd-3.0A.tar.Z
tar xvf w3c-httpd-3.0A.tar
```

This creates a directory called **WWW**, which you should make your current directory.

If you're not currently using a CERN server, you can go ahead and use the **make** command as long as **WWW** is your current directory. If you are using an older version of the CERN server, you need to run the following series of commands:

```
make clobber
make
```

The CERN Web server will detect what sort of UNIX operating system you're using and create an executable file named **httpd** in a subdirectory of **../WWW/Daemon/**. In addition, the utility programs (**htadm**, **htimage**, **cgiparse**, and **cgiutils**) go to the same directory.

The configuration file for the CERN server is stored as **/etc/httpd.conf**.

After installation, you'll want to check out the CERN server online documentation (*http://www.w3.org/pub/WWW/Daemon/User/Installation/Installation.html*) for more information on configuration and usage.

XS-HTTPD

XS-HTTPD is a WWW server with the following features:

- It doesn't take up much memory or disk space.
- Because of this, it runs quickly.
- It runs user CGI binaries under their own user ID!
- It gets users' pages under their own user ID, allowing them to really have protected pages (using the built-in authentication mechanism).

The file is **httpd.tar.gz**, and it's stored in the **internet/web_servers** directory on the CD-ROM.

You need to move it to your hard drive and then run the following commands:

```
gunzip httpd.tar.gz
tar xvf httpd.tar
```

You'll then want to read through the **Makefile**, which is self-documented. Next, adjust **config.h** (detailed instructions are in the file itself) to contain the necessary information for your system. You can run an automatic script for this process called **autodetect**, which creates a **config.h** file for you.

The resulting **make** command should compile the programs without any problems, after which you'd use **make install** to install the programs and data files in the correct locations. You might want to type **make -n install** first to see where the programs and the others files are going to be stored. If you do not like the directories, edit the **Makefile** and retry.

Other Web Servers Not on the CD-ROM

A number of other Web servers will run under Linux, but, for various legal and commercial reasons, they cannot be redistributed on the accompanying CD-ROM. Here are short summaries of these CD-ROMs and their Internet homes.

AOLserver

http://www.aolserver.com

The server formerly known as Navisoft and GNNserver is now marketed under the AOL banner. This server is available at no charge via the Internet in a Linux version (alas, AOL refused to let it be included in this book) and has many advanced features that are worth checking out, including a smooth SQL interface, a decent search engine, and the Illustra database.

Jigsaw

http://www.w3.org/pub/WWW/Jigsaw/

The Jigsaw Web server is a full HTTP Web server written in Java and available from the World Wide Web Consortium. While it has many promising features, Jigsaw is not included on the accompanying CD-ROM because only an early alpha version was available as this book was written.

Roxen Challenger

http://www.roxen.com

Roxen Commercial is a commercial Web server that's distributed under the GPL license and is available on a wide range of operating systems. It features Roxen-specific server-side includes and its own interpretive language.

TEAMate

http://www.mmb.com/TM/T7

TEAMate is commercial software that incorporates a Web server, among other Web-publishing applications.

Zeus

http://www.zeus.co.uk/

The Zeus Web server is a commercial Web server available in a Linux port.

Summary

This long chapter covered the installation and configuration of a Web server for your Linux Internet system. Most readers of this book will consider it a priority to have a Web server up and running; hence, we have provided the in-depth coverage here.

The majority of the time in this chapter was spent on the Apache Web server, which is the most popular Web server in the Internet world. It has many features, and best of all it ships as part of Slackware Linux. However, the WN is also a fine, full-featured Web server that has some features not found in the Apache Web server. Other Web servers covered included the NCSA, CERN, and XS-HTTP Web servers.

The next chapter covers Gopher and WAIS.

SETTING UP GOPHER

This chapter covers:

- Gopher
- A little Gopher history
- GN, a Gopher server
- Installing GN
- Setting up data directories
- Testing your Gopher
- Troubleshooting
- Using Web pages
- Using scripts
- Gopher data types

Gopher

The World Wide Web is only the beginning of the services that you can offer via the Internet, although most of users will be desiring the Web. In this chapter, we cover a predecessor to the World Wide Web, called Gopher.

Even though Gopher has been shoved aside lately because of the overwhelming popularity of the World Wide Web, it's still a viable Internet service. Developed at the University of Minnesota (where the school mascot is a Golden Gopher), Gopher is a menu-based interface to files and directories, much like the World Wide Web is nothing more than a graphical-based interface to files and directories. When a Gopher client connects to a Gopher server, the server returns a numbered set of lines. The user can choose one of the lines. If it's a Gopher text file, then the file will be displayed on the screen. If it's a link to another set of listings, then the listings will be displayed. If the line represents a downloadable file, the file will be downloaded to your machine.

If this sounds a lot like the World Wide Web in a stripped-down format, you're right. Basically, Gopher was designed for an assortment of machines, including dumb terminals, where the only input might be alphanumeric. The original Gopher system at the University of Minnesota was designed to be used in libraries with dumb terminals, and so users would need to scroll through the list or type in a number. Now, of course, when all you need to do is point and click on an item either using a Web browser or a newer Gopher client, these menus and text-based screen elements seem a tad antiquated, but you must remember that when Gopher was originally developed, it was on the cutting edge of technology—and one that contributed more than a few ideas and concepts to the World Wide Web.

But don't use Gopher because of its history; use Gopher because it can actually serve some of your computing needs. You may be working in a system that's put a lot of time and effort into existing Gopher menus and structures, and if you're moving them over to a Linux Internet server, you may want a way to continue offering them to the world. There's also a compelling reason to look at Gopher—it interacts easily with search engines like the Wide Area Indexing Service (WAIS), which will be covered later in this chapter. Quite honestly, it's simple to put together a Gopher-based front end to an indexed database. There are literally hundreds of those databases out there, all running very well using Gopher as a text- and menu-based interface. So Gopher can still be an important player in your Linux Internet computing arsenal.

NOTE This book doesn't cover the original Gopher server software. Why? Because the University of Minnesota made noises about wanting payment in order to use Gopher. While it's in my best interests on one level to go along with a payment schedule for Gopher (I am a Minnesota taxpayer, after all), it's not in my best interest to point you in the direction of quasi-commercial software when there's high-quality freeware that will also serve your purposes. If you want to check out Gopher source code for use on your Linux system, feel free to check out the Gopher home page at *http://boombox.micro.umn.edu/*.

GN: A Free Gopher

No Gopher ships natively as part of Slackware Linux. However, we have included GN 2.23 on the accompanying CD-ROM, in the **/cdrom/internet** directory. Developed by John Franks (*john@math.nwu.edu*) of the Department of Math at Northwestern University (and also the developer of WN, which you read about in the previous chapter), GN is a free multiprotocol server for both Gopher and HTTP. It has the following features:

- GN serves two protocols—gopher0 and HTTP/1.0, the protocol used by WWW clients. GN recognizes the protocol from the request and responds appropriately. This allows the use of Web browsers like Netscape Navigator in their native mode.

- Offers tools designed to ease migration from Gopher to the World Wide Web.

- Allows per-directory access control. You can have different access (by IP address or subnet) to every directory if you desire. You don't need to run different servers on different ports to have different levels of access.

- Supports WAIS index searches.

- Supports structured files.

- Supports compressed files.

- Allows built-in menu hierarchy searches.

It's distributed under the GNU license, which means that it can be used in both nonprofit and commercial situations.

The following information on GN comes from the GN documentation.

GN supports the standard text and binary types, including sound and image. Index types include programs (or shell scripts) that return virtual directories and also grep-type searches. GN runs under **inetd** or as a standalone daemon.

The GN gopher/http protocol server supports WAIS index searches. This means you can index a collection of files with the index software designed for use with WAIS, and the GN server will respond to user queries by providing a menu of those documents from your collection that contain a match for the user-supplied search term. Simple Boolean combinations like "horses and cows" or "fox not goose" are supported.

Installing the Software

You'll need to copy the **gn.tar.gz** file from the accompanying CD-ROM (it's stored in the **/internet** directory) and run the following commands on it:

```
uncompress gn.tar.gz
tar xvf gn.tar
```

This creates the GN **source** directory hierarchy. The top level of the directory created by untarring this file contains four directories: **gn**, **mkcache**, **waisgn**, and **docs**.

The next step is editing the **config.h** file in the top-level directory. You should enter the host name of the computer on which you plan to run GN and the complete pathname of your Gopher data directory. If you want to run at a port other than 70, also edit the DEFAULTPORT entry. You should also specify the complete path of the **mkcache/gn_mime.types** file on your system. You can put this file anywhere convenient (and give it any name). This file is used by the **mkcache** program; see the section later on Content-type for an explanation of the function of this file. Other customizations are possible but should not be needed.

Next, edit the **Makefile** file in the top-level directory. This allows you to specify the C compiler used if you wish to use something other than cc (and in the case of Slackware Linux, you'll need to specify **gcc**). You can also specify two directories in which things are placed when you do a **make install**. The first of these, SERVBINDIR, is the path of the directory in which you want the executable file for the GN server installed. The second, BINDIR, is the location for the **mkcache** program.

In the **gn-2.*** directory, do a **make** to produce the **gn** server and the **mkcache** utility. The **mkcache** utility produces cache files for use by the server (it is described later). The binary **gn** is the server and can be installed anywhere you choose. The binary **mkcache** is a utility program for maintainers and should be installed somewhere in your path, like **/usr/local/bin**.

You can now either run the server as a standalone daemon, the **sgn** executable, or run under **inetd**, the **gn** executable. We first describe the standalone version, and in most cases this is the version that you'll want to run. Launch it with the command:

```
sgn -p port [other options] /path/to/gnroot &
```

where *port* is the number of the port on which you wish the server to run. If this is a nonprivileged port (a port higher than 1024; if you're not clear about ports, you'll want to go back to Chapters 3 and 4 to review the discussions of ports), then **sgn** can be run as an ordinary user. However, for privileged ports like 70 or 80, you must run the preceding command as root. When **sgn** starts up, it will change its user ID to the one set in the **config.h** file line where USERID is defined.

It is important to run **gn** as *nobody* or some other user with no access privileges. It should never be necessary to run **gn** as root; to do so would be a serious mistake for maintaining security. Every attempt has been made to make **gn** as secure as possible, even if it is run as root; however, no program accessible to remote users on the Internet can be assumed perfectly secure.

Setting Up the Data Directory

In each directory of your data hierarchy, create a file called **menu** with one item for each file or directory you want **gn** to publish. Items in this file have a format like the following:

```
# This is a comment

Maintainer=mailto:gnperson@host.edu

Name=This description of the file will display on the client
Path=0/path/to/dir/file
Type=0
Host=YourHost.YourU.edu
Port=70

Name=This is a subdirectory
Path=1/path/to/dir/subdir
Type=1
Host=YourHost.YourU.edu
Port=70

Name=This is a remote link
Path=0/myfile/path
Type=0
Host=MyHost.MyUniv.edu
Port=70
```

The line starting with *Maintainer=* is optional (and provides information only to HTTP clients). It should contain a reference to the maintainer of this directory like the preceding one (technically any URL is permissible). The *Maintainer* line must be the first nonblank and noncomment line in the **menu** file.

There are several things to note about item entries in this file. The *Name* field must be first, the *Path* field starts with a **gn** type (e.g., 0 for a file or 1 for a directory; you'll learn more about this later in this chapter). It is followed by the pathname of the file or directory relative to the top-level data directory.

The *Type*, *Host*, and *Port* fields are optional for local items but required for remote links. If they are not present, the *Type* will be taken from the first character of the *Path* field, and the *Host* and *Path* fields will be those specified in **config.h** (or on the command line of **mkcache**). In general it is a good idea not to include the *Host* and *Port* fields for local items. This makes it much easier if at some future time you should wish to move your server to a new host or new port. (For more details on the format of menu files, see the man page called **mkcache.1** and the sample menu files in each directory of the source hierarchy.)

After the menu files have been created, you must run the **mkcache** program to produce a **.cache** file. This can be done once for each directory or once in the top data directory with the *-r* option to make all the **.cache** files for the hierarchy. You might want to look at a **.cache** file to see what it is like.

Testing Your Setup

After compiling and setting up the software, you can test it on a sample directory provided with the distribution. To do this, first make a symbolic link in your root data directory to the **docs** directory in the source distribution. The command line:

```
ln -s /your/src/dir/docs docs
```

executed in the root directory should do this.

Next, place a copy of the file **/docs/sample.root.menu** in your root data directory and name it **menu** (be sure to save the previous menu file if you have created one). Now in your root directory run the program **mkcache** with the command **mkcache -r**. This will produce some messages, including a warning about the file **docs/Install**, which you can ignore. (To understand the meaning of this warning, read the section on structured files later in this chapter.) Running **mkcache** with the -r option should produce two **.cache** files, one in your root directory and one in the **docs** subdirectory. Now change to the directory **docs/images** and run **mkcache** again to produce a **.cache** file here. Using the *-r* directory didn't take care of this directory because we don't want it to show on our menus and hence it isn't in any menu file. The image in this directory will appear inline in the menu for the root directory (if it is viewed with an HTTP client like Netscape Navigator); Gopher clients lack the capability to display it and will ignore it.

Now you are ready to test your server installation on this directory. Try it with your favorite Gopher or HTTP client.

Troubleshooting

If things are not working as they should, here are some tips to help you isolate the problems.

First, if the compilation of **gn** failed and produced an error message like:

```
ld: Undefined symbol
_putenv
```

it means that the C programming libraries on your system do not contain the function _putenv()_. For four functions, which seem to be less common than they should be, versions have been supplied. They are *putenv()*, *strncasecmp()*, *strstr()*, and *strftime()*. To use them, you will need to edit **config.h** and uncomment the line *#define NEED_PUTENV*, for example. If the compilation was successful, you can check the server itself by executing it from the command line. If you use the command **gn /full/path/of/root/dir**, it should run and pause for input. Type a return in response, and **gn** should print the *gopher protocol lines* of your top-level **.cache** file and exit. If instead of a return you type the selector for a file (i.e., the contents of the *Path= line* in the menu, like *0/dir/filename*), then **gn** should display the contents of that file and exit.

If this doesn't happen, there should be an error message that may be helpful. Better error messages are placed in the log file so you may want to run **gn** again with the additional arguments *-L logfile* and then examine the contents of the log file. Or if you run **gn -L /dev/tty**, the log entries will be printed to your screen instead of being put in a file. If it can't open a file, for example, the name of that file will be recorded in the log file. Check its permissions. Remember that all files that **gn** serves must be world-readable.

A second useful test is to telnet to your server at port 70. You should get a connection message and a pause for input. If you get a *Connection refused* message, it is likely that there is a problem with your **inetd** setup or for some reason your system can't find or can't execute the **gn** binary.

If your **image.gif** won't display, you probably forgot that **image.gif** must be in a menu file and the **.cache** file produced from it. Just putting a line like:

```
<img src="images/picture.gif">
```

in a file is not sufficient. For security reasons the server won't serve anything not in a **.cache** file. You must have your images in menu files.

Of course, if you don't want them to show on your clients' menus, you should use an *Attribute=invisible* line with them in the menu.

Limiting Access to Your GN Hierarchy

If you opt to limit access to your gopher, there are two ways to do this. For the first you use the *-a* option to **gn** (in the **inetd.conf** file). This will limit access to the server to those clients with an IP address or subnet address listed (and not excluded) in the file **.access** in the root data directory. The format of the **.access** file is one address per line, each line consisting of an IP address like 129.111.222.123 or a subnet address like 129.111.222 or 129.111. In case a subnet address is listed, any client with an IP address beginning with that subnet address will be allowed access.

You may also list the domain names of the machines using wildcards, provided the machines all have proper PTR domain name records. To allow access to all machines under **nwu.edu**, use the line **.nwu.edu*. Note that this will not allow access to a machine called *nwu.edu* if it exists. You would need to add in the record *nwu.edu* to allow access.

You can also exclude IP addresses or domain names by prefixing them with an exclamation mark (!), so if **.access** contained only the lines:

```
!speedy.acns.nwu.edu
*
```

access would be permitted to every machine except *speedy*. Likewise:

```
!129.111
*
```

would allow access to everyone except those on subnet 129.111. It is important to note that in determining access, **gn** reads the **.access** file only until it finds a match (with or without *!*) and then quits. So if **.access** consisted of the two lines:

```
*
!129.111
```

then access would be granted to everyone since the * comes first and it matches everyone.

The -*A* option is similar to the -*a* option except access is allowed on a per-directory basis. Each client request is processed by first looking for an **.access** file in the directory containing the requested item and comparing the IP address of the client with the addresses in this file. If no **.access** file exists in this directory, one is sought in the parent directory and then if necessary the parent of the parent, up to the root data directory. If no **.access** file is found by this process access is allowed to all clients provided the item requested exists in a **.cache** file.

It is possible with **gn** to attain even finer access discrimination than on a per-directory basis, even though it is somewhat cumbersome to do so. Nevertheless, if you need to make certain menu items visible (and accessible) to a select group of hosts, this is possible. Details on how to do it are in the last section of the document **/docs/technical.notes**.

Searching a Collection of Files

GN has two mechanisms to allow the user to create a small menu consisting of those items on a large menu whose files contain a particular search term. The first of these is described in this section. This method has the advantage of being much easier for the maintainer but will become slow if there are too many files being searched or the files are too large. It is appropriate if the number of files you wish to search is, say, less than 100 and the files themselves are at most a few hundred kilobytes (of course, this depends on your particular hardware, and your mileage may vary). If you have a large number of files or very large files, then using WAIS indexing may be a better choice. WAIS indexing is covered in a separate document that can be found online.

Using GN as a Web Server

GN can be used as a Web server (although it should be noted that if what you're primarily looking for is a Web server, you should be using the Apache Web server or WN, both of which were discussed in the previous chapter). GN will accept either Gopher requests or HTTP requests and respond appropriately. This takes place automatically with no action necessary on the part of the maintainer.

Once you have created a Web document, you can serve it with **gn** by giving it a filename ending in **.html** and making it available in the usual way as a text document. For example,

```
Name=A Sample of Hypertext Markup
Path=0/dir/dir2/sample.html
```

If this document is viewed with an HTTP browser, it will be displayed with the capabilities of that browser (i.e., nicely formatted in the ways prescribed by your HTML document). If it is viewed by a Gopher client, the HTML source (i.e., the unformatted document with markup tags) will be displayed. If you want to create two versions of a document—one in plain text and the other in HTML—this is easily handled by **gn**. Simply give the plain text file a name, say **sample**, and use the name **sample.html** for the HTML version. Then use the plain text name, but with a Path starting with *0h* (that's zero *h*). For example, a menu entry like:

```
Name=A Sample of Plain/Hyper text
Path=0h/dir/dir2/sample
```

will provide the file **sample** to Gopher clients and **sample.html** to HTTP clients. You can also name the plain text file **sample.txt**, and **gn** will automatically change the name to **sample.html** when putting it on a menu for an HTTP browser. This is only true for the suffix **.txt**, though. If you name the plain version **foo.tex**, then the HTML version must be named **foo.tex.html**. There is also a *1h* that works similarly. If a directory has path field **1h/dir/foo**, then Gopher clients will see it in the usual way, but for HTTP clients an HTML file **/dir/foo.html** will be served instead. However, the method described in the following paragraph is a better way to deal with putting HTML text into menus for most situations.

Adding HTML text to menus works slightly differently. You simply include the source in the menu file beginning with the keyword *httpText=* on a line by itself and ending with the keyword *endText=* on a line by itself. Here is an example from the main menu of the **gn** server at *hopf.math.nwu.edu*. It illustrates how to put graphic images into a menu:

```
httpText=
<title>The GN Server</title>
<img src="http:/I/image/fract2.gif">
<p>
This is the home of the <i>gn</i> Gopher/HTTP server.  It contains
documentation on <i>gn</i>, the source, and several examples of how
<i>gn</i> can be used.  To get the source distribution select the
compressed tar file listed below.
<p>
endText=


Name=Announcement of GN version 1.0
Path=0/announce-1.0
```

After the keyword *httpText=*, the first line creates a title for the document. All HTML tags that do the markup are contained in angle brackets <>. The line starting *<img src=....*says to insert the graphic image on *hopf* at port 70 with *Path=I/image/fract2.gif* at this point in the document. The tag *<P>* indicates a paragraph break. Any HTML text can be inserted in this way in a menu. There can be multiple insertions, and they can be anywhere in the text.

If you use the keyword *Text=* in place of *httpText=*, then **gn** will serve the text to HTTP clients exactly as with *httpText=* but will also put the text (with all HTML tags deleted) in the Gopher menus using the *i* or comment type supported by many clients. For the Gopher clients, no text formatting is done. The lines will have the same length they do in your menu file.

Sometimes it is desirable to actually put HTML constructs into a menu line itself. This can be accomplished by using *Hname=* instead of *Name=*. For example, the menu entry *Hname=Sample</A>* of:

```
<A HREF="http://host/hyper.html">Hyper text</A>
Path=0h/dir/sample
```

will produce a menu item for Gopher clients linked to **/dir/sample**, but for HTTP clients there will be two links—the first with anchor *Sample* to **/dir/sample.html** and the second with anchor *Hypertext* to **/hyper.html**. In an *Hname* line there must always be at least one closing anchor to close the anchor automatically opened at the start of the line, which provides a link to the item in the *Path* field.

HTML documents normally have a title given at the beginning of the document and set off by the tags *<TITLE>* and *</TITLE>*. This is displayed by most browsers. When **gn** menus are converted to HTML documents, the *Name=* entry from the parent menu is used as the title except for the root menu (which has no parent). The default root menu title is set in the **config.h** *#define ROOT_MENU_NAME*, but this can be changed executing **gn** or **sgn** with the *-t* option followed by a quoted title. For example, the command:

```
sgn -t "My Server"
```

will set the title to *My Server*.

The Attribute Field in Menus

The *HttpText* and *Hname* mechanisms described previously give a way to display more information to HTTP clients than to Gopher clients. Sometimes it is desirable to do the reverse—show a link to Gopher clients but hide it from Web clients. This can be done by using the *Attribute=* field for the menu item. Thus the entry:

```
Name=A file for gopher clients only
Path=0/dir/file
Attribute=gopheronly
```

will be displayed only to Gopher clients.

Similarly, there is a way to have a menu item displayed only for HTTP clients. The menu item would be:

```
Name=A file on this server for HTTP clients only
Path=0/dir/file
Attribute=httponly
```

This method will serve only local files. The next section discusses other ways to serve objects, including remote files, to HTTP clients.

Finally, you may wish for certain items never to be displayed on a menu but to be accessible to requests, for example an inline graphic file for an HTML document. To be accessible such a file must be referenced in a menu file (and the **.cache** file produced from it) so that the server has permission to serve it. Simply add the line *Attribute=invisible* to the menu item, and it will not be displayed. For example, the entry:

```
Name=My gif file for an inline image
Path=I/dir/file.gif
Attribute=invisible
```

will allow **file.gif** to be served but will never show in any client's menu. Hence what you put in the *Name* field is only a note to yourself, since the server should never allow it to be viewed.

Remote links are slightly problematical for **gn**. If a link to a remote server is made in the usual way by specifying *Name, Path, Type, Host,* and *Port*, then the **gn** server assumes by default that this is a link to a server capable of dealing only with the Gopher protocol and will present it as such. The determination of whether or not a link is remote is done at the time that **mkcache** is run, and a link is considered remote unless the *Host* and *Port* fields in the menu are omitted or agree exactly with the default values as specified on the **mkcache** command line or at compile time in the **config.h** file. For this reason it is important that whenever you run **mkcache** you specify the host on the command line, unless you have placed that name in the **config.h** file as *HOSTNAME*.

Of course, you may know that a remote link is running the **gn** server and therefore capable of handling HTTP requests as well as Gopher requests. In this case, to allow HTTP clients to get the best link, simply use *gnlink* attribute in your menu file entry. For example, a link to the Northwestern University Math server would look like:

```
Name=Northwestern University Mathematics Department
Path=1/
Attribute=gnlink
Type=1
Host=gopher.math.nwu.edu
Port=70
```

A final attribute value is *nosearch*. If a menu item contains the line *Attribute=nosearch*, then that item will be displayed for clients but its title will not be used when searches of menu items (as described in the next section) are done.

The only currently allowable values for the *Attribute=* field in a menu are *invisible, gopheronly, httponly, nosearch,* and *gnlink*. When entered in a menu attribute line, their case is not significant. It is not possible for a single menu item to have two attributes.

Serving Items to HTTP Clients

There are several ways to serve items to HTTP clients. The various methods are appropriate for different circumstances. In all cases, however, the selections will not be shown to Gopher clients and will be made available only to HTTP clients.

Perhaps the simplest and most natural is to use the *httpText=* and *endText=* keywords. These provide arbitrary HTML, including hypertext links, to the HTTP client.

When the object is a local file, an *Attribute=httponly* line may be used. This was discussed in the previous section.

Another method is to use a menu entry such as:

```
URLlink=A file for HTTP clients only on a remote server
Url=http://host.name.edu/0/dir/file
```

This provides arbitrary objects, including items from remote servers, to HTTP clients. The title for the item can use HTML by saying, instead,

```
URLHlink=File for HTTP clients <strong>only</strong></a> (on remote server)
Url=http://host.name.edu/0/dir/file
```

Note that when *URLHlink=* is used, you must furnish the <A> hyperlink terminator, similar to *HName=* lines.

Setting Up a "Search All Menus" Item

A built-in feature of **gn** is the ability to have a menu item that, when selected, prompts the user for a search term and returns a virtual menu of all menu items containing that term. In fact, such an item can occur at any level and return either all matches from all menus on that server or all matches at or below some chosen level.

Here's how to set it up. Create an entry like this in the menu file where you want the search item to occur:

```
Name=Search all menus on this server
Type=7
Path=7c/.cache
```

(If you want the search to cover only those items in directory **/foo/bar**, then the *Path* line should be *Path=7c/foo/bar/.cache*.) Now run **mkcache** to translate the new menu file to a **.cache** file, and you are done. The *Type*, *Host*, and *Port* lines are optional—if they are omitted, **mkcache** will use the default value or the value supplied on the command line. When you change any of the menus in your server and remake the **.cache** files, **gn** will automatically reflect this in menu searches. There is a maximum depth that **gn** will search into the **gn** hierarchy. Its value can be changed by editing the **config.h** file and recompiling.

If the directory tree you wish to search is not the same one whose menu you want to contain the search item, then you will need to place a search item in both menu files: one in the menu where the search item should appear and another in the menu of the directory to be searched (perhaps hidden with *Attribute=invisible*). The first puts the search item on the client's menu, and the second grants the server permission to do the search.

Compressed Files

If you wish, you can keep files on your server in a compressed format and uncompress them on the fly as a client requests them. You need a program to compress the files and a companion program to decompress them. Recommended are **gzip** and **zcat** from the GNU project. They are considerably more efficient than the UNIX standard **compress**.

When configuring **gn** for compilation, be sure to set the #*define DECOMPRESS* in the **config.h** file to the pathname of the program that will decompress the files you have compressed. The default value for this is **/usr/local/bin/zcat**. Another possibility would be **/usr/ucb/uncompress -c**.

If the file you want to make available is **rootdir/dir1/bigfile**, first you must compress it with the **compress** command, which will replace it with the **bigfile.gz** or **bigfile.Z** file. You then make a menu entry like the following (assuming **bigfile** was a text file and you have produced **bigfile.gz**):

```
Name=All the text in Bigfile
Path=0Z/dir/bigfile.gz
Type=0
```

The key here is the Z, which is the second character of the *Path* field. It indicates that the file is compressed. The *Path* would start with *0Z* (that's zero Z) for any compressed text file. It doesn't matter how the file was compressed or whether its name is **bigfile.Z** or **bigfile.gz** or something else. You have already told **gn** how to decompress the file by specifying the *DECOMPRESS* program in **config.h**.

Of course, if **bigfile** is a binary, the *Path* field would be *9Z/dir/bigfile.gz* and the Type would be *9*. For a sound file, *Path=sZ/dir/bigfile.gz*, *Type=s*, etc. Files of types 0, 4, 5, 9, s, and I can be compressed; structured files (type 1m) cannot be compressed.

You might want to let users download the file in compressed format. You could give them the option by having the menu item as above with *Path=0Z/dir/bigfile.gz* and also having a menu item:

```
Name=Bigfile in compressed format
Path=9/dir/bigfile.gz
Type=9
```

Note the *Type=9*, since compressed files are binaries (even though **bigfile** is text), and there is no Z as the second character of the *Path*, because now we do not want to decompress. Also note that two versions of **bigfile** show up on your menu (text and compressed binary), but there is only one file **bigfile.gz** on your disk.

Serving the Output of a Program or Script

Sometimes it is convenient to have the server return the output of a program or script. This capability is built into **gn**. Assuming that you have a program in a file **prog** that returns some text, you can make its output be an item on your server's menu with a menu entry like:

```
Name=Program output
Type=0
Path=exec0::/dir/prog
```

The phrase *exec* says to run the program **prog**, which must be executable by the **gn** userid (probably *nobody*). The *0* after the *exec* says this is a text file; *exec* can return most types, including 0 (text), 1 (menus), 9 (binaries), s (sound), and I (image). Scripts or programs returning type 1 documents must produce a document in the format of a **.cache** file. This format is described in the file **/docs/technical.notes**. To specify a type, the single character type is appended to the word *exec* in the path so that the *Type=0* line is not really necessary. Thus if you wanted to return the output of a program in the format of an image file you might have an entry like:

```
Name=Image program output
Path=execI::/dir/prog
ContentType=image/gif
```

The pair of colons in the path can contain arguments to the program.

There is also support in **gn** for scripts complying with the CGI (Common Gateway Interface) standard. This allows the use of a growing collection of scripts that are written for HTTP servers supporting the standard. The use of these scripts is similar to the *exec0* types described previously but with a somewhat different syntax. Your menu file entry might look like:

```
Name=A CGI script
Path=CGI/dir/script.cgi
```

The initial *CGI* in the *Path* field indicates that this is a CGI item. In some respects the syntax is rather awkward, but it is made necessary to comply with a standard really intended for servers with a quite different design.

In particular, the name of the script must end with the suffix **.cgi** (or a replacement set at compile time in the **config.h** file), and no directory above the script in the data hierarchy may end in this suffix. The reason for this is the unusual way in which arguments to CGI scripts must be transmitted to the script. Instead of enclosing them in colons as with the preceding *exec0* examples, the arguments are appended to the end of the path as if they were a filename. To execute the preceding script with argument *foo*, you would use the URL:

http://host/CGI/dir/script.cgi/foo

This URL is frequently generated by the script itself with the extra so-called path information (the *foo* in this example) used as a way of saving state. It is also possible to put this in the menu file so the script will be executed with that argument:

```
Name=A CGI script
Path=CGI/dir/script.cgi/foo
```

GN Internal Types

Each *Path* field in a **gn** menu file contains an entry known as a selector. The format of this selector is a **gn** internal type field followed by the path relative to the **gn** root directory of the file referenced. The **gn** internal type indicates to the server what kind of document or file is referenced. It can be a single character like *0* to indicate a text file or a more complicated string. Here is a list of the types and what they mean:

- **0—Plain text**. This is a normal ASCII text file; the MIME content type used is *text/plain*.

- **0h, 1h—Plain text and HTML (two files)**. Items of type 0h are represented by two files, **filename** or **filename.txt** and **filename.html**, which are plain text and HTML versions of the same document. The server will return the HTML version to HTTP clients and the plaintext version to Gopher clients. Content types are text/plain and text/html, respectively. Type 1h works similarly returning a menu corresponding to **dirname** to Gopher clients and an HTML document **dirname.html** to HTTP clients.

- **1—Menu**. Items of this type correspond to directories in the **gn** hierarchy. From the menu file in this directory, the server produces an HTML document for HTTP clients and a Gopher protocol directory for Gopher clients.

- **1m—Structured file**. Items of this type are files consisting of many smaller documents like a mail file. The server presents a menu of these smaller documents and when one is selected returns the appropriate part of the file.

- **1s—Searchable menu**. Like type 1 but allows items in this menu to be searched with grep searches.

- **2—CSO or "ph" URL (link)**. The **gn** server does nothing with these links except give the URL (or Gopher equivalent) to the client to handle.

- **3—Error**. This type is reserved for error messages. It should not be used in a menu file.

- **4, 5, 6—Binhex, DOS .exe, and uuencoded files**. These types refer to Mac binhex, DOS binaries, and UNIX uuencoded files, respectively. The server treats types 4 and 6 (binhex and uuencoded) exactly like text files and type 5 (DOS binaries) like type 9 binary files.

- **7—Maintainer-defined search or response to client-supplied string**. An item of this type refers to a program or script provided by the server maintainer. This program should take an input string and respond with output in the format of a **.cache** file.

- **7c—Menu keyword search**. This item refers to a directory in the **gn** hierarchy, typically the root directory. When it is selected, the user is prompted for a search term (any grep-like regular expression). The server returns a menu of all menu items in the hierarchy at or below the given directory containing matches for the regular expression.

- **7g—Grep searches**. This item refers to a directory in the **gn** hierarchy, containing a number of files. When this item is selected, the server prompts the user for a regular expression search term and returns a menu of all those files containing a match for that regular expression.

- **7m—Search a structured file**. This item refers to an item of type 1m. When this item is selected, the server prompts the user for a regular expression search term and returns a menu of all those documents in the referenced file containing a match for that regular expression.

- **7w, 7wc, 7wh, 7wr—WAIS index searches**. These items refer to a WAIS index in the **gn** hierarchy, containing an index of a collection of files in the hierarchy. When this item is selected, the server prompts the user for a search term and returns a menu of all those files containing a match. Type 7wc indicates that the menu item titles should be taken from the **.cache** files containing the documents rather than use what WAIS thinks the title should be (typically the filename). Type 7wh indicates that the indexed items should be type 0h (i.e., there is both a plaintext and an HTML version of each file). Type 7wr indicates a range type, where a single file is considered to contain a number of documents, like a mail file.

- **8—Telnet URL (link)**. The **gn** server does nothing with these links except give the URL (or Gopher equivalent) to the client to handle.

- **9, I, s—Binary files, image files, sound files**. These files are treated as binary data and downloaded appropriately. To determine its MIME content type, the file **gn_mime.types** is consulted and compared with the filename extension. This can be overridden by a *ContentType= entry* in the menu file.

- **0Z, 9Z, IZ, sZ—Compressed files**. These types refer to files of type 0, 9, I, and s, respectively, but the files in question are kept on the server in a compressed format. When a client requests one of these files, it is automatically uncompressed before transmission to that client.

- **exec0, exec1, exec7, exec9, execI, execs—Execute a command**. These types cause the server to execute a program provided by the maintainer. The last character indicates the type of item the program or script will return, like 0 for text, 1 for directory, and so on.

- **R123-345-1m, R123-345-range**. These types should not be entered in a menu file by the maintainer. They are used internally by the server for menu items that correspond to documents that consist of all the characters in a certain range of a file. *R123-345-1m*, for example, would refer to the document consisting of bytes 123 to 345 of a file with a type 1m menu entry. Similarly, *R123-345-range* refers to a document returned as a match of a WAIS index search (type 7wr).

Summary

This chapter covered Gopher, a text-based predecessor to the World Wide Web. Even though Gopher may seem a little creaky now, it can be an important part of your Linux Internet server arsenal.

In the next chapter, we cover search tools.

Indexing with Glimpse
and GlimpseHTTP

This chapter covers:

- Glimpse
- Creating indices with **glimpseindex**
- Options to **glimpseindex**
- Glimpse and **agrep**
- Glimpse search options
- Pattern
- Glimpse files
- GlimpseHTTP
- Installing GlimpseHTTP
- Other indexing tools

Search Tools for the Masses

After you're thrown up your Web and Gopher pages, you'll want a way for your users to be able to search through them. This isn't a trivial task—part of the Webmaster's challenge is to give users access to what they want and need, even if they have no clue about what they want or need or how to get it.

That's why a good search mechanism is a must for the well-maintained Linux Internet Web site. The accompanying CD-ROM comes with the Glimpse search engine, along with tools that allow you to integrate Glimpse with your Web pages. In this chapter, you'll learn about installing Glimpse, as well as implementing it on your Linux Internet server. You'll also learn about GlimpseHTTP, an add-on to Glimpse designed specifically for Web pages. Depending on your needs, you'll want to use Glimpse for a large-scale indexing job and GlimpseHTTP for a smaller-scale, local indexing job. The source code for both, as well as precompiled binaries for Glimpse, are on the accompanying CD-ROM, in the **/internet/glimpse** directory. Because GlimpseHTTP requires Glimpse to run, you'll want to start with Glimpse and then work your way to GlimpseHTTP. (Chances are that you'll want to use GlimpseHTTP for most tasks, since it seems to work best with Linux, but all options are presented here.)

NOTE When this book was written, an advanced tool named WebGlimpse was in development by the Glimpse development team. At that time, using WebGlimpse under Linux was a largely untested proposition. Check out the WebGlimpse Web pages at *http://glimpse.cs.arizona.edu/webglimpse/* to see if work on a Linux implementation has been completed.

Glimpse: A High-Powered Indexing Tool

Glimpse (short for GLobal IMPlicit SEarch) is a Perl-based tool for searching a filesystem or specific Web pages. Several programs make up the Glimpse distribution: **glimpse**, **glimpseindex**, **agrep**, **glimpseserver**, and more.

Using Glimpse is quite simple—all you need to do is combine the **glimpseindex** command with the directory you want to index:

```
glimpseindex directory
```

where *directory* is a specific directory. The **glimpseindex** command will index the entire directory tree. To index everything at or below your home directory, use

```
glimpseindex -o ~
```

There are actually three index types, relating to the size of the index file when compared to the source files:

- a very small (tiny) index (about 2 to 3 percent the size of the source files)
- a small index (about 7 to 9 percent the size of the source files)
- a medium-sized index (about 20 to 30 percent the size of the source files)

The larger the index, the faster the search, but in most situations, the small index will work well. This is created with the following command line:

```
glimpseindex -o directory
```

where *directory* is the directory to be indexed.

The options to **glimpseindex** are listed in Table 6.1.

Table 6.1 Glimpseindex Options

Option	Purpose
-a	Adds the given file(s) and/or directories to an existing index. Any given directory will be traversed recursively and all files will be indexed (unless they appear in **.glimpse_exclude**; see later in this chapter). Using this option is generally much faster than indexing everything from scratch, although in rare cases the index may not be as good. If for some reason the index is full (which can happen unless -o or -b are used) **glimpseindex -a** will produce an error message and will exit without changing the original index.
-b	Builds a medium-sized index (20–30 percent of the size of all files), allowing faster searches. This option forces **glimpseindex** to store an exact (byte level) pointer to each occurrence of each word (except for some very common words belonging to the stop list).

Table 6.1 Glimpseindex Options (continued)

Option	Purpose
-B	Uses a hash table that is four times bigger (256K entries instead of 64K) to speed up indexing. The memory usage will increase typically by about 2MB. This option is only for indexing speed; it does not affect the final index.
-d *filename(s)*	Deletes the given filename(s) from the index.
-D *filename(s)*	Deletes the given file(s) from the list of filename(s) but not from the index. This is much faster than -d, and the file(s) will not be found by **glimpse**. However, the index itself will not become smaller.
-E	Does not run a check on file types. Glimpse normally attempts to exclude nontext files, but this attempt is not always perfect. With -E, **glimpseindex** indexes all files, except those that are specifically excluded in **.glimpse_exclude** and those whose file names end with one of the excluded suffixes.
-f	Launches incremental indexing. **glimpseindex** scans all files and adds to the index only those files that were created or modified after the current index was built. If there is no current index or if this procedure fails, **glimpseindex** automatically reverts to the default mode (which is to index everything from scratch). This option may create an inefficient index for several reasons, one of which is that deleted files are not really deleted from the index. Unless changes are small, mostly additions, and -o is used, we suggest that you use the default mode as much as possible.
-F	Tells **glimpseindex** to receive the list of files to index from standard input.
-H *directory*	This puts or updates the index and all other **.glimpse** files (listed later) in *directory*. The default is the home directory. When **glimpse** is run, the -H option must be used to direct **glimpse** to this directory, because **glimpse** assumes that the index is in the home directory (see also the -H option in **glimpse**, in Table 6.2).
-i	Makes **.glimpse_include** (see Table 6.4) take precedence over **.glimpse_exclude**, so that, for example, you can exclude everything (by putting *) and then explicitly include files.
-I	Instead of indexing, only show (print to standard out) the list of files that would be indexed. It is useful for filtering purposes. (**glimpseindex -I dir | glimpseindex -F** is the same as **glimpseindex dir**.)
-M*x*	Tells **glimpseindex** to use *x* MB of memory for temporary tables. The more memory you allow, the faster **glimpseindex** will run. The default is 2. The value of *x* must be a positive integer. **glimpseindex** will need more memory than *x* for other things, and **glimpseindex** may perform some forks, so you'll have to experiment if you want to use this option. If *x* is too large you may run out of swap space.

Option	Purpose
-n	Indexes numbers as well as text. The default is not to index numbers. This is useful when searching for dates or other identifying numbers, but it may make the index very large if there are many numbers. In general, **glimpseindex** strips away any nonalphabetic character. For example, the string *abc123* will be indexed as *abc* if the -n option is not used and as *abc123* if it is used. Glimpse provides warnings (in the **.glimpse_messages** file) for all files in which more than half the words that were added to the index from that file had digits in them (this is an attempt to identify data files that should probably not be indexed). One can use the **.glimpse_exclude** file to exclude data files or any other files.
-o	Builds a small rather than tiny index (meaning 7–9% of the size of all files—your mileage may vary) allowing faster searches. This option forces **glimpseindex** to allocate one block per file (a block usually contains many files).
-R	Recomputes **.glimpse_filenames_index** from **.glimpse_filenames**. The file **.glimpse_filenames_index** speeds up processing. **Glimpseindex** usually computes it automatically. However, if for some reason you want to change the pathnames of the files listed in **.glimpse_filenames**, then running **glimpseindex -R** recomputes **.glimpse_filenames_index**. This is useful if the index is computed on one machine but is used on another (with the same hierarchy). The names of the files listed in **.glimpse_filenames** are used in runtime, so changing them can be done at any time in any way (as long as just the names not the content is changed). This is not really an option in the regular sense; rather, it is a program by itself, and it is meant as a post-processing step.
-s	Supports structured queries. This option was added to support the Harvest project, and it is applicable mostly in that context.
-Sk	The number *k* determines the size of the stop-list. The stop-list consists of words that are too common and are not indexed (e.g., *the* or *and*). Instead of having a fixed stop-list, **glimpseindex** figures out the words that are too common for every index separately. The rules are different for the different indexing options. The tiny index contains all words (the savings from a stop-list are too small to bother). With the small index (-o), the number *k* is a percentage threshold. A word will be in the stop list if it appears in at least *k* percent of all files. The default value is 80 percent. (If there are fewer than 256 files, then the stop-list is not maintained.) The medium index (-b) counts all occurrences of all words, and a word is added to the stop-list if it appears at least *k* times per megabyte. The default value is 500. A query that includes a stop list word is of course less efficient.
-t	Sets the order in which files are indexed is determined by scanning the directories, which is mostly arbitrary. With the -t option, combined with either -o and -b, the indexed files are stored in reversed order of modification age (younger files first). Results of queries are then automatically returned in this order. Furthermore, **glimpse** can filter results by age; for example, asking to look at only files that are at most five days old.

Table 6.1 Glimpseindex Options (continued)

Option	Purpose
-T	Builds the turbo file. Starting at version 3.0, this is the default, so using this option has no effect.
-X	Extracts titles from HTML pages and add the titles to the index (in **.glimpse_filenames**). This works only on files whose names end with **.html**, **.htm**, **.shtml**, and **.shtm**. The routine to extract titles is called **extract_info**, in **index/filetype.c**. This feature can be modified in various ways to extract info from many file types. The titles are appended to the corresponding file names with a space separator. **Glimpseindex** assumes that file-names don't have spaces in them.
-wk	**Glimpseindex** does a reasonable, but not a perfect, job of determining which files should not be indexed. Sometimes a large text file should not be indexed; for example, a dictionary may match most queries. The -w option stores in a file called **.glimpse_messages** (in the same directory as the index) the list of all files that contribute at least k new words to the index. The user can look at this list of files and decide which should or should not be indexed. The file **.glimpse_exclude** contains files that will not be indexed (see a more detailed discussion later). The recommended setting for k is about 1000. This is not an exact measure. For example, if the same file appears twice, then the second copy will not contribute any new words to the dictionary (but if you exclude the first copy and index again, the second copy will contribute).
-z	Allows customizable filtering, using the **.glimpse_filters** file to perform the programs listed there for each match. The best example is **compress/decompress**. If **.glimpse_filters** include the line `* . Z uncompress <` (separated by tabs), then before indexing any file that matches the pattern *.Z (same syntax as the one for **.glimpse_exclude**) the command listed is executed first (assuming input is from **stdin**, which is why **uncompress** needs <) and its output (assuming it goes to **stdout**) is indexed. The file itself is not changed (i.e., it stays compressed). Then if **glimpse -z** is used, the same program is used on these files on the fly. Any program can be used (we run **exec**). For example, we can filter out parts of files that should not be indexed. **glimpseindex** tries to apply all filters in **.glimpse_filters** in the order they are given. For example, if you want to uncompress a file and then extract some part of it, put the compression command (as shown in the preceding example) first and then another line that specifies the extraction. Note that this can slow down the search because the filters need to be run before files are searched.

Glimpse then uses the **agrep** command to search through these indexes. It's actually a fairly flexible system allowing for misspellings, Boolean queries, and excluded terms. There are a number of options:

```
glimpse -1 Linux
```

searches for every time *Linux* is used in a file, allowing for one misspelling.

```
glimpse -F emacs Linux
```

searches for every file containing *emacs* within the file and *Linux* in the name of the file.

```
glimpse 'Volkderding;Reichard'
```

searches for all lines that contain both *Volkdering* and *Reichard*.

```
glimpse -W 'Reichard;~Sean'
```

searches for all lines that contain *Reichard* in files that don't contain the word *Sean*.

```
glimpse -w -i `reichard'
```

searches for all instances of *reichard*, regardless of case (in this case, returning *Reichard*, *reichard*, *reicharD*, and more), as long as it's a complete word.

Table 6.2 lists all of the Glimpse search options.

Table 6.2 Glimpse Search Options

Option	Purpose
-#	# is an integer between 1 and 8 specifying the maximum number of errors permitted in finding the approximate matches (the default is zero). Generally, each insertion, deletion, or substitution counts as one **error**. It is possible to adjust the relative cost of insertions, deletions, and substitutions (see *-I, -D,* and *-S* options). Since the index stores only lowercase characters, errors of substituting uppercase with lowercase may be missed. Allowing errors in the match requires more time and can slow down the match by a factor of 2–4. Be very careful when specifying more than one error, as the number of matches tend to grow very quickly.
-a	Prints attribute names. This option applies only to Harvest SOIF structured data (used with **glimpseindex -s**).
-A	Used for **glimpse** internals.

Table 6.2 Glimpse Search Options (continued)

Option	Purpose
-b	Prints the byte offset (from the beginning of the file) of the end of each match. The first character in a file has offset 0.
-B	Best match mode. (Warning: -B sometimes misses matches. It is safer to specify the number of errors explicitly.) When -B is specified and no exact matches are found, **glimpse** will continue to search until the closest matches (i.e., the ones with minimum number of errors) are found, at which point the following message will be shown: *The best match contains x errors, there are y matches, output them? (y/n).* This message refers to the number of matches found in the index. There may be many more matches in the actual text (or there may be none if -F is used to filter files). When the -#, -c, or -l options are specified, the -B option is ignored. In general, -B may be slower than -#, but not by very much. Since the index stores only lowercase characters, errors of substituting uppercase with lowercase may be missed.
-c	Displays only the count of matching records. Only files with count > 0 are displayed.
-C	Tells **glimpse** to send its queries to **glimpseserver**.
-d *'delim'*	Defines *delim* to be the separator between two records. The default value is *'$'*, namely a record is by default a line. *Delim* can be a string of size at most 8 (with possible use of ^ and $), but not a regular expression. Text between two *delims*, before the first *delim* and after the last *delim*, is considered as one record. For example, -d *'$$'* defines paragraphs as records, and -d *'^From\ '* defines mail messages as records. **glimpse** matches each record separately. This option does not currently work with regular expressions. The -d option is especially useful for Boolean AND queries, because the patterns need not appear in the same line but in the same record. For example, `glimpse -F mail -d '^From\ ' 'glimpse;arizona;announcement'` will output all mail messages (in their entirety) that have the three patterns anywhere in the message (or the header), assuming that files with *'mail'* in their name contain mail messages. If you want to output a whole file that matches a Boolean pattern, you can use -d *'09g1Xs'* (or another garbage pattern). If the delimiter doesn't appear anywhere, the whole file is one record. Warning: Use this option with care. If the delimiter is set to match mail messages, for example, and **glimpse** finds the pattern in a regular file, it may not find the delimiter and will therefore output the whole file. (The -t option can be used to put the *delim* at the end of the record.) **agrep** (and **glimpse**) resorts to more complex search when the -d option is used. The search is slower and the limit of 32 characters is enforced.
-Dk	Sets the cost of a deletion to k (k is a positive integer). This option does not currently work with regular expressions.
-e	Useful when the pattern begins with a dash -.
-E	Prints the lines in the index (as they appear in the index) that match the pattern. Used mostly for debugging and maintenance of the index. This is not an option that a user needs to know about.

Option	Purpose
-f file_name	This option has a different meaning for **agrep** than for **glimpse**. In **glimpse**, only the files whose names are listed in file_name are matched. (The filenames must appear as in **.glimpse_filenames**.) In **agrep**, the file_name contains the list of the patterns that are searched.
-F file_pattern	Limits the search to those files whose name (including the whole path) matches file_pattern. This option can be used in a variety of applications to provide limited search even for one large index. If file_pattern matches a directory, then all files with this directory on their path will be considered. To limit the search to actual file names, use $ at the end of the pattern. file_pattern can be a regular expression and even a Boolean pattern. This option is implemented by running **agrep file_pattern** on the list of file names obtained from the index. Therefore, searching the index itself takes the same amount of time, but limiting the second phase of the search to only a few files can speed up the search significantly. For example, glimpse -F 'src#\.c$' needle will search for *needle* in all **.c** files with *src* somewhere along the path. The **-F file_pattern** must appear before the search pattern (e.g., **glimpse needle -F '\.c$'** will not work). It is possible to use some of **agrep**'s options when matching filenames. In this case all options as well as the file_pattern should be in quotes. (-B and -v do not work very well as part of a file_pattern.) For example, glimpse -F '-1 gopherc' pattern will allow one spelling error when matching **gopherc** to the filenames (so *gopherrc* and *gopher* will be considered as well). glimpse -F '-v \.c$' counter will search for *counter* in all files except for **.c** files.
-g	Prints the file number (its position in the **.glimpse_filenames** file) rather than its name.
-G	Outputs the (whole) files that contain a match.
-h	Does not display filenames.
-H directory_name	Searches for the index and the other **.glimpse** files in directory_name. The default is the home directory. This option is useful, for example, if several different indexes are maintained for different archives (e.g., one for mail messages, one for source code, one for articles).
-i	Launches a case-insensitive search (e.g., A and a are considered equivalent). Glimpse's index stores all patterns in lowercase. When -i is used together with the -w option, the search may become much faster. It is recommended to have -i and -w as defaults, for example, through an alias. Use the following alias in our **.cshrc** file: .br alias glwi 'glimpse -w -i'.
-Ik	Sets the cost of an insertion to k (k is a positive integer). This option does not currently work with regular expressions.
-j	If the index was constructed with the -t option, then -j will output the files last modification dates in addition to everything else. There are no major performance penalties for this option.
-J host_name	Used in conjunction with **glimpseserver** (**-C**) to connect to one particular server.

Table 6.2 Glimpse Search Options (continued)

Option	Purpose
-k	No symbol in the pattern is treated as a meta character. For example, **glimpse -k 'a(b|c)*d'** will find the occurrences of *a(b|c)*d*, whereas **glimpse 'a(b|c)*d'** will find substrings that match the regular expression *a(b|c)*d*. (The only exception is ^ at the beginning of the pattern and $ at the end of the pattern, which are still interpreted in the usual way. Use \^ or \$ if you need them verbatim.)
-K *port_number*	Used in conjunction with **glimpseserver (-C)** to connect to one particular server at the specified TCP port number.
-l	Outputs only the files names that contain a match. This option differs from the *-N* option in that the files themselves are searched, but the matching lines are not shown.
-L *x* | *x:y* | *x:y:z*	If one number is given, it is a limit on the total number of matches. Glimpse outputs only the first *x* matches. If *-l* is used (i.e., only filenames are sought), then the limit is on the number of files; otherwise, the limit is on the number of records. If two numbers are given (*x:y*), then *y* is an added limit on the total number of files. If three numbers are given (*x:y:z*), then *z* is an added limit on the number of matches per file. If any of the *x*, *y*, or *z* is set to 0, it means to ignore it (in other words, 0 = infinity in this case); for example, **-L 0:10** will output all matches to the first 10 files that contain a match. This option is particularly useful for servers that needs to limit the amount of output provided to clients.
-m	Used for glimpse internals.
-M	Used for glimpse internals.
-n	Each matching record (line) is prefixed by its record (line) number in the file. To compute the record/line number, **agrep** needs to search for all record delimiters (or line breaks), which can slow down the search.
-N	Searches only the index (so the search is faster). If *-o* or *-b* are used, then the result is the number of files that have a potential match plus a prompt to ask if you want to see the filenames. (If *-y* is used, then there is no prompt and the names of the files will be shown.) This could be a way to get the matching filenames without even having access to the files themselves. However, because only the index is searched, some potential matches may not be real matches. In other words, with *-N* you will not miss any file, but you may get extra files. For example, since the index stores everything in lowercase, a case-sensitive query may match a file that has only a case-insensitive match. Boolean queries may match a file that has all the keywords but not in the same line (indexing with -b allows **glimpse** to figure out whether the keywords are close, but it cannot figure out from the index whether they are exactly on the same line or in the same record without looking at the file). If the index was not built with *-o* or *-b*, then this option outputs the number of blocks matching the pattern. This is useful as an indication of how long the search will take. All files are partitioned into usually 200 to 250 blocks. The file **.glimpse_statistics** contains the total number of blocks (or **glimpse -N a** will give a pretty good estimate; only blocks with no occurrences of *a* will be missed).

Option	Purpose
-o	The opposite of -t: the delimiter is not output at the tail, but at the beginning of the matched record.
-O	Filenames are not printed before every matched record; instead, each filename is printed just once, and all the matched records within it are printed after it.
-p	Supports reading compressed set of filenames. The -p option allows you to utilize compressed neighborhoods (sets of filenames) to limit your search, without uncompressing them. (This is from version 4.0B1 only.) The usage is **-p** *filename:X:Y:Z*" where *filename* is the file with compressed neighborhoods, X is an offset into that file (usually 0, must be a multiple of *sizeof(int)*), Y is the length **glimpse** must access from that file (if 0, then whole file; must be a multiple of *sizeof(int)*), and Z must be 2 (it indicates that *filename* has the sparse-set representation of compressed neighborhoods: the other values are for internal use only). Note that any colon : in the filename must be escaped using a backslash \.
-P	Used for **glimpse** internals.
-q	Prints the offsets of the beginning and end of each matched record. The difference between -q and -b is that -b prints the offsets of the actual matched string, while -q prints the offsets of the whole record where the match occurred. The output format is @x{y}, where x is the beginning offset and y is the end offset.
-Q	When used with **-N**, **glimpse** not only displays the filename where the match occurs but also the exact occurrences (offsets) as seen in the index. This option is relevant only if the index was built with -b; otherwise, the offsets are not available in the index. This option is ignored when used not with -N.
-r	This **agrep** option is ignored in **glimpse**, unless **glimpse** is used with a filename at the end, which makes it run as **agrep**. If the filename is a directory name, the -r option will search (recursively) the whole directory and everything below it. (The **glimpse** index will not be used.)
-Rk	Defines the maximum size (in bytes) of a record. The maximum value (which is the default) is 48 KB. Defining the maximum to be lower than the default may speed up some searches.
-s	Works silently, that is, displays nothing except error messages. This is useful for checking the error status.
-Sk	Set the cost of a substitution to k (k is a positive integer). This option does not currently work with regular expressions.
-t	Similar to the -d option, except that the delimiter is assumed to appear at the end of the record. **Glimpse** will output the record starting from the end of **.I** *delim* to (and including) the next **.I** *delim*.
-T directory	Uses *directory* as a place where temporary files are built. (Glimpse produces some small temporary files, usually in **/tmp**.) This option is useful mainly in the context of structured queries for the Harvest project, where the temporary files may be nontrivial, and the **/tmp** directory may not have enough space for them.

Table 6.2 Glimpse Search Options (continued)

Option	Purpose
-U	Interprets an index created with the *-X* or the *-U* option in **glimpseindex**. Useful mostly for WebGlimpse or similar Web applications. When **glimpse** outputs matches, it will display the filename, the URL, and the title automatically.
-v	This **agrep** option will be ignored in **glimpse**, unless **glimpse** is used with a filename at the end, which makes it run as **agrep**. It outputs all records/lines that do not contain a match. (Glimpse does not support the NOT operator yet.)
-V	Prints the current version of **glimpse**.
-w	Searches for the pattern as a word—surrounded by nonalphanumeric characters. For example, **glimpse -w car** will match *car*, but not *characters* and not *car10*. The nonalphanumerics must surround the match; they cannot be counted as errors. This option does not work with regular expressions. When *-w* is used together with the *-i* option, the search may become much faster. The *-w* option will not work with $, ^, and _. It is recommended to have *-i* and *-w* as defaults, for example, through an alias. Use the following alias in our **.cshrc** file: `alias glwi 'glimpse -w -i'`.
-W	The default for Boolean AND queries is that they cover one record (the default for a record is one line) at a time. For example, **glimpse 'good;bad'** will output all lines containing both *good* and *bad*. The -W option changes the scope of Booleans to be the whole file. Within a file **glimpse** will output all matches to any of the patterns. So, **glimpse -W 'good;bad'** will output all lines containing *good* or *bad*, but only in files that contain both patterns. For structured queries, the scope is always the whole attribute or file.
-x	The pattern must match the whole line. (This option is translated to *-w* when the index is searched and it is used only when the actual text is searched. It is of limited use in **glimpse**.)
-X	Outputs the names of files that contain a match even if these files have been deleted since the index was built. Without this option glimpse will simply ignore these files. (New in version 4.0B1.)
-y	Do not prompt. Proceed with the match as if the answer to any prompt is **y**. Servers (or any other scripts) using **glimpse** will probably want to use this option.
-Y*x*	If the index was constructed with the *-t* option, then **-Y x** will output only matches to files that were created or modified within the last *x* days. There are no major performance penalties for this option.

Option	Purpose
-z	Allows customizable filtering, using the file **.glimpse_filters** to perform the programs listed there for each match. The best example is **compress/decompress**. If **.glimpse_filters** includes the line `*.Z    uncompress <` (separated by tabs), then before indexing any file that matches the pattern *.Z (same syntax as the one for **.glimpse_exclude**) the command listed is executed first (assuming input is from **stdin**, which is why **uncompress** needs <) and its output (assuming it goes to **stdout**) is indexed. The file itself is not changed (i.e., it stays compressed). Then if **glimpse -z** is used, the same program is used on these files on the fly. Any program can be used (we run **exec**). For example, we can filter out parts of files that should not be indexed. **glimpseindex** tries to apply all filters in **.glimpse_filters** in the order they are given. For example, if you want to uncompress a file and then extract some part of it, put the compression command (as shown in the preceding example) first and then another line that specifies the extraction. Note that this can slow down the search because the filters need to be run before files are searched.
-Z	No op.

Patterns

Glimpse supports a large variety of patterns, including:

- **Strings**, which are any sequence of characters, including the special symbols ^ for beginning of line and `$` for end of line. The following special characters ($, ^, *, [, |, (,), !, and \) as well as the following meta characters special to **glimpse** (and **agrep**): ;, „ #, <, >, -, and ., should be preceded by \ if they are to be matched as regular characters. For example, \^abc\ corresponds to the string ^abc\, whereas ^abc corresponds to the string abc at the beginning of a line.

- **Classes of characters**, a list of characters inside [] (in order) corresponds to any character from the list. For example, [a-ho-z] is any character between a and h or between o and z. The symbol ^ inside [] complements the list. For example, [^i-n] denotes any character in the character set except character i to n. The symbol ^ thus has two meanings, but this is consistent with **egrep**. The period symbol . (don't care) stands for any symbol (except for the newline symbol).

- **Boolean operations**, including an AND operation denoted by the symbol ;, an OR operation denoted by the symbol ,, or any combination. For example, **glimpse `pizza;cheeseburger'** will output all lines containing both patterns. The command **glimpse -F `gnu;\.c$' `define;DEFAULT'** will output all lines containing both *define* and *DEFAULT* (anywhere in the line, not necessarily in order) in files whose name contains *gnu* and ends with *.c*. The command **glimpse `{political,computer};science'** will match *political science* or *science of computers*.

- **Wildcards**, including the symbol #, used to denote a sequence of any number (including 0) of arbitrary characters. The symbol # is equivalent to .* in **egrep**. In fact, .* will work too, because it is a valid regular expression, but unless this is part of an actual regular expression, # will work faster.

- **Combination of exact and approximate matching**. Any pattern inside angle brackets <> must match the text exactly even if the match is with errors. For example, *<mathemat>ics* matches mathematical with one error (replacing the last *s* with an *a*), but *mathe<matics>* does not match mathematical no matter how many errors are allowed. (This option is buggy at the moment.)

- **Regular expressions**. Since the index is word based, a regular expression must match words that appear in the index for **glimpse** to find it. **glimpse** first strips the regular expression from all nonalphabetic characters and searches the index for all remaining words. It then applies the regular expression matching algorithm to the files found in the index. For example, **glimpse `abc.*xyz'** searches the index for all files that contain both *abc* and *xyz*, and then search directly for *abc.*xyz* in those files. (If you use **glimpse -w `abc.*xyz'**, then *abcxyz* will not be found, because **glimpse** will think that *abc* and *xyz* need to be matches to whole words.) The syntax of regular expressions in glimpse is in general the same as that for **agrep**. The union operation |, Kleene closure *, and parentheses () are all supported. Currently + is not supported. Regular expressions are currently limited to approximately 30 characters (generally excluding meta characters). Some options (-*d*, -*w*, -*t*, -*x*, -*D*, -*I*, and -*S*) do not currently work with regular expressions. The maximal number of errors for regular expressions that use * or | is four.

There are a number of files that are created by **glimpse** when an index is generated. They are listed in Table 6.3.

Table 6.3 Files Created by Glimpse

File	This file
.glimpse_include	contains a list of files that **glimpseindex** is explicitly told to include in the index even though they may look like nontext files. Symbolic links are followed by **glimpseindex** only if they are specifically included here. If a file is in both **.glimpse_exclude** and **.glimpse_include**, it will be excluded.
.glimpse_filenames	contains the list of all indexed filenames, one per line. This is an ASCII file that can also be used with **agrep** to search for a filename leading to a fast **find** command. For example, **glimpse `count#\.c$' ~/.glimpse_filenames** will output the names of all (indexed) .c files that have *count* in their name (including anywhere on the path from the index). Setting the following alias in the **.login** file may be useful: `alias findfile `glimpse -h :1 ~/.glimpse_filenames'`.
.glimpse_index	contains the index. The index consists of lines, each starting with a word followed by a list of block numbers (unless the -o or -b options are used, in which case each word is followed by an offset into the file **.glimpse_partitions**, where all pointers are kept). The block/file numbers are stored in binary form, so this is not an ASCII file.
.glimpse_messages	contains the output of the -w option (see Table 6.2).
.glimpse_partitions	contains the partition of the indexed space into blocks and, when the index is built with the -o or -b options, some part of the index. This file is used internally by **glimpse**, and it is a non-ASCII file.
.glimpse_statistics	contains some statistics about the makeup of the index. Useful for some advanced applications and customization of **glimpse**.
.glimpse_turbo	is an added data structure (used under **glimpseindex -o** or **-b** only) that helps to speed up queries significantly for large indexes. Its size is roughly a quarter of a megabyte. **glimpse** will work without it if needed.

Two files can be created by users. They are listed in Table 6.4. These files serve as compliments to other commands listed in the previous tables.

Table 6.4 User-Created, Optional Glimpse Files

File	This file...
.glimpse_exclude	contains a list of files that **glimpseindex** is explicitly told to ignore. In general, the syntax of **.glimpse_exclude/include** (explained in Table 6.3) is the same as that of **agrep** (or any other **grep**). The lines in the **.glimpse_exclude** file are matched to the filenames, and if they match, the files are excluded. Notice that **agrep** matches to parts of the string (e.g., **agrep /ftp/pub** will match **/home/ftp/pub** and **/ftp/pub/whatever**). So, if you want to exclude **/ftp/pub/core**, you just list it, as is, in the **.glimpse_exclude** file. If you put **/home/ftp/pub/cdrom** in **.glimpse_exclude**, every filename that matches that string will be excluded, meaning all files below it. You can use ^ to indicate the beginning of a filename and $ to indicate the end of one, and you can use * and ? in the usual way. For example, **/ftp/*html** will exclude **/ftp/pub/foo.html**, but will also exclude **/home/ftp/pub/html/whatever**; if you want to exclude files that start with **/ftp** and end with **html** use **^/ftp*html$**. Notice that putting a * at the beginning or at the end is redundant (in fact, in this case **glimpseindex** will remove the * when it does the indexing). No other meta characters are allowed in **.glimpse_exclude** (in other words, don't use ., *, #, or |). Lines with ? must have no more than 30 characters. Notice that, although the index itself will not be indexed, the list of filenames (**.glimpse_filenames**) will be indexed unless it is explicitly listed in **.glimpse_exclude**.
.glimpse_filters	is described in Table 6.2 for the -z option.

GlimpseHTTP

GlimpseHTTP is a version of Glimpse designed for Web sites (as opposed to the larger Glimpse distribution, which can be used with any text collection).

To install GlimpseHTTP on your system, you'll need to copy the source-code directory from the CD-ROM (the filename is **glimpseHTTP_2_0_src_tar.Z**). You'll also need to make sure that your Perl installation is up and running (a topic you'll learn more about in Chapter 11). It doesn't matter where you copy **glimpseHTTP_2_0_src_tar.Z**. Go to the directory containing **glimpseHTTP_2_0_src_tar.Z** and run the following command lines:

```
gunzip glimpseHTTP_2_0_src_tar.Z
tar xvf glimpseHTTP_2_0_src_tar
```

This will create a directory named **cgi-bin** and several other files, including a configuration script called **ghinstall**. Run this script after checking through the **ghinstall** documentation online (*http://glimpse.cs.arizona.edu/ghttp/*).

Next will come adding the **cgi-bin** directory as a script directory on the Apache Web server (assuming, of course, that you're using the Apache Web server). Do this by adding a line like the following to the **srm.conf** file:

```
ScriptAlias /cgi-bin/ /usr/local/glimpsehttp/cgi-bin/
```

Your directory may be different, of course.

With the installation complete, you can create an archive. Basically, GlimpseHTTP uses Glimpse and Glimpseindex files, as well as the following files:

- **ghreindex**, a file that calls **glimpseindex** to recreate the Glimpse index (and associated files), and will also call **ghgenhtml**.

- **ghindex.html**, a file that is generated by the ghgenhtml utility. This is an HTML file that contains the search form for GlimpseHTTP. Depending on how the archive is configured (done during the **makegharc** command), a separate **ghindex.html** file could be generated for each subdirectory or just for the root directory of the archive.

- **archive.cfg**, a file that is generated by the **ghgenhtml** utility. This file contains the configuration for the archive. The format of the file is *<archive title> <archive base URL> <subdirectory indices>*, where each field is specified by a *t* (tab character). The last field is a 1 (true) or a 0 (false), and denotes whether or not each subdirectory has a **ghindex.html**. If not, just the root directory has a search page.

- **.gheye.gif**, a GIF file used by the **ghindex.html** files generated by **ghgenhtml**.

Basically, the **makegharc** command is used to make an archive. This command configures an archive, generates the reindexing script **ghreindex**, and calls that script. This can be an involved process, so you'll want to consult the online documentation (*http://glimpse.cs.arizona.edu/ghttp/makegharc-man.html*) before running this command. When this command is executed, the proper files are generated for the GlimpseHTTP search interface.

Other Search Engines

There are other searching and indexing tools on the market. Some of these should be familiar, while others are obscure. The first two are actually available for Linux at the present time and have been superseded to an extent by the Glimpse and GlimpseHTTP tools; as a matter of fact, the Harvest system actually uses Glimpse internally. The third is a popular Web technology that might be available for Linux by the time you read this.

FreeWAIS

For a long time the Wide Area Information Server was the only decent indexing tool on the market. A freely available version, freeWAIS, is on the accompanying CD-ROM, as grabbed directly from *ftp://ftp.wsct.wsc.com/pub/freeWAIS-sf/Linux/* (the filename is **fwsf2062-elfbin.tgz**, and it's stored in the **/internet** directory). It's an older version of WAIS, but it's still serviceable. You'll want to check out freeWAIS if you want to link indexes to a Gopher server.

The documentation for freeWAIS can be found at *http://ls6-www.informatik.uni-dortmund.de/ir/projects/freeWAIS-sf/index.html*.

Harvest

The Harvest technology serves as the basis for the Glimpse tools detailed earlier in this chapter. In addition, Harvest is available in source-code form and binary format at *http://harvest.transarc.com/*. (This is also where the Harvest documentation is stored, so you'll want to check out this site thoroughly if you want to implement Harvest.) Technically, there's no work being done on Harvest at the present time, but the existing software is stable and usable. In the **/internet/harvest** subdirectory on the accompanying CD-ROM you'll find three files:

- **harvest-1.4.pl2-linux-ELF.tar.gz**, which contains precompiled binaries for Harvest.
- **harvest-1.4.pl2-src.tar.gz**, which contains the source code for Harvest, in case you want to compile Harvest on your own Linux system.
- **cached-1.4.pl2-linux-elf.tar.gz**, which contains the Harvest cache software (useful for setting up a cache of frequently served documents).

Excite

Excite for Web Servers is a high-performance, Perl-based tool. At the time this book was written, there was not a Linux version available, but according to Excite representatives, a Linux version was in the works. Check out the Excite Web site (*http://www.excite.com/navigate/download.cgi* or *http://www.excite.com*) to see if a Linux version is now available.

Summary

This chapter covered the installation and usage of Glimpse and GlimpseHTTP, two searching and indexing tools that can help you gain control of your Web site by providing your users the tools to search through indexes of portions of or all your Web site. Glimpse can take specific files or an entire file structure and index the contents in many different ways. Meanwhile, Glimpse and GlimpseHTTP give you the tools to send this information to users in many different methods.

Also mentioned in this chapter were additional indexing tools that you might want to check out, including freeWAIS, Harvest, and Excite.

In the next chapter, you'll learn about FTP and offering FTP access to your users.

WORKING WITH WU-FTP

This chapter covers:

- The WU-FTP server
- Working with FTP
- WU-FTP file locations
- Editing the **inetd.conf** file
- Launching the FTP server
- Configuration files
- The **ftpaccess** file
- Message files
- The **ftpconversions** file
- The **xferstats** script

399

FTP

One of the oldest protocols on the Internet—indeed, even predating the Internet—is the File Transfer Protocol (FTP). This protocol is a basic method for exchanging files between computers via the Internet. It doesn't matter what kinds of computers are talking to one another: A Macintosh can use FTP to transfer files from a Cray supercomputer, a Linux Internet server, a PC, or another Macintosh. (What the Mac does with the file after it's been transferred is another story, however.) Because the file-transfer mechanism is independent of the operating system, it's very easy to use, which is why it's so popular in the Internet world.

In addition to the fact that FTP is simple to access, any Web browser can be used to download files via FTP. In fact, the FTP is one of the protocols explicitly supported by all Web browsers. If you set up a link on a Web page to a file stored on your Linux Internet server and specify *ftp* in the URL instead of *http*, the Web browser will initiate a file transfer, usually prompting the user as to how to handle the file. From your end, these file transfers are ridiculously easy to set up, and for users they're ridiculously easy to use.

The Slackware Linux operating system ships with the Washington University FTP Server 2.4 (**wu-ftpd**), a more powerful version of the FTP server that usually ships with UNIX systems. This FTP server is very stable and respected, and unless your needs are *really* advanced, you won't need to look elsewhere for a replacement FTP server.

When you installed Slackware Linux as your Internet server in Chapter 3, the WU-FTP server should have been installed automatically. It uses the following files on your Linux system:

- /bin/ftpd
- /etc/ftpaccess
- /etc/ftpconversions
- /etc/ftpgroups
- /etc/ftpusers
- /usr/bin/ftpcount
- /usr/bin/ftpwho

- /usr/bin/ftpshut
- /usr/bin/xferlog
- /usr/bin/xferstats

 These file locations are specific to Slackware Linux. The default installation locations for WU-FTP are slightly different.

NOTE

We'll cover each of these files at the end of this chapter. In the meantime, we'll discuss the core FTP daemon and how it works.

Running FTP

You can launch the FTP daemon at any time from a command line:

```
ftpd
```

It's probably a better idea to launch it via **inetd**, since this will automatically launch the FTP daemon every time the system is booted. This means editing the **inetd.conf** file, a task you already learned about in Chapter 4. And, Slackware Linux is already set up to run the **ftpd** daemon, as you can see if you peruse the **/etc/inetd.conf** file, which contains information about Internet services.

The default directory for access is **/home/ftp**. Within that directory are six subdirectories and a text file called **welcome.msg**. The six directories are:

- **bin**, where you store the binary files that the incoming FTP clients can use. A copy of the **ls** command is within this directory by default.
- **etc**, where you can store files. This directory is empty by default.
- **incoming**, which is designed for incoming users to upload files. The permissions on this directory are set so that anyone with access to the FTP system can upload and download files.

- **lib**, where you can store files.
- **pub**, a public directory usually used to store files that can be downloaded by users.

These directory locations were set when WU-FTP was compiled for use on Slackware Linux. If you want to make some large-scale changes in these file locations, you'll need to recompile WU-FTP.

Configuration Files

For the most part, WU-FTP will run by itself; however, you might need to adjust a number of configuration files for security reasons. The beginning point for these configuration options is **/etc/ftpaccess**, which controls who has access to what files and directories. You can set up groups of users, and if you're running on an intranet, you can apply some Linux login group permissions to your FTP server. In addition, the file can control how much particular users can upload and download, and it also sets the log files.

The **ftpaccess** file is as follows:

```
loginfails 2

class   local    real,guest,anonymous *.domain 0.0.0.0
class   remote   real,guest,anonymous *

limit   local    20   Any                 /etc/msgs/msg.toomany
limit   remote   100  SaSu|Any1800-0600   /etc/msgs/msg.toomany
limit   remote   60   Any                 /etc/msgs/msg.toomany

readme  README*      login
readme  README*      cwd=*

message /welcome.msg          login
message .message              cwd=*

compress        yes           local remote
tar             yes           local remote
```

```
# allow use of private file for SITE GROUP and SITE GPASS?
private         yes


# passwd-check  <none|trivial|rfc822>  [<enforce|warn>]
passwd-check    rfc822  warn


log commands real
log transfers anonymous,real inbound,outbound
shutdown /etc/shutmsg


# all the following default to "yes" for everybody
delete          no      guest,anonymous        # delete permission?
overwrite       no      guest,anonymous        # overwrite permission?
rename          no      guest,anonymous        # rename permission?
chmod           no      anonymous              # chmod permission?
umask           no      anonymous              # umask permission?


# specify the upload directory information
upload  /home/ftp  *            no
upload  /home/ftp  /incoming    yes    root    daemon  0600 dirs
upload  /home/ftp  /bin         no
upload  /home/ftp  /etc         no


# directory aliases... [note, the ":" is not required]
alias   inc:    /incoming


# cdpath
cdpath  /incoming
cdpath  /pub
cdpath  /


# path-filter...
path-filter  anonymous  /etc/pathmsg  ^[-A-Za-z0-9_\.]*$  ^\.  ^-
path-filter  guest      /etc/pathmsg  ^[-A-Za-z0-9_\.]*$  ^\.  ^-


# specify which group of users will be treated as "guests".
guestgroup ftponly


email user@hostname
```

As you can tell, this complex file has many settings. Instead of spending excessive time on this file here, our advice is to check out the extensive online-manual page, either with the **man** command or via the Internet (*http://www.wustl.edu/ftp/*). There are a few settings to look at here, however.

```
message /welcome.msg            login
```

This line specifies the default login message—that is, the message that's sent to all users after they log on your FTP server. The default **welcome.msg** file is as follows:

```
Welcome, archive user!  This is an experimental FTP server.  If have
any unusual problems, please report them via e-mail to root@%L. If you
do have problems, please try using a dash (-) as the first character
of your password — this will turn off the continuation messages that
may be confusing your ftp client.
```

You'll probably want to change this message. For starters, it's a good idea to include the name of your own FTP server somewhere here, and you can probably take out the reference to WU-FTP as an "experimental FTP server," since it's not experimental any longer.

```
limit   remote  100 SaSu|Any1800-0600    /etc/msgs/msg.toomany
```

This line limits the number of remote users (100) and specifies the message sent when there are no available slots for additional users. The **msg.toomany** file is as follows:

```
Sorry, there are too many anonymous users using the system at this
time.  Please try again later.  There is currently a limit of %M
anonymous users.
```

This setting probably doesn't need to be changed, although you can always add more of an explanation.

```
# specify the upload directory information
upload  /home/ftp  *              no
upload  /home/ftp  /incoming      yes     root    daemon  0600 dirs
upload  /home/ftp  /bin           no
upload  /home/ftp  /etc           no
```

This specifies the directory where users can upload files. The default is **incoming**, and this is also the default in the FTP world as a whole.

You'll want to look through a number of other files. For instance, the **ftpconversions** file specifies which file types can be transformed into **tar** archives and compressed files. Its contents are as follows:

```
:.Z:  :  :/bin/compress -d -c %s:T_REG|T_ASCII:O_UNCOMPRESS:UNCOMPRESS
:    :  :.Z:/bin/compress -c %s:T_REG:O_COMPRESS:COMPRESS
:.gz:  :  :/bin/gzip -cd %s:T_REG|T_ASCII:O_UNCOMPRESS:GUNZIP
:    :  :.gz:/bin/gzip -9c %s:T_REG:O_COMPRESS:GZIP
:    :  :.tar:/bin/tar -cf - %s:T_REG|T_DIR:O_TAR:TAR
:    :  :.tar.gz:/bin/tar -czf -
%s:T_REG|T_DIR:O_COMPRESS|O_TAR:TAR+GZIP
```

The Ftpusers File

The **ftpusers** file is used to determine who cannot have access to your system via the FTP server. This might be a case where some specific users are causing problems and you wish to deny them access. In addition, this file also can be used to make sure that no one uses the FTP server as a back door into your Linux system.

```
#
# ftpusers          This file describes the names of the users that may
#          _*NOT*_ log into the system via the FTP server.
#          This usually includes "root", "uucp", "news" and the
#          like, because those users have too much power to be
#          allowed to do "just" FTP...
#
# Version:          @(#)/etc/ftpusers          2.00          04/30/93
#
# Author:          Fred N. van Kempen, <waltje@uwalt.nl.mugnet.org
#
# The entire line gets matched, so no comments or extra characters on
# lines containing a username.
#
root
uucp
news

# End of ftpusers.
```

The Xferstats Script

The **xferstats** file is a Perl script that analyzes user logs and presents the information in a more elegant format. You'll need to edit the script and make sure that your user logs are working before this script will work properly.

```perl
#! /usr/bin/perl
# ----------------------------------------------------------------------
#
# USAGE: xferstats <options>
#
# OPTIONS:
#       -f <filename>   Use <filename> for the log file
#       -r              include real users
#       -a              include anonymous users
#       -h          include report on hourly traffic
#       -d          include report on domain traffic
#       -t          report on total traffic by section
#       -D <domain>     report only on traffic from <domain>
#       -l <depth>      Depth of path detail for sections
#       -s <section>    Section to report on, For example: -s /pub will report
#          only on paths under /pub
#
# ----------------------------------------------------------------------

# edit the next two lines to customize for your domain.
# This will allow your domain to be separated in the domain listing.

$mydom1 = "wustl";
$mydom2 = "edu";

# edit the next line to customize for your default log file
$usage_file = "/usr/adm/xferlog";

# Edit the following lines for default report settings.
# Entries defined here will be overridden by the command line.

$opt_h = 1;
$opt_d = 0;
$opt_t = 1;
$opt_l = 3;
```

```
require 'getopts.pl';
&Getopts('f:rahdD:l:s:');

if ($opt_r) { $real = 1;}
if ($opt_a) { $anon = 1;}
if ($real == 0 && $anon == 0) { $anon = 1; }
if ($opt_f) {$usage_file = $opt_f;}

open (LOG,$usage_file) || die "Error opening usage log file: $usage_file\n";

if ($opt_D) {print "Transfer Totals include the '$opt_D' domain only.\n";
        print "All other domains are filtered out for this report.\n\n";}

if ($opt_s) {print "Transfer Totals include the '$opt_s' section only.\n";
        print "All other sections are filtered out for this report.\n\n";}

line: while (<LOG>) {

    @line = split;
    next if ($#line != 16);
    next if (!$anon && $line[12] eq "a");
    next if (!$real && $line[12] eq "r");

    $daytime = substr($_, 0, 10) . substr($_, 19, 5);
    $time = substr($_,11,2);

    if ($line[8] eq "\.") { $line[8] = "/unreadable/filename";}
    next if (substr($line[8],0,length("$opt_s")) ne "$opt_s");
    $line[8] = substr($line[8],length("$opt_s"));
    @path = split(/\//, $line[8]);

#
# Why was the original xferstats dropping leading 1 character path
# segments???
#
#   while (length($path[1]) <= 1) {
#       shift @path;
#       next line if ($#path == -1);
#   }

# Things in the top-level directory are assumed to be informational files
```

```
if ($#path == 1)
   { $pathkey = "Index/Informational Files"; }
   else {
        $pathkey = "";
        for ($i=1; $i <= $#path-1 && $i <= $opt_l;$i++) {
        $pathkey = $pathkey . "/" . $path[$i];
        }
   }


$line[6] =~ tr/A-Z/a-z/;


@address = split(/\./, $line[6]);


$domain = $address[$#address];
if ($domain eq "$mydom2" && $address[$#address-1] eq "$mydom1")
   { $domain = $mydom1 . "." . $mydom2; }
if ( int($address[0]) > 0 || $#address < 2 )
   { $domain = "unresolved"; }


$count = 1;
if ($opt_D)
   {if (substr($domain,0,length("$opt_D")) eq "$opt_D" ) { $count = 1;} else
   {$count = 0;}
   }


if ($count) {

$xferfiles++;                              # total files sent
$xfertfiles++;                             # total files sent
$xferfiles{$daytime}++;                    # files per day
$groupfiles{$pathkey}++;                   # per-group accesses
$domainfiles{$domain}++;


$xfersecs{$daytime}     += $line[5];       # xmit seconds per day
$domainsecs{$domain}    += $line[5];       # xmit seconds for domain
$xferbytes{$daytime}    += $line[7];       # bytes per day
$domainbytes{$domain}   += $line[7];       # xmit bytes to domain
$xferbytes              += $line[7];       # total bytes sent
$groupbytes{$pathkey}   += $line[7];       # per-group bytes sent
```

```
        $xfertfiles{$time}++;                    # files per hour
        $xfertsecs{$time}      += $line[5];      # xmit seconds per hour
        $xfertbytes{$time}     += $line[7];      # bytes per hour
        $xfertbytes            += $line[7];      # total bytes sent
        }
}
close LOG;

@syslist = keys(systemfiles);
@dates = sort datecompare keys(xferbytes);

if ($xferfiles == 0) {die "There was no data to process.\n";}

print "TOTALS FOR SUMMARY PERIOD ", $dates[0], " TO ", $dates[$#dates],
"\n\n";
printf ("Files Transmitted During Summary Period %12.0f\n", $xferfiles);
printf ("Bytes Transmitted During Summary Period %12.0f\n", $xferbytes);
printf ("Systems Using Archives                  %12.0f\n\n", $#syslist+1);

printf ("Average Files Transmitted Daily         %12.0f\n",
    $xferfiles / ($#dates + 1));
printf ("Average Bytes Transmitted Daily         %12.0f\n",
    $xferbytes / ($#dates + 1));

format top1 =

Daily Transmission Statistics

            Number Of    Number of    Average     Percent Of  Percent Of
Date        Files Sent   Bytes  Sent  Xmit  Rate  Files Sent  Bytes Sent
----------- ----------   -----------  ----------  ----------  ----------
.


format line1 =
@<<<<<<<<<<<<<<  @>>>>>>>>>  @>>>>>>>>>>  @>>>>>>>>>  @>>>>>>>  @>>>>>>>
$date,          $nfiles,    $nbytes,     $avgrate,   $pctfiles, $pctbytes
.

$^ = top1;
$~ = line1;
```

```
foreach $date ( sort datecompare keys(xferbytes) ) {

    $nfiles    = $xferfiles{$date};
    $nbytes    = $xferbytes{$date};
    $avgrate   = sprintf("%5.1f KB/s", $xferbytes{$date}/$xfersecs{$date}/1000);
    $pctfiles  = sprintf("%8.2f", 100*$xferfiles{$date} / $xferfiles);
    $pctbytes  = sprintf("%8.2f", 100*$xferbytes{$date} / $xferbytes);
    write;
}


if ($opt_t) {
format top2 =

Total Transfers from each Archive Section (By bytes)


                                        ---- Percent  Of ----
     Archive Section      Files Sent Bytes Sent  Files Sent Bytes Sent
------------------------ ---------- ----------- ---------- ----------
.

format line2 =
@<<<<<<<<<<<<<<<<<<<<<<<< @>>>>>>>>> @>>>>>>>>>> @>>>>>>>   @>>>>>>>
$section,                $files,    $bytes,     $pctfiles, $pctbytes
.

$| = 1;
$- = 0;
$^ = top2;
$~ = line2;


foreach $section ( sort bytecompare keys(groupfiles) ) {

    $files = $groupfiles{$section};
    $bytes = $groupbytes{$section};
    $pctbytes = sprintf("%8.2f", 100 * $groupbytes{$section} / $xferbytes);
    $pctfiles = sprintf("%8.2f", 100 * $groupfiles{$section} / $xferfiles);
    write;

}


if ( $xferfiles < 1 ) { $xferfiles = 1; }
if ( $xferbytes < 1 ) { $xferbytes = 1; }
}
```

```
if ($opt_d) {
format top3 =

Total Transfer Amount By Domain

              Number Of    Number of      Average     Percent Of  Percent Of
Domain Name   Files Sent   Bytes Sent     Xmit  Rate  Files Sent  Bytes Sent
-----------   ----------   ------------   ----------  ----------  ----------
.

format line3 =
@<<<<<<<<<<  @>>>>>>>>>  @>>>>>>>>>>>  @>>>>>>>>>  @>>>>>>>  @>>>>>>>
$domain,    $files,    $bytes,      $avgrate,  $pctfiles, $pctbytes
.

$- = 0;
$^ = top3;
$~ = line3;

foreach $domain ( sort domnamcompare keys(domainfiles) ) {

    if ( $domainsecs{$domain} < 1 ) { $domainsecs{$domain} = 1; }

    $files = $domainfiles{$domain};
    $bytes = $domainbytes{$domain};
    $avgrate  = sprintf("%5.1f KB/s",
                   $domainbytes{$domain}/$domainsecs{$domain}/1000);
    $pctfiles = sprintf("%8.2f", 100 * $domainfiles{$domain} / $xferfiles);
    $pctbytes = sprintf("%8.2f", 100 * $domainbytes{$domain} / $xferbytes);
    write;

}


print "\n";
print "These figures only reflect ANONYMOUS FTP transfers.  There are many\n";
print "sites which mount the archives via NFS, and those transfers are not\n";
print "logged and reported by this program.\n\n";

}


if ($opt_h) {

format top8 =
```

Hourly Transmission Statistics

```
                  Number Of    Number of    Average     Percent Of  Percent Of
       Time       Files Sent  Bytes  Sent  Xmit  Rate  Files Sent  Bytes Sent
---------------   ----------  -----------   ----------  ----------  ----------
.


format line8 =
@<<<<<<<<<<<<<<<   @>>>>>>>>>   @>>>>>>>>>>   @>>>>>>>>>   @>>>>>>>    @>>>>>>>
$time,            $nfiles,     $nbytes,      $avgrate,   $pctfiles, $pctbytes
.


$| = 1;
$- = 0;
$^ = top8;
$~ = line8;

foreach $time ( sort keys(xfertbytes) ) {

   $nfiles   = $xfertfiles{$time};
   $nbytes   = $xfertbytes{$time};
   $avgrate  = sprintf("%5.1f KB/s",
$xfertbytes{$time}/$xfertsecs{$time}/1000);
   $pctfiles = sprintf("%8.2f", 100*$xfertfiles{$time} / $xferfiles);
   $pctbytes = sprintf("%8.2f", 100*$xfertbytes{$time} / $xferbytes);
   write;
}
}
exit(0);


sub datecompare {

   $date1  = substr($a, 11, 4) * 4800;
   $date2  = substr($b, 11, 4) * 4800;
   $date1 += index("JanFebMarAprMayJunJulAugSepOctNovDec",substr($a, 4,
3))*400;
   $date2 += index("JanFebMarAprMayJunJulAugSepOctNovDec",substr($b, 4,
3))*400;
   $date1 += substr($a, 8, 2);
   $date2 += substr($b, 8, 2);
   $date1 - $date2;


}
```

```
sub domnamcompare {

    $sdiff = length($a) - length($b);
    ($sdiff < 0) ? -1 : ($sdiff > 0) ? 1 : ($a lt $b) ? -1 : ($a gt $b) ? 1 :
0;

}

sub bytecompare {

    $bdiff = $groupbytes{$b} - $groupbytes{$a};
    ($bdiff < 0) ? -1 : ($bdiff > 0) ? 1 : ($a lt $b) ? -1 : ($a gt $b) ? 1 :
0;

}

sub faccompare {

    $fdiff = $fac{$b} - $fac{$a};
    ($fdiff < 0) ? -1 : ($fdiff > 0) ? 1 : ($a lt $b) ? -1 : ($a gt $b) ? 1 :
0;

}
```

Summary

This chapter covers the WU-FTP server, which is a standard part of the Slackware Linux distribution. You don't need to do anything special to get the FTP server up and running, but you will want to check through its configuration files and its unconventional file locations if you plan to offer FTP services to your Internet or intranet users.

The next chapter is a brief introduction to the joys of **sendmail**.

SETTING UP A MAIL SERVER

This chapter covers:

- Electronic mail
- Simple Mail Transport Protocol
- Post Office Protocol
- **Sendmail**
- **Smail**
- Mail headers
- Mail and operating systems
- Mail clients
- The **sendmail.cf** file
- Aliases

Electronic Mail: Fueling the Internet Revolution

The World Wide Web may garner the headlines when it comes to the explosive growth of the Internet, but electronic mail is really the one application that unites *all* Internet users. In the course of Internet polls determining the most popular Internet applications, electronic mail almost always ranks as the top usage, with the World Wide Web closing the gap in recent years.

The allures of electronic mail are obvious, and unlike other Internet applications, electronic mail doesn't require you to be somewhat of a sophisticated or technologically savvy user. With most popular electronic-mail packages, all you need to do is know a few basic functions in order to send and receive mail. Many corporations that aren't fully integrated with the Internet have connected their e-mail systems to the Internet, which means that the actual number of people who can send and receive your users' e-mail actually exceeds the number of Internet users.

The role of your Linux Internet server is merely to distribute the mail. Because of this, we won't spend a lot of time on actually using electronic mail from the user point of view. The chances are that most of your users won't actually be using a Linux box for their daily tasks, which would make discussions of mail packages like **elm** and **pine** moot.

A Short Electronic-Mail Primer

Electronic mail is really nothing more than a chunk of text that's sent from one user to another user. There are two parts of the text: the body, which contains the message and any attachments (such as uuencoded or MIME attachments), and the header, which contains information about the route the mail took between users, the size of the body, the originator's mail message, a subject line, and so on. A typical header looks like this:

```
From mailnull Mon Jan 13 15: 52:08 1997
Return-Path: <ted@mecklermedia.com>
Received: from bastion.mecklermedia.com by riverside.mr.net (8.8.4/SMI-
4.1.R931202) id PAA05410; Mon, 13 Jan 1997 15:52:06 -0600 (CST)
Received: by bastion.mecklermedia.com; id QAA26164; Mon, 13 Jan 1997 16:51:59
-0500 (EST)
Received: from mozart.mecklermedia.com(10.1.1.5) by bastion.mecklermedia.com
via smap (3.2) id xma026147; Mon, 13 Jan 97 16:51:35 -0500
Received: from PC180.mecklermedia.com ([10.1.1.180]) by
mozart.mecklermedia.com (8.8.3/8.8.3) with ESMTP id QAA07556 for
<reichard@MR.Net>; Mon, 13 Jan 1997 16:52:01 -0500 (EST)
Message-ID: <32DAAEE5.27AB@iw.com>
Date: Mon, 13 Jan 1997 16:53:41 -0500
From: Ted Stevenson <ted@mecklermedia.com>
Reply-To: ted@mecklermedia.com
Organization: Internet World magazine
X-Sender: Ted Stevenson <ted@iw.com>
X-Mailer: Mozilla 4.0b1 (Win95; I)
MIME-Version: 1.0
To: reichard@MR.Net
Subject: Re: sorry...
X-Priority: Normal
References: <32CDE680.3828@mr.net>
Content-Type: multipart/alternative; boundary="————7B6F632C4B729"
Status: O
X-Mozilla-Status: 8011
```

For the most part, this information is generated by a electronic-mail package, not the mail server.

Electronic mail is independent of operating systems. Any electronic-mail client (any that conforms to Internet specifications, that is) can connect to any Internet mail server, provided that the client has an account on the server. Because of this, we won't spend time on the clients; we'll just look at the servers.

Mail is sent to the server via the Simple Mail Transfer Protocol, or SMTP. (For those of you into specs, check out RFC-788 and RFC-821.) Mail is usually sent to the client to the server via the Post Office Protocol, or POP. Newer mail servers make use of the Internet Mail Access Protocol, or IMAP.

Your E-Mail Tools: Sendmail and Smail

Basically, you have two major tools that can be used to transport electronic mail. Both have things to recommend them.

Sendmail is a venerable mail-transport tool in the UNIX world, and the most recent version is on the accompanying CD-ROM. (If you hearken back to Chapter 3, you were asked if you wanted to install and configure **sendmail** when installing Slackware Linux. At that point, you should have responded in the affirmative and supplied your IP address and other configuration for **sendmail**. If not, you can go back to the **setup** program and install **sendmail**.)

However, **sendmail** can be a pain to set up and configure. It's really meant for a larger Internet site that has complicated routing requirements, such as routings between different subnets. If you're running a smaller Linux Internet site, you may want to consider using **smail** instead. **Smail** is included with Slackware Linux on the accompanying CD-ROM, but isn't automatically configured upon installation.

There are additional Linux mail tools at *http://sunsite.unc.edu/pub/Linux/system/Mail/ news/INDEX.html*. You're encouraged to browse through this directory to see if there may be some other Linux tools to fit your needs. In addition, newer Linux **N O T E** tools are posted to this site periodically.

If you want to run **smail** as an SMTP daemon, add the following line to **/etc/inetd.conf**:

```
smtp stream tcp nowait  root  /usr/bin/smtpd smtpd
```

Mail is sent along automatically when your server is connected to the Internet. If not, the mail is spooled in **/usr/spool/smail/input** until the Internet connection is made, at which time **runq** runs and sends the mail.

Be warned that **smail** has some limitations. It was written for UUCP usage initially, but it has been adapted for SMTP. It's really meant for smaller Internet sites that don't do a lot of traffic in electronic mail.

Also, it's really convenient that **sendmail** is regarded as the de facto electronic-mail tool in the Linux Internet world, as well as in the greater Internet world. The advice here is to spend some time with your ISP, who should have experience with **sendmail** configurations and can help you in the configuration process. Also, you'll want to check out a **sendmail** text that covers the process in much greater detail. Such books are listed in Appendix A.

The Sendmail.cf File

Almost all of **sendmail** functionality is determined by the **sendmail.cf** file, found in the **/etc** directory:

```
#
# Copyright (c) 1983, 1995 Eric P. Allman
# Copyright (c) 1988, 1993
#     The Regents of the University of California.  All rights reserved.
#
# Redistribution and use in source and binary forms, with or without
# modification, are permitted provided that the following conditions
# are met:
# 1. Redistributions of source code must retain the above copyright
#    notice, this list of conditions and the following disclaimer.
# 2. Redistributions in binary form must reproduce the above copyright
#    notice, this list of conditions and the following disclaimer in the
#    documentation and/or other materials provided with the distribution.
# 3. All advertising materials mentioning features or use of this software
#    must display the following acknowledgement:
#       This product includes software developed by the University of
#       California, Berkeley and its contributors.
# 4. Neither the name of the University nor the names of its contributors
#    may be used to endorse or promote products derived from this software
#    without specific prior written permission.
#
# THIS SOFTWARE IS PROVIDED BY THE REGENTS AND CONTRIBUTORS ``AS IS'' AND
# ANY EXPRESS OR IMPLIED WARRANTIES, INCLUDING, BUT NOT LIMITED TO, THE
# IMPLIED WARRANTIES OF MERCHANTABILITY AND FITNESS FOR A PARTICULAR PURPOSE
# ARE DISCLAIMED.  IN NO EVENT SHALL THE REGENTS OR CONTRIBUTORS BE LIABLE
# FOR ANY DIRECT, INDIRECT, INCIDENTAL, SPECIAL, EXEMPLARY, OR CONSEQUENTIAL
# DAMAGES (INCLUDING, BUT NOT LIMITED TO, PROCUREMENT OF SUBSTITUTE GOODS
# OR SERVICES; LOSS OF USE, DATA, OR PROFITS; OR BUSINESS INTERRUPTION)
# HOWEVER CAUSED AND ON ANY THEORY OF LIABILITY, WHETHER IN CONTRACT, STRICT
# LIABILITY, OR TORT (INCLUDING NEGLIGENCE OR OTHERWISE) ARISING IN ANY WAY
# OUT OF THE USE OF THIS SOFTWARE, EVEN IF ADVISED OF THE POSSIBILITY OF
# SUCH DAMAGE.
#
```

```
######################################################################
######################################################################
#####
#####          SENDMAIL CONFIGURATION FILE
#####
##### built by root@darkstar on Sat May 11 18:32:32 CDT 1996
##### in /tmp/sendmail-8.7.5/cf/cf
##### using ../ as configuration include directory
#####
######################################################################
######################################################################


#####  @(#)cfhead.m4    8.3 (Berkeley) 9/15/95  #####
#####  @(#)cf.m4    8.24 (Berkeley) 8/16/95  #####


#####  linux for smtp-only setup  #####
#####  @(#)linux.m4    8.2 (Berkeley) 8/21/93  #####


#####  @(#)nodns.m4    8.1 (Berkeley) 8/6/93  #####


#####  @(#)nouucp.m4    8.1 (Berkeley) 6/7/93  #####


#####  @(#)always_add_domain.m4    8.1 (Berkeley) 6/7/93  #####


#####  @(#)proto.m4    8.100 (Berkeley) 12/3/95  #####


# level 6 config file format
V6/Berkeley


##################
#   local info   #
##################


Cwlocalhost
```

```
# my official domain name


# ... define this only if sendmail cannot automatically determine your domain
#Dj$w.Foo.COM


CP.


# "Smart" relay host (may be null)
DS


# place to which unknown users should be forwarded
#Kuser user -m -a<>

#DLname_of_luser_relay


# operators that cannot be in local usernames (i.e., network indicators)
CO @ %


# a class with just dot (for identifying canonical names)
C..


# Mailer table (overriding domains)
#Kmailertable dbm /etc/mailertable


# Domain table (adding domains)
#Kdomaintable dbm /etc/domaintable


# who I send unqualified names to (null means deliver locally)
DR


# who gets all local email traffic ($R has precedence for unqualified names)
DH
```

```
# class L: names that should be delivered locally, even if we have a relay
# class E: names that should be exposed as from this host, even if we
masquerade
# class M: domains that should be converted to $M
#CL root
CE root


# dequoting map
Kdequote dequote


# who I masquerade as (null for no masquerading) (see also $=M)
DM


# my name for error messages
DnMAILER-DAEMON


# Configuration version number
DZ8.7.3


##############
#   Options   #
##############


# strip message body to 7 bits on input?
O SevenBitInput=False


# 8-bit data handling
O EightBitMode=pass8


# wait for alias file rebuild (default units: minutes)
O AliasWait=10


# location of alias file
O AliasFile=/etc/aliases
```

```
# minimum number of free blocks on filesystem
O MinFreeBlocks=100


# maximum message size
#O MaxMessageSize=1000000


# substitution for space (blank) characters
O BlankSub=.


# avoid connecting to "expensive" mailers on initial submission?
O HoldExpensive=False


# checkpoint queue runs after every N successful deliveries
#O CheckpointInterval=10


# default delivery mode
O DeliveryMode=background


# automatically rebuild the alias database?
#O AutoRebuildAliases


# error message header/file
#O ErrorHeader=/etc/sendmail.oE


# error mode
#O ErrorMode=print


# save Unix-style "From_" lines at top of header?
#O SaveFromLine


# temporary file mode
O TempFileMode=0600
```

```
# match recipients against GECOS field?
#O MatchGECOS


# maximum hop count
#O MaxHopCount=17


# location of help file
O HelpFile=/usr/lib/sendmail.hf


# ignore dots as terminators in incoming messages?
#O IgnoreDots


# name resolver options
#O ResolverOptions=+AAONLY


# deliver MIME-encapsulated error messages?
O SendMimeErrors=True


# Forward file search path
O ForwardPath=$z/.forward.$w:$z/.forward


# open connection cache size
O ConnectionCacheSize=2


# open connection cache timeout
O ConnectionCacheTimeout=5m


# use Errors-To: header?
O UseErrorsTo=False


# log level
O LogLevel=9
```

```
# send to me too, even in an alias expansion?
#O MeToo


# verify RHS in newaliases?
O CheckAliases=False


# default messages to old style headers if no special punctuation?
O OldStyleHeaders=True


# SMTP daemon options
#O DaemonPortOptions=Port=esmtp


# privacy flags
O PrivacyOptions=authwarnings


# who (if anyone) should get extra copies of error messages
#O PostMasterCopy=Postmaster


# slope of queue-only function
#O QueueFactor=600000


# queue directory
O QueueDirectory=/var/spool/mqueue


# timeouts (many of these)
#O Timeout.initial=5m
#O Timeout.helo=5m
#O Timeout.mail=10m
#O Timeout.rcpt=1h
#O Timeout.datainit=5m
#O Timeout.datablock=1h
#O Timeout.datafinal=1h
#O Timeout.rset=5m
#O Timeout.quit=2m
#O Timeout.misc=2m
```

```
#O Timeout.command=1h
#O Timeout.ident=30s
#O Timeout.fileopen=60s
O Timeout.queuereturn=5d
#O Timeout.queuereturn.normal=5d
#O Timeout.queuereturn.urgent=2d
#O Timeout.queuereturn.non-urgent=7d
O Timeout.queuewarn=4h
#O Timeout.queuewarn.normal=4h
#O Timeout.queuewarn.urgent=1h
#O Timeout.queuewarn.non-urgent=12h


# should we not prune routes in route-addr syntax addresses?
#O DontPruneRoutes


# queue up everything before forking?
O SuperSafe=True


# status file
O StatusFile=/etc/sendmail.st


# time zone handling:
#   if undefined, use system default
#   if defined but null, use TZ envariable passed in
#   if defined and non-null, use that info
#O TimeZoneSpec=


# default UID (can be username or userid:groupid)
O DefaultUser=1:1


# list of locations of user database file (null means no lookup)
#O UserDatabaseSpec=/etc/userdb


# fallback MX host
#O FallbackMXhost=fall.back.host.net
```

```
# if we are the best MX host for a site, try it directly instead of config err
#O TryNullMXList


# load average at which we just queue messages
#O QueueLA=8


# load average at which we refuse connections
#O RefuseLA=12


# work recipient factor
#O RecipientFactor=30000


# deliver each queued job in a separate process?
#O ForkEachJob


# work class factor
#O ClassFactor=1800


# work time factor
#O RetryFactor=90000


# shall we sort the queue by hostname first?
#O QueueSortOrder=priority


# minimum time in queue before retry
#O MinQueueAge=30m


# default character set
#O DefaultCharSet=iso-8859-1


# service switch file (ignored on Solaris, Ultrix, OSF/1, others)
#O ServiceSwitchFile=/etc/service.switch
```

```
# hosts file (normally /etc/hosts)
#O HostsFile=/etc/hosts


# dialup line delay on connection failure
#O DialDelay=10s


# action to take if there are no recipients in the message
#O NoRecipientAction=add-to-undisclosed


# chrooted environment for writing to files
#O SafeFileEnvironment=/arch


# are colons OK in addresses?
#O ColonOkInAddr


# how many jobs can you process in the queue?
#O MaxQueueRunSize=10000


# shall I avoid expanding CNAMEs (violates protocols)?
#O DontExpandCnames


# SMTP initial login message (old $e macro)
O SmtpGreetingMessage=$j Sendmail $v/$Z; $b


# UNIX initial From header format (old $l macro)
O UnixFromLine=From $g   $d


# delimiter (operator) characters (old $o macro)
O OperatorChars=.:%@!^/[]+


# shall I avoid calling initgroups(3) because of high NIS costs?
#O DontInitGroups
```

```
###########################
#   Message precedences    #
###########################


Pfirst-class=0
Pspecial-delivery=100
Plist=-30
Pbulk=-60
Pjunk=-100



#####################
#   Trusted users    #
#####################


# this is equivalent to setting class "t"
#Ft/etc/sendmail.ct
Troot
Tdaemon
Tuucp



#########################
#   Format of headers    #
#########################


H?P?Return-Path: $g
HReceived: $?sfrom $s $.$?_($?s$|from $.$_) $.by $j ($v/$Z)$?r with $r$. id
$i$?u for $u$.; $b
H?D?Resent-Date: $a
H?D?Date: $a
H?F?Resent-From: $?x$x <$g>$|$g$.
H?F?From: $?x$x <$g>$|$g$.
H?x?Full-Name: $x
HSubject:
# HPosted-Date: $a
# H?l?Received-Date: $b
H?M?Resent-Message-Id: <$t.$i@$j>
H?M?Message-Id: <$t.$i@$j>
```

```
#####################################################################
#####################################################################
#####
#####                    REWRITING RULES
#####
#####################################################################
#####################################################################



###########################################
###  Rulset 3 — Name Canonicalization  ###
###########################################
S3


# handle null input (translate to <@> special case)
R$@                 $@ <@>



# strip group: syntax (not inside angle brackets!) and trailing semicolon
R$*               $: $1 <@>                    mark addresses
R$* < $* > $* <@> $: $1 < $2 > $3              unmark <addr>
R$* :: $* <@>     $: $1 :: $2                  unmark node::addr
R:include: $* <@> $: :include: $1              unmark :include:...
R$* : $* <@>      $: $2                         strip colon if marked
R$* <@>           $: $1                         unmark
R$* ;             $: $1                         strip trailing semi



# null input now results from list:; syntax
R$@                 $@ :; <@>



# strip angle brackets — note RFC733 heuristic to get innermost item
R$*               $: < $1 >                    housekeeping <>
R$+ < $* >          < $2 >                     strip excess on left
R< $* > $+          < $1 >                     strip excess on right
R<>               $@ < @ >                     MAIL FROM:<> case
R< $+ >           $: $1                         remove housekeeping <>



# make sure <@a,@b,@c:user@d> syntax is easy to parse — undone later
R@ $+ , $+        @ $1 : $2                    change all "," to ":"
```

```
# localize and dispose of route-based addresses
R@ $+ : $+            $@ $>96 < @$1 > : $2         handle <route-addr>


# find focus for list syntax
R $+ : $* ; @ $+      $@ $>96 $1 : $2 ; < @ $3 >   list syntax
R $+ : $* ;           $@ $1 : $2;                  list syntax


# find focus for @ syntax addresses
R$+ @ $+             $: $1 < @ $2 >                focus on domain
R$+ < $+ @ $+ >      $1 $2 < @ $3 >                move gaze right
R$+ < @ $+ >         $@ $>96 $1 < @ $2 >           already canonical


# do some sanity checking
R$* < @ $* : $* > $*     $1 < @ $2 $3 > $4         nix colons in addrs


# if we have % signs, take the rightmost one
R$* % $*             $1 @ $2                       First make them all @s.
R$* @ $* @ $*        $1 % $2 @ $3                  Undo all but the last.
R$* @ $*             $@ $>96 $1 < @ $2 >           Insert < > and finish


# else we must be a local name
R$*                  $@ $>96 $1


#################################################
###   Ruleset 96 — bottom half of ruleset 3   ###
#################################################


S96


# handle special cases for local names
R$* < @ localhost > $*        $: $1 < @ $j . > $2      no domain at all
R$* < @ localhost . $m > $*   $: $1 < @ $j . > $2      local domain
R$* < @ [ $+ ] > $*           $: $1 < @@ [ $2 ] > $3   mark [a.b.c.d]
R$* < @@ $=w > $*             $: $1 < @ $j . > $3      self-literal
R$* < @@ $+ > $*              $@ $1 < @ $2 > $3        canon IP addr
```

```
# look up domains in the domain table
#R$* < @ $+ > $*           $: $1 < @ $(domaintable $2 $) > $3



# pass to name server to make hostname canonical
R$* < @ $* $~P > $*        $: $1 < @ $[ $2 $3 $] > $4



# local host aliases and pseudo-domains are always canonical
R$* < @ $=w > $*        $: $1 < @ $2 . > $3
R$* < @ $* $=P > $*     $: $1 < @ $2 $3 . > $4
R$* < @ $* . . > $*        $1 < @ $2 . > $3



# if this is the local hostname, make sure we treat is as canonical
R$* < @ $j > $*           $: $1 < @ $j . > $2



##################################################
###   Ruleset 4 — Final Output Post-rewriting   ###
##################################################
S4


R$* <@>                $@                        handle <> and list:;



# strip trailing dot off possibly canonical name
R$* < @ $+ . > $*      $1 < @ $2 > $3



# eliminate internal code — should never get this far!
R$* < @ *LOCAL* > $*      $1 < @ $j > $2



# externalize local domain info
R$* < $+ > $*          $1 $2 $3                  defocus
R@ $+ : @ $+ : $+      @ $1 , @ $2 : $3          <route-addr> canonical
R@ $*                  $@ @ $1                   and exit



# delete duplicate local names
R$+ % $=w @ $=w        $1 @ $j                   u%host@host => u@host
```

```
################################################################
###    Ruleset 97 — recanonicalize and call ruleset zero    ###
###                (used for recursive calls)              ###
################################################################


S97
R$*              $: $>3 $1
R$*              $@ $>0 $1



#####################################
###    Ruleset 0 — Parse Address    ###
#####################################


S0


R<@>              $#local $: <@>          special case error msgs
R$* : $* ; <@>    $#error $@ 5.1.3 $: "list:; syntax illegal for recipient
addresses"
R<@ $+>           $#error $@ 5.1.1 $: "user address required"
R$* <$* : $* > $* $#error $@ 5.1.1 $: "colon illegal in host name part"
R$* < @ . > $*    $#error $@ 5.1.2 $: "invalid host name"


# handle numeric address spec
R$* < @ [ $+ ] > $*    $: $>98 $1 < @ [ $2 ] > $3          numeric internet
spec
R$* < @ [ $+ ] > $*    $#smtp $@ [$2] $: $1 < @ [$2] > $3   still numeric:
send


# now delete the local info — note $=O to find characters that cause
forwarding
R$* < @ > $*        $@ $>97 $1          user@ => user
R< @ $=w . > : $*   $@ $>97 $2          @here:... -> ...
R$- < @ $=w . >     $: $(dequote $1 $) < @ $2 . >    dequote "foo"@here
R$* $=O $* < @ $=w . >   $@ $>97 $1 $2 $3          ...@here -> ...


# handle local hacks
R$*              $: $>98 $1
```

```
# short circuit local delivery so forwarded email works
R$=L < @ $=w . >        $#local $: @ $1          special local names
R$+ < @ $=w . >         $#local $: $1            regular local name


# not local — try mailer table lookup
#R$* <@ $+ > $*        $: < $2 > $1 < @ $2 > $3     extract host name
#R< $+ . > $*          $: < $1 > $2                 strip trailing dot
#R< $+ > $*            $: < $(mailertable $1 $) > $2     lookup
#R< error : $- $+ > $*     $#error $@ $1 $: $2         check — error?
#R< $- : $+ > $*       $# $1 $@ $2 $: $3         check — resolved?
#R< $+ > $*            $: $>90 <$1> $2              try domain


# resolve fake top level domains by forwarding to other hosts


# pass names that still have a host to a smarthost (if defined)
R$* < @ $* > $*             $: $>95 < $S > $1 < @ $2 > $3     glue on smarthost
name


# deal with other remote names
R$* < @$* > $*           $#smtp $@ $2 $: $1 < @ $2 > $3
user@host.domain


# if this is quoted, strip the quotes and try again
R$+                  $: $(dequote $1 $)          strip quotes
R$+ $=O $+           $@ $>97 $1 $2 $3            try again


# handle locally delivered names
R$=L                 $#local $: @ $1          special local names
R$+                  $#local $: $1            regular local names


#########################################################################
###    Ruleset 5 — special rewriting after aliases have been expanded    ###
#########################################################################
```

```
S5


# deal with plussed users so aliases work nicely
R$+ + *                 $#local $@ $&h $: $1
R$+ + $*                $#local $@ $2 $: $1 + *


# prepend an empty "forward host" on the front
R$+             $: <> $1


# send unrecognized local users to a relay host
#R< > $+ + $*           $: < $L . > $( user $1 $) + $2
#R< > $+                $: < $L . > $( user $1 $)      look up user
#R< $* > $+ <> $*       $: < > $2 $3                   found; strip $L
#R< $* . > $+           $: < $1 > $2                   strip extra dot


# handle plussed local names
R< > $+ + $*            $#local $@ $2 $: $1


# see if we have a relay or a hub
R< > $+                 $: < $H > $1            try hub
R< > $+                 $: < $R > $1            try relay
R< > $+                 $@ $1                  nope, give up
R< $- : $+ > $+         $: $>95 < $1 : $2 > $3 < @ $2 >
R< $+ > $+              $@ $>95 < $1 > $2 < @ $1 >


##################################################################
###  Ruleset 90 — try domain part of mailertable entry     ###
##################################################################


#S90
#R$* <$- . $+ > $*      $: $1$2 < $(mailertable .$3 $@ $1$2 $@ $2 $) > $4
#R$* <$- : $+ > $*      $# $2 $@ $3 $: $4      check — resolved?
#R$* < . $+ > $*        $@ $>90 $1 . <$2> $3          no — strip & try again
#R$* < $* > $*          $: < $(mailertable . $@ $1$2 $) > $3      try "."
#R<$- : $+ > $*         $# $1 $@ $2 $: $3      "." found?
#R< $* > $*             $@ $2                  no mailertable match
```

```
####################################################################
###   Ruleset 95 - canonify mailer:host syntax to triple     ###
####################################################################


S95
R< > $*                $@ $1                        strip off null relay
R< $- : $+ > $*        $# $1 $@ $2 $: $3            try qualified mailer
R< $=w > $*            $@ $2                        delete local host
R< $+ > $*             $#relay $@ $1 $: $2          use unqualified mailer


####################################################################
###   Ruleset 93 - convert header names to masqueraded form    ###
####################################################################


S93
R$=E < @ *LOCAL* >     $@ $1 < @ $j . >             leave exposed
R$=E < @ $=M . >       $@ $1 < @ $2 . >
R$=E < @ $=w . >       $@ $1 < @ $2 . >
R$* < @ $=M . > $*     $: $1 < @ $2 . @ $M > $3     convert masqueraded doms
R$* < @ $=w . > $*     $: $1 < @ $2 . @ $M > $3
R$* < @ *LOCAL* > $*   $: $1 < @ $j . @ $M > $2
R$* < @ $+ @ > $*      $@ $1 < @ $2 > $3         $M is null
R$* < @ $+ @ $+ > $*   $@ $1 < @ $3 . > $4          $M is not null


####################################################################
###   Ruleset 94 - convert envelope names to masqueraded form    ###
####################################################################


S94
#R$+              $@ $>93 $1
R$* < @ *LOCAL* > $*     $: $1 < @ $j . > $2


####################################################################
###   Ruleset 98 - local part of ruleset zero (can be null)    ###
####################################################################
```

```
S98
#
######################################################################
######################################################################
#####
#####                  MAILER DEFINITIONS
#####
######################################################################
######################################################################



##################################################
###   Local and Program Mailer specification   ###
##################################################



#####  @(#)local.m4     8.21 (Berkeley) 11/6/95  #####



Mlocal,          P=/usr/bin/procmail, F=lsDFMAw5:/|@ShP, S=10/30, R=20/40,
         T=DNS/RFC822/X-Unix,
         A=procmail -a $h -d $u
Mprog,           P=/bin/sh, F=lsDFMoeu, S=10/30, R=20/40, D=$z:/,
         T=X-Unix,
         A=sh -c $u



#
#  Envelope sender rewriting
#
S10
R<@>            $n                errors to mailer-daemon
R$+             $: $>50 $1        add local domain if needed
R$*             $: $>94 $1        do masquerading



#
#  Envelope recipient rewriting
#
S20
R$+ < @ $* >         $: $1              strip host part
```

```
#
#  Header sender rewriting
#
S30
R<@>                $n                  errors to mailer-daemon
R$+             $: $>50 $1          add local domain if needed
R$*             $: $>93 $1          do masquerading


#
#  Header recipient rewriting
#
S40
R$+             $: $>50 $1          add local domain if needed
#R$*            $: $>93 $1          do all-masquerading


#
#  Common code to add local domain name (only if always-add-domain)
#
S50
R$* < @ $* > $*     $@ $1 < @ $2 > $3       already fully qualified
R$+             $@ $1 < @ *LOCAL* >         add local qualification


####################################
###   SMTP Mailer specification   ###
####################################


#####  @(#)smtp.m4     8.32 (Berkeley) 11/20/95  #####


Msmtp,          P=[IPC], F=mDFMuX, S=11/31, R=21, E=\r\n, L=990,
        T=DNS/RFC822/SMTP,
        A=IPC $h
Mesmtp,          P=[IPC], F=mDFMuXa, S=11/31, R=21, E=\r\n, L=990,
        T=DNS/RFC822/SMTP,
        A=IPC $h
Msmtp8,          P=[IPC], F=mDFMuX8, S=11/31, R=21, E=\r\n, L=990,
        T=DNS/RFC822/SMTP,
        A=IPC $h
Mrelay,          P=[IPC], F=mDFMuXa8, S=11/31, R=61, E=\r\n, L=2040,
        T=DNS/RFC822/SMTP,
        A=IPC $h
```

```
#
#   envelope sender rewriting
#
S11
R$+                  $: $>51 $1              sender/recipient common
R$* :; <@>           $@                      list:; special case
R$*                  $: $>61 $1              qualify unqual'ed names
R$+                  $: $>94 $1              do masquerading


#
#   envelope recipient rewriting -
#   also header recipient if not masquerading recipients
#
S21
R$+                  $: $>51 $1              sender/recipient common
R$+                  $: $>61 $1              qualify unqual'ed names


#
#   header sender and masquerading header recipient rewriting
#
S31
R$+                  $: $>51 $1              sender/recipient common
R:; <@>              $@                      list:; special case


# do special header rewriting
R$* <@> $*           $@ $1 <@> $2            pass null host through
R< @ $* > $*         $@ < @ $1 > $2          pass route-addr through
R$*                  $: $>61 $1              qualify unqual'ed names
R$+                  $: $>93 $1              do masquerading


#
#   convert pseudo-domain addresses to real domain addresses
#
S51


# pass <route-addr>s through
R< @ $+ > $*         $@ < @ $1 > $2                  resolve <route-addr>
```

```
# output fake domains as user%fake@relay


#
#   common sender and masquerading recipient rewriting
#
S61


R$* < @ $* > $*       $@ $1 < @ $2 > $3          already fully qualified
R$+                   $@ $1 < @ *LOCAL* >          add local qualification


#
#   relay mailer header masquerading recipient rewriting
#
S71


R$+              $: $>61 $1
R$+              $: $>93 $1
```

For the most part, this file will be gibbering to you. We reproduce the file here so that you can refer to it if you're making changes to it. Most of what you'll need to worry will be worked out with your ISP.

Aliases

One aspect of **sendmail** that might require some immediate attention is aliases. Basically, aliases allow you to redirect mail from one name to another. For example, it's handy to use **sendmail** to redirect message from a general name to a specific name. Most larger Web sites will ask that mail be sent to the Webmaster, using an address like *Webmaster@kreichard.com*. Similarly, most Internet sites don't designate a specific person as the postmaster (the person overseeing the electronic mail); instead, they use a name like *postmaster@kreichard.com*.

For these situations, you'll want to set up an **aliases** file. One already exists in your Slackware Linux installation, under **/etc/aliases**. However, the default is to have nothing in the file except the following:

```
# put any sendmail aliases in here
```

(Remember that any line beginning with # is a comment and isn't actually acted upon.)

So, if you want to name the user *kevin* as the Webmaster, you would add the following line to the **/etc/aliases** file:

```
Webmaster: kevin
```

You could also name the *root* user as the postmaster:

```
postmaster: root
```

You can put in as many aliases as you want. After you're done adding aliases, save the file.

Your next step is to run the **newaliases** command:

```
newaliases
```

The **newaliases** command runs and tells you how many new aliases were created.

Summary

Slackware Linux ships with several electronic-mail tools, including **sendmail** and **smail**. In this chapter, we briefly run through **sendmail** and some options that you might need to look at, such as aliases.

In the next chapter, we cover setting up a news server.

SETTING UP A NEWS SERVER

This chapter covers:

- The Usenet
- Newsgroups
- Evaluating the Usenet
- Hardware and network considerations
- Installing news software
- Cnews
- Cnews files
- InterNetNews (INN)
- INN and **cron**
- INN files

All the News That Fits

The Usenet is the world's largest bulletin board. With hundreds of thousands of people participating all over the world, the Usenet can be seen as the collective wisdom of the Internet.

The Usenet is organized by newsgroups, which are specialized discussion groups. Some of the groups are *very* specialized, such as scientific groups devoted to one small area of biology or computer-science groups devoted to one small aspects of an operating system. (There are many newsgroups connected with Linux; see Appendix A for details.)

A First Decision

Before deciding on which Usenet software to use, you'll first need to decide if you even want to offer it locally. Handling a Usenet newsfeed is not an insignificant chore, as one day's postings can run into 400 or 500 megabytes, and typically you're looking at keeping these postings for seven days. That's a lot of traffic, and in most situations a separate machine is needed to handle the Usenet feed. Typically, a Usenet feed is checked once an hour, with new messages going out and coming in. This can eat up a lot of your bandwidth, particularly if you're trying to use a lower-speed link (like ISDN or a dialup link) for your Internet server.

Most ISPs will offer access to their news server to their clients. In this situation, a user will connect directly to the ISP news server to check the newsgroups. It doesn't make much difference for the user, unless you're running your Internet server on a slow link (such as a dialup link).

Deciding which course to take is probably more difficult than it looks. Let's face it—most of your users won't bother with newsgroups, since newsgroups perfectly illustrate Sturgeon's Law (90 percent of everything is crap). There will always be a small and vocal minority who will want a full Usenet feed, mainly so they can waste time in their cubicles exchanging conspiracy theories or what really was the meaning behind that cryptic statement on last week's episode of *The X Files*.

If you've figured out that the feeling here is that a full Usenet feed is a waste of time and computing resources, you win the jackpot.

Evaluating Your Needs

If you do decide to go with a Usenet feed, you'll need to make sure that you have the correct resources:

- **Do I have enough hard-disk space?** As mentioned earlier, a full Usenet feed can into 400 or 500 megabytes per day, and as the Usenet descends into a fractured world where a single message can appear in 10 newsgroups (an event called *crossposting*), that number is probably on the conservative side.

- **Do I have enough network capacity?** Most Usenet servers are set up to suck a feed once an hour or so. If we're talking about tens of thousands of megabytes at that time, you're looking at a serious crimp in your network capacity. (You can avoid this by only performing a feed at off hours, like in the middle of the night. However, this detracts from the immediacy of the Usenet.)

- **Do I really need to offer a full newsgroup feed?** If you're using your Linux Internet server and offering paid access to the rest of the world, you'll need to offer a Usenet feed—your clients will expect it. But if you're running a Linux Internet server in a corporate situation, there are very few compelling corporate reasons to offer full Usenet access to your users. (Exceptions occur in the high-technology field, where you might want employees to monitor newsgroups related to your business.)

- **Do I have a machine for offering Usenet access?** You'll want to dedicate a machine for a Usenet server. Usenet software isn't always the most stable software in the Internet world, and it's not unheard of for a large feed to overwhelm a server. You don't want a Usenet server to drag down the rest of your Linux Internet server, even if you only have a partial feed.

If you do decide to offer Usenet access on a local Usenet server, you can use one of the many Linux Usenet servers that ship with Slackware Linux.

Maintaining a Usenet feed is a little complicated than just installing a server and creating some content. You'll need to know how to use scheduling commands like **cron**, and you'll need to know something about the networking aspects of Linux. You'll want to check out a UNIX command reference like *UNIX in Plain English* (MIS:Press) or find a good Linux tutorial.

N O T E

There are two main Linux news servers: INN and Cnews. When you installed Slackware Linux, you were asked to make a decision between the two. In some ways, it doesn't make a difference which you chose; both work, but they're configured in different ways. Cnews is a more basic server that's easier to configure, but INN is know for having more advanced capabilities.

You can't run both of these news servers. Disaster will ensue.

WARNING

Cnews

Installation was automatic for Cnews when you installed Slackware Linux. (If not, run the **setup** program again and install in that fashion.) There are a number of files to peruse after installation, and they're listed in Table 9.1.

Table 9.1 Cnews Files

File	Purpose
/usr/local/lib/news/active	Lists the active newsgroups; this file is not to edited manually.
/usr/local/lib/news/batchparms	Lists the batch parameters.
/usr/local/lib/news/explist	Defines when articles expire.
/usr/local/lib/news mailname	Specifies the name in mailed replies.
/usr/local/lib/news/mailpaths	Sets the mail address for posting to moderated groups.
/usr/local/lib/news/organization	Defines your organization.
/usr/local/lib/news/sys	Lists other linked systems.
/usr/local/lib/news/whoami	Defines your hostname.

If you want to add newsfeeds, use the **addfeed** program; if you want to add newsgroups, use the **addgroup** program. The documentation details how to add scheduling via a **crontab** file.

InterNetNews (INN)

In a more perfect world, you'd go with INN right away. However, INN is a more "difficult" news server, in that it takes a little more skill to set up and configure, and that it needs to be running at all times with its own daemon (**innd**; as opposed to Cnews, which can be set up to grab the news at specific times). On the flip side, INN is regarded as a speedier news server, in that it takes less time to grab a feed.

Working with your Crontab File

You'll want to add INN information to your **crontab** file. The INN distribution comes with a file called **crontab-news**, which contains information to add to your **crontab** setup:

```
SHELL=/bin/sh
#
MAILTO=ROOT
#
#=====================================================================
#
# INN-1.4 (Inter Net News)
#
#     Sample crontab file by andreas@knobel.knirsch.de (Andreas Klemm)
#
#     copy it to /usr/spool/cron/crontabs/news
#
#     Reboot your system or
#     kill and restart the crond job, to activate this file
#
#=====================================================================
#
#---------------------------------------------------------------------
# send news batches to your news feed
#---------------------------------------------------------------------
```

```
#
0,15,30,45 * * * *    /usr/lib/news/bin/sendbatch - manlobbi > /dev/null
#
#--------------------------------------------------------------------
# Daily housekeeping ... expires news and other things ...
#--------------------------------------------------------------------
#
0 22 * * *          /usr/lib/news/bin/news.daily < /dev/null
#
#--------------------------------------------------------------------
# offer spooled news - that was spooled into the incoming directory when
# the INNd server wasn't available - again to the INNd server.
#--------------------------------------------------------------------
#
15 * * * *          /usr/lib/news/rnews -U
```

This file is pretty simple to analyze:

- **SHELL=/bin/sh**, as you should know by now, is the notation for launching a **sh** shell.
- **MAILTO=root** forwards mail from users to the **root** user.
- **0,15,30,45 * * * *   /usr/lib/news/bin/sendbatch - manlobbi > /dev/null** tells **cron** to get every 15 minutes. The *manlobbi* is the generic term used in the configuration file; you'll need to change this to an alias for your service provider's newsfeed.
- **0 22 * * *   /usr/lib/news/bin/news.daily < /dev/null** runs the tasks in the **news.daily** file at 10 p.m. (22:00 in military time). These tasks would include expiring news items.
- **15 * * * *   /usr/lib/news/rnews -U** sends spooled news to INN server in those situations when the server wasn't available. The default is every hour, at 15 minutes past the beginning of the hour.

Other Configuration Files

There are a number of configuration files used by INN. For the most part, you'll need to edit some of these files. They are all found in **/usr/lib/news**.

NOTE The INN documentation will refer to these files being in the **/usr/local/lib/news** directory, and this directory is specified in some of these configuration files. Instead of changing all of these references, it's easier to set up a link for **/usr/local/lib/news** to **/usr/lib/news**.

The **expire.ctl** file is used to specify when newsgroup items expire (that is, how long items are to be stored before they are purged from the system). The default is to purge all groups within five days. However, it's possible to never let any news item be purged, and it's also possible to set up specific newsgroups to be purged at different intervals.

The **inn.conf** file specifies the domain, moderator mailer, host, server, and organization for an INN news server.

The **hosts.nntp** specifies where the news is grabbed from.

The **newsfeeds** file is used if you send along a newsfeed to another site. (Related to this file are the **nnrp.access** and **nntpsend.ctl** files.)

The **moderators** file is used to send messages along to moderated newsgroups, instead of being posted directly to the newsgroup.

Summary

This chapter briefly discussing setting up Usenet software, and whether or not you actually want to run a Usenet server on your Internet system. Two choices are detailed: Cnews and INN.

In the next chapter, you'll learn about other miscellaneous tools and services for your Linux Internet server.

MISCELLANEOUS SERVICES

This chapter covers:

- Squid
- ATM and Linux
- Cyber Radio 1
- The Mbone and Linux
- Whiteboard software
- The **wb** software
- Commercial software
- StreamWorks
- Sybernet

Odds and Sods: Miscellaneous Topics

Not all the offerings in the Linux Internet world fall so smoothly into the chapter headings found elsewhere in this book. This chapter covers miscellaneous topics that are important enough to warrant some level of coverage, but not necessarily their own chapters. This includes such useful software as the Squid Internet object cache, as well as commercial software meant for Linux Internet servers.

Squid

If performance is an issue for you, then you'll want to consider using Squid, a high-performance cache. As the documentation states:

> *Squid offers high performance proxy caching for Web clients. It supports FTP, Gopher, and HTTP requests. The cache software, available only in source, is more than an order of magnitude faster than the CERN httpd and other popular Internet caches, because it never needs to fork (except for FTP), is implemented with nonblocking I/O, keeps meta data and hot objects in VM, caches DNS lookups. Squid caches can be arranged hierarchically for an improvement in response times and a reduction in bandwidth usage.*

The use of this software is *highly* recommended. You can get more information about Squid at *http://squid.nlanr.net/Squid/*. The accompanying CD-ROM contains the source code (**squid-1_1_5-src_tar.gz**) as grabbed from *ftp://squid.nlanr.net*.

ATM

ATM technology is new, and support within Linux is even newer. There are efforts to allow Linux servers to access ATM technology, but as this book was written the technology was in a very early stage. For more information, check *http://lrcwww.epfl.ch/linux-atm/*.

Cyber Radio

Cyber Radio 1 was originally written for live Internet audio broadcasts at the Georgia Tech student radio station, WREK Atlanta 91.1 FM. It's been made available to the greater Internet in several UNIX versions, including a Linux version.

It's a simple tool: Digital information is read from an audio device (like **/dev/audio**) and then sent to any number of connected clients. These users must be using a Cyber Radio 1 client program, which comes in Microsoft Windows and Linux versions.

The file is **CyberRadio1.tar.gz**, and it can be found on the accompanying CD-ROM and at *ftp://sunsite.unc.edu/pub/Linux/apps/sound/*.

The Mbone and Linux

The Mbone is a high-bandwidth Internet tool that's used to transmit live audio and video. You can implement the Mbone on your Linux server, but you'll need to make sure that it support multicasting, and you'll need to make some adjustments to your network setup.

You can find more information at *http://www.teksouth.com/linux/multicast/*.

Whiteboard Software

Whiteboard software allows two or more machines to be linked via the Internet to a whiteboard, which allows shared drawings to be created and disseminated in real time. On the accompanying CD-ROM is **wb** from the Network Research Group of Lawrence Berkeley National Laboratory.

The filename is **linux-wb-1.59.tar.Z**. It was grabbed from *ftp://ftp.ee.lbl.gov/conferencing/wb/*.

Commercial Software

So far in this book we've covered the free offerings that are part of the accompanying CD-ROM. For the most part, these offerings will take you very far as you make your way through the Internet with your own Linux server.

However, the size of the Linux community is growing to the point where it's attracting the attention of some commercial software developers. While the commercial software for Linux isn't nearly on the scale as it is for the UNIX and Windows NT worlds, there are still some interesting offerings that you may want to consider. In the rest of this chapter, we look at some of these offerings.

StreamWorks

Audio is a trendy Internet application, in the form of *streaming audio*, where digitally encoded audio is sent from a server to an audio-capable computer on the Internet. There, decoding software translates the digital stream into audio. The appeal here is that streaming decoding takes place on the fly; there's no need to download huge files, and real-time audio broadcasts (like sporting events) can be broadcast via the Internet in a relatively efficient fashion.

A more challenging task is streaming video, which applies the previous concepts to video. Of course, video is a much more bandwidth-intensive application than audio.

It takes entire suite of products to create streaming audio and video, but you can purchase server software to send encoded video and audio from your Linux Internet server. The StreamWorks Server from Xing uses MPEG compression to send digital audio and video from your server.

There are other competing products on the market, such as Real Audio, but none that offer a Linux version. While Real Audio is the most popular encoder on the market, in a sense it doesn't really matter which encoder you use, since all of the vendors give away the client software at no charge. Therefore, you could supply your users with client software at no cost to you or them.

Since the StreamWorks Server is a commercial product, we're not going to spend a lot of time on it, but you should know that it's the only commercial streaming-audio product that's been developed for use on a Linux Internet server. For more information (including pricing information), check the Web site at *http://www.xingtech.com/products/sw_server.html*.

Sybernet

If you need to link UNIX or Windows databases—specifically, Sybase databases—you may want to look at Sybernet, which links an Apache Web server on Linux with Sybase databases. More information can be found at *http://linux.sri.com/*.

Summary

This short chapter details miscellaneous tools that you'll want to consider implementing on your Linux Internet server.

In the next chapter, you'll be exposed to HTML and Web pages.

SECTION III

Creating Content

Your server and services are in place. Now it's time to look at the tools and methods for creating content to transmit on said Internet services.

Chapter 11 covers HTML, the *lingua franca* of the World Wide Web. You don't need to actually create your own Web pages using Slackware Linux (indeed, the more advanced page-design tools are found on the Macintosh and Windows operating systems), but Slackware Linux does ship with a wide variety of tools for creating Web pages. In addition, the chapter covers how to implement imagemaps using the Apache Web server.

Chapter 12 described programming tools for the Apache Web server. These tools include Perl, Tcl, Java, and other service-side includes. Programming can be an advanced topic, and this chapter provides an overview of tools, rather than an in-depth description of programming topics.

HTML AND WEB PAGES

This chapter covers:

- HyperText Markup Language
- Linux and HTML
- Text editors
- HTML editors
- A basic Web page
- HTML tags
- The **imagemap** program
- The imagemap module for Apache
- Directives
- Client-side imagemaps

What is HTML?

If you don't know the answer to this question, you had best go back to school for a lesson on exactly why you've gone to the trouble to set up a Linux Internet server. However, chances are pretty good that you already have a good idea about HTML and why you need to have some working knowledge of it, if only to put up some basic Web pages.

 We're not going to spend a lot of time delving into the nuances of Web-page design. To be honest, there are a ton of competent books on the subject in the marketplace. Check Appendix A for a listing of HTML-design books that can help **N O T E** you if you want to learn more about Web-page design. Here, we'll spend time explaining some Web-page design tools and techniques unique to Linux and the Apache Web server.

HTML, which stands for HyperText Markup Language, is the lingua franca of the World Wide Web. A page that's formatted using HTML tags will be read by a Web browser, which will then supply the appropriate formatting. For instance, you would place a bold (<*B*>) before text that you want to be in bold type, while you would place a bold-off marker (</*B*>) after the text you want to be in bold type. The Web browser doesn't display these tags, but rather applies them to the text at hand. This is how headlines, bullets, subheads, and formatted text occurs. (If this looks suspiciously like the tags formerly used in the typesetting world, you're exactly correct. As a matter of fact, desktop-publishing programs with some lineage from the old typesetting days, like QuarkXPress, will choke on these tags.) The resulting file is a combination of HTML tags and text, making it totally a text file. There's no special encoding, no special formatting—an HTML file is merely a text file with some hidden tags.

Reduced to this limit, an HTML file becomes just another Linux text file, if you choose to look at it like that. Since you're already used to editing text files during the course of setting up a Slackware Linux Internet server, creating a basic Web page won't be any big deal for you.

Using Linux to Create HTML Pages

The issue here—and one that you might want to consider—is whether you want to use a Linux system to create Web pages. You probably won't want to actually use the server for page creation on a large scale; if the server has any sort of traffic at all; there's no reason to launch X Window and an HTML editor to work on Web pages and detract from the Web-server performance. And while there are good page-editing tools available on Linux (which we'll cover a little later), there are more advanced site-management tools available for the Windows 95 and Macintosh platforms.

On the other hand, you may have no other choice but to use your Linux server to create Web pages, or you may just want to stick to an all-Linux system. In this situation, you can use some of the standard Linux tools to create and edit HTML files. You could use one of the text editors that ship with Slackware Linux. We're not going to spend a lot of time on these editors here; if you want more information on them, check out Appendix A for a listing of additional Linux/UNIX texts.

All of these editors can be used to edit text files. These include **elvis**, which can be launched with the following command lines:

```
elvis
```

or

```
vi
```

The **elvis** text editor is a **vi** clone. If you're a UNIX or Linux user, you know that **vi** is a basic text editor; not terribly fancy, but functional. It's not an X Window application, but it can be launched under X. An X Window application—at least with Slackware Linux—is **emacs**, which can be launched in an **xterm** window with the following command line:

```
emacs
```

Linux HTML Editors

The accompanying CD-ROM contains a number of HTML editors in the **internet/editors** directory. These are decent editors and will get the job done for most basic HTML editing jobs. They're all stored in the Linux **tar** and **gzip** format. They're in the same exact form as stored on FTP sites on the Internet.

You're on your own when using these editors. We haven't tested all of them; they're included here as a service to you. You may want to check out some of the home pages listed here before diving in and using these packages.

N O T E

TkHTML

http://www.cobaltgroup.com/~roland/tkHTML/tkHTML.html

ftp://ftp.cobaltgroup.com:/pub/liem/tkHTML

TkHTML is a simple HTML editor based on the Tcl script language and the Tk toolkit for X11. It allows quick composition and editing of HTML-format documents, as well as a rapid way of converting existing text documents to the HTML format. To use tkHTML 3.1 from the accompanying CD-ROM, you don't need Tcl or Tk installed on your Linux system, as these libraries are statically linked to the binary. It was developed by Liem Bahneman (*roland@cobaltgroup.com*).

The filename is **tkHTML-3.11-Linux-ELF.gz.**

Amaya

http://www.w3.org/pub/WWW/Amaya/

ftp://ftp.w3.org/pub/amaya/amaya-linux-elf_0_9a_tar.gz

Amaya is a joint Web browser and HTML editor from the World Wide Web Consortium.

The filename is **amaya-linux-elf_0_9a_tar.gz.**

ASHE (A Simple HTML Editor)

http://www.cs.rpi.edu/~puninj/TALK/head.html

ftp://ftp.cs.rpi.edu/pub/puninj/ASHE

This is a small and simple HTML editor developed by John Punin (*puninj@cs.rpi.edu*) and Mukkai Krishnamoorthy (*moorthy@cs.rpi.edu*) of Rensselaer Polytechnic Institute.

The filename is **xhtml-1.3-linux-elf.gz.**

AsWedit 3.0

http://www.advasoft.com/

ftp://sunsite.doc.ic.ac.uk/packages/www/asWedit/

AsWedit is a HTML and text editor for X Window System and Motif. It offers three independent modes: a plain text editing mode and two context-sensitive, validating modes for authoring of HTML documents as used on the Internet and intranets. The two HTML modes are standard and experimental.

The filename is **asWedit-3.0-i386.linux.tar.gz.**

A Basic Web Page

Here we'll assume that you've launched an editor and you want to create a basic Web page. It's actually very simple. The easiest way to create a page in a text editor is just to type the text you want and then add the tags later. You can follow along with your own text editor, or else you can read through this section and apply them to your own pages. Let's say we want our Web page to have the following text:

```
This is our home page.
We want it to look really spiffy.
We want a headline here.
We want some bold text here.
Finally, we want a link to Kevin's home page.
```

This page, as typed, won't look too hot. As a matter of fact, it looks pretty crummy, as you can see in Figure 11.1, with our text displayed in the Arena Web browser.

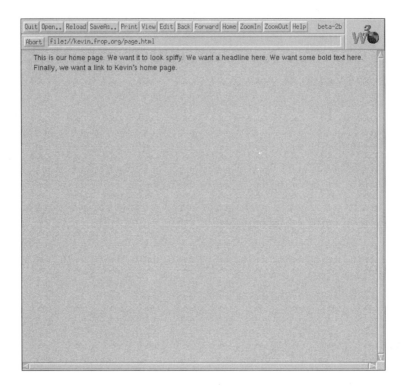

Figure 11.1 Our unformatted text.

Why does this look so lousy? Because there are no HTML tags to tell the Arena Web browser how to display the text. We're missing a lot of formatting commands here; as a matter of fact, there aren't even tags to tell the Web browser where the end of a line is. In this brief example, we can insert the major tags.

For starters, we need to have a title for our page. This title appears on the title bar of the Web browser—at the top of the window, basically—and looks something like this:

```
<TITLE>This is the title.</title>
```

If the title isn't part of the Web page, the browser will use the URL as the title.

From this basic line you can learn some things about the HTML language:

- **HTML tags usually appear in pairs.** The first part of the HTML tag "turns on" the formatting, while the second part of the tag turns off the formatting. In our example, the *<TITLE>* tag tells the Web browser that the beginning of the title is forthwith, and the *</TITLE>* tag signifies the end of the title. (The beginning tag lacks a slash.) Almost all HTML tags appear in pairs.

- **Case doesn't matter.** HTML tags don't have case requirements, unlike Linux as a whole. *<TITLE>*, *<TitLe>*, and *<title>* are the same thing as far as a Web browser is concerned.

We can add our title to our Web page:

```
<TITLE>This is the title.</title>
This is our home page.
We want it to look really spiffy.
We want a headline here.
We want some bold text here.
Finally, we want a link to Kevin's home page.
```

Still, this doesn't do a lot for our document layout. A Web page needs a declaration that tells the Web browser what follows is, well, a Web page. This is done by placing *<HTML>* at the beginning of the Web page and *</HTML>* at the end of the Web page. Most newer Web browsers don't require these tags to accurately lay out a Web page, but it doesn't hurt to include them for the sake of users of older Web browsers.

You can include information about the Web page using the *<HEAD>/</HEAD>* tag. This information isn't displayed as part of the Web page, but is seen when a user views the document source, or when the page is edited in a text or Web-page editor. This might include the name of the person creating the page, or the department where the document originated (in those cases where a larger corporation is implementing a Linux Internet server). A *<HEAD>* tag might look like this:

```
<HEAD>This is Kevin's test page.</HEAD>
```

The *<TITLE>* tag must appear within the *<HEAD>*/*</HEAD>* tag.

Some Web experts argue that you should also include the URL of the page within the document. This can be a pain if you're creating Web pages manually and moving them around, but many newer HTML editors will track this automatically. Such a tag would look like:

```
<BASE HREF="http://www.kreichard.com/test.html">
```

Throwing this all together gives us the following text file:

```
<HTML>
<HEAD>
<TITLE>This is the title.</title>
<BASE HREF="http://www.kreichard.com/test.html">
</HEAD>
This is our home page.
We want it to look really spiffy.
We want a headline here.
We want some bold text here.
Finally, we want a link to Kevin's home page.
```

Finally, we need to tell the Web browser where the actual body text of the Web page appears. This is done with the *<BODY>*/*</BODY>* tag. If we apply these tags to our test Web page, the resulting HTML text would look like this:

```
<HTML>
<HEAD>
<TITLE>This is the title.</title>
<BASE HREF="http://www.kreichard.com/test.html">
</HEAD>
<BODY>
This is our home page.
We want it to look really spiffy.
We want a headline here.
We want some bold text here.
Finally, we want a link to Kevin's home page.
</BODY>
```

The resulting Web page is shown in Figure 11.2.

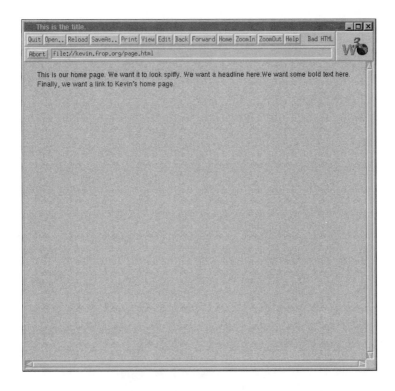

Figure 11.2 Adding some formatting to our Web page.

The resulting Web page is still pretty rough. That's because we need to insert some line breaks and paragraph breaks in our page. The *<P>* tag is used to specify the beginning of a paragraph. We can insert it into our test file as follows:

```
<HTML>
<HEAD>
<TITLE>This is the title.</title>
<BASE HREF="http://www.kreichard.com/test.html">
</HEAD>
<BODY>
<P>This is our home page.
<P>We want it to look really spiffy.
<P>We want a headline here.
<P>We want some bold text here.
<P>Finally, we want a link to Kevin's home page.
</BODY>
```

The resulting Web page is shown in Figure 11.3.

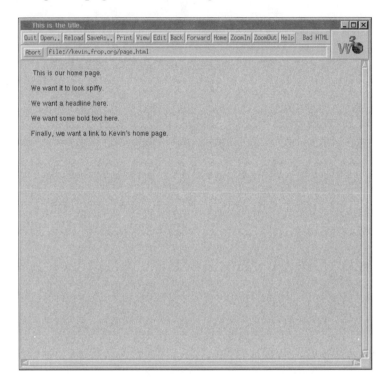

Figure 11.3 Adding paragraph breaks to the Web page.

This is better, but you'll notice that the *<P>* tag does something that detracts from the beauty of our prose: It inserts a line after every paragraph. This is rather unsightly, so it may be best if you use the *
* tag at the end of lines where you don't want a line inserted. We'll do so with a few lines in our test file:

```
<HTML>
<HEAD>
<TITLE>This is the title.</title>
<BASE HREF="http://www.kreichard.com/test.html">
</HEAD>
<BODY>
<P>This is our home page.<BR>
We want it to look really spiffy.
<P>We want a headline here.
<P>We want some bold text here.<BR>
Finally, we want a link to Kevin's home page.
</BODY>
```

The resulting Web page is shown in Figure 11.4.

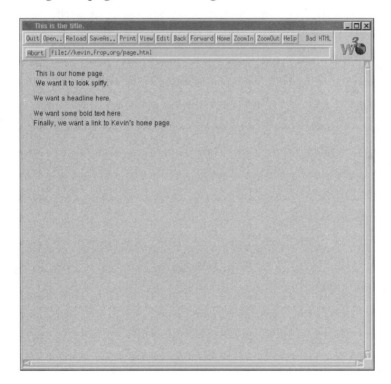

Figure 11.4 Line breaks instead of paragraph breaks.

This improves the formatting greatly.

However, as you can tell by the text in the file itself, there are a few other formatting tricks we want to perform on the test file. The line about bold text is a giveaway, and as you might expect, there's a simple tag for doing this—*<B>/</B>*. We can place it within the line as follows:

```
<P><B>We want some bold text here.</B><BR>
```

You can also specify *italic* formatting with the *<I>/</I>* tags, as well as a fixed-width font (known as *typewriter* in the HTML world) with the *<TT>/</TT>* tags. In addition, the *<U>/</U>* tags can be used to underline text, but this isn't a widely accepted practice; it's confusing to users because underlined text usually signifies hyperlinks, and as a result many Web browsers won't even display underlined text.

The next thing that pops out about our test file is the headline. There are actually six headline styles:

- *<H6>/</H6>*
- *<H5>/</H5>*
- *<H4>/</H4>*
- *<H3>/</H3>*
- *<H2>/</H2>*
- *<H1>/</H1>*

The order is from smallest to largest; the largest headline is *<H1>/</H1>*, while the smallest headline is *<H6>/</H6>*. These are shown in Figure 11.5.

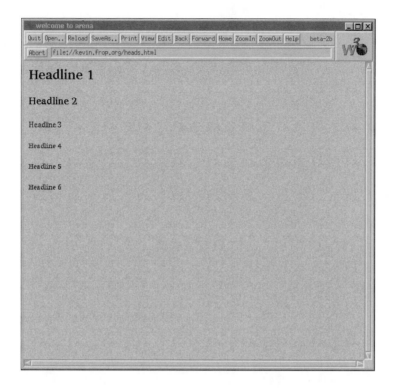

Figure 11.5 HTML heading styles.

You can also apply the bold and italic formatting to headlines.

Here are the previous tags applied to our test file:

```
<HTML>
<HEAD>
<TITLE>This is the title.</title>
<BASE HREF="http://www.kreichard.com/test.html">
</HEAD>
<BODY>
<P>This is our home page.<BR>
We want it to look really spiffy.
<P><H2>We want a headline here.</H2>
<P><B>We want some bold text here.</BR><BR>
Finally, we want a link to Kevin's home page.
</BODY>
```

The rendered Web page is shown in Figure 11.6.

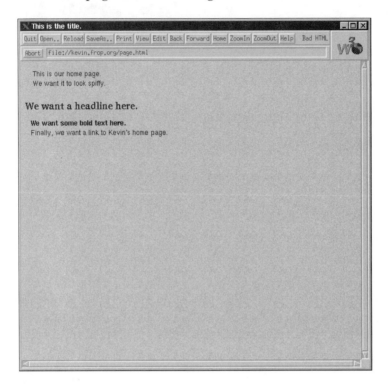

Figure 11.6 Our final Web page.

With these tags, you can get a functional Web page out to your users, especially if as a Webmaster your goal in Web pages is to give users brief pieces of information, such as when Web pages have been moved or when a page is under construction. Mind you, we've not gotten into 90 percent of the possible HTML formatting commands out there; you'll want to check out Appendix A for a listing of books that cover HTML formatting.

In the rest of this chapter, we'll cover a topic specific to the Apache Web server and, by default, to the specific use of Linux as an Internet server: imagemaps.

Using Apache Imagemaps

The following information on imagemaps is from *Apache Week*.

Imagemaps can provide a graphical interface to a web site. If the mouse is clicked over an imagemap image the coordinates of that click are sent to the server. The server can decide what page to return based on the location of the click.

Traditionally, imagemaps have been implemented at the server end with a CGI program (usually called **imagemap**). This is configured with a map file listing what regions on the image correspond to what documents to return. Apache can use CGI imagemaps, but it is more efficient to use the internal imagemap module. This module, compiled in by default, means that the server does not need to run a separate process to handle the image clicks. It is fully upwardly compatible and also adds some new features. Both of these approaches implement what are called server-side imagemaps, because all of the processing happens on the server.

The main problem with server-side imagemaps is that the user does not get any indication of which areas of the image contain links. An extension to HTML allows client-side imagemaps to tell the browser what areas on the image correspond to what documents. The browser can then highlight or show the active areas as desired. It is possible to use both client-side and server-side imagemaps at once, so that the maximum number of browsers are supported.

The Imagemap CGI Program

Older versions of Apache came with an imagemap program in the **cgi-src** directory. This could be compiled and placed into a CGI directory (typically **cgi-bin**). The internal imagemap module is faster than using the CGI program and it has replaced all of the functionality.

If you are using the **imagemap** program, you can easily move over to using the imagemap module. First, ensure that an appropriate *AddHandler* line is enabled in your **srm.conf** file (see the following section). Then all you need to do is update the HTML documents that refer to the imagemap program. You will probably be using something similar to this:

```
<A HREF="/cgi-bin/imagemap/maps/mapfile">
<IMG SRC="image.gif" ISMAP></a>
```

First of all, you need to rename your mapfile to have a suitable extension (as given on the *AddHandler imap-file* line, for example, *.map*) if it does not already have this extension. Then change the HTML line to read:

```
<A HREF="/maps/mapfile.map">
<IMG SRC="image.gif" ISMAP></a>
```

The HREF is now simpler because the **/cgi-bin/imagemap** part is not given.

The Imagemap Module

The imagemap module is a core part of Apache and is compiled in by default. To use it, you first need to configure the Apache server. You should pick a file extension to use for imagemap configuration files, typically *.map*. The *AddHandler* command below should be added to your **srm.conf** file:

> *AddHandler imap-file map*

You will need to restart the server after making this change, by sending it a -HUP signal. Now, any request for a file ending in *.map* will be treated as an imagemap request.

To actually create an imagemap you need to do two things:

1. Create a map file that maps areas of the image onto documents.
2. Add the code to an HTML page to tell the browser which image to use and what mapfile.

Creating the Map File

The map file is a text file containing the information needed for the server to map points on the image onto documents to return (or URLs to redirect to). It can also contain statements to control the behavior of the imagemap. The imagemap module uses map files in standard NCSA format, with optional extensions.

Areas and positions on the image can be mapped onto documents or URLs with the following commands. All coordinates start at the top-left of the image, position *(0,0)*. These statements can be modified to make use of Apache imagemap extensions (such as to give a menu text). This will be covered later.

> *rect url x1,y1 x2,y2*
>
> The rectangle (x1,y1) to (x2,y2).
>
> *poly url x1,y1 x2,y2 ....*
>
> The polygon formed by the points given.
>
> *circle url x1,y1 x2,y2*
>
> The circle with its center at (x1,y1) and point (x2,y2) on the circumference.
>
> *point url x1,y1*
>
> The closest point to the clicked position, if the click is not inside any circle, poly, or rect.

The *url* part of each of these statements is the document to return if the point clicked was inside the respective area (or in the case of *point*, the closest). It can be either an absolute URL (starting *http://*), a URL relative to the document root (starting /), or a relative URL (not starting with a /, and possibly including ../ components to go to parent directories).

If the URL is relative, it is taken relative to the directory containing the imagemap configuration file, not the original HTML document (if different). However, this can be changed by the base statement (see below).

There are various ways to create the coordinates for the map file. One is to do it by hand, using positions obtained by an image-editing program. Alternatively there are various programs available that will let you mark the shapes on an image and then write out the correct statements, such as those listed in Yahoo's Imagemaps category.

The statements that can be used to control the behavior of the imagemap are:

base [url | map | referer]

Use *url* as the base for any relative URLs within the map file. Alternatively, the word *map* can be used, which makes URLs relative to the directory containing the map file (this is the default). Alternatively, relative URLs can be made relative to the HTML document that included the imagemap image, with referer. This only works with browsers supporting the Referer request header (most modern browsers support this).

default [url | error | nocontent | referer | menu]

This tells the server what to do if the point clicked was not inside any rect, poly, or circle, and there were no point statements. It can be done by a URL, or one of these values: error: return a 500 Server Error status; nocontent: return a 204 No Content status, which will cause most browsers to keep the current document; referer: return the document given by the Referer request header, which will be the HTML document that contained the imagemap; menu: return a text (HTML) version of the URLs in the map file. The default is *nocontent*.

HTML For an Imagemap

The final part of creating an imagemap is to add suitable HTML code to an HTML document. Images are placed using the code *<IMG SRC="...">*. To place an imagemap, surround this tag with a *<A HREF...>* tag referring to the map file, and include the attribute *ISMAP* in the *<IMG SRC...>*. For example:

```
<A HREF="/docs/home.map"><IMG SRC="/graphics/image.gif" ISMAP></A>
```

where **docs/home.map** is the URL of the map file, relative to the server's document root. The *ISMAP* attribute in the *<IMG SRC...>* tag tells the browser that this is an imagemap. When the image is clicked, it sends a request for the given HREF URL, followed by the position of the image click, such as:

```
GET /docs/home.map?20,35
```

if the image was clicked at position (20,35).

Map Menu Document

One of the big problems with imagemaps in the past has been that they do not work with text-only browsers. The imagemap module is written to provide support for text-only browsers, which usually ignore the *ISMAP* attribute. The imagemap module recognizes this and will return a text (HTML) document containing a menu of the possible selections from the map file. In addition, a menu document can be returned if the user of a graphical browser selects a point outside any of the defined areas, if the statement "default menu" is given in the map file.

The type of menu returned can be configured with the *ImapMenu* directive. This can be placed in a *<Directory>* or *<Location>* section, or in a **.htaccess** file. It takes a single argument that gives the type of menu to return:

- *none* (do not show a menu)
- *formatted* (output a formatted document, with a suitable heading and with the map lines shown as *<pre>* text)
- *semiformatted* (format the map lines as *<pre>* text, and also show comment text on other lines [comments start with a hash character, #], but do not output a header)
- *unformatted* (do not format map lines as *<pre>* text and output text from comment lines, but do not output a header)

The semiformatted and unformatted options let you add additional text and mark-up to the map document. The difference between these two is that with semiformatted, the map links are output as *<pre>* sections, which forces them onto separate lines. The unformatted option does not impose any restrictions, so it is possible to build up a map document with multiple links on a line, for instance.

The links in the menu document correspond to the URLs for each of the areas defined in the map file. The text of the link will be the URL itself. However, this can be replaced with more meaningful text by giving this text as an argument before or after the coordinates. For example:

```
rect /welcome.html 1,1 20,20 "Welcome to this site"
```

Directives

The imagemap module supports three directives: the first configures the type of menu to return (if any). This is the *ImapMenu* directive already covered. The other two directives provide alternate ways of setting the base and default actions (see the base and default map configuration statements, above). The corresponding directives are *ImapBase* and *ImapDefault*, and they take the same arguments.

The directives can be given in *<Directory>* and *<Location>* sections, and in **.htaccess** files.

Examples

You have an image that contains two areas you want to make active: a circle, which should lead onto a contents page (**contents.html**) and a square that gives information about your company (**about.html**). The basic map file to do this would be:

```
circle contents.html 25,25 0,25
rect   about.html    50,0 100,50
```

This would be included in a HTML document like this:

```
<A HREF="/maps/home.map"><IMG SRC="/img/logo.gif" ISMAP></A>
```

If the user clicks inside the circle or square area, they will get the associated document, relative to the mapfile location. The requested files would be: **/maps/contents.html** and **/maps/about.html**. This probably is not what is wanted. The URLs in the map file could be given as relative to the document root, for example:

```
circle /contents.html 25,25 0,25
rect   /about.html    50,0 100,50
```

Alternatively, the base statement could be used to set the base URL, as in:

```
base /
```

```
circle contents.html 25,25 0,25
rect   about.html    50,0 100,50
```

Rather than putting the URL in the map file like this, it might be better to make all of the URLs relative to the location of the HTML document containing the imagemap, with:

```
base referer
```

If the user clicks an area outside the circle and the square the user will, by default, get a HTML menu of the URLs in the map file. Users of nongraphical browsers will also get this menu. To make it more readable, add some descriptions:

```
base referer
```

```
circle contents.html 25,25 0,25  "Contents"
rect   about.html    50,0 100,50 "About our company"
```

which will produce the following map document links as text:

```
Contents
```

```
About our company
```

The map document produced will just contain these two links. To make
it more elaborate, you can either include your own mark-up text (on
comment lines), or set the *ImapMenu* directive to the value formatted. To
include your own mark-up, put it on lines that start with a # character:

```
base referer
```

```
# <h1>Menu Bar</h1>
```

```
circle contents.html 25,25 0,25  "Contents"
rect    about.html    50,0 100,50 "About our company"
```

```
# Select one of the options above
```

This produces:

```
Menu Bar
```

```
Contents
```

```
About our company
```

```
Select one of the options above
```

This works because the default value for the *ImapMenu* option is
semiformatted, which outputs comment text (after the # symbol) as part
of the map document. For more elaborate formats, you could include
ImapMenu unformatted in your **access.conf** or **.htaccess** file, and use:

```
base referer


# <h1>Menu Bar</h1>


# Select an option:
circle contents.html 25,25 0,25  "Contents"
# or
rect    about.html    50,0 100,50 "About our company"
```

which produces:

```
Menu Bar


Select an option: Contents or About our company
```

Client-Side Imagemaps

Client-side imagemaps move the processing of the coordinate information to the browser. The HTML code includes the information about the areas on the image and the documents they lead to. This means the browsers can give positive feedback when the mouse is over an active area. This can only works in browsers that support the option, but it is possible to use a single image as both a server-side and client-side imagemap. Here is an example image setup for both server- and client-side imagemap:

```
<A HREF="/docs/home.map"><IMG SRC="/graphics/image.gif" ISMAP
      USEMAP="#thismap"></A>


<MAP NAME="thismap">
<AREA SHAPE=CIRCLE COORDS="25,25,25" HREF="contents.html">
<AREA SHAPE=RECT COORDS="50,0,100,50" HREF="about.html">
</MAP>
```

The circle here uses the center point and a radius, rather than a point on the circumference.

Summary

This chapter covered two basic topics: Creating rudimentary Web pages and the use of imagemaps within documents served by the Apache Web server. You can use a text editor from Linux (like **elvis** or **emacs**), a Linux-based HTML editor (like TkHTML), or an HTML editor from another operating system to create Web pages that are served by your Linux Internet server. A topic that was covered in detail was the use of imagemaps within documents served by the Apache Web server, as this topic is specific to the use of Slackware Linux as a Web server and differs slightly from how imagemaps are served by other Web servers.

In the next chapter, you'll learn about programming tools available under Slackware Linux for use on an Internet server.

PROGRAMMING, CGI, AND YOUR WEB SERVER

This chapter covers:

- Programming tools
- A CGI overview
- Perl
- Tcl
- Java
- Python
- Server-side includes
- Apache and SSI
- SSI commands
- Extended SSI

A Range of Programming Tools

So far in this book we've spent our time on discussing how your Internet server responds to various requests by shipping out files. If a Web browser requests a file, then the Apache Web server sends out the file. If a Gopher client requests a Gopher menu, then the Gopher server sends it out. If an FTP client requests a file, then the FTP server sends the file. And if a mail client requests mail, then the mail server sends out the mail.

However, the Apache Web server—as well as the other Web servers that ship as part of this book—is capable of much more. Instead of merely sending out a Web document, the Apache Web server can take input from a Web browser and then tailor the output, running an application or even two along the way. In addition, Web-browser users have the option of running an application through a link on a Web page.

This is implemented on the Apache Web server through the use of the Common Gateway Interface, or CGI. Basically, a Web page has a link to a CGI script; the script is run, and then the output is sent to the user. The process looks something like this:

- A request is made to the Web server from a Web browser.
- The request is sent to a CGI script.
- The CGI script processes the request, usually using input from the Web browser. This could range from asking for some simple return (like a calculation) or something.
- The information generated by the CGI script is formatted (usually in the form of a Web page, but sometimes in the form of an electronic-mail message) and then sent to the requesting Web browser.

Where would you use CGI scripts? Anyplace where you want some data input from a user to be inserted into a database, for example. This could be forms that allow people to register for a product or a service. Input could be provided with any number of elements: data-entry fields, radio buttons, and the like. If you peruse the Internet long enough, you'll see the wide range of uses for CGI scripts.

NOTE In this book, we're not going to spend a lot of time on each of these programming tools. There are reams of books on each of the topics discussed here, and if any of the programming tools pique your interest, you're encouraged to check out Appendix A for a list of books that cover these topics. A script created for one Web server can usually be run directly on the Apache Web server or any of the other Web servers that are on the accompanying CD-ROM. In addition, there are some example scripts in the Apache Web-server directory.

Running Down Your Choices

Slackware Linux and the Apache Web server contain several tools for creating CGI scripts and applications. We'll introduce them here.

Perl

Perl is a free scripting tool developed by Larry Wall for the UNIX operating system. There's a full Perl implementation with Slackware Linux and the Apache Web server.

A Perl script created for one environment can be used on any other Web-server environment, for the most part. Perl is a rather forgiving programming environment, so that small errors in syntax will be ignored or handled by the operating system.

Perl is probably the most popular programming tool on the Internet. It's amazingly powerful, while at the same time not that difficult to implement. Appendix A contains a list of Perl books that should help you implement your own Perl scripts on your Web server. In addition, there is an extensive set of online-manual pages that accompany Perl in Slackware Linux.

Tcl

The Tool Command Language, or Tcl, is similar to Perl in that it can be used to script almost anything. Tcl is a little more idiosyncratic than Perl when it comes to syntax, but all in all it's pretty much as easy to learn as Perl. Like Perl, Tcl was written for the UNIX operating system and transferred to the Internet environment due to the popularity of Web servers that run on the UNIX and Linux operating systems.

Appendix A contains a list of Tcl books that should help you implement your own Tcl scripts on your Web server. In addition, there is an extensive set of online-manual pages that accompany Tcl in Slackware Linux.

Java

Java is a glorified scripting language that's become one of the hotter development languages on the Internet. It's definitely worth your attention for use for development on a Linux Internet system.

Karl Asha and crew have done a fine job of porting the Java Development Kit (JDK) to Linux. You can find the most recent version in **/internet/java** on the accompanying CD-ROM.

Python

Python is an intriguing programming language that's been steadily gaining in popularity. It's really a hybrid between a true programming language and a scripting language, with object-oriented overtones. There are some tricks to using Python on a Web server; the February 1997 issue of Linux Journal (*http://www.ssc.com/lj*) has an excellent introduction to both Python and using Python on an Apache Web server.

You can find the most recent version in **/internet/python** on the accompanying CD-ROM.

Using Server-Side Includes

The following information is from *Apache Week*, which can be found at *http://www.apacheweek.com*.

While standard HTML files are fine for storing pages, it is very useful to be able to create some content dynamically. For example, to add a footer or header to all files, or to insert document information such as last modified times automatically. This can be done with CGI, but that can be complex and requires programming or scripting skills. For simple dynamic documents there is an alternative: server-side-includes (SSI).

SSI lets you embed a number of special commands into the HTML page itself. When the server reads an SSI document, it looks for these commands and performs the necessary action. For example, there is an SSI command that inserts the document's last modification time. When the server reads a file with this command in, it replaces the command with the appropriate time.

Apache includes a set of SSI commands based on those found in the NCSA server. This is implemented by the **includes** module (**mod_includes**). An extension of the standard SSI commands is available in the XSSI module, which will be a standard part of the Apache distribution from the next release.

Telling Apache to Use SSI

By default, the server does not bother looking in HTML files for the SSI commands. This would slow down every access to a HTML file. To use SSI you need to tell Apache which documents contain the SSI commands.

One way to do this is to use a special file extension; *.shtml* is often used, and this can be configured with this directive:

```
AddHandler server-parsed .shtml
AddType    text/html     shmtl
```

The *AddHandler* directive tells Apache to treat every *.shtml* file as one that can include SSI commands. The *AddType* directive makes such that the resulting content is marked as HTML so that the browser displays it properly.

An alternative method of telling the server which files include SSI commands is to use the so-called *XBitHack*. This involves setting the execute bit on HTML files. Any file with a content type of *text/html* (i.e. an extension *.html*) and with the execute bit set will be checked for SSI commands. This needs to be turned on with the *XBitHack* directive. (This directive was covered in Chapter 4.)

For either method, the server also needs to be configured to allow SSIs. This is done with the *Options Includes* directive, which can be placed in either the global **access.conf** or a local **.htaccess** (although the latter must first be enabled with *AllowOverride Options*). Since some SSI commands let the use execute programs which could be a security risk, an alternative option, *IncludesNOExec*, lets SSI commands work except for any which would execute a program.

SSI Commands

All SSI commands are stored within the HTML in HTML comments. A typical SSI command looks like this:

```
<!-#flastmod file="this.html" ->
```

In this case the command is **flastmod**, which means output the last modified time of the file given. The arguments specify the file **this.html** (which might be the name of the file containing this command). The whole of the command text, including the comment marker <!— and —>, will be replaced with the result of this command.

In general, all commands take the format:

```
<!-#command arg1="value1 arg2="value2 ... ->
```

where *arg1*, *arg2*, and so on are the names of the arguments, and *value1*, *value2*, and so on are the values of those arguments. In the **flastmod** example, the argument is *file* and it's value is **this.html**. Often commands can take different argument names. For example, **flastmod** can be given a URL with the argument *virtual*, to get the last modified time from the server. For example:

```
<!-#flastmod virtual="/" ->
```

to get the last modification time of the home page on the server (this is useful if the page being accessed might have a different filename, for instance).

Besides flastmod, there are SSI commands that get the size of a file or URL, the contents of a variable (passed in by the server), the contents of another file or URL, or the result of running a local file. These are documented in the NCSA tutorial on server-side includes, as well as the XSSI documentation.

When SSI commands are executed, a number of environment variables are set. This include the CGI variables (*REMOTE_HOST*, etc.), and some more, such as *DOCUMENT_NAME* and *LAST_MODIFIED*. These can be output with the **echo** command (so a better way of getting the last modification time of the current file would be **<!—#echo var="LAST_MODIFIED" —>**).

Extended SSI (XSSI)

The optional XSSI Apache module extends the server-side includes with:

- *Variables in commands*: XSSI allows variables to be used in any SSI commands. For example, the last modification time of the current document could be obtained with **<!—#flastmod file="$DOCUMENT_NAME" —>**.
- *Setting variables*: the **set** command set be used within the SSI to set variables.
- *Conditionals*: SSI commands **if**, **else**, **elif**, and **endif** can be used to include parts of the file based on conditional tests. For example, the *$HTTP_USER_AGENT* variable could be tested to see the type of browser and different HTML codes output depending on the browser capabilities.

To use XSSI, copy the file from the accompanying CD-ROM (in the */internet* directory), extract the files from the archive and follow the instructions in the **INSTALL** file.

Examples

Here are some examples of using SSI (the final one assumes you are using the XSSI module).

Displaying Document Information

The following code puts the document modification time on the page:

```
Last modified: <!—#echo var="LAST_MODIFIED" —>
```

Adding a Footer to Many Documents

This adds the following text to the bottom of each of the documents:

```
<!--#include file="footer.html" -->
```

Hide Links from External Users

Using the XSSI **if** command and the *REMOTE_ADDR CGI* variable to see if the user is in the local domain is done with the following:

```
<!--#if expr="$REMOTE_ADDR != /^1.2.3./" -->
 <a href="internal-documents.html">Internal Documents</a>
<!--#endif -->
```

where *1.2.3* is the IP address prefix of the local domain.

Summary

The Apache Web server that ships with Slackware Linux contains a number of programming tools that allow you to create your own applications or scripts. These tools include Perl and Tcl.

In the next chapter, you'll learn about security.

SECTION IV

Security

Security is one of the more important issues you'll face in your Internet usage. Chapter 13 covers security tools that ship with Slackware Linux and describes some basic methods for ensuring basic system security.

SECURITY

This chapter covers:

- Security
- Server security
- Document security
- User security
- Shadowing passwords
- Firewalls
- Three kinds of firewalls
- Firewall tools
- SATAN
- Specific Linux system vulnerabilities

Are Any of Us Truly Secure?

For a while, it seemed as though coverage of the Internet was limited to stories about security breeches on the Internet, with hordes of unprincipled hackers gleefully rifling through the files on a supposedly "secure" Internet site, grabbing hundreds of thousands of credit card numbers for God only knows what.

Of course, the real Internet isn't exactly like that; to be totally honest, the best place to find usable credit card numbers is behind the dumpster of a bank, not on someone's Web server. Still, there are Internet users out there who consider it great sport to go where they're not supposed to go. But the greater danger is from disgruntled ex-employees who would love nothing more than to wreak a little havoc on the company that laid them off.

In this chapter, we'll cover the many facets of security on the Internet, ranging from limitations on access to your Internet server to secure transactions. Your attitude should be simple: That your Internet site is unsecure and at risk, and that if you want to protect your transactions, your employers, and your users, you should take whatever steps you need to make your Internet Web server more secure.

This task can be broken down into three areas:

- Server security
- Document security
- User security

We'll run down each briefly.

NOTE   Security and networks is an involved and technical topic. You'll want to peruse your local bookstore for a more complete guide to Internet security.

Server Security

Basically, a secure server means that no unauthorized user has access to your system. If you don't want another Internet user reading the content of your Internet site, you should have the ability to prevent their access.

Document Security

Some documents on your Web server should be accessible to the bare minimum of people (that is, only to someone logged on as the administrator), while other documents should be limited to a small group of people (such as personnel report accessible only to upper management). This can mean outside Internet users, as well as internal users on an intranet.

User Security

When a user sends something to your Linux Internet site, they should have a reasonable expectation that the transaction should be secure; that is, no one should be able to read the contents of the transaction. This can range from registration information on a sensitive Internet site, to financial information from a bank.

Each of these security issues requires a different solution, although there is certainly overlap between the issues. These solutions will be covered in the remainder of this chapter.

NOTE You can stay informed about security risks. There's the very real chance that some hacker will find a security hole in Linux and your Internet server, so you should make an effort to stay informed by subscribing to the RISKS Forum (which details the issues raised by computers in society, including security concerns) and to CERT advisories, which will then be sent directly to you. To do so, you'll need to send a one-line message to the appropriate e-mail address (*risks-request@csl.sri.com* or *cert-advisory-request@cert.org*), with the word SUBSCRIBE as the text of the message. In addition, you should peruse Lincoln Stein's excellent WWW Security FAQ at *http://www.genome.wi.mit.edu/WWW/faqs/www-security-faq.html*, as well as the Linux Security Page (*http://207.237.120.45/linux/*) and alerts from the Linux Emergency Response Team (*http://www.redhat.com/linux-info/security/people/*).

Maintaining Server Security

The most secure Internet server is going to be the one where there are no other users. Of course, running a Linux Internet server for your own pleasure tends to be a tad limited in the amount of enjoyment it provides—what's the point of creating those really cool maps if no one else is going to see them?

Opening up your server to the rest of the company in the form of the intranet means that you're automatically increasing the chances of a security breech; some Internet security experts argue that the biggest threat of server security lies with disgruntled workers, not with malicious hackers. The threat increases when you connect to the outside Internet—besides those disgruntled workers, there are also the malicious hackers to worry about. And if you incorporate CGI scripts or Java applets into your Web pages, you're increasing the chances of a security breach.

What can you do? Be careful. Basically, if you don't need a service, then don't start one. This is easy to do with Linux, since you have total control over Internet services. Subscribe to the notion that less is more.

Watching the Scripts

When you're in a rush and under some severe deadlines, you might do things that are convenient, rather than smart.

Working with CGI scripts can make your life easier. However, if you're not careful with your scripts, you can inadvertently introduce a number of security holes on your own server. And if you don't follow some simple rules, you could end up with a downed machine and a boss screaming at you on the other end of the phone. These guidelines include:

- **Keep CGI scripts in one place**. You shouldn't keep scripts in multiple locations on your server; they'll be hard to remember, and inevitably you'll lose track of one in a directory where the permissions are not as strict as they should be. If you keep all the scripts in one place, you can set restrictive permissions for that directory, meaning that users will be able to only run the scripts, not change them or add their own.

- **Don't allow users to store CGI scripts in their own space.** This is really a variation of the first rule.

- **Watch your code carefully.** If you're not a coding veteran, you may not realize when you introduce an error that could open a security hole. That goes for CGI scripts you may grab from other sources. Any outside script that reads or writes files on your system should be examined more closely. And if a script is too complex for you to understand, you may be better off passing on it.

- **Make frequent backups.** If a hacker does bring your system to its knees, you should be able to restore the system quickly.

Perl and Security

Perl, like the rest of the Internet, was designed to be open and usable by all. However, Perl isn't as secure as it should be—and you may be making the problem worse than it can be. For starters, *never* place the Perl executable in your **cgi-bin** directory. (The default in Slackware Linux is not to have the Perl executable in that directory.) This allows *any* Perl script to be run on your machine, and since Perl allows access to the innards of your system, this means that any smart Perl hacker could grab important information about your system.

Secure Transactions

If you're planning on charging on your Web site for anything, you'll want to institute some sort of secure-transaction mechanism. This can take the form of secure transactions between the Web browser and the Web server. On a more speculative level, it can take the form of digital cash in the future.

There are several vendors pushing their version of digital cash; their names are listed at the end of this chapter. In addition, there are mechanisms in most Web server for secure transactions. The exact route you take will depend on the Web server you use and the authentication schemes they are pushing.

Shadowing Passwords

One of the more common ways for someone to hack onto a Linux Internet server—or a Linux system in general—is to try and get into the **/etc/passwd** file. To prevent easy access, you can set up Shadow passwords, which takes the **/etc/passwd** file and encrypts it. There is a downside: you will need to recompile the WU-FTP server if you plan on using Shadow passwords, and you'll need to use a different command to add users.

Login as root, and then copy the file **shadow-current_tar.gz** from the accompanying CD-ROM. You can unarchive the file with the following command line:

```
tar zxfv shadow-current_tar.gz
```

This creates an directory called **shadow-mk**. Make this the current directory and then run the following command lines in sequence:

```
make save
```

This command line saves the old binaries, should you want to uninstall Shadow passwords later. The old binaries are saved in **shadow-mk/save**.)

```
make all
```

This command line compiles the software. It could take a while, so relax.

```
make install
```

This command line installs the software.

```
/usr/sbin/pwconv
```

This command line program converts old passwords to Shadow passwords.

```
mv ./npasswd /etc/passwd
```

This command line replaces the original password file with a new file that contains no passwords, but a reference to Shadow passwords stored elsewhere on the system.

```
mv ./nshadow /etc/shadow
```

This command line moves the new password file to **etc**.

```
chmod 644 /etc/passwd
```

This command line changes the new password file to a file that's readable by the world, but writable only by you.

```
chmod 640 /etc/shadow
```

This command line changes the **Shadow** file to a file that's not readable by the world, only readable to the group, and writable only by the owner.

```
chown root.shadow /etc/shadow
```

This command line changes the ownership of the file to **root.shadow**.

```
touch /var/adm/lastlog
touch /var/adm/ftmp
touch /var/adm/faillog
touch /var/adm/sulog
```

This command line creates logfiles.

If you're running X, you'll need to add the following line to your **/usr/X11R6/lib/X11/config/linux.cf** file:

```
#define HasShadowPasswd        YES
```

To add users, you'll need to use the **useradd** command, not the standard **adduser** command.

Firewalls

A firewall is a separate Web server that allows and prevents access to and from your Web site. Sometimes this is a separate PC sitting between your network and the Internet, while at other times it can be a separate process running on your Web server.

Where to Place the Firewall

There are three places to put your server in conjunction with the firewall:

- The server can be connected directly to the outside world, with the firewall set up to protect your internal network.
- The server be connected only to the firewall, which handles both incoming and outgoing Internet requests
- The server can be installed directly on the firewall.

There are some advantages to each.

If you're running an Intranet and want to allow your users access to the outside world without allowing the outside world access to your Intranet, you'll want to place the firewall directly on the Internet and your server on your internal network. Users who want access to the Internet at large go through the firewall. (Of course, your users who may want access to your server from afar won't be able to get into your server.)

Placing your server directly on the Internet with the firewall protected an inner network means that the server is vulnerable (in the Internet world, this is called the "sacrificial-lamb" approach), but that the inner network—where sensitive data is kept—is always protected.

The idea of placing the firewall on the server generally isn't a good one, but there are financial situations where this is your only choice.

Three Types of Firewalls

Basically, there are three types of firewalls, as defined by the Internet world:

- application proxy gateway
- circuit level relay
- packet filter

Your security tools can include all three of these tools, or any combination.

A proxy is the most commonly used firewall. Basically, a proxy server sit between an internal network and the outside world. When a user on the internal network wants to communicate with the outside world, it first contacts the proxy server, which then reaches out to the outside world (i.e., the greater Internet). The advantage here is that you can log transactions and apply some limits to specific Internet protocols; for instance, you can allow outside FTP clients to grab software from your site, but you can prevent them from any uploads.

A circuit-level relay is a cruder tool that performs some low-level gateway functions, but doesn't allow you to track transactions or apply specific rules to specific Internet protocol. The SOCKS technique is a good example.

Packet filtering has traditionally been a popular firewall technique, as it offers a high level of control through rules. These rules can be applied to IP addresses (incoming and outgoing), port numbers, specific protocols being transported, and more. The actual IP address of the internal-network user isn't revealed to the Internet, but the IP address of the proxy server is.

Firewall Tools

There are a number of tools that you can use to create your own firewall.

The first is the Cern server that was described in Chapter 4 and contained on the accompanying CD-ROM. It's set up to be used as proxy server. Documentation for using the Cern server is at *http://www.w3.org/pub/WWW/Daemon/User/Installation/Installation.html*.

The second is the TIS Firewall Toolkit, which is freely available software in source-code form. Because of legal reasons, however, this product is not contained on the accompanying CD-ROM. You can read more about it at *http://www.tis.com/docs/products/fwtk/*. Using this toolkit is not a simple matter, and if you're not a byte wizard that knows everything about TCP/IP, you should avoid it. In addition, there's no Linux-specific help with this product.

SATAN

Sometimes the best way to find holes in your system is to look for them yourself. That's the theory behind SATAN, the Security Administrator Tool for Analyzing Networks. Its home page is *http://www.cerf.net/cerfnet/security/satan/index.html*. We're not going to go into installation and such—the home page covers that stuff more than adequately—but we will point out that it's an essential tool for system security, and one that you should consider using.

Be warned that Linux support for SATAN isn't absolute. We're including SATAN on the accompanying CD-ROM (the filename is **satan-1.1.1.Linux.tgz**) but the official SATAN site doesn't promote this port to Linux.

Linux Security Vulnerabilities

No system is every truly secure. The folks at the Linux Emergency Response Team— and specifically Alexander O. Yuriev—have put together a list of alerts that are applicable to Linux systems. This information comes from *http://www.redhat.com/linux-info/security/Linux-Security-FAQ/*, and it's there that you should search for more information and a link to the original alert message. Vulnerabilities include:

- vixie cron
- lpr
- sendmail

- dip
- mount/umount from linux-util 2.5
- suid perl
- NCSA cgi-bin applications.
- root's crontab
- fvwm 1.24.
- rxvt
- telnetd(8) and login on systems with shared libraries
- adduser-1.0
- Ghostscript
- Cipher 3.0 and GCC 2.7.0 -O flag incompatibility
- vacation 1.0
- wu.ftpd 2.4
- rpc.ugidd
- hash sign in the hostname
- at/atrun prior to 2.7
- Trojan Satan 1.0 binaries for Linux
- UNFS 2.0

Summary

Security is an involved topic in the Linux Internet server world. This overview provides basic information for increasing system security, as well as the tools you'll need to better protect your Linux Internet server. Remember, no site is absolutely secure.

For More Information

Since you're reading a book about setting up an Internet site via Linux, it's only natural that you would turn to the Internet for more information about setting up and maintaining your Web site. This appendix contains other sources of information that should augment your Internet experience.

World Wide Web Sites

Here are some World Wide Web (WWW) sites that feature information about Linux and the Internet, as well as Linux in general. These sites are bookmarked at *http://www.kreichard.com*, if you don't want to type in these URLs and want to merely jump between Web sites.

Apache Week

http://www.apacheweek.com/

This Web site, which is updated weekly, covers in-depth topics concerning the Apache Web server. Some portions of this book came from this Web site.

Linux Journal

http://www.ssc.com/lj

This Web site is associated with the excellent magazine, *Linux Journal*. (If you're not a subscriber, definitely get out the checkbook and subscribe.) Excerpts from the magazine are featured here, as well as archives of past issues.

Linux Gazette

http://www.ssc.com/lg/

This online guide to Linux comes courtesy of the folks who bring you the Linux Journal.

Linux Documentation Project

http://sunsite.unc.edu/mdw/linux.html

The mothership of Linux Web sites. If a Linux site or Web resource isn't listed here, it probably doesn't exist.

Linux is Business

http://www.m-tech.ab.ca/linux-biz/

A listing of Linux business applications.

Linux Security WWW

http://bach.cis.temple.edu/linux/linux-security/

This site covers security issues related to Linux, which includes Internet connectivity.

Linux Applications and Utilities

http://www.xnet.com/~blatura/linapps.shtml

As the title says—links to Linux software.

Linux Newsgroups

There are literally hundreds of newsgroups dedicated to Linux on the Usenet. Most of them are of limited use, however; newsgroups like *alt.fan.linus-torvalds* and *alt.sex.fetish.linux* (yes, this group really exists!) don't add a lot to the pool of Linux knowledge. Here's a listing of the newsgroups that you'll actually find useful. Be warned that some of these newsgroups are not English-centric; unless you have the right fonts installed on your system, the postings in *tw.bbs.comp.linux* and other foreign-language newsgroups will appear to be gibberish.

> *alt.linux*
>
> *alt.os.linux*
>
> *alt.os.linux.slackware*
>
> *alt.uu.comp.os.linux*
>
> *alt.uu.comp.os.linux.questions*
>
> *aus.computers.linux*
>
> *comp.os.linux*
>
> *comp.os.linux.admin*
>
> *comp.os.linux.advocacy*
>
> *comp.os.linux.announce*
>
> *comp.os.linux.answers*
>
> *comp.os.linux.development*
>
> *comp.os.linux.development.apps*
>
> *comp.os.linux.development.systems*
>
> *comp.os.linux.hardware*
>
> *comp.os.linux.help*
>
> *comp.os.linux.misc*
>
> *comp.os.linux.networking*
>
> *comp.os.linux.questions*
>
> *comp.os.linux.setup*
>
> *comp.os.linux.x*

computer42.mail2news.linux-alert

linux.admin.isp

linux.dev.admin

linux.dev.apps

lnux.dev.config

linux.dev.diald

linux.dev.isdn

linux.dev.kernel

linux.dev.net

linux.dev.newbie

linux.dev.ppp

linux.dev.raid

linux.dev.scsi

linux.dev.serial

linux.dev.x11

linux.net.atm

linux.test

local.linux-isp

mailing-list.isdn4linux

maus.os.linux

nl.comp.os.linux

no.linux

sfnet.atk.linux

tw.bbs.comp.linux

ucb.os.linux

uk.comp.os.linux

utah.linux

uw.linux

There are two newsgroups that should be of particular interest to you as you set up an Linux Internet site: *linux.admin.isp* (which is geared toward Internet Service Providers, or ISPs, who use Linux; they'll have a lot of useful information for you as you set up and maintain a site) and *comp.infosystems.www.servers.unix* (which is where official news and tips about the Apache Web server is disseminated).

In addition, the following newsgroups cover the arcane world of electronic mail as it applies to your Linux Internet server:

comp.mail.elm

comp.mail.mh

comp.mail.mime

comp.mail.misc

comp.mail.multi-media

comp.mail.sendmail

comp.mail.smail

Books

This book should be only the beginning of your work to bring a Linux Internet server to fruition. These books will come in handy as you extend your education.

Linux

Linux Configuration and Installation, second edition, by Patrick Volkerding, Kevin Reichard, and Eric F. Johnson, MIS:Press, 1996, ISBN 1-55828-492-3.

Linux Programming, by Patrick Volkerding, Eric F. Johnson, and Kevin Reichard, MIS:Press, 1996, ISBN 1-55828-507-5.

The Linux Database, by Fred Butzen, and Dorothy Forbes, MIS:Press, 1997, ISBN 1-55828-491-5.

Internet Site Management

Communications Systems and Networks, by Ray Horak, MIS:Press, 1996, ISBN 1-55851-485-6.

Managing Internet Information Services, by Cricket Liu, Jerry Peek, Russ Jones, Bryan Buus & Adrian Nye, O'Reilly & Associates, 1994, 1-56592-062-7.

WebMaster in a Nutshell, by Stephen Spainhour & Valerie Quercia, O'Reilly & Associates, 1996, ISBN 1-56592-229-8.

Network Management

DNS and BIND, second edition, by Paul Albitz and Cricket Liu, O'Reilly & Associates, 1996, ISBN 1-56592-236-0.

Linux Network Administrator's Guide, by Olaf Kirch, SSC, 1994, ISBN 0-916151-75-1.

TCP/IP Network Administration, by Craig Hunt, O'Reilly & Associates, 1992, ISBN 0-937175-82-X.

HTML

HTML in Plain English, by Sandra E. Eddy, MIS:Press, 1996, ISBN 1-55828-511-3.

CGI Programming

CGI Programming on the World Wide Web, by Shishir Gundavaram, O'Reilly & Associates, 1996, ISBN 1-56592-168-2.

Instant Web Scripts with CGI/Perl, by Selena Sol and Gunther Birznieks, MIS:Press, 1996, ISBN 1-55851-490-2.

Introduction to CGI/Perl by Steven E. Brenner and Edwin Aoki, MIS:Press, 1996, ISBN 1-55851-478-3.

Perl

Cross-Platform Perl, by Eric F. Johnson, M&T Books, 1996, ISBN 1-55851-483-X.

Programming Perl, 2nd Edition, By Larry Wall, Tom Christiansen, and Randal L. Schwartz, O'Reilly & Associates, 1996, ISBN 1-56592-149-6.

The Webmaster's Handbook: Perl Power for Your Web Server, by Christian Neuss and Johan Vromans, Thomson Publishing, 1995, ISBN 1-85032-253-8.

Tcl

Graphical Applications with Tel and Tk, by Eric F. Johnson, M&T Books, 1995, ISBN 1-55851-471-6.

Tcl and the Tk Toolkit, by John K. Ousterhout, Addison-Wesley Professional Computing Series, 1994, ISBN 0-201-63337-X.

Python

Internet Programming with Python, by Aaron Watters, Guido van Rossum, and James C. Ahlstrom, M&T Books, 1996, ISBN 1-55851-484-8.

Sendmail

Sendmail, second edition, by Bryan Costales and Eric Allman, O'Reilly & Associates, 1997, ISBN 1-56592-222-0.

Security

Building Internet Firewalls, by D. Brent Chapman and Elizabeth D. Zwicky, O'Reilly & Associates, 1995, ISBN 1-56592-124-0.

Practical UNIX and Internet Security, second edition, by Simson Garfinkel and Gene Spafford, O'Reilly & Associates, 1996, ISBN 1-56592-148-8.

HARDWARE SUPPORTED BY SLACKWARE LINUX

This is a listing of the hardware supported by Slackware 96, which can be found on the accompanying CD-ROM. It's based on the Linux Hardware Compatibility HOW-TO, which can be found at *http://sunsite.unc.edu/ mdw/linux.html*. This appendix doesn't cover all the possible hardware options for Slackware Linux; instead, only those hardware issues pertaining to using Linux as an Internet server are covered. (For instance, a discussion of using a Mattel Powerglove with Linux isn't really of interest when discussing Internet servers.)

Bus

ISA, VLB, EISA, and PCI buses are supported. PS/2 MicroChannel buses are not supported in the Slackware 96 distribution.

CPU

All the major CPUs from the major manufacturers (Intel, AMD, and Cyrix) are supported. There's no reason for a separate math coprocessor with Linux, as it supports FPU emulation.

Hard-Drive Controllers

Slackware Linux works with standard IDE, MFM, and RLL controllers. In addition, Enhanced IDE (EIDE) interfaces (with up to two IDE interfaces and up to four hard drives and/or CD-ROM drives) are supported. Explicitly supported are the following EIDE interfaces: CMD-640, DTC 2278D, FGI/Holtek HT-6560B, RZ1000, and Triton (82371FB) IDE (with busmaster DMA). Also supported are ESDI controllers that emulate the ST-506 (MFM/RLL/IDE) interface; generic 8-bit XT controllers also work.

SCSI Controllers

The following SCSI controllers are supported: AMI Fast Disk VLB/EISA (BusLogic compatible); Adaptec AHA-1505/1515, AHA-1510/152x, AHA-154x, AHA-174x, AHA-274x, AHA-2940/3940; Always IN2000; all BusLogic models; DPT PM2001, PM2012A, Smartcache; DTC 329x; Future Domain TMC-16x0, TMC-3260, TMC-8xx, TMC-950; Media Vision Pro Audio Spectrum 16 SCSI; NCR 5380 generic cards, 53c400 (Trantor T130B), 53c406a (Acculogic ISApport/Media Vision Premium 3D SCSI), 53c7x0, 53c8x0; Qlogic/Control Concepts SCSI/IDE (FAS408); Seagate ST-01/ST-02; SoundBlaster 16 SCSI-2; Trantor T128/T128F/T228; UltraStor 14F/24F/34F; and Western Digital WD7000 SCSI.

If you deviate from this list, be careful. There are some cheap sound boards on the market that purport to be SCSI interfaces, but these are used mainly with CD-ROM drives and not other SCSI devices (such as a hard-disk storage system).

There are special kernel patches available for the following SCSI controllers: AMD AM53C974, AM79C974 (PCI; used for Compaq, H-P, and Zeos onboard SCSI) (*ftp://sunsite.unc.edu/pub/Linux/kernel/ patches/scsi/AM53C974-0.3.tgz*); Adaptec ACB-40xx SCSI-MFM/RLL bridgeboard (*ftp://sunsite.unc.edu/pub/Linux/kernel/patches/scsi/ adaptec-40XX.tar.gz*); Always Technologies AL-500 (*ftp://sunsite.unc.edu/pub /Linux/kernel/patches/scsi/al500-0.2.tar.gz*); BusLogic (*ftp://ftp.dandelion.com/ BusLogic-1.0-beta.tar.gz*); Iomega PC2/2B (*ftp://sunsite.unc.edu/pub/*

Linux/kernel/patches/scsi/iomega_pc2-1.1.x.tar.gz); Qlogic (ISP1020) (*ftp://sunsite.unc.edu/pub/Linux/kernel/patches/scsi/isp1020-0.5.gz*); and Ricoh GSI-8 (*ftp://tsx-11.mit.edu/pub/linux/ALPHA/scsi/gsi8.tar.gz*).

Parallel-port SCSI adapters are not supported.

Hard Drives

If the controller is supported, the hard drive should work with no problems. However, all-direct access SCSI devices with a block size of 256, 512, or 1024 bytes should work, although other block sizes will not work (this can often be fixed by changing the block and/or sector sizes using the **MODE SELECT SCSI** command).

I/O Controllers

Virtually all standard serial, parallel, and joystick I/O controllers are supported, including those featuring 8250, 16450, 16550, and 16550A UARTs. In addition, cards that support nonstandard IRQs (like IRQ > 9) can be used.

Multiport Controllers

Multiport controllers come in the form of intelligent cards and nonintelligent cards. Supported nonintelligent cards are AST FourPort and clones (4 port); Accent Async-4 (4 port); Arnet Multiport-8 (8 port); Bell Technologies HUB6 (6 port); Boca BB-1004, 1008 (4, 8 port), BB-2016 (16 port), IO/AT66 (6 port), IO 2by4 (4 serial/2 parallel, uses 5 IRQs); Computone ValuePort (4, 6, 8 port) (AST FourPort compatible); DigiBoard PC/X (4, 8, 16 port); Comtrol Hostess 550 (4, 8 port); PC-COMM 4-port (4 port); SIIG I/O Expander 4S (4 port, uses 4 IRQs); STB 4-COM (4 port); Twincom ACI/550; and Usenet Serial Board II (4 port).

Support intelligent cards are Cyclades Cyclom-8Y/16Y (8, 16 port) and Stallion EasyIO/EasyConnection 8/32, 8/64/ONboard/Brumby/Stallion.

There are kernel patches supporting the following multiport controllers: Comtrol RocketPort (8/16/32 port) (*ftp://tsx-11.mit.edu/pub/linux/packages/comtrol/*); DigiBoard PC/Xe (ISA) and PC/Xi (EISA) (*ftp://ftp.digibd.com/drivers/linux/*); Moxa C218 (8 port) and C320 (8/16/24/32 expandable) (*ftp://ftp.moxa.com.tw/drivers/c-218-320/linux/*), and Specialix SIO/XIO (modular, 4 to 32 ports) (*ftp://sunsite.unc.edu/pub/Linux/kernel/patches/serial/sidrv0_5.taz*).

Network Adapters

In general, newer network adapters work without a lot of fuss with Linux. Older network adapters may require a little configuration work on your part.

Supported Ethernet adapters are 3Com 3C503, 3C505, 3C507, 3C509/3C509B/3C579; AMD LANCE (79C960)/PCnet-ISA/PCI (AT1500, HP J2405A, NE1500/NE2100); AT&T GIS WaveLAN; Allied Telesis AT1700; Ansel Communications AC3200 EISA; Apricot Xen-II; Cabletron E21xx; DEC DE425/DE434/DE435, DEPCA, and EtherWORKS; Hewlett-Packard PCLAN (27245 and 27xxx series), PCLAN PLUS (27247B and 27252A), and 10/100VG PCLAN; Intel EtherExpress and EtherExpress Pro; NE2000/NE1000; New Media Ethernet; Racal-Interlan NI5210 (i82586 Ethernet chip), and NI6510 (am7990 lance chip); PureData PDUC8028, PDI8023; SEEQ 8005; SMC Ultra; Schneider & Koch G16; Western Digital WD80x3; and Zenith Z-Note/IBM ThinkPad 300 built-in adapter.

There are two things to note regarding network cards in the Hardware HOW-TO: avoid 3Com 3C501 cards like the plague, and beware of NE2000/NE1000 clones.

Supported pocket and portable adapters are AT-Lan-Tec/RealTek parallel-port adapter and D-Link DE600/DE620 parallel-port adapter.

Slotless connections include SLIP/CSLIP/PPP (serial port), EQL (serial IP load balancing), and PLIP (parallel port) using a LapLink cable or bi-directional cable.

All ARCnet work with Linux.

The IBM Tropic chipset Token Ring cards work with Linux.

Drivers are available for the following Ethernet cards: 3Com Demon Ethercards 3C592 and 3C597 (*http://cesdis.gsfc.nasa.gov/linux/ drivers/vortex.html*); 3Com Vortex Ethercards 3C590 and 3C595 (*http://cesdis.gsfc.nasa.gov/linux/drivers/vortex.html*); DEC 21040/21140 Tulip/SMC PCI EtherPower 10/100 (*http://cesdis.gsfc.nasa.gov/linux/ drivers/tulip.html*); and H-P J2585 and J2573 (*http://cesdis1.gsfc.nasa.gov:80/ linux/drivers/100vg.html*).

ISDN Cards

In general, ISDN cards that emulate standard modems or common Ethernet adapters don't need any special drivers. You'll need patches to the Linux kernel to use the following ISDN cards: 3Com Sonix Arpeggio (*ftp://sunsite.unc.edu/pub/Linux/kernel/patches/network/sonix.tgz*); Combinet EVERYWARE 1000 ISDN (*ftp://sunsite.unc.edu/pub/Linux/ patches/network/combinet1000isdn-1.02.tar.gz*); Diehl SCOM card (*ftp://sunsite.unc.edu/pub/Linux/kernel/patches/network/isdndrv-0.1.1.tar.gz*); and ICN ISDN/Teles ISDN/Creatix AVM ISDN cards (*ftp://ftp.franken.de/ pub/isdn4linux/*).

ATM Interfaces

Slackware Linux does not support any ATM adapters right out of the box. There is only one patch, and that is for the Efficient Networks ENI155P-MF 155 Mbps ATM adapter; you can find it at *http://lrcwww.epfl.ch/linux-atm/*.

Frame Relay Cards

Slackware Linux does not support any frame relay cards right out of the box. There is a driver for the Sangoma S502 56K frame relay card at *ftp://ftp.sovereign.org/pub/wan/fr/*.

Tape Drives

A number of tape drives are supported by Slackware Linux. Tape devices will come in handy for an Internet server—those backups might come in handy at some point.

In general, SCSI tape drives are supported with no problems.

Also supported with no problems are QIC-02 drives, as well as drives with dedicated controllers, including the Colorado FC-10/FC-20, Mountain Mach-2, and Iomega Tape Controller II.

You'll need a kernel patch (*ftp://sunsite.unc.edu/pub/Linux/kernel/tapes*) to use tape drives that run from the floppy diskette controller, including QIC-117, QIC-40/80, QIC-3010/3020 (QIC-WIDE) drives.

Unsupported tape drives include Emerald, Tecmar QIC-02, Colorado Trakker, Colorado TC-15, Irwin AX250L/Accutrak 250, IBM Internal Tape Backup Unit, and COREtape Light.

UPS Devices

Most UPS devices work in conjunction with PC hardware; as such, they'll work with Linux with few problems. You'll want to check the UPS HOW-TO for more information.

To use the APC SmartUPS, you'll need to install this package: *ftp://sunsite.unc.edu/pub/Linux/system/UPS/apcd-0.1.tar.gz*. To use UPS divices with RS-232 monitoring port (the "unipower" package), you'll need to install this package:*ftp://sunsite.unc.edu/pub/Linux/system/UPS/unipower-1.0.0.tgz*.

Video Cards

For the purposes of a Web server, any graphics card will work just fine—you won't need much more than text mode or perhaps standard VGA resolution when working with the X Window System on a limited basis.

If you want to use the X Window System on a more regular basis, however, you'll want to make sure you're using one of the following cards or chipsets for high-resolution graphics: Actix GE 32, GE 64 VLB, and Ultra; ARK Logic ARK1000PV/2000PV; ATI VGA Wonder, ATI Mach8, ATI Mach32, ATI Mach64; Avance Logic AL2101/2228/2301/2302/2308/2401; Cirrus 542x, 543x, 6420/6440; Chips & Technologies 65520/65530/65540/65545; Compaq AVGA; Diamond Viper VLB/PCI, Stealth 24 VLB, and Stealth 64; ELSA Winner 1000, Winner 1000 PRO VLB/PCI, Winner 1000AVI, Winner 2000PRO/X, and Winner 2000 PRO PCI; Genoa GVGA and VideoBlitz III AVI; Hercules Terminator 64 and Terminator Pro 64; IBM 8514/A, IBM XGA, XGA-II; IIT AGX-010/014/015/016; MCGA; JAX 8231; Miro 10SD VLB/PCI, 20SD, Crystal 20SV PCI, and Crystal 40SV; MX MX68000/MX68010; NCR 77C22, 77C22E, 77C22E+; #9 GXE Level 10/11/12, Level 14/16, GXE64 PCI, FX Motion 771, FX Vision 330, and GXE64 Pro VLB/PCI; Oak OTI-037/67/77/87; Orchid P9000 and Fahrenheit 1280+; RealTek RTG3106; S3 911, 924, 801, 805, 928, 864, 964, Trio32, Trio64, 868, 968; SPEA Mirage, Mirage VLB, Mirage P64, Mercury 64, and Mercury VLB; STB Pegasus VL, Velocity 64V, PowerGraph 64, and PowerGraph X.24; Trident TVGA8800/ A8900/A9xxx; Tseng ET3000/ET4000/ET4000AX/W32/W32i/W32p; Video 7/Headland Technologies HT216-32; Weitek P9000; and Western Digital/Paradise PVGA1, WD90C00/10/11/24/30/31/33. The following monochrome cards are supported: Hercules, Hyundai HGC-1280, and Sigma LaserView Plus. The following cards are unsupported at higher resolutions: Compaq Qvision and Number Nine Imagine 128.

PCMCIA Cards

Support for PCMCIA cards—used predominantly on laptops, which won't often be used for Linux Internet servers—comes through David Hinds' Card Services, which ships as part of Slackware Linux. The following PCMCIA Ethernet cards are supported: 3Com 3c589, 3c589B; Accton EN2212 EtherCard; CNet CN30BC Ethernet; D-Link DE-650; EFA InfoExpress SPT EFA 205 10baseT; EP-210 Ethernet; Farallon Etherwave; GVC NIC-2000P Ethernet Combo; Hypertec HyperEnet; IBM CreditCard Ethernet Adapter; IC-Card Ethernet; Katron PE-520 Ethernet; Kingston KNE-PCM/M; LANEED Ethernet; Linksys EtherCard; Maxtech PCN2000 Ethernet; Network General "Sniffer";

New Media Ethernet; Novell/National NE4100 InfoMover; Proteon Ethernet; PreMax PE-200 Ethernet; RPTI EP400 Ethernet; Socket Communications Socket EA LAN Adapter; Thomas-Conrad Ethernet; and Volktek Ethernet.

The following memory cards are supported: New Media SRAM, Epson 2-MB SRAM, and Intel Series 2 and Series 2+ Flash.

The following PCMCIA SCSI adapters are supported: Adaptec APA-1460 SlimSCSI, New Media Bus Toaster SCSI, and Qlogic FastSCSI PCMCIA.

Xircom Ethernet and Ethernet/modem cards are not supported.

All modem PCMCIA cards should work.

Sound Cards

Even though you're unlikely to need sound capabilities on your Linux Internet server, you might be interested in knowing that Slackware Linux supports the following sound chipsets and boards: 6850 UART MIDI; Adlib (OPL2); Audio Excell DSP16; Aztech Sound Galaxy NX Pro; Crystal CS4232 (PnP) cards; ECHO-PSS cards (Orchid SoundWave32, Cardinal DSP16); Ensoniq SoundScape; Gravis Ultrasound, Ultrasound 16-bit sampling daughterboard, and Ultrasound MAX; Logitech SoundMan Games, SoundMan Wave, and SoundMan 16; MPU-401 MIDI; MediaTriX AudioTriX Pro; Media Vision Premium 3D, Pro Sonic 16, and Pro Audio Spectrum 16; Microsoft Sound System; Oak OTI-601D cards; OPTi 82C928/82C929 cards (MAD16/MAD16 Pro); SoundBlaster, SoundBlaster Pro, and SoundBlaster 16; Turtle Beach Wavefront cards (Maui, Tropez); and Wave Blaster (and other daughterboards).

CD-ROM Drives

Slackware Linux supports a wide range of CD-ROM drives. In general, all SCSI CD-ROM drives are supported. Explicitly supported are the following CD-ROM drives: EIDE (ATAPI) CD-ROM drives; Aztech CDA268, Orchid CDS-3110, Okano/Wearnes CDD-110, Conrad TXC;

GoldStar R420; LMS Philips CM 206; Matsushita/Panasonic, Creative Labs, Longshine, Kotobuki (SBPCD); Mitsumi; Optics Storage Dolphin 8000AT; Sanyo H94A; Sony CDU31A/CDU33A, CDU-535/CDU-531; and Teac CD-55A SuperQuad.

You'll need kernel patches to use the following CD-ROM drives: LMS/Philips CM 205/225/202 (*ftp://sunsite.unc.edu/pub/Linux/ kernel/patches/cdrom/lmscd0.3d.tar.gz*); Mitsumi FX001D/F (alternate drivers) (*ftp://ftp.gwdg.de//pub/linux/cdrom/drivers/mitsumi/mcdx-1.0a.tar.gz*); NEC CDR-35D (*ftp://sunsite.unc.edu/pub/Linux/kernel/patches/cdrom/ linux-neccdr35d.patch*); and Sony SCSI multisession CD-XA (*ftp://tsx-11.mit.edu/ pub/linux/patches/sony-multi-0.00.tar.gz*).

Removable Drives

All SCSI drives should work if the controller is supported, including optical (MO), WORM, floptical, Bernoulli, Zip, SyQuest, PD, and others.

To use parallel-port Zip drives, you'll need to grab a kernel patch from *ftp://gear.torque.net/pub/*.

Mouse

Basically, Slackware Linux supports any mouse that's connected to a parallel port, a serial port, or a PS/2 (mouse) port; during installation, it will be up to you to tell Linux where the mouse is. Supported mice include Microsoft serial mouse, Mouse Systems serial mouse, Logitech serial mouse (including the Mouseman), ATI XL Inport busmouse, C&T 82C710 (QuickPort; used on (Toshiba and TI Travelmate laptops), Microsoft busmouse, Logitech busmouse, and PS/2 (auxiliary device) mouse.

The following models require kernel patches: Sejin J-mouse (ftp://sunsite.unc.edu/pub/Linux/kernel/patches/console/ jmouse.1.1.70-jmouse.tar.gz) and MultiMouse ftp://sunsite.unc.edu/ pub/Linux/system/Misc/MultiMouse-1.0.tgz).

Printers/Plotters

Slackware Linux should work with pretty much any printer or plotter connected to a parallel port (or, in a pinch, a serial port).

Printing out PostScript files requires the use of Ghostscript. Since this topic isn't really germane to a book about using Linux on an Internet server, it won't be covered here; you're encouraged to check Appendix A for a complete book on Linux installation and configuration.

INDEX

X

Z

What you will find on the CD-ROM

The accompanying CD-ROM contains a full implementation of the Slackware Linux operating system; details for installing and configuring Slackware Linux can be found in Chapter 3 of this book. Slackware Linux ships with many tools that youíll find useful for developing your own Linux Internet server, including the Apache Web server, Perl, and Tcl.

In addition, there are a number of directories specific to this book and using Linux as an Internet server. These programs are detailed through the course of this book. The contents of these directories are as follows.

/internet:
The CyberRadio audio server (**CyberRadio1.tar.gz**)
FreeWAIS (**fwsf2062-elfbin.tgz**)
The GN Gopher server (**gn.tar.gz**)
SATAN (**satan-1.1.1.Linux.tgz**)
Shadow passwords (**shadow-current_tar.gz**)
The Squid object cache (**squid-1_1_5-src_tar.gz**)
WhiteBoard (**linux-wb-1.59.tar.Z**)

/internet/editors:
Amaya (**amaya-linux-elf_0_9a_tar.gz**)
ASHE (**xhtml-1.3-linux-elf.gz**)
AsWedit (**asWedit-3.0-i386.linux.tar.gz**)
TkHTML (**tkHTML-3.11-Linux-ELF.gz**)

/internet/glimpse:
Glimpse (**glimpse-4_0_bin_Linux-2_1_10-i486_tar.Z**)
GlimpseHTTP (**glimpseHTTP_2_0_src_tar.Z**)
WebGlimpse (**webglimpse-1_1_src_tar.gz**)

/internet/harvest:

Harvest, compiled for Linux (**harvest-1.4.pl2-linux-ELF.tar.gz**)

Harvest source code (**harvest-1.4.pl2-src.tar.gz**)

Cache files needed for Harvest (**cached-1.4.pl2-linux-elf.tar.gz**)

/internet/java:

Java Development Kit, for systems with Motif (**linux.jdk-1.0.2-pl1. common.tar.gz**)

Java Development Kit, for systems without Motif (**linux.jdk-1.0.2-pl1. static-motif-bin.tar.gz**)

/internet/python:

Python (**python1_4-i486-linux2_0-elf_tar.gz**)

/internet/web_servers:

CERN Web server (**w3c-httpd-3.0A.tar.gz**)

NCSA Web server (**httpd_1_5_2a-export_linux2_0_0_tar.Z**)

WN Web server (**wn_tar_gz**)

XS-HTTPD (**httpd.tar.gz**)

Every month *Linux Journal* brings you the most complete information on what this powerful system can do for you and your work.
Linux Journal tells you what you need to know to make Linux work for you:

- Stay informed about current trends in Linux technologies
- Interviews with Linux developers and other personalities
- Keep up with the latest release in Linux software
- Avoid common mistakes by reading our tutorials
- Reviews of Linux-related products
- Columns on GNU, programming, technical support and more
- *LJ* Annual Buyer's Guide free with subscription (13th issue)

Questions?	FAX:	URL:
Call (206) 782-7733	+1 (206) 782-7191	http://www.ssc.com/

For a free catalog of other SSC publications, e-mail info@ssc.com

Just by returning this card I will automatically receive a free issue of Linux Journal, compliments of

MIS:Press
The LINUX Internet Server

Please fill out this form and return to:
Linux Journal
P.O. Box 55549 • Seattle, WA 98155-0549

I also want to subscribe.

By subscribing today, I will save over 50% of the newsstand price.

1 YEAR
- ❏ $22 US
- ❏ $27(USD) Canada
- ❏ $32(USD) Other countries

2 YEARS
- ❏ $39 US
- ❏ $49(USD) Canada
- ❏ $54(USD) Other countries

Please allow 6-8 weeks for processing

NAME _____

COMPANY _____

ADDRESS _____

CITY _____ STATE _____ POSTAL CODE _____

COUNTRY _____ TELEPHONE _____

FAX _____ E-MAIL _____

❏ Visa   ❏ MasterCard   ❏ American Express   ❏ Check Enclosed

CREDIT CARD # _____ EXP. DATE _____

SIGNATURE _____